INSTRUCTIONAL SYSTEMS DEVELOPMENT

INFORMATION LIFELINE

TIPS, TOOLS, AND INTELLIGENCE FOR TRAINERS

AN INFOLINE
COLLECTION

 ASTD Press

Need a trainer's lifeline? Visit infoline.astd.org.

Infoline is a real got-a-problem, find-a-solution publication. Concise and practical, *Infoline* is an information lifeline written specifically for trainers and other workplace learning and performance improvement professionals. Whether the subject is a current trend in the field, or tried-and-true training basics, *Infoline* is a complete, reliable trainer's information resource. *Infoline* is available by subscription and single copy purchase.

Ordering information: ASTD Press books, *Infolines*, and *Infoline* subscription can be purchased by visiting our Website at store.astd.org or by calling 800.628.2783/703.683.8100.

ISBN: 1-56286-313-4

ISBN -13:978-1-56-286313-5

Library of Congress Catalog Card No. 2002102061

Printed in the United States of America.

Instructional Systems Development

Basics of Instructional Systems Development.............................1

Instructional Design for WBT 19

Be a Better Needs Analyst 37

Conducting a Mini Needs Assessment.............................55

Needs Assessment by Focus Group 73

Task Analysis 91

Course Design and Development.............................109

Lesson Design and Development.............................127

Instructional Objectives.............................145

Write Better Behavioral Objectives 159

Teach SMEs to Design Training 177

Create Effective Job Aids.............................195

Effective Classroom Training Techniques.............................213

Enhance Learning Retention.............................231

Essentials for Evaluation 249

Managing Evaluation Shortcuts 267

Evaluation Data: Planning and Use.............................285

Editor
Tora Estep

Copyeditor
Ann Bruen

Production
Kathleen Schaner

 ASTD Press

Basics of Instructional Systems Development

Issue 9706

Basics of Instructional Systems Development

AUTHOR

Chuck Hodell
The George Meany Center
for Labor Studies
10000 New Hampshire Ave.
Silver Spring, MD 20903
Tel. 301.431.5440
E-mail: hodell@umbc.edu

Chuck Hodell serves on the faculty of the University of Maryland Baltimore County in the Instructional Systems Development graduate program. He is the author of the ASTD Press title, *ISD from the Ground Up,* as well as numerous other publications.

Editor
Cat Sharpe Russo

Associate Editor
Patrick McHugh

Copy Editor
Kay Larson

ASTD Internal Consultant
Dr. Walter Gray

Production Design
Kathleen Schaner

Instructional Systems Development 3
What Is ISD? 3
Do You Need Subject Matter Experts? 4

The ADDIE Model of ISD 5
Analysis 6
Design 9
Development 9
Implementation 10
Evaluation 10
Objectives 11
Evaluation Tasks 14
Putting It All Together 15

References & Resources 16

Job Aid
A Training Program Instructional Systems Design Checklist 18

Instructional Systems Development

If you had to choose one metaphor to help describe the Instructional Systems Development (ISD) process, you might consider the humble road map. You know the one—the one that shows countless destinations and endless ways to get your destination. On your road map your destination is a city, town, or possibly a major intersection. In training and education, the destination is a successful training program, a multimedia courseware, or a distance education course.

As simple as a real road map is to use, there are still hapless millions who refuse to take the time to look at one before leaving home. On any given day you can easily spot the mapless—they can usually be identified by the puzzled look on their faces and the familiar arched back silhouette as they lean from their minivan windows asking for directions. In the world of instructional design, the ISDless can typically be identified by the puzzled look on their faces as learners fail to reach their desired training destination—all the while wasting valuable organizational resources on unsuccessful programs.

Traveling provides many opportunities to use different kinds of maps. Observing the daily numbers of subway riders traveling the Metro Rail System in the Washington, D.C., area is an ever continuous example of people who would rather get off at the wrong stop than look at the highly visible and easy-to-read maps posted in each Metro railcar and station. This doesn't just apply to the many tourists who stream in to visit the D.C. area either—it's also the wave of blue suits and denim that daily invades the subway to emerge from the darkness just in time to be late for work. The net result of these individuals' failure to follow the simple navigational system is a loss of valuable and irreplaceable time, a confusion about where they are at any given moment, a loss of momentum from starting and stopping, and a loss of confidence in their ability to travel successfully at all. Applying this metaphor to training and education, these same symptoms exist in learners and other stakeholders when designers fail to use a system of instruction as a road map. Instructional Systems Development provides the means by which a road map can be created and followed, leading learners down the path of success.

ISD is not a cure for the common cold or the answer to world peace but it *is* a valuable tool to be used in the fight against mediocre training efforts that bore or frustrate participants and rarely provide the sponsoring organization anything more than a bad day in the training department. Current challenges in training will not be sufficiently addressed by industrial age approaches that appear as out of date in the training world as the steam engine does in the space program.

Today, ISD is used in every imaginable type of training and education. From preschool classes to multimedia courseware for the masses, ISD is the strength behind the product and the process that ensures compliance with best practices in the field of instructional design. The ISD map to success is paved with methodological milestones, quality markers, and mega opportunities for creativity.

What Is ISD?

Instructional Systems Development, or ISD as we will refer to it, is a systems approach to analyzing, designing, developing, implementing, and evaluating any instructional experience. It may also be called Instructional Development (ID), Curriculum Development (CD), Instructional System for Training (IST), or a variety of other acronyms. The differences between the many systems are usually modest in scope and tend to be linked to terminology and procedural issues.

Regardless of what you call them, each of these systems operates on certain basic principles. If you are a "systems" thinker you already know that systems are present in every facet of our lives. We elect our representatives in the political system and we prosecute them in the legal system. We pay taxes as a result of the legislative system and we travel from place to place as a result of a transportation system. Instructional systems are no different in theory than any other system; only the details change.

The reason training and education work so well in a systems environment goes to the very essence of systems themselves. The systems that seem to work best are those that have observable, measurable, and replicable elements. In the case of ISD, these elements include analytical methods, objectives, evaluation schemes, design plans, and a number of other system components.

While ISD is a system, it is not so rigid that it lacks flexibility. In fact, the more you work with ISD, the more you realize that the system allows you greater opportunities to be creative. For example, a system-less training organization with an intra-organizational communications problem might decline to pursue that "analysis and evaluation stuff" and concentrate on creating very attractive participant materials and a video that features the company CEO looking casual, sitting on the corner of his or her desk. This is what I refer to as the four-color and Hollywood approach to training—all flash and no substance. A systems approach that contains analysis and evaluation allows for creativity necessary to focus on the real workplace issues and provide solutions that can be evaluated and replicated organization wide, proffering some assurance that the intervention was worth the monies and resources expended.

Before going any further into ISD, it is important to herald the universality of this process. The notion that ISD only works in training environments is as accurate as saying that maps only work if you are driving a red sports car in towns with a population of fewer than 500. The process of assembling a curriculum is built on the same concepts and principles. This applies to whether you are designing an English as a second language course, a third grade reading lesson, or a jet airline simulator. The variables that exist in any curriculum design process, including population variables, delivery systems, and resources, are just that—variables.

Do You Need Subject Matter Experts?

The myth of having to be a subject matter expert (SME, pronounced *sh-mee*) to design curriculum is exactly that—a myth. One of the first questions usually asked by new ISD students relates to a common misconception concerning whether you need to be a subject matter expert before you can design curriculum in any given subject matter. While a little subject matter expertise may be helpful, it is not a requirement for success. Every day, ISD practitioners design exciting and successful curricula in subject areas that are only vaguely familiar to them. Remember, ISD is a systems approach to developing training, and the "system" includes methods of working with folks that are SMEs. Most SMEs, in fact, really appreciate the ISD process; once freed of the responsibility of designing curricula, they can concentrate on the subject matter while you worry about that "design stuff."

This is analogous to the relationship many of us have with machinery—especially cars and computers. For the most part, we have no *real* knowledge of these technologies beyond what is called the "appliance operator" mode. In other words, we can turn them on, hope they work, and then use them to our own selfish ends. We don't need to know how many volts of electricity power a certain microprocessor or how many pints of green stuff needs to be in our car's radiator. We only need to know whom to ask when we need help, especially when we get the "fatal error" message on our computer monitor or when the green stuff that was once happily circulating in our cars is now dripping onto our driveway.

The ADDIE Model of ISD

There are a number of ISD models named after individuals and institutions, but we are going to use the generic, or ADDIE, model as our point of reference. Although a nice name for a cat, ADDIE actually represents the first letter contained in each of the five separate elements of this model: Analysis, Design, Development, Implementation, and Evaluation. Most instructional designers use the ADDIE model or some variation of it as a basis for their work. Eventually, most experienced designers adopt their own unique models—one that fits their work styles and the demands of their clients or organizations.

Below is a short profile of each component. A more detailed and in-depth explanation follows.

Analysis

The who, what, where, when, why, and by whom of the design process. In this element you must determine:

- if a problem exists that can be appropriately addressed by training

- what goals and objectives the training should address

- what resources are available for the project

- who requires the training and their needs (population profiles)

- all additional data needed to successfully complete the project.

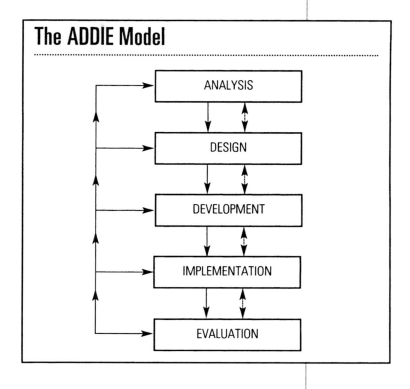

The ADDIE Model

Design

This is the real heart of the instructional design process. Here the designer will:

- prepare instructional objectives

- develop instructional evaluation techniques and tasks

- develop a program evaluation plan

- develop the sequence and structure of the course

- prepare logic and objectives maps

- determine and prepare draft copies of necessary materials.

Development

In this phase the designer will:

- prepare all participant and instructor materials for the course

- prepare all support materials including audio, video, and other media

- program any computer-based materials

- field or beta test the project.

Implementation

In this phase a project is:

- put into service
- evaluated by learners, facilitators, and funders
- changed, restructured, or improved as necessary.

Evaluation

This phase actually takes place throughout the instructional design process. The major evaluation elements demand that a designer:

- confirm that all subject matter is correct and reviewed by SMEs

- consult with stakeholders to ensure adherence to established project goals

- adhere to the design plan and procure sign-off on all critical design elements

- review and act on all evaluations from participants, facilitators, and other end users of the project

- ensure quality control of the process by constant and thorough evaluation of all remaining project elements.

Analysis

Just as *A* is the first letter in the alphabet, analysis should be the first item addressed in instructional design. Without analysis, you really have nothing to work from or any information to work with. There are as many analysis techniques as there are analysts and it can be very confusing to the uninitiated. There are, however, several basic building blocks in analysis that designers need to consider.

Getting Started

The first question that must be asked in analysis is critical to the success of any training endeavor: "Is there a problem that can be reasonably remedied by a training intervention?" Many a novice designer has turned enthusiasm into disaster by assuming that a problem was training related and later discovering that no appreciable change took place in the target population because the cure was not training but in solving the nature of the problem itself. While this may seem to be *too* obvious to take seriously as a critical first step, here is an example that might make you change your mind.

A rather large manufacturing company called a training consultant in to bid on what they perceived as a blueprint reading problem in their maintenance department. It seemed that every time a major piece of equipment broke down, the maintenance crews were constantly making mistakes when repairing the equipment. This suggested that the crews could not read the blueprints.

Being a good instructional designer, the consultant asked about the process of repairing broken equipment. He learned that a crew initially visited the broken machinery, returned to the blueprint room, wrote down the needed information, returned to the broken equipment and attempted to repair it. When asked to be shown the blueprint room, the consultant discovered a small, windowless room, illuminated by a single, low wattage incandescent bulb. The consultant also observed a sign posted in the room, which reminded everyone that no blueprints could leave the room. In less than a day, the entire problem was fixed by installing new lighting and providing extra copies of the blueprints for repair crews to take on site. This consultant could have trained everyone, everyday for a year on blueprint reading and still not have improved the maintenance efficiency to a measurable level.

Other first-step analysis issues you may want to consider include:

■ A Target Population Profile

This includes every variable that might affect outcomes: education levels, cultural influences, language skills, learning styles, levels of participants' motivation, organizational political streams, and relevant past experience with the subject matter.

■ Types of Training

Preliminary categorization of a training assists in narrowing the range of options available for instructional design. This should not be confused with training platforms (see next entry). Types of training include skills enhancement, technical, marketing, managerial, cross-cultural, sensitivity, second language acquisition, organizational change, literacy, and traditional academic training.

■ Training Platforms

These are the delivery systems for any training. Examples include classroom, on-the-job, multimedia, computer-based, distance learning, teleconferencing, and seminars.

■ Resources

These are the resources available for the project and might include access to subject matter experts, sources for print materials including manuals, books, videos and other reference materials, funds procurable for the project, existing courseware and materials, facilitators on hand for implementation, and support equipment such as overhead projectors and video playback equipment.

■ Constraints

These are issues that might cause problems including unreasonable deadlines, limited access to training facilities, platform-related deficiencies including broken or aging equipment, and anything else that can influence a project's success or failure.

A number of methods are used during the analysis phase to gather and review data including:

- surveys
- focus groups
- materials review
- subject matter expert panels
- existing programs review
- Internet and Web-based searches.

For more detailed information on analysis methods and how to gather and review data, refer to the following *Infolines*: No. 258612, "Surveys From Start to Finish"; No. 259008, "How to Collect Data"; No. 259705, "Essentials for Evaluation"; No. 258903, "Be a Better Job Analyst"; No. 258502, "Be a Better Needs Analyst"; and No. 259713, "The Role of the Performance Needs Analyst."

Types of Structure

Plans for sequencing and structuring a lesson, course, or instructional program are made during the design phase. Sequence and structure are very closely related. Sequence is the order in which skills or information is taught, while structure refers to the relationships among skills and topics. Structure is important because it provides a framework for learning; structured information helps you learn more quickly and allows you to remember what you have learned more efficiently. You can prove this by trying the following experiment:

Look at the words listed below for 30 seconds, cover the list up, then try to rewrite it.

orange	beef	cabbage	pea
grapefruit	lemon	fish	chicken
apple	pork	lettuce	bean

Now look at this structured word list for 30 seconds, cover, and rewrite it.

Food	*Furniture*	*Animals*
apple	bed	cow
cookie	chair	dog
pear	desk	elephant
toffee	sofa	horse

Which list did you remember better? There were exactly the same number of words to remember, but the second list was structured by main topics and alphabetized within topics.

Task-Centered Structure

A task-centered structure arranges skills and knowledge by their relationships to job tasks. This type of structure is particularly helpful when there is a specific order in which tasks must be done on the job. The structure tends to reinforce the order in a training participant's mind.

The following example shows a task-centered training program for a gas station attendant. The topics have been divided into units according to tasks that were identified by the program designer. The design might have used a variety of different task classifications as the program structure.

Training Topic	Task
Greeting	Welcome customer
Determining customer need(s)	Welcome customer
Windshield cleaning	Regular service
Gas pumps	Regular service
Gas tanks	Regular service
Oil maintenance	Regular service
Wiper fluid refill	Regular service
Air pumps	Repair
Tires	Maintenance
Tire patches	In-stock
Jacks	In-stock
Tow truck operation	Towing
Tow bar attachment	Towing
Prices	Payments
Cash registers	Payments
Credit card transactions	Payments

Topic-Centered Structure

This structure arranges instruction by topic. Main topics are divided into unit headings. This is useful when training participants are required to learn a lot of information—this framework makes it easier for participants to learn and retain related information. There are many possible ways to arrange a topic-centered structure. Consider how you would rearrange the topics from the task-centered example if you use the following topical titles as unit headings:

- gas
- oil
- windshields
- tires
- towing
- customer contact
- billing and payment.

Problem-Centered Structure

This type of structure is helpful when training participants are expected to learn how to solve problems. Structuring a course around the problems learners have faced or will face on the job helps them focus on finding solutions. For example, a training program designed to prepare a mechanic to diagnose car problems might have unit headings as follows:

- stalling
- not starting
- slow pick-up
- bucking
- vibrations
- low gas mileage.

This structure is based on symptoms of car problems. The instructional emphasis will be on diagnostics. If the program were structured by topic or task, training participants might not learn to think in terms of diagnosing a car problem from its symptoms.

Design

In this phase the designer provides the basic foundation and structure for the training project. The foundation consists of the goals, objectives, and evaluation tasks that must be developed and how they are sequenced. The structure comes from the many decisions that must be made regarding training platforms and other implementation questions.

A design plan will be developed that includes a working map for the project. This will serve as the blueprint for developing the training and will also list all of the objectives written for the training program along with a list of additional items needed such as:

- printed support materials including manuals and handouts

- audio and video support materials

- scripts and storyboards for computer-based projects

- evaluation materials including tests, quizzes, and other formal evaluations

- lesson plans and other forms of facilitator support

- program documentation strategies

- staff assignments and responsibilities

- project management plan with milestones and deadlines.

Development

It is in this phase that the tangible and most easily recognized components of the training begin to take shape. The project moves from the blueprint to construction stage using the design plan as a guide.

Major development phase elements are as follows:

1. Manuals and materials are prepared in draft form and reviewed by SMEs and designers for accuracy.

2. Nonprint media such as audio, video, and computer-based programs are prepared and reviewed.

Mapping

Instructional designers frequently use a mapping process to guide them during the curriculum design process. The most common types of maps used are: course, lesson, and topic. Each map serves the same purpose—it provides a visual element to help simplify the design process for SMEs and other individuals not as familiar with the ISD process.

Course maps provide an overview of an entire class such as English 101 or Math 215. The course map will usually display a listing of the terminal objectives for the course and the sequence in which they will be presented.

Lesson maps represent a smaller unit of instruction—typically a single lesson that is offered in a single session. Lesson maps commonly display one or more terminal objectives as well as supporting enabling objectives.

Topic maps are often limited to one concept or principle and provide more in-depth detail to the structure of an instruction unit. A topic map might be used to represent the steps necessary to perform a single, simple skill such starting a car or answering a telephone.

3. Programs are pilot tested, changes are incorporated into the final program, and materials modified as necessary.

4. Programs are packaged and distributed in preparation for implementation.

Implementation

This is the traditional time when projects are placed in service and the evaluation process begins in earnest. In most implementations you can expect to see the following:

- evaluation of learner's ability to meet program objectives

- evaluation of program design by facilitators

- review of materials prepared for the program

- review of implementation-specific elements such as class size, format, and so on

- modification of design and materials as suggested by evaluation.

Evaluation

While the evaluation element of the ADDIE model appears to be the last function, in reality, evaluation takes place at every point throughout the ISD process. In fact, every action in the ISD process has an equal and counterbalancing evaluation element associated with it.

In the **analysis** phase, evaluation usually consists of the following:

- review of all research data by SMEs and the design team

- survey, focus group, or other analytical method to validate population, delivery systems, course design, and other important training components

- evaluation of resources and constraints data based on reviews by key decision makers

- review of process issues such as deadlines and deliverables.

During the **design** phase, evaluation is usually done on the following:

- objectives and evaluation tasks

- materials and medium plans

- process issues associated with deadlines and deliverables.

Development phase evaluations include the following:

- review of materials by SMEs, the design team, and the target audience

- pilot testing of training components and materials

- review of deadlines and deliverables in preparation for implementation.

During **implementation,** evaluations usually consist of the following:

- full course reviews based on evaluations of learners and facilitators

- review of deadlines and deliverables based on targets set in the design element.

Objectives

The use of objectives in curriculum design is identical to the use of a road map to show our intended destination and the best way to get there. You will not find too many people who just get in their cars and drive toward a new destination without knowing how to get there. Objectives are the destination points in the curriculum design adventure and without them, learners and designers have no reference point for any single destination.

An objective must be stated clearly and describe the intended exit competencies for the specified unit, lesson, course, or program that it has been written to identify. There are two general categories of objectives: terminal and enabling. The classification of an objective is determined by where it falls in the curriculum design. If it describes an exit behavior for the unit of instruction, it is usually a terminal objective. If it describes a behavior that supports a terminal objective, it is considered an enabling objective. For example, if writing a terminal objective for a unit of instruction in the subject area "Learning the Internet," it might look like this:

Given a computer system, modem, and software, the Internet 101 student should be able to access the Internet and check for any email messages waiting on the system at least five times without error.

This objective must have several building blocks or enabling objectives to provide additional concepts and skills needed to meet this objective. One enabling objective might be as follows:

Given prompts for account name and password, the Internet 101 learner should be able to correctly enter this information without error in five successive attempts.

This enabling objective breaks down the expected exit competency into more manageable chunks or enabling objectives. Using our road map metaphor again, if we are traveling from Annapolis, Maryland, to Dallas, Texas, the terminal objective would be arriving in Dallas, the enabling objectives would be arriving in St. Louis and Oklahoma City.

Four Components of an Objective

The four building blocks of an objective are:

1. Audience.

2. Behavior.

3. Condition.

4. Degree.

When objectives are written in this format they are cleverly called A-B-C-D objectives. These four components are used to clearly and succinctly describe the learning environment and desired outcome for terminal or enabling objectives.

While some might consider the level of detail involved in four-part objectives either terminal banality or a behaviorist's dream, designers consider them the real foundation of "best practices" grade design work. There are several reasons for this philosophy, but the most persuasive is that without objectives you really have nothing to evaluate—objectives provide all the building blocks for gauging success. Until you define success (in this case with objectives) you can never hope to reach it.

An example of a four-part objective might be as follows:

Given a complete copy of the Infoline *on Instructional Systems Development, the Introduction to ISD participant (UMBC course number EDUC 602) should be able to accurately describe the four components of an objective without error when given at least three opportunities to do so.*

Course Mapping

Mapping is a visual representation of a unit of instruction. It usually depicts either terminal or enabling objectives. A map can be drawn for any number of different instructional units including courses, units, and lessons. The map seen below represents all of the terminal objectives for EDUC 602, a graduate course in Instructional Systems Development.

Maps drawn for ISD projects use a bottom-up format with the lowest level depicting the first objective, in this case *Systems & Models* as shown in the lowest box. Each higher level of objectives builds up from the level below. In this particular case, you must complete the module on *Systems & Models* before you can take the module *Generic ISD Model,* and so on.

When a level has more than one box, the boxes can be taken in any order, but all of them must be taken before progressing on to the next level. For example, a learner must complete both the *Evaluation Tasks* and *Objectives* modules before progressing to the *Syllabus Elements* module. Learners then progress through the modules on Gagne's *Nine Events* and then *Lesson Plans* in preparation for the final project.

The larger boxes outlined with dotted lines represent the three main course areas and the objectives associated with each. The first two objectives are required for both the research project and the final project, whereas the remaining enabling objectives relate to **Element One** and **Element Two** of the final project.

Terminal objectives for this course are depicted in hexagonal boxes. In EDUC 602, participants are required to successfully prepare two portfolio projects to meet the objectives for the course.

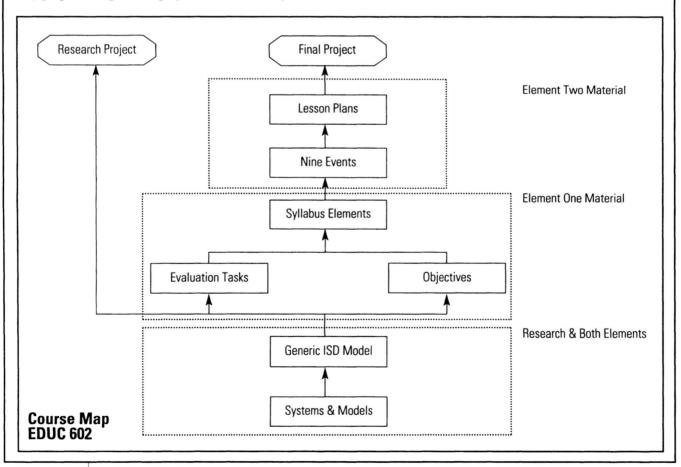

Let's look at the four components of this objective:

1. Audience: The Introduction to ISD Learner (UMBC course number EDUC 602).

2. Behavior: Should be able to accurately describe the four components of an objective.

3. Condition: Given a complete copy of the *Infoline* on Instructional Systems Development.

4. Degree: Without error when given at least three opportunities to do so.

Now let's look at what each of these components really tells us about the objective.

■ *Audience*
The first element of an objective must offer as complete a description of the intended learner as possible. At first, the audience component might seem simple to produce, but this is a deception. Defining a population for an objective requires a designer to really picture the intended audience and then describe that audience in concise terms. It's not good enough just to say "the learner" because that could refer to anyone.

The audience component of an objective provides a lot of information. It should begin to narrow the focus of the objective and offer important clues concerning possible prerequisites and the sequencing and placement within a larger series of objectives. In our objective we learn several important things concerning the intent of the objective. First, our learner is going to be working at the introductory level of this subject (Introduction). Second, this learner is taking a course in Instructional Systems Development (ISD). Third, this course may be one in a series of courses since it has been assigned a designating number (UMBC course number). Fourth, it is probably being offered by the Education Department (EDUC). Fifth, it is probably a graduate-level course (602).

■ *Behavior*
The behavior component is the core of an objective. It is here that we define the real work to be accomplished by the learner. Behaviors must be observable and measurable, and then written as concisely as possible. Commonly misused behaviors such as *learn* and *understand* really do not provide much information and should be avoided.

In our objective, the behavior is both observable and measurable as the learner is required to accurately describe the four components of the objective. This objective leaves little doubt about what is required, and it builds a solid platform for the evaluation task necessary to ensure mastery.

■ *Condition*
The condition component of an objective provides the learning environment that supports the intended outcome. Conditions can be as simple as providing physical elements such as books or tools or as complex as requiring learners to successfully complete a series of lessons or courses before attempting a particular objective.

In our objective, the condition statement, "given a complete copy of the *Infoline* on Instructional Systems Development," ensures that each learner will be given the tools necessary to meet the objective, thereby eliminating the issue of environmental support if a learner fails to meet the objective.

■ *Degree*
This component designates the required efficiency level to successfully complete the objective. Examples of degree include the following:

● four out of five times

● with a score of 80 percent or greater without error

● in an hour or less.

In our degree statement there is little doubt concerning the objectives' requirements for success, "without error when given at least three opportunities to do so."

Evaluation Tasks

For every objective (terminal or enabling) there should be a corresponding evaluation task. Some are formal, others are informal. Formal evaluation tasks include taking tests or quizzes and writing an essay. Informal evaluation tasks might include having a learner describe a given concept or principle or state a rule in mathematics or grammar.

Objectives should closely match evaluation tasks in two important areas: behavior and condition. When these elements match, an objective is said to have performance agreement. The performance agreement principle ensures consistency between what we expect of learners in the objective and what we require them to do in an evaluation.

In our objective for the Internet class, we call for the learner to access the Internet and check for waiting messages using the supplied computer system, modem, and software. A corresponding evaluation task might include the following:

Using any computer station located in the classroom with a modem and software installed for telecommunications, access the Internet and retrieve any waiting messages in your account.

This evaluation task matches the objective in both behavior and condition. It ensures that the learner will be evaluated in a way that is consistent with the intent of the objective.

Performance agreement problems usually exist when either the behavior or condition (or both) are inconsistent with the objective. In our Internet example, requiring the learners to write an essay on how they would access their email accounts is not the same behavior as actually requiring them to get on the computer system and meet the objective. This evaluation lacks performance agreement. It is important to remember that it makes no difference which behaviors and conditions you specify in your objectives and evaluation tasks, only that they match and provide performance agreement for the objective.

Objective Domains

It is useful to define objectives by the primary domain in which they are intended to be implemented. By domain we mean the classification of the objective into one of four general categories: cognitive, affective, psychomotor, and interactive. The divisions represented by each domain typically have these characteristics:

Cognitive: skills and knowledge relating to intellectual activity.

Affective: attitudes, feelings, and values.

Psychomotor: skills related to physical activity.

Interactive: skills related to interactive and interpersonal exchanges.

Objective domains assist you in writing objectives and evaluation tasks and also help ensure performance agreement. Inappropriate use of domains in training can cause dissonance in learners and threaten the success of any program. An illustration of this principle would be using an objective written for one domain and an evaluation task written for another domain. An example might be having an objective that requires a learner to successfully operate a piece of equipment and the evaluation task that asks for an explanation of the theory of operation.

Putting It All Together

Now that we have covered the basics of ISD, it is time to pull it all together in a way that makes sense for you. All of the discussion about the ADDIE model and A-B-C-D objectives starts to sound like alphabet soup until you have a way to make it work for you. Remember our road map analogy! You need to be sure of your destination and how you will get there. Here are some suggestions that might help you get started.

1. Always use a systems approach like ISD in your curriculum development work. This is true if you are designing training you will implement yourself or training that will be distributed to a thousand sites around the world. Nothing substitutes for the power of ISD. The ADDIE model is an easy and proven way to use ISD for almost any training situation.

2. Never, ever start a curriculum design project without doing analysis. Your first question should always be "Can I address the problem with training?" Next, be sure that you have gathered all the data you can about your population. Determine your training type and then analyze your resources and constraints.

3. Always establish clear, observable, and measurable objectives. Writing great objectives will establish a clear foundation for everything you design. No matter how simple or complex the subject matter and other details of your training, objectives will always get you started in the right direction.

4. Create evaluation tasks that accurately determine a learner's ability to meet objectives. Remember, it is important that evaluations match objectives in terms of behavior and condition. Then, objectives and evaluation tasks are said to have performance agreement.

5. Use the *Accumulation of Advantages* principle to guide your decisions regarding instructional design. Every successful training effort is the result of a number of separate decisions that support the "best practices" approach to curriculum design. Since no single element of any training project will ensure success, it takes a systems approach like ISD to ensure victory in the battle against mediocre curriculum design efforts.

Set your goals, write your objectives, evaluate your results, and accumulate the advantages that Instructional Systems Development offers new millennium training organizations.

References & Resources

Articles

Benefit, Arian B. "Instructional Design Process: A Case Example." *Performance & Instruction,* September 1995, pp. 40-42.

Carolan, Mary D. "Seven Steps for Back-to Basics Training, Nineties-Style." *Training & Development,* August 1993, pp. 15-17.

Chapman, Bryan L. "Accelerating the Design Process: A Tool for Instructional Designers." *Journal of Interactive Instruction Development,* Fall 1995, pp. 8-15.

Cook, Marvin J. "How to Structure Technical Training." *Technical & Skills Training,* May/June 1992, pp. 8-12.

Evers, Linda M. "Designing an Informational/Instructional Strategy." *Technical & Skills Training,* November/December 1992, pp. 25-31.

Filipczak, Bob. "To ISD or Not to ISD?" *Training,* March 1996, pp. 73-74.

Gramiak, Lori H. "Maintenance: The Sixth Step." *Training & Development,* March 1995, pp. 13-14.

Holton, Elwood F. III, and Curt Bailey. "Top-to-Bottom Curriculum Redesign." *Training & Development,* March 1995, pp. 40-45.

Huang, Zhuoran. "Making Training Friendly to Other Cultures." *Training & Development,* September 1996, pp. 13-14.

Katz, Michael, and Jacob Rosenberg. "From Complex Expert Thinking to Lucid Learning Methods." *Performance & Instruction,* July 1996, pp. 12-13.

McDowell, Callie. "What Can You Do to Align Employee Training With Business Strategy?" *Bank Marketing,* December 1996, pp. 12-15.

Moller, Leslie, "Working With Subject Matter Experts." *Techtrends,* November/December 1995, pp. 26-27.

Orlin, Jay M. "The Mix That Makes a Good Instructional Designer." *Technical & Skills Training,* October 1992, pp. 13-17.

Reid, Robert L. "On Target: Designing Training." *Technical & Skills Training,* January 1994, pp. 27-30.

Rogers, Eric, and Anthony Kalupy. "SPC Training." *Technical & Skills Training,* October 1993, pp. 11-14.

Shultz, Fred, and Rick Sullivan. "A Model for Designing Training." *Technical & Skills Training,* January 1995, pp. 22-26.

"Three Factors to Consider When Developing Courses." *Training,* December 1995, p. S3.

Books

Cortada, James W., and John A. Woods. *The ASTD Training and Performance Yearbook.* Alexandria, VA and New York: ASTD and McGraw-Hill, 1997.

Ford, Donald J., editor. *ASTD's In Action Series: Designing Training Programs.* Alexandria, VA: ASTD, 1997.

Harless, Joe H. *Analyzing Human Performance Tools for Achieving Business Results.* Alexandria, VA and Annapolis, MD: ASTD and Human Performance Technologies, 1997.

Head, Glenn H. *Training Cost Analysis: A How-To Guide for Trainers and Managers.* Alexandria, VA: ASTD, 1993.

Kirkpatrick, Donald L. *Evaluating Training Programs.* San Francisco: Berrett-Koehler, 1994.

Tracey, William R. *Designing Training and Development Systems.* 3rd edition. New York: American Management Association, 1992.

References & Resources

Infolines

Butruille, Susan. "Lesson Design and Development." No. 258906 (revised 1999).

Long, Lori. "Surveys From Start to Finish." No. 258612 (revised 1998).

Overfield, Karen. "Developing and Administering Training: A Practical Approach." No. 259201 (revised 1997).

Sharpe, Cat, ed. "Be a Better Needs Analyst." No. 258502 (revised 1998).

Waagen, Alice. "Essentials for Evaluation." No. 259705.

Internet Sites

ASTD. Available at http://www.astd.org

Job Aid

A Training Program Instructional Systems Design Checklist

Use this checklist as a guide to track your progress in developing lessons, courses, or training programs. You can also use the completed checklist as a reminder of program aspects that need to be evaluated.

Course/Program Title: _____

Analysis

☐ Organizational needs have been determined.
☐ Program goals have been set.
☐ Training population needs have been defined.
☐ On-hand resources have been determined.
☐ Constraints have been identified.
☐ Job(s) have been broken down into tasks or responsibilities.
☐ Tasks have been broken down into skills and knowledge.
☐ Job performance standards have been identified.

Design

☐ Objectives reflect organizational needs and goals.
☐ Objectives reflect training population's needs.
☐ Test item(s) have been written for each objective.
☐ Each test item matches its related objective.
☐ Training strategies reflect resource constraints, but honor population needs.
☐ Logical training sequence has been determined.

Development

☐ Training materials support objectives.
☐ Media selection is appropriate for objectives.
☐ Media selection reflects resource constraints.
☐ Evaluation forms are prepared.
☐ Training documentation tracks participant's progress.
☐ Course documentation meets organizational documentation needs (for planning, legal, other purposes).

Implementation

☐ Qualified instructors have been selected.
☐ Problems with the training design or materials are recorded.
☐ As they become necessary, revisions are made in the program—up to and throughout implementation.

Evaluation

☐ Evaluation plan was carried out.
☐ Evaluation data were used to make refinements or corrections in the course or program.

■INFORMATION LINE■
THE TOOLS AND TECHNIQUES FOR TRAINERS

Instructional Design for WBT

Issue 0202

Instructional Design for WBT

AUTHORS

Philip M. Harris
Vignette Corporation
200 N. Kings Canyon Dr.
Cedar Park, TX 78613
Tel: 512.741.4722
Fax: 512.741.4403
Email: pharris@vignette.com

Philip M. Harris is the certification program lead for the Vignette Corporation. He has edited a guide on certification and is a certified instructional designer/developer. He also has developed several Web-based and instructor-led training programs.

Orlando S. Castillo
Reliant Energy
8814 Bryce Canyon Ct.
Spring, TX 77379
Tel: 713.448.5704
Fax: 713.448.5724
Email: castillo@texas.net

Orlando S. Castillo is a senior training consultant with Reliant Energy. Previously, he was a senior training developer for the Vignette Corporation, where he was the lead for the Web-based training group. Castillo also has worked for United Training Services, and Compaq Computers Tandem division and Texas A&M University.

Managing Editor
Stephanie Sussan
ssussan@astd.org

Production Design
Kathleen Schaner

Instructional Design for WBT 21
    Analysis 22
    Design..29
    Development 30
    Implementation 30
    Evaluation..31

References & Resources.....................................33

Job Aid
    Media Selection Matrix 35

Instructional Design for WBT

More and more organizations are expanding across the oceans, so it's imperative to find ways to address learners located all over the world. As a result, organizations need to not only manage and disseminate knowledge in a localized setting, but also find ways of increasing and disseminating information to learners across the globe.

Tools, such as videophone conferencing and computer-based training (CBT) have been around for years. Why then would an organization need to find new ways or use new technology? The answer is simple: For the global workforce to remain competitive, organizations and learners must work in real time, in multinational arenas, and with multiple formats of information. The medium that supports a company's desire for competitive advantage is the World Wide Web.

With this relatively new medium and continually expanding technology, it is important to understand the process of sound instructional design that, when applied to the Web, can facilitate a great learning experience.

To address the above business challenge, your organization must have a process in place that:

- analyzes customers and business behavior

- adapts technology design and delivery to facilitate learner satisfaction by anticipating learners' current business and technology environment and future learning needs

- utilizes a process that enables training developers to create, design, develop, implement, evaluate, and measure customer satisfaction.

Instructional design is a systems approach to analyzing and designing an instructional experience. The traditional process, also commonly referred to as the Analysis, Design, Development, Implementation and Evaluation (ADDIE) model, consists of the process and tools instructional designers use to determine the who, what, when, where, why, and how of training instruction.

When designing instruction for the Web, you can use the same model and tools. However, be aware that some differences and issues arise in the Web environment. A diagram of the ADDIE model can be found on the next page.

Special Considerations

Designing Web-based training presents several special considerations and opportunities. There are many questions that organizations, as well as individuals, need to answer before using the Web to instruct learners. Some of the additional things to consider when designing instruction for the Web include:

- authoring systems
- content management systems
- delivery systems
- learner analysis
- media analysis
- Web-based project team analysis
- task analysis
- Web usability
- graphic design.

This chapter provides a breakdown of the ADDIE model adapted for Web-based training, specifically focusing on analysis and design, as well as the special considerations and opportunities of each phase.

The ADDIE Model

This ISD model shows the basic phases of ISD and the relationship of the phases to one another.

The lines and arrows show that the phases interrelate and may be changed during development. Lines and arrows leading back to each phase from the evaluation phase show that evaluation may turn up some problems that make it necessary to go back to a particular phase and make changes.

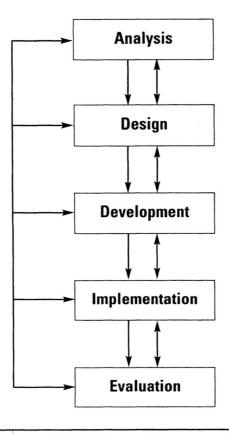

Analysis

There are two critical areas to analyze in any training. First, you and your organization need a strong business reason for implementing the training. Second, you must justify the cost of the training, more commonly referred to as showing a return-on-investment (ROI).

You can assess both of these areas by asking a series of Web-centric questions. You also should reference traditional instructional design knowledge bases. (For more information on traditional ISD, see *Infoline* No. 259706, "Basics of Instructional Systems Development.") You will need to complete the business justification and assess the costs once you have received the necessary management support.

■ *Business Need*
When analyzing your organization's need for Web-based training, ask the following questions:

1. Why are we doing this training?

2. Is there current training available in a different format?

3. Who will control the knowledge assets?

4. Is there management support?

5. Are there enough potential learners to justify the costs?

6. Do the learners currently use computers to learn?

7. Will the learners accept Web-based training?

8. What kinds of resources are available?

If the answers to questions 4–7 are yes, then Web-based training will meet your business need. Assuming all of the answers for questions 4–7 are yes, the business need and customer requirements need to be expanded to understand the ROI.

If you are not in the position to analyze business need, there are several places to turn. Generally, the first stop is with the chief operating officer and/or the person in charge of new business development. Together you can determine if your collective analysis is thorough enough or if you should turn to outside business consultants.

■ *Return-on-Investment*
ROI is the measurement of cost vs. benefit. The formula for ROI is:

$$(Benefits - Costs)/Costs = ROI$$

While costs are easier to identify than benefits, you can determine benefits by conducting a market analysis. Start by comparing the different costs associated with Web-based training and traditional classroom training. There typically are three main costs that make up Web-based training:

- authoring
- content management
- delivery.

You will gain a greater understanding of the costs as more of the analysis questions are answered. However, to fully understand the costs, each skill set should be defined—especially when choosing the tools and suppliers.

For more information on costs and ROI, see the sidebar on the next page, *Cost-Benefit Analysis.*

If your role as an instructional designer does not extend to ROI analysis, your first stop for help is the head of market research. This person likely will have the tools to determine the necessary information. Together you can decide if you need to contact outside consultants to aid in the research and analysis.

Authoring

Authoring refers to creating the content. There are two types of authoring: programming and non-programming. As the name indicates, programming authoring systems are those that require some form of programming language or a specific skill to build the content. Conversely, non-programming systems require little or no programming skills. Keep in mind that currently there are more than 200 e-learning systems on the market. Make sure you thoroughly research a system before investing in it.

The Blended Potential

Blended learning techniques can save you time and money, but only if you design them for that purpose. By designing and developing Web-based training (WBT) to be used in a classroom environment, you can offer several substantial benefits. Those can include a "build once, use often" product that can be effective in a stand-alone mode as well as being taught by an instructor. Another benefit is that development time and money can be spent on creating more lessons. Also, both the online and classroom students can use the same evaluation instruments.

Build once, use often

If the WBT is primarily designed and developed for the online participant, with the graphics, animations, and interactivity visible on a large scale, then it is possible to produce quality multiuse instruction.

Time and money

By focusing on the objectives and the means by which they will be met, you can focus your energies on building a WBT that can also be used in a classroom setting.

Evaluation

If you are hosting WBT in a system that has testing, and you allow your students access to your evaluations then you can look at the statistical disparity between the online learners and the instructor on a teacher-by-teacher basis, as well as a WBT vs. an instructor-led situation.

Blended instruction has its caveats. First, decide whether your WBT could, and should, be available to an instructor-led course. Second know your evaluation limitations before promising any statistical reporting. And third, treat blended learning as you would change management. Get early buy-in from management and the instructors who are going to use the techniques so that every effort is made to be successful with your blended training solutions.

Cost-Benefit Analysis

Cost-benefit analysis is a two-fold calculation process. The first calculation, done before a project is undertaken, will yield an *estimated* return-on-investment of the training solution.

The second calculation, done after the training, will yield the *actual* return-on-investment. If the training solution is being created for non-economic reasons, then ROI is not a factor in the analysis phase of the ISD process. If the training solution is created for economic reasons, then the higher the ROI, the greater the dollar yield. When calculating the ROI, management, not the training developer, should determine the appropriate minimum ROI. To determine ROI, use the following formula:

$$(\text{Benefits} - \text{Costs}) \div \text{Costs} = \text{ROI}$$

There are two methods to determine the costs of training: actual itemized costs, or the 2 percent rule. The 2 percent rule is simply taking 2 percent of the average annual salary of the person/role that will attend the proposed training solution. To calculate this cost, use this formula:

Salary (daily while on training)	x
Benefit package	.33x
Lost Production/Replacement Cost	1.5x
Organizational Overhead	1.25x
Tuition	actual
Travel	actual

Total Cost

There is no specific formula or method to determine the benefits of training. In fact, it is difficult to determine a benefit for a knowledge deficit because there are few, if any, measurable events. However, this does not mean that the benefit cannot be determined if the proposed training solution results in a knowledge or behavioral adjustment, and if running it more than once it can justify its existence.

To determine the benefit of training a skill, you must know the required skill. If you know the required skill and can assess the current skill, you can calculate the benefit of training. For example, an assembly line worker makes three products per hour, and each product is worth $100. If after training each assembly worker can make six products, the formula would be:

Increase in x multiplied by **the value of x** multiplied by **# of employees to train** multiplied by **# of days per year** = **Benefit.**

Non-programmatic and programmatic authoring systems may be associated with other systems, like content management systems.

For assistance in this department, the first stop should be the IT department. They will have the knowledge and skills to help you determine the best system to use.

Content Management

Content management refers to the management of pieces of subject matter. Content in these systems have the following three characteristics:

- hierarchical
- retrievable
- reusable.

Once the content has been entered into a system, it must have a way of being delivered to the learner.

For more information on content management, see the sidebar, *LMS or LCMS?*

The IT department also can help you in this department. Those folks will have the knowledge about all the competing systems out there and can help you determine the best system for your company's needs.

Delivery

Delivery refers to how the learners access the material. Delivery also is known as course hosting. Course hosting refers to who will host and deliver the content to the learner. There are two types of hosting: either by the organization or by an outside supplier. The different cost considerations of both environments must be reviewed as well as other considerations, such as security and control of proprietary information.

A method for estimating cost can come from the analysis conducted to determine your business need. For example, if the analysis shows that management wants to manage the content internally and no programmers are available to help design

LMS or LCMS?

What is the difference?

To the untrained eye a learning management system (LMS) and a learning content management system (LCMS) might seem like the same thing. This, however, is not he case. LMS and LCMS are different things with different audiences. Below is a breakdown of the differences.

What Are They?

LMS is used to manage training resources—activities such as: schedule courses, register students, maintain student records, provide assessment capabilities, provide for the organization of courses, maintain security and in some cases provide reports.

LCMS is use to create and manage content in an e-learning environment.

Who Are the Target Audiences?

LMS is targeted at administrators or training managers.

LCMS is targeted at training developers and instructional designers.

or code the content, an organization's IT department will need knowledge of the authoring, content management, and delivery systems. You would then select a variety of systems and tools that could meet this criterion.

At this point, the cost is only an estimate because no specific tools and systems have been selected. Tools and system selection will take place as the analysis continues.

Once you have an idea of the tools and systems you will use, it is time to start assembling a training team. Traditional classroom training teams need a variety of members to be successful, including project managers, learners, subject matter experts, instructional designers (who often play more than one role), technical writers, and editors. Web-based design teams have similar members, as well as a host of others, such as:

- multimedia designer
- content entry specialist
- quality assurance tester
- management information systems specialist
- programmer
- graphic designer.

For each new skill, factor the costs into the ROI equation.

Learner Analysis

After you have justified the business need through the ROI analysis, you need to conduct a more thorough analysis of the learners. This allows for the instruction to be tailored to the target audience. The learner analysis consists of the following questions:

1. What operating systems does the learner know?

2. Which browser does the learner use?

3. What type of connection to the Web does the learner have?

4. How much time does the learner spend online?

5. Are Java or plug-ins enabled on the learner's computer?

6. Does the learner have sound capabilities?

7. What is the learner's screen resolution?

8. How long does the learner have to complete the training? Is this continuous time?

9. What knowledge, skills, and applications (KSAs) does the learner possess?

10. How much time does the learner have to prepare for the course?

11. Does your budget allow the individual to travel to acquire the KSAs required for the job?

12. How many people will you hire over the next month to fill this job or similar roles?

13. What is the reading level of the learner?

14. What is the highest level of education attained by the learner?

15. What is the expected audience size?

16. What resources are available (for example, people, facilities, supports)?

17. How frequently will the training be offered?

Upon completion of the learner analysis, you should have a clear picture of what kind of media the learners will best utilize. However, to fully assess what is needed to deliver Web-based training, you also need to conduct a task/content analysis.

Task/Content Analysis

The task/content analysis lets you know what the learner needs to know. This information may be a job task or a piece of content needed to perform a certain job task or tasks. This analysis will create the course objectives, and you will now know what the content should look like. This analysis is performed for all delivery methods. Project managers are a good place to turn for help with this task. These people will best know what information their staff needs to gain in order to accomplish their jobs in the most efficient manner.

What is different in a Web-environment is how the objective is presented and measured. You will need to keep in mind the type of media being used as you create and develop the course objectives. You also should keep in mind the learner analysis and what type of system and tools the learners have. In doing so, you will be able to determine if the learners can have certain types of animation, sounds, or examples to enhance their learning. An easy way to track what can be included is to keep a task/content user interface design checklist as the objectives are being created and analyzed.

For an example of a list, see the sidebar *Design Checklist*.

The finished task/content analysis will help to determine the system needed for the specific training and narrow the possible options that each system provides.

Media Analysis

The media analysis helps you select which tools and system you want to use to deliver your training. The analysis has the following two main components:

1. A review of the constraints of the organization, (a constraints matrix).

2. The selection of the system for authoring, content management, and delivery (a media selection analysis).

■ Constraints Matrix

You need to ask questions about budget, time, and resources, and rate the answers on a scale to determine if this is a plausible solution.

Check out the *Web-Based Training Matrix* sidebar on the next page to see how to determine if the training solution should be developed in a Web-based medium.

■ Media Selection Analysis

After you have determined the constraints, the next step is to determine the best delivery system. A possible solution may have taken shape from questions asked during the analysis phase. You should now ask more specific questions and review answers from the learner analysis.

Design Checklist

It is important to keep track of what can be included in a Web-training class. Following is a checklist to aid you in that task. Check all that apply:

1. Will the instruction need to have:

☐ Animation

☐ Video

☐ Graphics

2. Will you conduct testing with the learner, and if so, will you:

☐ Give responses

☐ Provide feedback

☐ Track scores

3. Will the instruction need to have:

☐ Practice

☐ Simulations

☐ Case studies

☐ Multiple-choice questions

☐ Demonstrations

From these questions, you can determine if an authoring, content management, and delivery system is needed and if it will require programming or non-programming skills. The questions to ask and review are:

1. Who will control the knowledge assets?

☐ The organization

☐ Outside suppliers

2. What kinds of resources are available for this project?

☐ Multimedia designer

☐ Content entry

☐ Tester

☐ MIS

☐ Programmer

☐ Graphic designer

Also, ask all the questions from the learner analysis.

To aid in the selection of the system, complete a media selection matrix. The media selection matrix is a checklist that draws its questions and selection criteria from user interface design principles. The user interface design principles are areas that you will need to evaluate.

For an example, see the *Media Selection Matrix* job aid at the back of this issue.

Everyone from the chief operating officer to the IT department to the individual product managers should aid in this process. As a group you can determine if it is necessary to outsource the analysis to a business consultant group.

Once the system has been selected, it is time to finalize a Web development team and get a more accurate cost for the ROI calculation.

With a team forming and the system selected, you can move into the design phase. Most of the work completed in the analysis phase will have a direct impact on the design phase, and the same is true in reverse. As you begin to design the course, you may have to go back and look at or revise the analysis.

Web-Based Training Matrix

The following is a matrix to aid in determining if the solution should be developed in a particular medium.

Medium	Time	Budget	Resources
Web-based	High	High/Low	High
Computer-based	High/Medium	High/Medium	High/Low
Other Distance	High/Medium	High/Low	High/Low
Instructor-led	Medium/Low	Medium/Low	Medium/Low

If management or the client said that this solution is needed in three to six months (high under the time category) and there are ample resources available (high under the resources category), then the instructional designer would look at this matrix and determine that Web-based training is the appropriate solution.

Design

The design phase involves organizing the previously gathered analysis data and building the structure for training. In this phase, the instruction and semifinal training will start to take form. There are three things that will define the design phase, which will be carried into the development phase:

1. Project planning.

2. Functional specification.

3. Testing.

■ *Project Planning*

Project planning is a fundamental part of any training design. The information from the analysis phase will help you define what the project plan will look like. The information needed to complete this task consists of the following:

Development ratios: This is based on industry averages. For Web-based training it is 150 to 200 resource hours for every hour of instruction. This compares with the standard for instructor-led of 40 resource hours for each instruction hour.

Project team skills: This is based on the resources available from management and the system selected.

Project time: This is based on what management or the instructional designer has determined.

■ *Functional Specification*

The functional specification is determined when you build the actual content and functionality of the training. It provides a framework for proceeding into development. At this point, the system selected will be critical. Each function (authoring, content management, and delivery) has specific information that will, along with the content, create tasks. These are:

1. Content design.

2. Content expansion.

3. Storyboard design.

4. Scheme.

Content Design

This is part of the hierarchical structure of the content defined during the analysis. You can present this information by using an outlined text document. The following is an example.

Example: Content Design

Job: *Sales consultant.*

Task: *Communicate products and services.*

Activities: *Multiple-choice questions and practice examples.*

Material presented using: *Text, animation, and graphics.*

Objective: *Given all the necessary historical information about the products and services, the learner will be able to communicate how these products and services are used as solutions to a particular business need.*

Subtasks: *Overview of the content, the integration of content, and the analysis.*

Content Expansion

This provides an even greater breakdown of each task. It will become a written description of what the end-user will see. The text, animation, graphics, video, and other multimedia elements are described in full detail. If any questions, practices, simulation, or scenarios are to be presented, they need to be defined and documented. At this point the material should be edited for content validity, spelling, grammar, internationalization, and cultural sensitivity.

Storyboard Design

The storyboard design mirrors the presentation environment. It is a facsimile of how the training will appear to the end-user. It also is the visual representation of the content expansion task. This is much like an artist's storyboard. It should be based directly on the system that will be used to deliver the content. If the authoring system is programmatic, the storyboard should reflect elements that may have to be programmed. For example, if the content is to be tested by multiple-choice questions, the corresponding feedback may need to be a pop-up window.

If the environment is non-programmatic, there still should be a storyboard for each subtask created during the content expansion. This will help guide the individual responsible for content entry in the development phase. It also directs a programmer to options that may need to be programmed to add functionality for the learner. This part of the functional specification will be used with the scheme provided to the content entry team. Having this in front of them will let them know exactly what they are supposed to see and what should happen.

Scheme

The scheme details the sequence of the storyboards. Each storyboard should be tagged to identify the order. If the authoring system that has been selected needs programming, then a more technically oriented scheme needs to be created. These schemes are made up of symbols familiar to the programmer.

■ *Testing*

A testing plan details how the testing will take place. It also highlights how each test or specific functionality needs to be tested and how it should be measured. Testing can occur at different times during the development phase. The environment in which the learner will receive the training needs to be documented and built into the test plan. A common mistake is to test the material on a machine with a different configuration than the learner's. In doing so, the learner may experience problems not foreseen by the development team.

Development

It is in this phase that the most tangible and most easily recognized components of the training begin to take shape. The project moves from the blueprint to construction stage, using the design plan as a guide. The development phase, or content entry, is a two-fold process.

First, the content must be entered into the environment (authoring, content management systems). Manuals and materials are prepared and reviewed by subject matter experts, and computer equipment and other media are also prepared and reviewed. Second, the content must be tested (delivery system). Both of these steps can happen in unison or one could be completed before the other.

The keys to testing are version control, tracking, and iterations. The tester should have the functional specification, test plan, and any other relevant documents to ensure a thorough test. Another editing check also is necessary. This process of matching written text to the visual presentation should be tracked and each error recorded. Realizing that nothing is ever right on the first try, you should plan enough time for several revisions before releasing the training solution.

A pilot release of the program should take place during the testing and should have an audience that comes from the proposed training population. If no such audience is available, a pilot should be run with any small group. This will give the tester and training developer test data on the functionality and content. After the last round of testing, the training solution should be released.

Implementation

This is the point when projects are placed in service and the evaluation process begins in earnest. In most implementations, you can expect to see the following:

● evaluation of the learner's ability to meet program objectives

● evaluation of program design by facilitators

- review of materials prepared for the program

- review of implementation-specific elements such as format

- modification of design and materials as suggested by the evaluation.

You should create a release plan for those who may take part in the training or administrator the training.

A release plan is a formal document that states how the training will be delivered, when the training will be available, where the training should not be accessible from (restrictions, like operating systems that are unsupported), and what content should be released to the learners. This document is extremely important, especially when an outside delivery supplier is involved. A release plan will guide the system and improve content dissemination.

Evaluation

The evaluation for Web-based training uses the four levels of traditional training evaluation developed by Donald Kirkpatrick. While the evaluation element of the ADDIE model appears to be the last function, in reality evaluation takes place at every point throughout the process. In fact, every action in the ISD process has an equal and counterbalancing evaluation element associated with it. Evaluations are conducted at the beginning, middle, end, and sometimes after training. Evaluations are conducted for several reasons, including showing retention, ensuring customer satisfaction, and measuring ROI. The four levels of evaluation are:

Level 1—Reaction: how the learner feels or reacts to the training; a form of a customer satisfaction survey.

Level 2—Learning: how the learner improves in KSAs from the beginning to the end of class.

Level 3—Behavior: how the learner improves in performance back on the job.

Level 4—Results: the measure of increase in what learners came to training to acquire.

Web-Based Project Management

Is there a difference in how you manage a Web-based project and a non-Web-based project?

There are considerations specific to the Web that come into play when managing a Web-based project, but on the whole, Web and non-Web projects are managed in the same manner. There are three critical factors any project manager must manage:

1. Time.

2. Quality.

3. Cost.

In the Web environment, these factors are harder to **predict**. However, if you possess the basic project management **skill** set, you should be able to manage a Web-based project team. Common skills and abilities that a project manager might want to have are the ability to:

- delegate
- make decisions
- motivate
- adapt.

Technical knowledge and adaptability are especially important for Web-based project managers. For example, it will help if they know what effects using HTML over DHTML may have on the project and programmers. And they will be able to adapt to changes in the technology if they are more technically versed.

Possibly two of the most important skills a Web-based project manager can have are patience and flexibility. These can be critical, especially if the technology that is being used is new to the market or if it needs to be changed to improve quality and decrease time or cost.

In the **analysis** phase, evaluation usually consists of the following:

- review of all research data by subject matter experts and the design team

- survey, focus group, or other analytical method to validate population, delivery system, course design, and other important training components

- evaluation of resources and constraints data based on reviews by key decision makers

- review of process issues such as deadlines and deliverables.

During the **design** phase, evaluation usually is done on the following:

- objectives and evaluation tasks

- materials and medium plans

- process issues associated with deadlines and deliverables.

Development phase evaluations include the following:

- review of materials by subject matter experts, the design team, and the target audience

- pilot testing of training components and materials

- review of deadlines and deliverables in preparation for implementation.

During **implementation**, evaluations usually consist of the following:

- full course reviews based on valuations of learners and facilitators

- review of deadlines and deliverables based on targets set in the design element.

Go Beyond Traditional Training

The Web-based design process provides an opportunity to go beyond traditional methods of ISD to provide the learner with a portable, personal, and a highly engaging learning experience. There are even greater gains from the business view. With a systematic approach to Web learning, a company can experience greater customer satisfaction and brand recognition.

The key to the Web-based design process is simply to remember that this is a systematic process that is highly customizable. Some of the suggestions provided in this *Infoline* may not be applicable to each situation. Instructional designers should know the basics of the ISD process and then apply them based on the situation they are in.

The most important thing to remember is that no matter how streamlined the process is or what management dictates, the learner is the customer, and the material created is a reflection of your professionalism as an instructional designer.

References & Resources

Articles

Barron, T. "The New Universe of Multi-media Courseware." *Technical and Skills Training,* May/June 1997, pp. 8-11.

Benson, A.D. "Evaluating WBT: Seven Lessons from the Field." *Technical Training,* September/October 1999, pp. 26-28.

Coné, J. "How Dell Does It." *Training & Development,* June 2000, pp. 58-70.

Dobbs, K. "Who's in Charge of E-Learning?" *Training,* June 2000, pp. 54-58.

Galagan, P., and P.F. Drucker. "The E-Learning Revolution." *Training & Development,* December 2000, pp. 24-30.

Goff, L. "Intranet-based Training: Seeing Is Believing." *Computerworld,* March 23, 1998.

Hartley, D. "All Aboard the E-Learning Train." *Training & Development,* July 2000, pp. 37-42.

———. "Evaluation: Pricing E-Learning." *Training & Development,* April 2001, pp. 24-27.

Khirallah, D.R., and S. Swanson. "New Schools of Thought." *Informationweek,* November 20, 2000, pp. 22-24.

Kruse, K. "Five Levels of Internet-based Training." *Training & Development,* February 1997, pp. 60-61.

Masie, E. "Seizing Your Intranet." *Training & Development,* February 1997, pp. 51-52.

Spitzer, D.R. "Rediscovering the Social Context of Distance Learning." *Educational Technology,* March/April 1998, pp. 52-56.

Suessmuth, P. "A Rule-of-Thumb Way to Determine Quickly the Real Cost of Any Training Program." *Training,* October, 1976, pp. 285–286.

Zvacek, S.M. "Effective Affective Design for Distance Education. *Tech Trends,* January 1991, pp. 40-43.

Books

Ary, D., et al. *Introduction to Research in Education.* 5th edition. Orlando: Harcourt Brace, 1996.

Beer, V. *The Web Learning Fieldbook: Using the World Wide Web to Build Workplace Learning Environments.* San Francisco: Jossey-Bass Pfeiffer, 2000.

Bloom, B.S. *Taxonomy of Educational Objectives: Book 1: The Cognitive Domain.* White Plains, NY: Longman, 1956.

Driscoll, M. *Web-based Training: Using Technology to Design Adult Learning Experiences.* San Francisco: Jossey-Bass Pfeiffer, 1998.

England, E., and A. Finney. *Managing Multimedia.* 2nd edition. Essex, England: Addison Wesley Longman Ltd., 1999.

Gagne, R.M. *The Conditions of Learning.* 4th edition. New York: Holt, Rinehart, Winston, 1985.

Haladyna, T. M. *Writing Test Items to Evaluate Higher Order Thinking.* Needham Heights, MA: Allyn & Bacon, 1996.

Hall, B. *Web-based Training Cookbook.* New York: John Wiley & Sons, 1997.

Hartley, D. *On-Demand Learning: Training in the New Millennium.* Amherst, MA: HRD Press, 2000.

———. *Selling E-Learning.* Alexandria, VA.: ASTD, 2001.

Horton, W. *Designing Web-based Training.* New York: John Wiley & Sons, 2000.

Kirkpatrick, D.L. *Evaluating Training Programs: The Four Levels.* 2nd edition. San Francisco: Berrett-Koehler, 1998.

Kelly, K. *New Rules for the New Economy: 10 Radical Strategies for a Connected World.* New York: Penguin, 1999.

Lee, W.W., and D.L. Owens. *Multimedia-Based Instructional Design: Computer-based Training, Web-based Training, Distance Broadcast Training.* San Francisco: Jossey-Bass Pfeiffer, 2000.

Lipnack, J., and J. Stamps. *Virtual Teams: People Working Across Boundaries with Technology.* New York: John Wiley & Sons, 2000.

Mager, R.F. *Preparing Instructional Objectives.* 3rd edition. Atlanta: Center for Effective Performance, 1997.

McArdle, G.E. *Training Design and Delivery.* Alexandria, VA: ASTD, 1999.

McCain, D.V. *Creating Training Courses: When You're Not a Trainer.* Alexandria, VA: ASTD, 1999.

Milano, M., and Ullius, D. *Designing Powerful Training: The Sequential-Iterative Model.* San Francisco: Jossey-Bass Pfeiffer, 1998.

Moore, M.G., and G. Kearsley. *Distance Education: A Systems View.* Belmont, CA: Wadsworth Publishing, 1996.

Morgan, C., and M. O'Reilly. *Assessing Open and Distance Learners.* London: Kogan Page Ltd., 1999.

References & Resources

Piskurich, G.M. *Self-Directed Learning: A Practical Guide to Design, Development, and Implementation*. San Francisco: Jossey-Bass, 1993.

Piskurich, G.M., et al. eds. *The ASTD Handbook of Training Design and Delivery*. New York: McGraw-Hill, 2000.

Rossett, A. *First Things Fast: A Handbook for Performance Analysis*. San Francisco: Jossey-Bass Pfeiffer, 1999.

Rosset, A., and K. Sheldon. *Beyond the Podium: Delivering Training and Performance to a Digital World*. San Francisco: Jossey-Bass Pfeiffer, 2001.

Senge, P., et al. *The Fifth Discipline Fieldbook: Strategies and Tools for Building a Learning Organization*. New York: Doubleday, 1994.

Smith, P.L., and T.J. Ragan. *Instructional Design*. 2nd edition. Upper Saddle River, NJ: Simon & Schuster, 1999.

Thomsett, M.C. *The Little Black Book of Project Management*. New York: AMACOM, 1990.

Journal

Cyrs, T.E., ed. "Teaching and Learning at a Distance: What It Takes to Effectively Design, Deliver, and Evaluate Programs." *New Directions for Teaching and Learning*. San Francisco: Jossey-Bass, 1997.

Infolines

Elengold, L.J. "Teach SMEs to Design Training." No. 250106.

Hodell, C. "Basics of Instructional Systems Development." No. 259706.

Phillips, J. "Level 1 Evaluation: Reaction and Planned Action." No. 259813.

———. "Level 2 Evaluation: Learning." No. 259814.

Phillips, J., and R.D. Stone. "Level 4 Evaluation: Business Results." No. 259816.

Phillips, J., W. Jones, and C. Schmidt. "Level 3 Evaluation: Application." No. 259815.

Phillips, J., P.F. Pulliam, and W. Wurtz. "Level 5 Evaluation: Mastering ROI." No. 259805.

Sanders, E. "Learning Technologies." No. 259902.

Tanquist, S. "Evaluating E-Learning." No. 250009.

Waagen, A.K. "Essentials for Evaluation." No. 259705.

Media Selection Matrix

The following matrix will help you determine whether Web-based training is appropriate for your training needs.

Is this a (or some combination of):

☐ Authoring System

☐ Content Management System

☐ Delivery System

Directions: Rate the Importance Level of Each as either:

2 = "must have" or 1 = "like to have"

Upon completion, add up the checks or number of criteria meet. This and the cost of the system will help you select the appropriate system.

Criteria	Importance	Vendor or System Name			
Animation • Importing • Exporting					
Video • Importing • Exporting • Streaming					
Programming Capabilities • Java • VB Script • HTML • XML					
User Testing • Give responses • Provide feedback • Track scores					

(continued on next page)

Job Aid

		Vendor or System Name			
Criteria	**Importance**				
Features ● Back button ● Next button ● Glossary button ● Home button					
Administration ● Track learner progress ● Assign username and passwords					
Support ● Technical support ● Instructor/SME Support					
3rd Party Integration ● Existing or legacy systems ● Plug-ins ● Programs					
Total Criterion Meet					
Cost ● Product ● Support ● Enhancements					
System(s) Selected					

Be a Better Needs Analyst

Issue 8502

Be a Better Needs Analyst

Be a Better Needs Analyst 39

Conducting the Needs Analysis 39

Needs Analysis Guidelines 42

Data Collection Instruments 44

Designing and Using Instruments 45

Questionnaires 46

Interviews 48

Observations 50

Work Samples 51

Records and Reports 52

References & Resources 53

Job Aid

Checklist for Designing Instruments 54

Editorial Staff for 8502

Editor
Madelyn R. Callahan

ASTD Internal Consultants
Ron Zemke
Allison Rossett

Revised 1998

Editor
Cat Sharpe

Contributing Editor
Ann Bruen

Be a Better Needs Analyst

Question:
What is the last thing a needs analyst should be expected to do?

Answer:
Read minds.

In today's business market, analysts must have strong communication and technical skills, proficiency in the use of time-tested assessment instruments, and a fair amount of ingenuity. If they possess these qualities and have a firm commitment from their client, they will not need to be clairvoyant.

Successful needs analyses rely on good strategies and the support of the client organization. This is the ideal foundation for beginning a needs study. Effective analysts can start out with a clear focus: to find the right problem and the right solution.

The classical approach to determining needs or problems is **identifying the discrepancy between the desired and actual knowledge, skills, and performance (and specifying root causes).** That difference is the training need. A variety of methods including interviews, observations, questionnaires, and tests may lead to identifying needs.

Using these methods effectively involves accurate gathering, analyzing, verifying, and reporting of data. Critical competencies for the analyst's role include the following:

- understanding organizational structure, power, culture, and communication systems

- understanding the factors that contribute to and hinder group and individual changes in organizations

- identifying the knowledge and skills necessary to perform jobs; assessing individuals' abilities

- using technology (such as computers, Web-based training, the Internet, intranets, CD-ROM) to assist training and evaluation

- observing and describing behavior objectively

- developing sound data collection and analysis methods

- processing, synthesizing, and forming appropriate conclusions about the data

- providing constructive feedback

- designing presentations and communicating information, recommendations, suggestions, and ideas.

What this means is that skilled analysts are now among the most important professionals in the training, development, and performance fields. Technological advances and expanding industries continually create new workplace training requirements, increasing the demand for skilled analysts and accurate assessment methods. With unrelenting budget cuts hitting training departments, today's trainers have bigger jobs, yet correspondingly smaller budgets than they did in the past. For many organizations, a sound needs analysis is essential to a return on training investment dollars and reduces the risk of funding inappropriate programs.

This chapter will help you improve your needs analysis techniques, paying special attention to administering interviews and questionnaires. It provides a beginning for the trainer who wants to conduct, report, and justify effective needs assessments.

Conducting the Needs Analysis

As with any analysis, there are procedures to be followed in order to produce a useful product. Here are six basic steps to help you focus your needs analysis.

Step 1: Define Your Objectives

Determine your purposes and objectives for the analysis. These factors are the bases for management planning and development decisions. Some objectives for conducting a needs analysis are as follows:

- Distinguish employees who need training.

- Identify performance problems, deficiencies, and the root causes.

- Determine whether training is the best solution to the problems.

Nailing Down Needs Assessment

Across the nation trainers hear words like these:

Brad, in just a little over five weeks, our new blockbuster sandwich will be available to the public in 2,600 stores and franchises across the nation. I want to be certain that this sandwich is done right everywhere. It has to taste exactly the same in Boise and Boston. That's where you come in. Get some training ready to go so that our people know how to make that sandwich and make it good. Start with a needs assessment. But don't spend too long before you start writing that training.

Wilma, see that box over there? It's full of illustrated manuals that pretty much describe how the new system will work. Well, actually, that documentation is for the hospital, which is one-third our size, but the vendor swears that we'll be able to use it here. And here's Sharon Murray's number. She is the vendor rep who can help you out. We need this course and we need it fast. No time for a whatchamacallit, a needs assessment, this time.

The phrase *needs assessment* is everywhere, and everywhere it means something different. That makes it difficult to learn about, challenging to do well, and nearly impossible to explain to a skeptical colleague.

Fortunately there are some things about needs assessment that most experts recognize:

1. It comes at the beginning of any systematic approach to training, prior to teaching anybody anything in any setting or technology.

2. It is done to understand more about a performance problem—some gap between what is happening and what ought to be happening. This means that needs assessment is the systematic search for details about the difference between optimal and actual.

3. There is a lot of verbal support for the idea of needs assessment, far more than for the time and resources it takes to do it well. When people want trainers to solve problems, they want them solved yesterday. If a needs assessment stands between the problem and a snappy new course, then needs assessment is suspect.

4. People who conduct needs assessments usually do so using in-person and telephone interviews and questionnaires. Training literature clearly presents the leading characteristics of these two techniques: ease of data analysis, anonymity, opportunity to follow up responses, and cost.

5. Needs assessments usually ask for people's feelings. The inquiry should focus on what sources feel is causing the performance problem and whether or not the trainees could perform successfully under pressure. Training resources should not be used on problems that better supervision or powerful incentive plans can dispatch.

6. Training and therefore needs assessment is not about performance problems as much as it used to be. Now it is about new systems and technologies, necessitating expanded ways of understanding the situation before training.

These areas of accord provide little solace to people like Wilma and Brad who need to know what needs assessment is, why it is important, and how to do it. It is not just one act like sending out a survey. It is several stages of assessment, using several techniques, each of which gets you closer to knowing what is going on, and why.

Needs assessments are used to discover the following things:

Optimal performance. Both of the trainers described above need to seek out the details of what constitutes excellent performance.

Actual performance. How well is each employee performing? How have middle managers conducted their performance appraisals? New systems and technologies involve little examination of current, actual performance. These training needs assessments will be based primarily on information about optimals.

Attitudes on subject, skills, or technology. This search is crucial for training design. Will Wilma walk into the hospital training center and be greeted with hostility? Do middle managers believe that the old appraisal system was perfectly adequate? Are they confident of their ability to master a computerized behavioral rating scale?

The cause or causes of the problem. There are still those old-fashioned performance problems caused by poor incentives, motivation, skills, knowledge, or work environment. Which of these is the obstacle in Wilma's situation? Needs assessment must tell you that.

Trainers perform needs assessments until they know, in detail and conclusively, the nature of the mission (optimal minus actual); the attitudes or feelings; and the causes of problems. The search for information varies, depending on what got you started: a performance problem, or a new task, system, or technology.

Allison Rossett

- Secure the support and commitment of management in the process of building and evaluating effective training programs.

- Generate data that will be useful in measuring the impact of the training program.

- Provide specific recommendations for training programs: scope, methods, frequency, cost, and location.

- Decide priorities for the upcoming year and for long-range strategic planning.

- Justify spending to top management by determining the value and cost of training. Calculate the difference between "no training" costs (the expenses incurred or monies lost by continuing with the same problems) and the costs of the training solution.

Step 2: Identify the Necessary Data

A thorough needs assessment requires information to identify:

- the need
- the solution
- the population requiring training
- the strategies for delivering training.

Know the nature and quantity of the information you require for a useful assessment study. You may need opinions, attitude surveys, financial statements, job descriptions, performance appraisals, work samples, or historical documents from the company's archives.

Step 3: Select Data Collection Method

Choose or design a method for gathering data. Use various combinations of the following methods, alternating between their structured and unstructured versions: interviews, questionnaires, observation, group discussion, key consultation, work samples, records, reports, and tests.

Base structured or formal assessment methods on the necessary data as outlined in step two and also on a comparison of each method's degree of effectiveness for gathering the data. Validate all instruments (questionnaires, surveys, and so forth) used in this approach.

Step 4: Collect the Data

If you are dealing with a sample or study group, administer the questionnaires, conduct the interviews, observe performances, and so forth.

Step 5: Analyze and Confirm the Data

Compare the new data with past years' information and analyze to uncover problems and related trends or patterns. Confirm results and check for accuracy by consulting with the persons who originally provided the information.

Step 6: Prepare the Final Report

Point out problems, needs, weak areas, and recommend strategies for improvement. Using tables, graphs, and other support data for findings, design a clear and interesting presentation with well-written materials and attractive visuals. Some presentation skills are also necessary. Refer to *Infolines* No. 258410, "How to Prepare and Use Effective Visual Aids," and No. 259409, "Improve Your Communication and Speaking Skills."

Needs Analysis Guidelines

Following are a number of guidelines to keep in mind as you undertake a needs analysis. While all these suggestions may not be appropriate for your situation, many can help ease the task and simplify the process.

1. Use a model of human performance that is relevant and useful for your particular organization. The model should take into account the company's culture, climate, objectives, availability and allocation of resources, and specific factors that affect performance.

2. Use a comprehensive and flexible approach. A good needs analysis should address the total organization, a department, division, group, or a single individual.

3. Plan a well-timed analysis. Do not schedule assessments during difficult periods of structural change, transfer of ownership or executive management, or major policy revisions that affect all organizational levels. Analysts must assess the current needs of individual departments and divisions on their own terms but also on the basis of how these groups can be affected by changes in other areas of the organization.

4. Use your analysis to indicate if an actual, significant problem or need exists and, if it does, to develop an appropriate solution. Start by identifying the concerned members of the organization:

   ● Why are they interested in the problem?
   ● How do they perceive the problem?
   ● Why do they support training as a solution?

   To find the individuals responsible to that problem or need, begin at the top of the organizational structure and continue through the lower levels. Include the concerned individuals in every step of the process; they must assist in determining the needs and approve the analysis results.

5. Know your study subjects. To reduce the possibility of prescribing inappropriate training, analyze the performance level of your group. Do this by identifying discrepancy factors, the important differences between high and lower performers. Use this information in determining training program content and emphases. Enhance strong points discovered during the analysis.

6. Vary techniques for gathering data. Habitual use of a few approaches may trap you into inappropriate applications. Several kinds of independent performance studies are more likely to produce accurate needs assessments than one. For example, surveys may indicate a number of needs, but multiple group or one-on-one interviews may negate those findings.

7. Keep studies short. It is preferable to survey a small sample of high and low performers than to attempt an analysis of the entire workforce. Large-scale studies create unrealistic expectations of your work and high costs to the client. One good rule of thumb is that studies should be completed within 20 to 40 working days.

8. View front-end analysis costs as an investment in the future. Strong technical skills, effective assessment methods, accurate scoring, and a lucid, substantial final report are vital for successful analyses. Always schedule enough time to prepare a good presentation of your needs analysis results, even if you must stop the process before completing some additional data analyses. At the end, it is better to spend time and money on polishing rather than hastily constructing a presentation.

9. In reports and presentations, convey the right amount of information to the appropriate audience at the appropriate time. Reports are typically long and comprehensive, indicating results of surveys, questionnaires, and other methods for gathering data. They may also include explanations of methods and samples of data-gathering devices. Following are some groups that may be in your presentation audience:

- study subjects
- employees of the client organization
- funding agencies
- top and middle management
- professional colleagues
- other needs analysts.

10. In presentations, use a variety of strategies for presenting results. Some include:

Graphics. Illustrations, photographs, boxes, different typefaces, and white space are effective design elements and contribute to the appearance of all printed material. Slides, overheads, and videotapes are useful for large presentations.

Needs Analysis Planning Checklist

Unfortunately, many companies lose time, effort, and funds on unsuccessful needs studies, and all too often, their failures can be traced to poor planning. Sound decisions at the beginning guarantee a strong foundation throughout the analysis. Start making wise choices by thinking through the following issues:

☐ Who is being trained? What are their job functions? Are they from the same department or a variety of areas in the organization?

☐ What are their deficiencies? Why are they deficient?

☐ What are the objectives of the needs analysis?

☐ How will a needs analysis assist in solving problems and benefit the organization?

☐ What are the expected outcomes? Will they have a pervasive effect on many organizational levels (departmental, divisional, regional, and corporate)?

☐ Will assessment instruments (questionnaires, surveys, tests, and so forth), interviews, or a combination be most appropriate? Who will administer these, in-house personnel or external consultants?

☐ Will the analysis interrupt the work process? What effect will this have on the workforce and on productivity?

☐ Will there be a confidentiality policy for handling information? Will the individuals working with the information honor this policy?

Summaries. A separate sheet of research briefs or condensed sections of the text can be the most important information for fast, easy reading. These may be executive (introductory) or report (concluding) summaries, abstracts, or overview quotations.

Oral Reports. A short presentation of essential information should give the highlights of results, clarify questions concerning methods or findings, and encourage all concerned to act on the recommendations of the report with interest and commitment.

Data Collection Instruments

Instruments are tools such as questionnaires, tests, checklists, surveys, and scales that systematically gather data about individuals, groups, or entire organizations. In a needs analysis they indicate both weak and strong areas. Answer the following questions to determine your needs, and then you can select the type(s) that best suits your needs, time constraints, and budget requirements from the below-listed descriptions of the most commonly used instrument types.

- What are the stated goals or expectations of the personnel being studied? How do they relate to the organizational goals?

- What is the organizational climate?

- What are the backgrounds and educational profiles of the personnel being studied?

- Who will administer, score, and interpret results?

- Does the use of follow-up of instruments require special training? If so, is this training available?

- Is the scoring objective, or will it require special skills? (Objective scoring eliminates the need for such skills, and respondents more easily accept the results as accurate.)

- How complicated is the scoring? Complex scoring scales are costly and time consuming.

Instrument Formats

All instruments share certain characteristics. They can be easily and quickly administered, usually without special training; they can be administered in groups and do no disrupt the workplace; they can be scored quickly and accurately using computer software designed for data collection; and the results obtained are objective, so training departments do not need to interpret them. Here is a listing of several instrument formats from which you can select to conduct your data collection.

■ *Likert Scale*
This is a linear scale used to rate statements and attitudes. Respondents receive a definition of the scale ranging from one to 10 with, for example, one indicating least important and 10 indicating most important.

■ *Semantic Differential*
In this format, participants rate two contrasting ideas or words that are separated by a graduated line, either numbered or unnumbered. They indicate frequency of behavior or depth of opinion by circling points on the line. An example measuring the value of new equipment would be:

VALUABLE – – – – – – – – – – – – – – – – – USELESS
1 2 3 4 5 6 7 8 9 10

■ *Alternate Response*
This is an inventory format that forces respondents to choose between two acceptable statements. The choices present a pattern of responses indicating tendencies toward particular behaviors or attitudes. This is the hardest type of instrument to construct because both statements must be plausible enough to present a difficult choice, but sufficiently different to distinguish two separate sets of beliefs and attitudes.

■ *Multiple-Choice*
Also difficult to construct, this format consists of choosing one item or statement from several well-planned and well-written choices. Each choice must be logically consistent with all elements of the instrument. The results indicate a person's style, behavioral patterns, and attitudes. For example, with this format it is possible to identify and analyze styles of leadership, communication, training, problem solving, management, and sales.

■ *Open-Ended*
This essay question format also may be difficult to construct. Questions must be objective, free of the questioner's biases, and clear enough for respondents to complete the questionnaires or surveys without a great deal of assistance. These questions are not limited to preselected responses.

■ *Completion*

This format presents well-designed completion questions that encourage participants to disclose opinions and perceptions about themselves, their jobs, careers, and other workers and managers. Some experts have found that completion helps to focus and stimulate respondents' thinking, more so than the open-ended format, because it forces them to use their own thoughts and language to complete or fill in the blanks.

Designing and Using Instruments

Before you begin your needs analysis, you must do considerable planning. Follow these suggestions to achieve optimum results:

Become familiar with instruments. Study the different formats and respond to a variety of instruments. Analyze for style, tone, word choice, and language patterns. How do the words stimulate thoughts and feelings?

Gather preliminary information for your instrument. Interviews, observations, reports, and print media will provide excellent background material. From these sources select key issues for your focus.

Choose the most important issues and arrange them in logical sequence. For example, assessing sales skills would require organizing ideas on communication, presentation, and negotiation.

Select an appropriate format. If this is your first effort, use an easy format such as the completion questionnaire or rating scale.

Write questionnaire items and statements clearly and logically. Write clear and simple instructions: "Read through the list of duties and indicate how often you perform these jobs by circling 'frequently,' 'occasionally,' 'infrequently,' or 'never.'" Do not ask wordy or combined questions such as, "Do you have sufficient time to keep up with production standards, or should you petition for weekend overtime and temporary outside assistance?" Separate these into two questions.

Provide spaces for comments next to or following each question.

Focus your questions to gather information and responses that are more specific than "yes" or "no." For example: "What training exercises are most useful to you on the job?" "What practice activities would improve the training program?"

Emphasize important distinctions to avoid mis-interpretations of questions. For example, "What exercises are *not* helpful?" "Does the training program address both problems *and* workers' needs?" "Are the statements true *or* false?"

Assign descriptions to numerical scales to help participants answer questions. For example: "In comparison to your old machinery, how helpful are the new computer terminals?"

1	2	3	4	5
not helpful	less helpful	no change	more helpful	very helpful

Carefully examine the instrument and items it is designed to measure; these should be clearly and logically related.

Administer the instrument at different times to the same participants under the same conditions to establish the tool's reliability. If the results are the same, the instrument is reliable.

Look for valid content. The instrument should measure the items as it promises.

Evaluate instruments based on whether they are appropriate for the study subjects: For example, is the instrument written in a clear, jargon-free style? Are there any statements or questions in it that will cause negative reactions? How well known is this particular instrument? Will participants be familiar with the format? Too familiar?

Introduce participants to the instrument by pointing out that it is not an examination form but an assessment tool for determining training needs. The instruments help individuals assess department operations, managers' performance, and their own individual job performance.

Provide a simple scoring system. Complex systems may cause confusion and frustration. Systems that subtract points for unacceptable answers will be seriously questioned. Use *general* scores to call attention to tendencies or patterns. Precise computations and percentages are not meaningful in this context. Inform respondents that scores are general guidelines indicating patterns rather than final judgments.

De-emphasize the numbers. Groups must understand that the objective is to focus on behavior, attitude, and values. Provide precise scoring instructions if groups are more comfortable with numbers and "how much" qualifiers.

Periodically try different procedures. Get a feel for when precise or general scoring is most useful, depending on the background of the group, the training goals, and your own training standards.

Questionnaires

In this instrument, individuals respond to a printed question-and-answer format—such as surveys, polls, and checklists—by choosing from lists of prepared answers or writing in original responses. Questionnaires may solicit factual information ("How many overtime hours do you work per week?") or opinions ("How do you feel about working two shifts?").

Use questionnaires to accomplish the following goals:

● reach a large or geographically dispersed population in a limited period of time

● determine areas of inquiry that require further investigation through other assessment methods

● verify information gathered from other sources.

Following are the advantages and disadvantages of using questionnaires:

Advantages

● Comparatively inexpensive to administer and easy to construct, questionnaires yield data that can be tabulated and reported without difficulty.

● Respondents may freely give confidential information without fear of reprisal.

● No special training is necessary to administer the questionnaire or tabulate results.

● Many standard questionnaires are available, eliminating development time and effort.

Disadvantages

● Since communication is one way, respondents may not properly interpret questions. Results may also be misinterpreted.

● The questionnaire may not get at causes of and solutions to problems. It may not ask the most effective questions, missing the point of the analysis.

● The development of effective and reliable instruments requires strong technical skills and may be costly.

● Low return rates and inappropriate responses hinder the accuracy of questionnaires.

Electronic Questionnaires

The increased use of email and intranets has opened new options for gathering information. The electronic questionnaire can be completed online, promising a quick turnaround of responses. The information can be submitted directly to a database, thereby reducing or eliminating data entry. There are, however, disadvantages to using electronic questionnaires. Your target population is limited to those who have access to email or the intranet, and therefore, your results may be biased. In addition, the investment of time and money necessary to purchase the necessary software and learn how to use it may be prohibitive.

Tips for Effective Questionnaires

When preparing and administering questionnaires, follow these tips for success:

1. Before developing the questionnaire, gather preliminary information. Interview a small sample of people to get a sense of the language and emphases that must be part of the questionnaire.

2. Determine the kind of results you expect from the questionnaire. Then identify the questions that will produce this information.

3. During development, clearly focus the questionnaire. Lengthy and broad questionnaires will be answered grudgingly and hastily, if at all. Developers should establish a reasonable amount of time for gathering necessary information.

4. When considering formats and questionnaire design, keep the following factors in mind: the background and job of the respondent, the kind of information that is required, the purpose for gathering the information, and its application.

5. Select the appropriate type of questionnaire based on the number of respondents. With large groups, use a checklist or alternate response questionnaire for simple processing and data comparison. Checklists are suitable for presenting data in quantified form.

6. Avoid using open-ended questionnaires with large groups. The responses are very difficult to quantify. Small groups benefit most from this format. Questionnaires provide them with substantial information worth the processing time and effort.

7. If you plan to use questionnaires on a regular basis, develop question files for the companies and jobs you will be assessing most often. The files will help you construct questionnaires to suit the particular requirements for each job; ascertain the effectiveness of the questions in prior situations; and adjust the questions according to current changes in the organization or department.

8. Give every assurance to respondents that the questionnaire is confidential. Besides verbal assurances, you can offer them the opportunity to use code numbers instead of their names on the questionnaires. Avoid asking for biographical data such as age, gender, or marital status. If this data is required, however, word the question in general terms. For example, a question about age would be:

Indicate the age bracket to which you belong.

(a) 18 to 35   (b) 35 to 50   (c) over 50

9. If responses are grievances and complaints, address these in a straightforward manner. Explain your plans to improve or alleviate problem situations and let respondents know that management recognizes and understands the problems, including those they may not have the power to solve.

10. Keep questionnaires simple and relevant to employees' performances. Do not use the questionnaire as an opportunity to gather information about other segments of the organization. This wastes time and creates doubts in respondents' minds about the stated purpose of the questionnaire.

11. Always use questionnaires in conjunction with a variety of other methods.

12. Do not regard questionnaire results as ends in themselves but as stimulation for additional discussion and analysis of problems. For example, during interviews solicit participants' opinions with questions based on the questionnaire results. Do participants agree with the findings? What are their reasons for agreeing or disagreeing?

13. Do not administer questionnaires to low literacy groups. A negative experience with this method will set the tone for your entire study. Choose instead interviews or observation—methods that do not involve reading or writing—or use questionnaires as outlines in structured interviews.

14. Be sure that respondents are able to supply the required answers before administering the questionnaire. For example, word processing assistants would not be able to offer an improved software design for their computer work. They could make useful recommendations for more efficient software options, but they should not be expected to have program design skills.

15. To determine if the data will be usable, test the questions by anticipating possible responses. Well-designed questions receive few unproductive responses, such as: "I can run this department better than my supervisor;" or "This new equipment keeps me from doing a better job—I suggest buying other machinery by a different manufacturer."

16. Always test the questionnaire. Ask a sample group or at least two individuals to comment on clarity and format. This feedback indicates which questions and instructions should be reworded or edited, reducing the possibility of misinterpretation. Questionnaires going to more than 200 people should be tested by 10 to 20 respondents, and the results subsequently analyzed. Easily misinterpreted or leading questions should be reworded as well as any questions that solicit strictly positive or negative responses.

17. When appropriate, share the results with respondents ether in a letter to them or by addressing them in small groups. Their valuable feedback on the quality of the data and the experience of analyzing and discussing the data establishes trust and confidence, essential qualities for additional successful activities. If you cannot share the results with participants, send a letter thanking them for their participation and telling them how you intend to use the information they contributed.

18. Investigate using a commercially prepared questionnaire for standard assessments.

Interviews

The interview is an active interchange, either in person or via telephone with one individual or a group. It may be a first step or the central means of gathering data in a needs analysis program. Interviews may be formal and highly structured, with prepared questions, or they may be casual and flexible, directed mainly by the interviewee and focused on topics that may evolve spontaneously during conversation. Suggested discussion topics include the following: problems on the job; ideas for improvement or solutions; the most and least liked parts of the job; working relationships with co-workers, managers, and staff; job achievements; personal goals; and interest in obtaining more knowledge and skills.

Use interviews to accomplish these goals:

- gather background data at the beginning of analysis or supplement and expand data from instruments and observations

- obtain input from those people who better express their views in person than on written surveys or questionnaires (this input can be used to construct more effective instruments)

- identify causes of problems and possible solutions by encouraging interviewees to reveal their feelings and opinions on these matters

- give participants pride of ownership in the analysis process by inviting them to provide the data for diagnosing training needs.

Following are the advantages and disadvantages of using interviews:

Advantages

- Interviews clarify expectations and assumptions about the process for both the analyst and the group being studied. They enable parties to become familiar with one anothers' language and jargon and help uncover root problems yet untreated.

- Interviews are good opportunities to build rapport. They demonstrate that decision makers value employees' opinions and empathize with staff. In open-ended and nondirective interviews, participants and interviewers can relax and be themselves.

● Interviewers receive additional information in the form of nonverbal messages. Interviewees' behaviors, their gestures, eye contact, and general reactions to questions are additional data or cues for the next questions.

● Good questioning techniques focus data and produce solid, manageable evidence. Interviewers use these techniques to probe ambiguous responses and unexpected leads.

Disadvantages

● Interview-generated data can be affected by the interviewer's biases. In some cases interviewers become too involved with clients' problems and turn the interviews into counseling sessions.

● It can be very difficult to organize and analyze the data results accurately, especially with unstructured interviews. Frequently, wide variation exists between clients' self-assessed and actual performances.

● Unskilled interviewers sometimes make clients feel self-conscious. In such cases, interviewees will say whatever they think the interviewer wants to hear.

Tips for Conducting Effective Interviews

Interviews require thorough preparation. You must plan out in detail exactly what you want to accomplish during the interview and the steps you will take to accomplish those goals. Here are some tips for success:

1. Conduct interviews in private, comfortable environments, such as conference rooms, that are free of traffic and interruptions. Opt for a neutral space instead of a work site or supervisor's office where having a desk between you and the interviewee may be an obstacle.

2. Prepare for the interview by observing the department and gathering information. What are the specific problems and difficulties that are immediately apparent? How frequently do they occur?

3. Determine the number of interviews required for a successful study. If interviews are your only source of data, schedule more than the amount needed to develop questionnaires and surveys. Experts suggest conducting only four to six interviews when studying a homogeneous group. The first interviews may give you up to 98 percent of the necessary information.

4. Be well prepared with solid interviewing techniques and a plan for conducting the interview. Decide whether you want it to be structured or flexible and open ended.

5. Prepare participants and allay their anxieties by fully explaining the purpose of the interview and the process. Let them know that you have been asked by management to prepare a training program based on information derived from these interviews.

6. Set the climate for the interview and put interviewees at ease with general questions that can be easily answered by the interviewee, such as "What does your job entail? What do you like most about it?" Gradually incorporate more specific inquiries about problems, for example: "If you had the authority, what changes would you make in the organization?"

7. As interviewees enter the room, ask them if note-taking, audio- or videotaping during the interview will make them uncomfortable. If they do not feel self-conscious about recording, proceed carefully. If you tape the interview, use a counter so you can access salient information without running through the entire tape.

8. Keep questions broad based enough not to indicate how they should be answered. They should be short and to the point.

9. Create a good environment for understanding and communication. Strong listening skills help you gather detailed and accurate information.

10. Keep the interview focused and stay on course. To avoid having your interview change into a counseling session, maintain a friendly distance from clients' serious personal problems by suggesting they speak in detail with qualified professionals such as counselors, personnel specialists, advisers, or therapists.

11. Never make interviews mandatory. If participants feel threatened, the interview data will reflect their self-consciousness and half-hearted cooperation.

12. Conduct group interviews when *group* behavior determines job performance. Although individual interviews may give you the information you need, they may also signal an effort to break up the group, resulting in reduced morale and effectiveness.

13. Make necessary provisions for group interviews during *and* after work. If the workday must be interrupted for interviews, affecting workers with interdependent jobs, provide assistance such as rescheduling the extra workload or bringing in temporary help.

14. Clarify misunderstandings about interviews scheduled after work hours. Assumptions that administrators do not think the process warrants company time sharply reduce the validity of findings and data. Determine whether to compensate off-the-clock interviewees with pay or compensatory time.

15. Remember to get the entire, accurate story and all the facts. If an interviewee requests that information be kept off the record, accommodate that wish.

16. If appropriate, interview at least three other persons who can offer useful information about a participant in an individual needs assessment. Others, such as supervisors, subordinates, and customers, may provide valuable insights into the subject's behavior.

17. Never betray your clients' trust. Confidentiality is crucial for a successful analysis; it is also the basis of your credibility.

18. End the interview in a comfortable, straightforward manner.

19. Analyze and summarize the data. Maintain objectivity; do not let your analysis be overshadowed by your own theories.

20. Report the analysis of the data. Follow a confidential reporting procedure that is comfortable for each interviewee.

Observations

The needs analyst obtains data directly by observing behavior and interacting with the workforce (employees, managers, clients, and field representatives). Observation is a fundamental tool with both broad and highly specific applications. Use observation to accomplish the following objectives:

- obtain background information on topics such as group dynamics, the organization's culture, or the work climate

- supplement interviews and questionnaires

- validate information derived from interviews and questionnaires

- investigate possible communication problems; inefficient use of time, resources, and personnel; declining operational standards; ineffective procedures; and conflicts between management and staff

- identify positive or strong characteristics.

Following are the advantages and disadvantages of using observation as a data-collection tool:

Advantages

- Observation gives observers an idea of a typical workday.

- Observation is unobtrusive; it may be as unstructured as a walk down the hall or a casual chat with workers. It minimizes disruptions of the work process and activity.

- Observation provides direct contact with situations. It yields on-the-job reports and is, therefore, highly relevant and valid.

- Administrative costs may be low if the observation is casual and relatively unstructured.

Disadvantages

- It is difficult to record data and to observe large numbers of people when using this tool.

- Employees may feel that they are being scrutinized and consequently may alter their performance.

- When observation is restricted to the work setting, data may be limited.

- It can be time consuming. Many jobs are part of cyclical operations that take place on a weekly, monthly, or yearly basis. A great deal of time would be necessary to observe all of these operations.

Tips for Effective Observation

To get an overall sense of the organizational climate, you can observe the work environment and interact with personnel. Following are some suggestions for successfully using observation as an information-gathering tool:

1. Explain the purpose and process of the observation to all supervisors and subordinates. This will alleviate any fears about "spying."

2. Describe actions with narrative statements or checklists.

3. Stay close to activity but remain unobtrusive.

4. Check at various points during the process to make sure that you are gathering meaningful and accurate information. Cross-check for validity by consulting reports, records, and staff.

5. Avoid returning for additional observation. This is disruptive and nonproductive, particularly in plant or factory environments where the work routine varies only slightly from day to day.

6. Reduce false expectations and waste in training expenditures by using observation to distinguish those employees who are most likely to benefit from training.

7. Restrict activity to *watching* the workforce. In cases where individual coaching would improve and raise performance to company standards, ask supervisors to handle the coaching. This will let supervisors know you are not trying to usurp their responsibilities.

8. Assess reliability of the data. Two or more observers of the same operations should have coinciding ratings. Agreement among raters is the basis for determining the validity of the data.

9. Share the results of the observation with the group *before* this data becomes part of the needs analysis report.

Work Samples

This frontline information can be in the form of tangible work samples such as the manager's reports, a secretary's typing, a repairman's mending of equipment, or a computer programmer's new software design. Or, it can be less tangible, for example, a teacher's presentation of a lesson or a manager conducting a meeting. Work samples can also be advertising layouts, market analyses, training designs, or program proposals.

Use work samples to identify problem areas that may require further analysis. If a department's or individual's products are found unsatisfactory on a regular basis, then an investigation may be necessary. Work samples also may be used to supplement other assessment methods, to validate other data, and to gather preliminary information for the study.

Here are some of the advantages and disadvantages to using work samples for gathering data:

Advantages

- The method is unobtrusive.

- As is the case with records and reports, this method provides clues to trouble spots.

- It also provides direct data on the organization's actual work.

Disadvantages

- Using this method may be costly and time consuming. The wrong sample will provide little or no information.

- In order to use this data-gathering method, the trainer's skills must include specialized content analysis.

- Workers may alter their behavior if they know that some kind of observation is in progress.

Records and Reports

Company archives contain useful historical data in the form of the following: personnel, productivity, and financial records; government, planning, audit, budget, and program reports; policy handbooks; organizational structure charts; program evaluations; minutes of meetings; memorandums; documents explaining the organization's history; exit interviews; grievance files; quality control; career development information; and conference proceedings.

Use records and reports to accomplish the following goals:

- gather background information and acquire a general sense of the organization's culture and traditions

- verify information generated by other assessment methods

- understand how particular problems have influenced individuals and organizational competency.

Following are the advantages and disadvantages of using this method of information gathering:

Advantages

- It can indicate potential problem areas.

- This method is unobtrusive; researchers work on their own schedules without interrupting the workplace and routine.

- If stored, filed, and updated at the work site, this data can be collected easily, quickly, and inexpensively.

- This method has high validity, because the data is quantifiable, historical, and objective evidence.

Disadvantages

- Reports may be adjusted or "selectively edited."

- It may be difficult to obtain materials if access is restricted to authorized persons or if record-keeping procedures have changed over time.

- Documents are limited to a historical focus. This method requires skilled analysts to apply pertinent information to current problems.

- This method risks misinterpretation by unskilled analysts. Patterns and trends may be difficult to interpret from the data. Causes of problems and solutions may be unclear.

Tips for Using Records and Reports Effectively

In order to successfully employ this method of data gathering, do the following:

1. Find out what kinds of records and reports are kept in the company archives.

2. Decide whether these particular documents will give you the necessary information. For example, minutes from the monthly directors' planning meetings and studies of the turnover rate may not offer direct insight into the impact of the word processing training program.

3. Use reports such as turnover studies to indicate trouble spots. For example, if the turnover rate is higher than the average, a problem may exist requiring a needs analysis. Other kinds of documents, such as planning reports or career development materials, may directly identify training needs.

4. If the material is not immediately accessible, determine whether it is worth spending the time searching through files.

5. Use production records to find information about sales, customer complaints, back orders, and other production data.

6. In non-manufacturing companies, look for documents, such as strategic planning reports, explaining how the company is achieving its mission and objectives.

References & Resources

Articles

Brethower, Dale M. "Rapid Analysis: Matching Solutions to Changing Situations." *Performance Improvement,* November/December 1997, pp. 16-21.

Darraugh, Barbara. "It Takes Six." *Training & Development Journal,* March 1991, pp. 21-24.

Kaufman, Roger. "Auditing Your Needs Assessment." *Training & Development,* February 1994, pp. 22-23.

———. "A Needs Assessment Audit." *Performance & Instruction,* February 1994, pp. 14-16.

Kimmerling, George. "On Target: Needs Assessments and Organizational Goals." *Technical & Skills Training,* May/June 1992, pp. 26-30.

McClelland, Sam. "A Systems Approach to Needs Assessment." *Training & Development,* August 1992, pp. 51-53.

Moseley, James L., and Mary J. Heaney. "Needs Assessment Across Disciplines." *Performance Improvement Quarterly,* vol. 7, no. 1 (1994), pp. 60-79.

Rossett, Allison. "Have We Overcome Obstacles to Needs Assessment?" *Performance Improvement,* March 1997, pp. 30-35.

Sleezer, Catherine M. "Training Needs Assessment at Work: A Dynamic Process." *Human Resource Development Quarterly,* Fall 1993, pp. 247-264.

Watkins, Ryan, and Roger Kaufman. "An Update on Relating Needs Assessment and Needs Analysis." *Performance Improvement,* November/December 1996, pp. 10-13.

Zemke, Ron. "How to Do a Needs Assessment When You Think You Don't Have Time." *Training,* March 1998, pp. 38-44.

Books

ASTD Trainer's Toolkit: Needs Assessment Instruments. Alexandria, VA: ASTD, 1990.

Bartram, Sharon, and Brenda Gibson. *Training Needs Analysis: Resource for Identifying Training Needs, Selecting Training Strategies, and Developing Training Plans.* Aldershot, Hampshire, UK: Gower Publishing, 1994.

The Best of Needs Assessment. Alexandria, VA: ASTD, 1992.

Goldstein, Irwin L. *Training in Organizations: Needs Assessment, Development, and Evaluation.* 3rd edition. Pacific Grove, CA: Brooks/Cole Publishing, 1993.

Kaufman, Roger, et al. *Needs Assessment: A User's Guide.* Englewood Cliffs, NJ: Educational Technology Publications, 1993.

McClelland, Samuel B. *Organizational Needs Assessments: Design, Facilitation, and Analysis.* Westport, CT: Quorum Books, 1995.

Phillips, Jack J., and Elwood F. Holton, eds. *In Action: Conducting Needs Assessments.* Alexandria, VA: ASTD, 1995

Reay, David G. *Identifying Training Needs.* East Brunswick, NJ: Nichols Publishing, 1994.

Robinson, Dana Gaines, and James C. Robinson. *Performance Consulting: Moving Beyond Training.* San Francisco: Berrett-Kohler, 1995.

Swanson, Richard A. *Analysis for Improving Performance: Tools for Diagnosing Organizations and Documenting Workplace Expertise.* San Francisco: Berrett-Kohler, 1994.

Warfel, Sam L., and Robert L. Craig, eds. *The ASTD Training and Development Handbook: A Guide to Human Resource Development.* New York: McGraw-Hill, 1996.

Wilcox, John, ed. *ASTD Trainer's Toolkit: More Needs Assessment Instruments.* Alexandria, VA: ASTD, 1994.

Infolines

Austin, Mary. "Needs Assessment by Focus Group." No. 259401 (revised 1998).

Eline, Leanne. "How to Prepare and Use Effective Visual Aids." No. 258410 (revised 1997).

Gupta, Kavita. "Conducting a Mini Needs Assessment." No. 259611 (revised 1999).

Plattner, Francis B. "Improve Your Communication and Speaking Skills." No. 259409 (revised 1997).

Sparhawk, Sally, and Marian Schickling. "Strategic Needs Analysis." No. 259408 (revised 1999).

Job Aid

Checklist for Designing Instruments

When designing a needs analysis, it is very important to select the instrument or combination of instruments that best support your analysis objectives as well as your respondents' objectives. Regardless of your choice, however, each type of item requires special consideration during the design phase. The checklist that follows will help you determine whether your items are well written and are likely to help you gather the data you need for your analysis.

Directions: Complete the checklist appropriate to each type of item included in your analysis. Note that "no" answers may indicate potential problems in item construction that may bias your results.

	Yes	No	Comments
Multiple-Choice Items			
1. The central question or problem is stated in the stem of each item.			
2. The response choices for each item are grammatically correct.			
3. All the response choices within each item are approximately the same length.			
4. There are no ambiguous statements in the stems or the choices.			
5. All the choices for each item are feasible.			
6. The items are written at the language level of the respondents.			
7. The items are constructed so that clues cannot be obtained from other items.			
8. The items are constructed to measure the level of knowledge, specific skills, or attitudes.			
Completion Items			
1. Only significant words, feelings, or attitudes are omitted in incomplete sentence items.			
2. Each item is grammatically correct.			
3. Any question asked is explicit enough to be easily understood by the respondent.			
True-False Items			
1. All statements are entirely true or entirely false.			
2. No trivial details are included in any of the statements.			
3. The statements are concise without more elaboration than is necessary to give clear meaning.			
4. The statements avoid using specific determiners that signal the desired response.			
Essay Items			
1. The language in each item is precise and unambiguous.			
2. All problems or tasks are clearly stated.			
3. All special conditions are stated.			
4. The items clarify any additional directions needed beyond the general set of directions.			
5. No item may be answered with a simple "yes" or "no" response.			
6. All items are written at the respondent's comprehension level.			
Oral Items			
1. The possible response could not be a simple "yes, I agree," or "no, I don't agree."			
2. The response will not be embarrassing for the respondent to make.			
3. Specific directions are planned that would be helpful to the respondent in structuring a response.			
4. Wording of the oral question is at the respondent's level of comprehension.			
5. Possible follow-up questions are planned.			
Structured Interview Items			
1. The items for the interview are in a logical sequence.			
2. Each item is worded at the respondent's comprehension level.			
3. A method of recording responses is specified.			
4. Possible follow-up questions are planned.			
Attitude Scales			
1. All items are at the comprehension level of the respondent.			
2. Directions are clearly stated and define or describe the ratings to be used.			
3. Items are logically sequenced.			
4. The scale includes at least three, but no more than seven, ratings for each statement or set of words or ideas.			

The material appearing on this page is not covered by copyright and may be reproduced at will.

Conducting a Mini
Needs Assessment

Issue 9611

Conducting a Mini Needs Assessment

A U T H O R

Kavita Gupta
Consultant
Targeted Training
28 Pilgrim Drive
Winchester, MA 01890
Tel: 617.721.6440
Fax: 617.721.0406

Kavita Gupta has more than nine years' experience as a teacher, instructional designer, and consultant to several New England universities, Citicorp, and a performance improvement company. She holds an MS in instructional systems technology from Indiana University.

Conducting a Mini Needs Assessment 57

Defining a Mini Needs Assessment 57

Mini Versus Classic Needs Assessment 58

Advantages and Limitations 58

Mini Needs Assessment Steps 61

Step 1: Pinpoint the Problem 61

Step 2: Confirm the Problem 65

Step 3: Seek Solutions 68

References & Resources 70

Job Aid

Sample Client Interview Form 71

Editorial staff for 9611

Editor
Cat Sharpe

Associate Editor
Patrick McHugh

Copy Editor
Leanne Eline

Revised 1999

Conducting a Mini Needs Assessment

"The world is running on HST—or hare standard time," according to Tom Peters in his book, *The Pursuit of Wow! Every Person's Guide to Topsy-Turvy Times*. If you want to lead in the future, you will have to develop faster ways for getting the job done. Those who do not quickly pursue their business goals will lose the race. Human resource, development, and performance professionals can improve their sprinting speed by exploring new processes and determining where miniaturization can improve efficiency. The material presented in this *Infoline* explores one way to do that.

A mini needs assessment is a process for identifying training problems and solutions in a condensed timeframe. In addition to presenting the model itself, this *Infoline* provides sample forms and checklists you can use to implement a mini needs assessment in your organization. The process can be used by both internal and external training consultants with one caveat: Traditional needs assessment experience is recommended before you attempt a mini needs assessment.

Defining a Mini Needs Assessment

Consider the following situations:

You are the vice president of human performance improvement for a large software development company. You have been assigned the task of developing and implementing a competency-based sales training program for all marketing personnel in your new Internet division.

You head a small family-owned business. Your business has grown and you have added staff to fill new customer needs. Old-timers feel threatened by new staff and morale has fallen. Some of your long-standing customers are beginning to drift away. You need to get to the roots of these problems quickly and fix them.

You are the training director of a prestigious law firm. You must develop a communication skills training program for the partners and associates within the firm. Which aspects of communication to include in the training is unclear, but the firm has recently lost several clients to rival firms because of the brash behavior of a few junior attorneys. The partners and associates all have limited time for training because of their need to maintain a quota of billable hours.

You are the HRD leader of a financial services company. Customer service representatives lack product knowledge. Foreclosure specialists are unable to process loans because of the implementation of a new computer system. You are tasked with implementing a new diversity training program within two weeks.

While there is no denying that the first situation warrants a traditional in-depth approach to needs assessment such as a competency study, there is little doubt that comprehensive needs assessments may not be feasible in the other situations. The reason? Everyone appears to be hard-pressed for time—from the business owner to the HRD leader of the financial institution. For these professionals, diverse sources must be tapped quickly, if information relating to the performance or training needs of their organizations is to be obtained.

Thus, despite the well-documented advantages of a conventional needs assessment, it is often impossible or impractical to conduct the kind of in-depth data gathering associated with this method. In many situations similar to those presented earlier, organizations are faced with constraints that make an in-depth needs assessment impossible.

At its most basic level, **a mini needs assessment is an intervention that results in a set of action plans to help solve performance problems.** It condenses the needs assessment process into three essential steps:

1. Pinpoint the problem.

2. Confirm the problem.

3. Seek solutions.

One or two individuals can easily implement a mini assessment. The emphasis is on short interviews and focus group discussions to elicit a broad range of views about the problem. This information can then be distilled to identify problems and develop appropriate solutions. Because of the non-quantitative nature of the information, sophisticated statistical skills are not required of those doing the data gathering. Good analytical skills for identifying the problem and then summarizing the information gathered into correct solutions are imperative for those implementing the process.

Mini Versus Classic Needs Assessment

The main objective of a mini needs assessment is to gather needed information with as little fuss as possible. Its low-profile approach enables you to be in and out of an organization quickly. The classical approach to needs assessment, however, typically involves a larger sample size and has broad-ranging objectives.

A traditional needs assessment also employs a wider variety of tools such as surveys, task analyses, nominal group techniques, observations, or action research to solve performance problems. A mini assessment focuses mainly on firsthand information as its primary data collection tool. For additional details on methods and techniques for conducting in-depth needs analysis, see the following *Infolines*: No. 259713, "The Role of the Performance Needs Analyst"; No. 259408, "Strategic Needs Analysis"; No. 258502, "Be a Better Needs Analyst"; No. 258612, Surveys from Start to Finish"; and No. 259401, "Needs Assessment by Focus Group."

A traditional needs assessment—with its global scope and multitiered approach—can take several months to a year to complete. The chief reason for this relates to the dynamics of the approach. Assembling work teams and committees; developing and administering formal data collection instruments; and analyzing, refining, and preparing conclusions are all labor-intensive tasks. A mini needs assessment, on the other hand, eliminates the requirement for this infrastructure because its underlying premise is that only a few individuals will be available to conduct the assessment.

The number of specialists (internal or external) and level of organizational resources needed to execute a traditional needs assessment initiative also result in elevated costs. A mini needs assessment, however, makes few demands on an organization. Consequently, the costs are far more modest.

The classical approach to needs assessment ensures that training is clearly linked to defined outputs. It provides comprehensive data that can be used for job profile and competency model development. It also allows more time to determine the validity of training needs and to probe underlying issues related to performance problems. All this is necessary to leverage management

acceptance for high-cost performance interventions. For more information about interventions, refer to *Infoline* No. 259714, "The Role of the Performance Intervention Specialist."

In contrast, a mini needs assessment tries to address problems that require prompt attention. The mini action plan developed in Step 3: Seek Solutions, which follows below, immediately begins helping your client address the problems you are investigating. A mini needs assessment enables you to provide what all clients are looking for: rapid, effective results at minimal cost.

Advantages and Limitations

It is important to recognize that a mini assessment is not a replacement for an in-depth needs assessment. Rather, it is useful to think of it as a partner, or other alternative you can employ if the circumstances warrant. Each approach is designed to meet specific organizational needs in a given situation. The needs of the organization should dictate which approach will be most appropriate. In light of this, the benefits of employing an approach in a given situation can, therefore, become drawbacks to that same approach elsewhere. Let us consider the traditional approach first.

Traditional Approach: Benefits and Limits

■ *Validation of Results*
Perhaps the greatest benefit of a conventional needs assessment is validation of results. The rigorous and painstaking process permits an organization to have a great deal of confidence in the conclusions derived from a study. Assuming there is sufficient time to conduct such an analysis, its conclusions will be supported by extensive documentation and analytical expertise. When time is short, however, the rigors of validation can become serious drawbacks to this method.

■ *Organization-Wide Participation*
The conventional approach also encourages widespread organizational participation. The various work teams and committees that participate in an in-depth needs assessment ensure that a significant cross-section of the organization has a stake in the process. This widespread involvement and

visibility also enhances management and employee acceptance of the process and outcomes. In situations where work-flow requirements are rigid, the level of organizational participation required by an in-depth assessment can be a hindrance.

■ *Cross-Functional Data Generation*

The vast quantity of multipurpose data generated in an in-depth needs assessment can be employed for a variety of purposes. It can be the basis for competency modeling, job profiling, or performance review development. It can also identify the need for and development of comprehensive training programs. Applying the data from one project to serve as the basis of many others can, in the long run, justify the high costs associated with an in-depth assessment. For an organization with an isolated or short-term problem, however, the benefits of cross-functional data may be compromised by the data's lack of focus on the immediate problem.

Mini Approach: Benefits and Limits

■ *Quick to Complete*

The primary value of a mini needs assessment is its short duration. Mini assessments can take from a few days to a week, can focus on an immediate problem, and can get quick results. In situations where a problem causes a serious financial drain on the organization, a mini assessment can put action plans in place much faster—often well before a traditional assessment can even get organized. The trade-off is validity of data and the inability of assessors to undertake thorough analyses of problems.

■ *Low Risk*

A mini assessment is also low risk. Given its modest cost and the fact that it requires only a few people to implement, a mini assessment is more easily justified than a traditional approach. A mini assessment does not have the high profile and broad-based participation of an in-depth assessment, but if it fails, it will not have cost a year of effort or hundreds of thousands of dollars.

■ *Little Commitment Required*

A third advantage is the low level of client or organizational commitment needed for success. The flip side of broad-based participation is that some organizations, even if they can afford the price tag of an in-depth assessment, cannot afford to disrupt work flow and production, or place additional demands on the time of key employees. An in-depth assessment can easily fail if the necessary people in the organization cannot or will not get involved.

In this respect, a mini assessment imposes minimal demands on the organization, its people, and productivity. The main limitation of this low-profile approach is that the initiative does not receive the widespread visibility often associated with in-depth assessments.

■ *Minimizes Paperwork*

Mini assessments require minimal paperwork. By avoiding the painstaking data-gathering, analysis, and refinement steps of an in-depth assessment, a mini assessment manages documentation of findings, records, and report preparation on a simplified level. While having highly validated multipurpose data is enviable, if the assessment produces so much paperwork that no one wants to use the data, then the project is considered a failure. The short data-gathering phase of a mini assessment makes its results more focused and usable for dealing with problems at hand.

■ *Catalyst for Further Study*

Despite their short-term focus on a specific problem, mini assessments can serve as catalysts for further study by uncovering issues that prompt additional attention and research. It is not hard to imagine a series of mini needs assessments that deal with a number of problems or explore the ramifications of one problem. In any case, the mini assessment leaves the door open for further study when time or resources can be allocated.

■ *Delivery of Concise Action Plans*

This approach delivers concise action plans. While a global examination of a problem is often beneficial, it is easy to study a problem and never develop a solution. Because a mini assessment is so focused on a particular problem, it is more likely to identify practical action-steps to solve it.

When to Use a Mini Needs Assessment

A deciding factor is time. Consider using the approach for the following types of situations:

- The client will fund a short-duration analysis only.

- The client or stakeholders only have a small window of opportunity available to complete a needs assessment.

- A problem has brought productivity to a halt and immediate action is critical.

- The presence of any outside agency (including your needs assessment team) must be kept to a minimum in order to create the least amount of distraction to productivity.

- Several different areas need to be quickly evaluated to effect a collective solution. (In this situation, a series of mini needs assessments can be performed and the information consolidated into a collective solution.)

- The client does not require quantitative "numbers" justification during the analysis stage.

Process Model

Process Steps	How to Do the Steps	What Tools to Use	What Results You Want to Achieve
Step 1: Pinpoint the Problem	• Interview client • Uncover issues • Identify key stakeholders	• Process Model Checklist • Client Interview Form	Problem definition (client-defined only)
Step 2: Confirm the Problem	• Interview stakeholders • Assess the effect of the problem on the organization	• Process Model Checklist • Stakeholder Interview Questions • Focus Group Questions	Mini findings
Step 3: Seek Solutions	• Consider appropriate solutions • Gain consensus on mini action plan	• Process Model Checklist	Mini action plan

Copyright © Targeted Training, 1996. Used with permission.

Mini Needs Assessment Steps

The *Process Model* shown opposite defines the steps, identifies the tools to use, and shows desired end results. The *Process Model Checklist* depicted on the next page provides a list of reminders you can use to plan each step of your mini needs assessment. It also provides time-saving tips for each step in the process. An overview of the process follows.

Step 1: Pinpoint the Problem

Three activities are involved in pinpointing the problem:

1. Interviewing the client.

2. Exposing underlying issues.

3. Identifying the key stakeholders.

Interviewing the Client

You begin to identify the problem by interviewing the client. Recognizing the problem may seem like the simplest part of the needs assessment because clients almost always "know" what the problem is when they request your help. For example, you might hear:

"There is a backlog of policies in the underwriting department. Writers need to complete insurance policies faster."

or

"Sales for product X have fallen off. Sales associates need to develop a better understanding of product X so they can sell more of it."

Both these examples not only pinpoint the problem (the backlog and the reduction in sales), they also assume a solution (write faster and know more about the product). The danger here is twofold:

1. The problem singled out by the client may not be the true problem at the heart of the matter.

2. The solution suggested by the client may be irrelevant to the actual problem once it is correctly identified.

Exposing Underlying Issues

Let's assume you are faced with the first example—there is a backlog of policies in the underwriting department. This can easily be substantiated by asking your client relevant questions that not only help to crystallize the issues at hand but also establish standards for performance. For instance:

- How many policies should underwriters complete in a day? In a week?

- How many policies constitute a backlog?

- What is your definition of a backlog? (Terms are slippery characters. What constitutes a "backlog" to your client may be a "temporary surge" to the underwriters. Clarifying the terms used in your interviews sets a precedent for performance standards, which serve as a benchmark for gauging discrepancies or gaps, and also prevents misunderstandings.)

- What effect does the backlog have on your operations? On your customers?

You don't have to actually define the problem in the course of the client interview; you only have to be sure you have asked enough pertinent questions to elicit a fair notion of what the problem might be. Remember, the information gathered in this first step is strictly the client's perception of the problem. Step 2: Confirm the Problem, which you do with other stakeholders, may uncover conflicting information about the problem. Before you can move on to solutions, you will have to reconcile the two observations to identify the real problem.

The *Sample Client Interview Form* shown in the job aid at the end of this chapter identifies a number of general questions you can use in a client interview. As you begin to assess what the client thinks the problem is, you can tailor your general questions into more specific requests for clarification. Tom Peters says that the five most important words in an interviewer's arsenal are "Please give me an example." Examples are your track shoes. They speed you toward a solution, providing good traction so you don't misstep. Another simple strategy that can be used is the "Five Whys" approach. By asking a series of questions that

Process Model Checklist

Step 1: Pinpoint the Problem

What is the problem? Use the following questions as guides to get at the answer:

☐ Have you scheduled an interview with your client or sponsor?

☐ Can any documents or reports be read prior to the meeting?

☐ Have you established standards for performance?

☐ Have you included a few additional names in your master list of interviewees?

Timesaving Tips

● Limit questioning to one or one and one-half hours.

● Keep the discussion on track by paraphrasing and summarizing.

● Separate opinions from facts; ask for concrete examples to substantiate opinions.

● Avoid using documents or reports that are dated, have no relevance to the specific nature of your assessment, or are difficult to obtain.

● Quantify standards for performance.

● When drawing up a list of interviewees, include one or two high and low performers, department heads (supervisors or managers), and back-up candidates in the event key persons are unavailable.

● If a confidentiality waiver is required, ask what can be done to expedite its approval.

● Write problem definition statements in a bulleted list instead of prose.

● Summarize the meeting and provide the client with written feedback on pertinent conclusions.

Step 2: Confirm the Problem

What evidence exists of the problem? Use the following questions to ascertain this information:

☐ Have you determined which method (interviews or focus groups) will produce the desired results?

☐ Have you scheduled interviews, focus groups, or informational meetings?

☐ Do you have evidence to show how the problems are affecting the unit or organization?

☐ Do the problems warrant further investigation?

Timesaving Tips

● Consider using electronic communication such as e-mail, fax, or phone instead of formal letters to notify participants about the assessment (where appropriate have department supervisors undertake this task).

● Have the department manager distribute a copy of the questions ahead of time.

● Consider talking to people before work or during lunch if they are unavailable during work hours (never schedule information-gathering meetings after work).

● If a pattern of responses begins to emerge (such as a knowledge, skill, or motivation problem), ask other interviewees about questions related to these problems first.

Step 3: Seek Solutions

What is the most viable solution? Use the following questions to arrive at an answer:

☐ Have you identified the most cost-effective solution for each problem?

☐ Have you prioritized the solutions?

☐ Are the solutions consistent with the strategic or business goals of the organization?

☐ Have you categorized the solutions into immediate and short-term action plans?

Timesaving Tips

● Avoid recommending interventions that have already been tried and failed, or are incompatible with the culture and business goals of the organization.

● Run solutions and estimated costs by your client before preparing final recommendations.

● Present immediate and short-term action plans in a one- or two-page executive summary.

begin with "Why" and building on each previous question, a great deal of insight can be gained into the root of a problem. For a discussion of the questions you should ask yourself when undertaking a mini needs assessment, see the sidebar *Quick Answers to Tough Questions.*

Identifying Key Stakeholders

Stakeholders have a vested interest in solving problems. They may be directly or indirectly affected by the specific problems. In turn, this can interfere with their ability to successfully complete work assignments. Because they deal with them on a daily basis, stakeholders are often in the best position to give you excellent examples of how these problems impair an organization's functioning capacity. Stakeholders can also be people such as managers and high, medium, or low performers.

You will need to identify these stakeholders in your client interviews. Even if your client provides only one name, that individual may lead you to others. When you begin Step 2, these stakeholders may provide input to support your client's view of the problem, or they may declare a false start to the race by revealing startling examples of the real issue at hand—a problem that goes beyond the description presented by your client. Remember, your main objective at this point is to determine key people who are credible and knowledgeable about the problem(s), or who can provide insight about performance needs.

Once you have completed your client interview, catch your breath. Review your notes and, if you have not already done so, identify key conclusions from the interview. Document these in one page and send a copy to the client. If there is disagreement about any of your results, discussing them with the client will uncover them. You can never have too much communication. This exchange of information will not slow down your process; you can go on to Step 2 while awaiting your client's reaction to the conclusions from Step 1. This first step provides you with a definition of the situation from your client's perspective. If others were involved during the client interview, you will also be able to include their input.

Quick Answers to Tough Questions

To help you tackle a mini needs assessment, here are some answers to questions you may have about the process.

Question:
What if I have never undertaken a conventional needs assessment before? Does this preclude me from sprinting through a mini assessment?

Answer:
It is useful to have a broad understanding of the concepts and principles associated with needs assessment so that you can do a mini needs assessment should the occasion arise. A good starting point is the references and resources section.

Question:
Do I need to track all the steps in a mini needs assessment to cross the finish line successfully?

Answer:
No! The hallmark of a professional athlete is the ability to use the right blend of slow, medium, or fast steps, while eliminating those that may hinder progress in the race to success. On occasion, it may be necessary to improvise or use innovative strategies in realizing these goals. The same steps should be followed when undertaking a mini needs assessment initiative.

Question:
What if I must change course midway through my mini needs assessment and realize that a maxi assessment is called for instead?

Answer:
It is not uncommon to discover after a small-scale assessment has been completed that the situation warrants further exploration, or that a different approach needs to be taken. Should this happen, alert your client to the situation you have encountered. Have solid reasons and some hard data to substantiate your plan for a new course of action. Typically, the client's purse strings, logistical factors, and time availability will dictate whether you can proceed further.

Question:
What if interviews or focus groups are inadequate for obtaining the information that I require, and observations must be included as part of my mini needs assessment?

Answer:
By all means integrate observations along with the data-collection method that best meets your needs. Observations can be performed quickly and effectively using a checklist. If appropriate, document completion times for various activities too.

Question:
People have a tendency to clam up when questioned about their on-the-job performance. What if people are unwilling to reveal—or deny having—job, performance-related, or other knowledge or skill "deficiencies"?

Answer:
First, convey the fact that confidentiality will be maintained. This usually puts people at ease and dispels fears about retribution. It also allows for more open communication. Second, show what's in it for them, how they can benefit from improved performance (promotions, higher salaries, and so forth), and how poor performance can be detrimental to both themselves and the organization. This not only helps open the door for further dialogue but also leads to discourse about strategies for performance enhancement.

Question:
What guarantee do I have that people will provide honest ratings or will not inflate ratings when asked about items listed in the *Sample Stakeholder Interview Questions,* or items that I have added to this list?

Answer:
Once again, emphasize confidentiality and show what's in it for them up front prior to seeking information. In addition, asking for specific examples can help corroborate ratings, or reveal "holes" in stories.

Step 2: Confirm the Problem

Begin Step 2 by speaking with stakeholders identified by the client in order to obtain their input. Following are the two key actions for this step:

1. Interview stakeholders.

2. Assess the problem's effect on the organization.

Interviewing Stakeholders

Plan out your stakeholder's involvement to ensure the success of this step. You will decide which format—interviews, focus groups, or informational meetings—provides the best material. You should also consider how to diversify the mix of stakeholders to include everyone's viewpoint on the problem. Sometimes the best approach is to put everyone in a room together, ask questions, and see what happens. This approach allows you see the impact of the problem across functions.

At other times, it may be politically expedient to keep the different stakeholders separate in order to control the progress of the meeting. The scope of the problem as well as the information you glean from your initial client interviews should give you some hints as to whether you have been handed the race baton or a political hand grenade. Exercise sound judgment and trust your intuition when planning this stage of your assessment.

Communication is another key element to succeed with Step 2. Tell the stakeholders what is expected of them and the value of their contribution. Keep the setting of your meeting as informal as possible and resist the urge to use training jargon in your interactions.

To prepare for your stakeholder interview, compose a list of questions. Some questions can be as general as those outlined in the *Sample Client Interview Form,* but be selective about the questions—make sure they help focus stakeholders' input, thereby helping you focus and confirm the problem.

One way to focus the problem is to ask questions that help determine exactly what kind of situation you are dealing with. The list of sample stakeholder questions in the *Mini Needs Assessment*

Stakeholder Interview Guide on the next page identifies categories of problems and offers a partial list of questions that can help you explore them. This is not an exhaustive list, but it will give you a start. Based on the information you have already obtained, you can create specific queries to add to this outline.

If you are conducting focus groups rather than interviews, you might ask the same kind of questions but in a slightly expanded format. For example, the knowledge or skill problem issues might be rephrased as follows:

● How would you rate your current knowledge of job-related responsibilities?

● How would you rate your ability to perform job-related skills?

● How would you rate your proficiency in the technical skills required for your job?

As in the client interview, listen for any recurring themes in your stakeholder dialogues. If you find one, tailor your questions to probe for more details. And remember your track shoes! Ask for specific examples to support all assertions. The *Process Model Checklist* will help you plan your stakeholder interviews and offer some techniques to maximize time as well.

Assessing the Problem's Effect

During and after your stakeholder interviews, you need to assess the problem's effect on the organization. In what ways does the problem hinder productivity, disrupt relationships, or create barriers to success? Examples from stakeholders can be particularly useful to identify the situation's impact on day-to-day workload and are vital to achieving success with a mini needs assessment.

Often, a simple cost-benefit analysis can be enlightening to a client as you unveil the consequences of a performance gap left unattended. For instance, remember the underwriters in the first problem example who were experiencing a backlog in writing insurance policies? When presented as a loss of revenue to the insurance company, this gap will assuredly precipitate the need for immediate action.

Mini Needs Assessment Stakeholder Interview Guide

Stakeholder #: _____ Name: _____

Date: _____ Dept./Unit: _____

Purpose: To obtain a stakeholder's perspective of a performance problem.

Instructions: Ask each stakeholder to rate each of the following items. The scale is as follows: 1=very poor, 2=poor, 3=average, 4=high, 5=very high. If an item is not applicable, mark "NA." Space has been provided for additional notes. Use a separate form for each stakeholder.

Note: Items that receive a rating of 1-3 are indicators of potential performance problems. Possible solutions to a stated performance problem appear next to each problem indicator. You may consider a given solution if it is appropriate for your situation.

Key: Training is not always the recommended solution for every performance problem. Only problems for which training is considered an appropriate solution are highlighted in bold with the words "provide training."

Sample Stakeholder Interview Questions

Problem Indicator	Poor			High		Possible Solution
A. Knowledge or skill problem?						
1. Knowledge of job-related responsibilities.	1	2	3	4	5	Will job aids help? If not, provide training.
2. Proficiency in technical skills needed to perform job or tasks.	1	2	3	4	5	Provide training.
B. Job performance problem?						
1. Availability of documents such as job aids, reference guides, or manuals.	1	2	3	4	5	Increase number.
2. Knowledge of how performance will be measured.	1	2	3	4	5	Provide information or conduct briefing.
C. Existing training problem?						
1. Quality of prerequisite training.	1	2	3	4	5	Provide training.
2. Quality of training personnel.	1	2	3	4	5	Provide train-the-trainer training.
3. Quality of training material.	1	2	3	4	5	Audit and revise materials.
D. Environmental problem?						
1. Accessibility to internal customers.	1	2	3	4	5	Improve communication channels.
2. Availability of internal customers.	1	2	3	4	5	Improve work flows.

Mini Needs Assessment Stakeholder Interview Guide

Problem Indicator	Poor				High	Possible Solution
E. Attitude problem?						
1. Value of job/tasks.	1	2	3	4	5	Increase job responsibilities.
2. Opportunity for feedback on performance from peers.	1	2	3	4	5	Build periodic assessment and feedback schedule between manager and individuals or groups.
3. Opportunity for feedback on performance from managers.	1	2	3	4	5	Same as above.
F. Motivation problem?						
1. Ability of group to meet unit goals.	1	2	3	4	5	Evaluate unit goals. Provide rewards.
2. Tolerance for mistakes by management.	1	2	3	4	5	Change organizational culture.
3. Quality of cooperation between units.	1	2	3	4	5	Promote cooperation through inter- or intragroup activities.
G. Compensation/incentives problem?						
1. Value for compensation scales.	1	2	3	4	5	Increase pay scales.
2. Value for incentive structures.	1	2	3	4	5	Change incentive structures.
3. Knowledge about incentive/reward structures.	1	2	3	4	5	Provide information.

The solutions you develop in Step 3: Seek Solutions need to be commensurate with the scope of the gap, and the only way to determine the scope is to assess its impact on the organization.

As you are speeding down the track to win the race, don't lose sight of the finish line. You are assessing the need to change something in the organization. At this point, you have enough information to assess the problem's effect on the organization. One key consideration is whether the problem is worth solving. In most cases, yes; but occasionally, you may find a situation in which the solution is more cumbersome than the problem, the problem is too small to address, or there is no problem at all.

Let us consider the case of the underwriters again. Your interviews might reveal that, within the last two months, several underwriters had left the company without notice, one of whom was the most experienced underwriter; the computer system developed a problem that took four working days to fix; and new requirements for insurance policies mandated two days of redesign work on the computer program, including one day of retraining for underwriters. Aside from hiring replacements, and ensuring that turnover does not escalate, it appears as if the problems can be fixed easily.

Step 3: Seek Solutions

With the finish line in sight, you can now begin to consider what steps to follow to arrive at a solution. You have two objectives in this step:

1. Consider appropriate solutions.

2. Gain consensus on a mini action plan.

Find Appropriate Solutions

Solving the problem is, of course, the heart of a needs assessment. It can also be the most difficult step. You may find you have several solutions to the problem. If so, prioritize them by placing the most cost-effective answers at the top of the list.

Be sure that your solutions are appropriate for the organization. They should be consistent with the company's mission or vision, and their implementation should not cause any discomfort. If your client and stakeholders are uncomfortable with your conclusions, they will not implement them. A group that cherishes old school management ideals is an unlikely candidate for change. In such situations, sensitivity to values and culture can prevent clashes with intrinsic or business objectives.

Obtain Unanimous Support

One way to make sure your client and the stakeholders are comfortable is to turn "your" solutions into "their" solutions. Present your ideas to them, listen for their reactions, and incorporate their suggestions (as appropriate) into the final solution. Build ownership for the solution by reiterating that the client and stakeholders are the source of these ideas and that their contributions will guide implementation of the solution.

The mini action plan identifies the actions needed to improve the situation. It should also identify the person responsible for spearheading each action, the date by which the action is to be completed, and some measure to assess whether or not the action has been completed.

The process of seeking solutions can seem overwhelming, but you can simplify it by dividing the mini action plan into short-term projects that can be done immediately and actions that require more time to complete. For instance, in the second problem example stated earlier, sales for product X have fallen off. Let's say that in the course of your client interview and stakeholder interactions, you discover (as the client suspects) that the sales associates are not well versed in the attributes of product X and as a result, they avoid discussing the product in conversations with potential buyers. You also discover this is only one of the problems associated with product X. Your mini action plan might look like the *Sample Mini Action Plan* on the next page. Planning steps and timesaving tips for this can also be found in the *Process Model Checklist*.

The Finish Line

The mini needs assessment process is not difficult if you have some experience with the traditional needs assessment process. By condensing the steps and the timeline for completion, you are simply running a shorter race, allowing you to finish faster without depleting all your energy or overtaxing the resources of your client. Your shoes may be smoking, but your rapid results and the success of your efforts will not only ensure that you continue to win the race toward the future but also that you earn a place of honor in the Hare Racing Hall of Fame!

Sample Mini Action Plan

Problem: Sales of Product X Have Declined.

Short-Term Solutions	Person Responsible	Date of Completion	Measures of Success
Provide sales associates with sample product to take home and questionnaire to fill in and return.	L. Bliss, marketing manager	xx/xx/xx	All sales associate questionnaires returned.
Move product display to front counter.	R. Ramirez, store manager	xx/xx/xx	Product moved.
Provide all sales associates with a laminated card detailing product X attributes.	D. Lee, product specialist	xx/xx/xx	All sales associates have received card.

Long-Term Solutions	Person Responsible	Date of Completion	Measures of Success
Provide formal training to sales associates on product X.	O. Villhalla, training director	xx/xx/xx	All sales associates have completed product X training.
Provide training materials (including laminated cards) to all sales associates on all new products.	O. Villhalla, training director / J. Meganson, new product development	xx/xx/xx	Formal process exists for creating training materials for all new products.
Include sales associates in the product development testing cycle.	O. Villhalla, training director / J. Meganson, new product development	xx/xx/xx	Formal process exists for including sales associates in the product development testing cycle.

References & Resources

Articles

Brethower, Dale M. "Rapid Analysis: Matching Solutions to Changing Situations." *Performance Improvement,* November/December 1997, pp. 16-21.

Kaufman, Roger. "Auditing Your Needs Assessment." *Training & Development,* February 1994, pp. 22-23.

Reichheld, F. F. "Learning from Customer Defections." *Harvard Business Review,* March/April 1996, pp. 64-65.

Rossett, Allison. "Have We Overcome Obstacles to Needs Assessment?" *Performance Improvement,* March 1997, pp. 30-35.

Watkins, Ryan, and Roger Kaufman. "An Update on Relating Needs Assessment and Needs Analysis." *Performance Improvement,* November/December 1996, pp. 10-13.

Zemke, Ron. "How to Do a Needs Assessment When You Think You Don't Have Time." *Training,* March 1998, pp. 38-44.

Books

ASTD Trainer's Toolkit: Needs Assessment Instruments. Alexandria, VA: ASTD, 1990.

Beckley, J. L. *Power of Little Words.* Fairfield, NJ: The Economics Press, 1984.

Dubois, D. *Competency-Based Performance Improvement.* Amherst, MA: HRD Press, 1993.

Gilbert, T. F. *Human Competence: Engineering Worthy Performance.* New York: McGraw-Hill, 1978.

Harless, J. *An Ounce of Analysis (Is Worth a Pound of Objectives).* Newnan, GA: Harless Performance Guild, 1975.

Kaufman, R., et al. *Needs Assessment: A User's Guide.* Englewood Cliffs, NJ: Educational Technology Publications, 1993.

Peters, T. *The Pursuit of Wow! Every Person's Guide to Topsy-Turvy Times.* New York: Vintage, 1994.

Phillips, J., and E. F. Holton III, eds. *In Action: Conducting Needs Assessments.* Alexandria, VA: ASTD, 1995.

Mager, R. F., and P. Pipe. *Analyzing Performance Problems: Or You Really Oughta Wanna.* Belmont, CA: Lake Publishing, 1984.

Robinson, D. G., and J. Robinson. *Performance Consulting: Moving Beyond Training.* San Francisco: Berrett-Kohler, 1995.

————. *Training for Impact.* San Francisco: Jossey-Bass, 1989.

Rossett, A. *Training Needs Assessment.* Englewood Cliffs, NJ: Educational Technology Publications, 1987.

Zemke, R., and T. Kramlinger. *Figuring Things Out: A Trainer's Guide to Needs and Task Analysis.* Reading, MA: Addison-Wesley, 1982.

Infolines

Austin, Mary. "Needs Assessment by Focus Group." No. 259401 (revised 1998).

Callahan, Madelyn. "The Role of the Performance Intervention Specialist." No. 259714.

Kirrane, Diane. "The Role of the Performance Needs Analyst." No. 259713.

Long, Lori. "Surveys from Start to Finish." No. 258612 (revised 1998).

Sharpe, Cat, ed. "Be a Better Needs Analyst." No. 258502 (revised 1998).

Sparhawk, Sally, and Marian Schickling. "Strategic Needs Analysis." No. 259408 (revised 1999).

Presentations

Cava, J. "Developing Competencies and Organizational Applications." In *1995 Proceedings of 2nd International Conference on Using Competency-Based Tools and Applications to Drive Organizational Performance.* Boston, MA: Linkage, Inc., and Case Western Reserve University.

Gupta, Kavita. "How to Do a Mini Needs Assessment Effectively." Paper presented at the 1996 ASTD International Conference, in Orlando, FL.

Regalbuto, Gloria. "The Front-End of Front-End Analysis." Paper presented at the 1995 ASTD International Conference, in Dallas, TX.

Sample Client Interview Form

Date: _____   Name: _____

Interviewer: _____   Title/Dept./Unit: _____

Sample Interview Questions

1. What are the problems?

_____

_____

_____

2. What is causing the problems?

_____

_____

_____

3. Can any external factors be causing the problems?

_____

_____

_____

4. When did the problems first occur?

_____

_____

_____

5. When do the problems typically occur?

_____

_____

_____

6. What has been done to resolve the problems?

_____

_____

_____

7. What are the standards for performance?

_____

_____

_____

8. Which stakeholders are affected by the problems?

_____

_____

_____

9. How are the stakeholders affected by the problems?

_____

_____

_____

10. Which other units or departments are being affected by the problems?

_____

_____

_____

11. How is the organization as a whole being affected by the problems?

_____

_____

_____

INFORMATION
LINE

TIME, TOOLS, AND INTELLIGENCE FOR TRAINERS

Needs Assessment by Focus Group

Issue 9401

AUTHOR

Mary Austin

Needs Assessment by Focus Group

Editorial Staff for 9401

Editor
Barbara Darraugh

ASTD Internal Consultant
Michele Brock

Revised 1998

Editor
Cat Sharpe

Designer
Steven M. Blackwood

Copy Editor
Kay Larson

Needs Assessment by Focus Group 75

    Managing Focus Groups 75

The Facilitator's Skill Set 76

    Preparation: Identifying the Issues 76

    Preparation: Selecting the Resources 79

    Leadership: Presenting the Task 80

    Leadership: Directing the Activities 81

    Documentation Activities 82

References & Resources 88

Job Aid

    Facilitation Checklist 90

Needs Assessment by Focus Group

Why haven't our production goals been met? Why does it take so long to develop and implement a new training course? We have excellent employees who have adequate training—or have they? Perhaps it's time to see what new training is needed.

Before investing in new training initiatives, training administrators should review the results of a complete training needs assessment. There are several assessment strategies that provide accurate information about training needs, and the more accurate the information, the greater the return on the training investment. This is where the interactive concept plays a role.

Interactive is a concept that can be applied to the needs analysis portion of a training program before it is applied to a course. This *Infoline* provides a step-by-step guide for conducting interactive focus groups and obtaining legitimate "insider" information for a needs analysis.

The Focus Group Strategy

An employee focus group assessment is one strategy for discovering real and perceived training deficiencies. Focus groups can help identify the types of training necessary for employees and the required conditions for providing efficient and effective training from an internal perspective.

Training needs assessment involves examining issues or dilemmas that do not necessarily have a clear or procedural solution. It involves and affects all those persons who have a stake in the training problem and its resolution. Known as "stakeholders," these are the people who need to be part of an interactive focus group, a group that uncovers the root causes for training deficiencies and suggests possible solutions.

Interactive group work, however, is not inherently productive. Unless effective resources are allocated and managed properly, it will be a classic example of wasted time, effort, and money. Some focus group sessions offer a pretense of interactive group work while using a "tell and sell" format. These are focus groups that do no more than distribute a survey, collect data, and report biased results. A mailing, of course, might serve the same purpose.

Many focus groups offer a plan for meaningful assessment work by using a highly structured agenda, limited interactions, and well-defined individual tasks. Individual tasking, however, is not the best exercise for group work.

Managing Focus Groups

Some focus group meetings call for a disparate group to examine tough, uncertain training needs. Under these circumstances focus group sessions can be even more troublesome to manage. Those in charge may encounter difficulty helping the group members exchange ideas, uncover needs, and suggest effective training options. Then there are those in the group who may feel their time and energy was wasted on pursuing an unattainable goal. In any event, effective focus group work does not happen easily. When group work focuses on existing training problems and future training needs, productivity is at great risk.

The very nature of performing a difficult assessment or finding the best training solution sets the stage for contrasting opinions, lengthy discussions, possible resolutions, and change. If handled poorly, this type of group work can expose conflict, cause meetings to end with a sense of frustration, and result in flawed assessments.

The situation requires a detailed plan, the ability to manage group dynamics, and methods to help the group focus on goals. The plan will be unique; it must reflect situation-specific goals. The control valve for managing the work and the interactions within a focus group is an effective facilitator. This professional can avoid chaos and bring the appropriate methodologies to group work. The benefits of interactively focusing on a training problem come from the products of successful group work that include an honest assessment of training needs and people with training needs becoming advocates of training solutions.

The Facilitator

Guiding face-to-face interactions, selecting assessment strategies, and helping the group uncover the basic causes of training deficiencies involve both management skills and human relations skills. A competent focus group facilitator is an agent capable of managing collaborative activities, allowing groups to generate a complete snapshot of present training deficiencies and to produce a comprehensive list of real training needs.

The job of coordinating group member interactions and directing their work can be an equally difficult assignment. It may be an impossible task if group members feel that the facilitator is biased or inflexible. The focus group facilitator, therefore, must be autonomous, as well as knowledgeable about group problem-solving methodologies. In addition, he or she must gain the confidence of group members by valuing the time and talents of all participants equally.

Often the person called upon to facilitate a focus group is not properly trained or experienced in this type of work. In some cases, the only prerequisites for facilitating group work are having a calm nature, being literate, having legible writing skills, and being available. While these attributes are valuable, a professional focus group facilitator will have a needs assessment background, a significant amount of previous task experience, and interactive group-work proficiency on which to draw. Possessing these attributes, he or she has a better chance of conducting successful focus group sessions.

Glossary of Terms

Brainstorming: spontaneous idea generation.

Delphi: distance idea generation.

Groupthink: controlled idea development.

Idea structuring: idea analysis and prioritization.

Idea writing: silent idea generation.

Interpretive structural modeling: pairwise comparison of items.

Nominal group technique: structured idea generation.

Options field method: pairwise comparison of solutions.

Options profile method: solutions selected from categories.

Trade-off analysis: options implementation feasibility.

The Facilitator's Skill Set

The three key components for facilitating focus group work are preparation, leadership, and documentation. What may appear to be a straightforward assignment is actually a series of activities involving considerable needs analysis, skilled negotiation, leadership in collaborative processes, and communications skills.

On the following pages, 14 skill steps delineate the core responsibilities of the facilitator in the areas of planning, directing, and reporting (another way of saying preparation, leadership, and documentation). The descriptions of these skills may serve as a guide for staging focus group sessions. This set is not meant to be a comprehensive list of all the strategies or skills necessary for facilitating group work. It may, however, help those responsible to understand the scope of the facilitator's task and the need for selecting an experienced facilitator to manage complex group work.

The focus group facilitator will spend about one-third of his or her scheduled task time analyzing a situation and planning appropriate activities. Thus, the preparation phase for the focus group includes carefully defining the issues involved and selecting appropriate resources. The next third of the task, the leadership phase, involves presenting the task to the group and directing its activities. The final third of the task, the documentation phase, consists of analyzing and reporting the results. The chart on the next page illustrates these components and their steps. The explanation that follows describes how these steps are an integral part of one dynamic approach to training needs assessment: the focus group.

Preparation: Identifying the Issues

The first phase is to identify the training issues or dilemma the group will address in the focus session. Because the problem situation does not originate with the facilitator, a representative must be responsible for initiating the needs assessment work, informing and advising the facilitator, and implementing outcomes. This representative or "owner" contributes the information needed up front: the who, what, where, why, and when for the focus group work. After the representative triggers the assessment procedure, the facilitator begins structuring a series of probing questions. Then he or she becomes familiar with all aspects of the training problem that group members will confront.

■ *Step 1: Define the Task*

The focus group facilitator and the representative must define the group task in very specific terms. Often, the initial task statement is excessively long or contains several training problems embedded in one lengthy statement. This, in itself, becomes a problem: how to ferret out the basic task, how to determine which part has priority. The facilitator and the owner must analyze the task statement thoroughly and determine if it truly represents the basic training issue to be investigated. If more than one issue is present, the facilitator may suggest other focus group sessions.

■ *Step 2: Establish the Objectives*

Objectives define what the focus group will achieve by the end of the session. Accomplishing the objectives should provide a more complete understanding of the training problem. As the focus group facilitator outlines the objectives, he or she will further define the extent of the group work. Deciding whether the group needs to analyze only the origins of the training problem or the origins and ramifications of various resolutions helps to determine the breadth and depth of the needs analysis.

A strategy for generating suitable objectives is to list them and then carefully review the necessity for each inclusion. If the objective is realistic and directly confronts the training problem, it stays. Otherwise, throw it out. After defining the task, the facilitator will concentrate on developing some triggering questions that help motivate the group to think about the training problem in objective terms, to help group members analyze different aspects of the problem. As group members share their insights, they may begin to understand the training problem from other perspectives.

For example, the facilitator might begin with a question that asks group members to do the following:

● List the training required to increase job skills.

● Name the obstacles to increasing job skills.

● Identify the barriers, parts, or limiting forces that add to the dilemma of, failure in, or increased difficulties within current training practices.

Focus Group Facilitation

Preparation Activities

Identifying the Issues

1. Define the task.

2. Establish the objectives.

3. Choose the participants.

Selecting the Resources

4. Determine the strategies.

5. Organize the agenda.

6. Prepare the facility.

Leadership Activities

Presenting the Task

7. Introduce the participants.

8. Review the objectives.

9. Clarify participation.

Directing the Activities

10. Explain the procedures.

11. Manage input/output activities.

12. Record and share data.

Documentation Activities

13. Report the results.

14. Evaluate group performance.

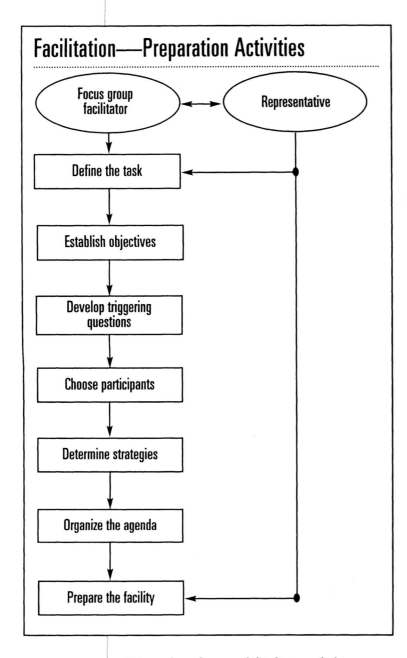

Facilitation—Preparation Activities

Using selected parts of this list may help generate a complete overview of the problem, while trying to address every item may overwhelm the group and waste time.

■ *Step 3: Choose the Participants*
As stated previously, individuals who have a personal stake in the outcome of training are the prime candidates for focus groups. Overlooking or omitting key people may eliminate important perspectives and insights. After the facilitator and representative establish a comprehensive list of

participants, they should determine if there are adequate facilities to accommodate everyone. Crowded conditions do not create an atmosphere that promotes serious reflection or encourages individuals to contribute.

Actually, it would be better to get a bigger room or more chairs than to exclude key people. There is, however, a limit to the number of people who, as a group, can interact fully, communicate effectively, develop ideas efficiently, and work productively. The magic number appears to be 12, although there is some evidence that larger groups can work productively with the aid of electronic meeting rooms.

If the room will not hold everybody that should be involved or if the number of people becomes prohibitive, the facilitator and representative should consider alternatives, such as arranging for a rotating schedule of participants or repeating the sessions with alternate groups of stakeholders.

It also helps to know if there are detractors, hostilities, or hidden agendas that may surface during group work. People who always disagree may be distracting or contentious during group work, but they also may stimulate others to speak out. Groups of people who always tend to agree may complete tasks quickly, but harmony alone does not always lead to better insights, reliable assessments, or successful results.

Once the facilitator is aware of the types of people contributing to the group work, he or she can arrange the setting and develop strategies leading to more constructive interactions. Even something as simple as planned seating may be useful in building focus group rapport. Persons who are known to disagree can be seated apart from each other. Someone who is introverted can be seated near a sympathetic individual. A person who dominates others or assumes an authority role may be placed toward the edges of the group where his or her influence is not the focal point.

Similar to managing personality types, managing the focus group climate is equally important. If some group members have tried to examine training deficiencies and failed, they may be less supportive of the assessment agenda. If group members have met with success through other interactive sessions, they may be more optimistic and receptive to current efforts.

At times more seasoned group members may try to shortcut procedures by skipping intermediate steps or arriving at premature assessments. They may assume a course of events based on previous focus group meetings. Familiarity with a process, or past experience, does not necessarily improve group work. Thus, some participants may lose interest quickly because they "have seen it all before," while others may become so comfortable taking part in activities that they become complacent. The focus group facilitator constantly monitors the climate for tell-tale signals of positive and negative reactions.

Careful observations of group dynamics, prompt interventions at key moments, and positive reinforcements for insights help to keep the participants' attention focused. In most cases, the facilitator need only make a group member aware of his or her negative influence on the group to make a positive change. In addition, creating a variation for a conventional activity may renew interest in that activity and help to keep all group members on task.

Preparation: Selecting the Resources

The second phase of preparation involves selecting the resources that will help the participants accomplish the focus group assessment goals. The facilitator will determine the strategies best suited for the situation, organize the agenda, and arrange for a workable meeting area.

■ Step 4: Determine the Strategies
There are many possible solutions for every training problem, probably several that are equally effective, just as there are several approaches to finding solutions. Brainstorming, Nominal Group Technique (NGT), idea writing, groupthink, consensus methodologies, Interpretive Structural Modeling (ISM), Delphi, and idea structurings are a few methods used in focus group work. The goal is to find training solutions that are both effective and efficient, that gain and maintain the learner's attention.

Selecting the best strategies for a specific assessment situation is an important ingredient of facilitating focus group work. For example, when generating training ideas, the group may use one of several methodologies. Examining the situation with the representative will give the facilitator insight into which methodology will be most useful. And, knowing how each method operates and assessing the climate accurately will help determine the most valuable strategies to use in each situation.

A potentially volatile or tense focus group situation may require a procedure that initially uses limited verbal exchanges. The silent generation of ideas might be the most appropriate opening strategy for that situation. Therefore, if the facilitator selects NGT, group members will have little opportunity to become confrontational. If the facilitator uses idea writing, each participant will share information using an idea-exchange format (computerized or paper and pencil). If the facilitator selects brainstorming, the group will exchange information spontaneously and orally. Consequently, they will need to exhibit supportive behaviors toward fellow group members.

■ Step 5: Organize the Agenda
The agenda should detail each phase of group work and the approximate duration of that work. Consequently, the focus group facilitator needs to estimate, as accurately as possible, how long it will take the group to complete each activity. This timetable will serve as the organizing tool, a way of reminding the group where they are going and what they already accomplished.

Most group members will follow a posted agenda studiously. Updating completed procedures within the agenda actually helps to focus attention on the next scheduled task.

■ Step 6: Prepare the Facility
Ideally, the setting for group work will be a well-designed workroom with assessment-support technology, as well as display and projection areas. Also, the facility may include smaller workrooms, break areas, and areas for technical equipment and support personnel. At the other end of the spectrum, the meeting room simply may be a comfortable, private conference area that will accommodate the group and the large displays of group-process work. More important, all tools for group work need to be accessible and in good working order, be they writing materials or computer hardware and software.

Attention to details—such as maintaining a comfortable room temperature, providing good lighting, and supplying functional, comfortable

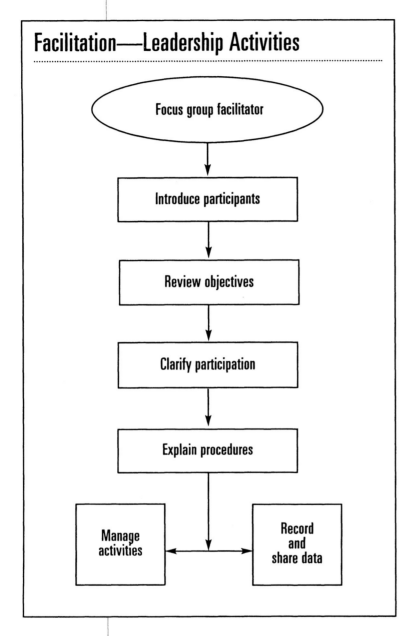

Facilitation—Leadership Activities

Focus group facilitator

↓

Introduce participants

↓

Review objectives

↓

Clarify participation

↓

Explain procedures

↓

Manage activities ←→ Record and share data

---

unexpectedly. What if a group member is interrupted frequently by other work demands? What if a member of the support team is not available when needed? A veteran at managing group work prepares for "Murphy's Law"—what can go wrong, will go wrong—then plans a simple alternative or intervention for each unusual event.

Leadership: Presenting the Task

The first phase of leadership activities involves implementing the plan: describing the focus group task, the interactive processes, and the group's responsibility. This step includes the first formal encounter between the facilitator and each group member. This initial stage of interpersonal communication affects each group member's perception of the facilitator's ability to lead the group. Therefore, the facilitator needs to be enthusiastic, articulate, and thorough. The facilitator should also project a sense of confidence in the plan and in each member's ability to contribute to the needs assessment process.

■ *Step 7: Introduce the Participants*
The facilitator will make all the formal introductions, including that of the representative responsible for acting upon the results of the group work. As the facilitator introduces each group member, he or she should add a statement that clarifies why each was chosen to participate. Before the first meeting, the facilitator may send each member a statement of purpose for the focus group session and an outline of the proposed activities. After the introductions, the facilitator will review the significance of the problem and the scope of the work, even when group members have prior knowledge of the agenda.

Finally, the facilitator will introduce the support team members and explain their involvement in the group work. All persons involved in any capacity should wear name tags, and participants should have tent name plates identifying their place within the work environment. Such identification is especially important when group members are not close associates. In fact, group members will interact more openly if they are addressed individually by name and not linked to a hierarchy of title or position.

seating—will help keep participants focused on their task. The facilitator should remove any items that are not necessary. Contradictory or distracting props may result in confusing the participants. For example, if group members must record all data in a computerized format for subsequent processing, writing materials should not be provided.

The facilitator should identify contingency plans. These are the "what if" alternatives to the agenda. The experienced facilitator will be in control of events even if equipment malfunctions, key people do not show, or the schedule changes

To understand the problem, engage in dialogue, and make rational assessments, each participant must fully understand the issues involved. In addition to reviewing the problem and the key issues, the facilitator should present the history of the training problem, including how long the problem has existed and other solutions that have been attempted previously.

■ *Step 8: Review the Objectives*

Displayed objectives will help group members clarify the goals of the needs assessment work. A complete outline of specific tasks and procedures will help the group to accomplish those objectives. The facilitator should review each item carefully so group members understand where they are going, how they will get there, and when they are due to arrive. This, in turn, will help group members to organize their thoughts and their personal agendas.

Typically, the facilitator will detail the agenda as an hour-by-hour plan. Without sharing this information, group members may experience outside interruptions and may become distracted by other concerns.

■ *Step 9: Clarify Participation*

To function effectively, the facilitator must be accepted as a knowledgeable and neutral guide. To establish credibility in this role, the facilitator will explain his or her part: as one who is familiar with the task, but is not responsible for generating training-needs information. The facilitator must convey the idea that he or she has no vested interest in any one particular assessment outcome. Focus group members should be aware that the facilitator will encourage active listening and active participation in the assessment activities.

The facilitator should also emphasize that each person is responsible for generating ideas, responding to questions, making assertions, comparing statements, and uncovering important issues. Group members also need to feel confident that the facilitator can direct their work in a manner that will maximize their efforts.

Leadership: Directing the Activities

The second phase of leadership, directing activities, involves initiating interactions and managing group-member communication during various events. The facilitator's attitude and actions during these events should be a model of proper conduct. The group will reflect the demeanor that the facilitator exhibits. If the facilitator is casual, the participants may not consider the activity serious work. If the facilitator is aloof or pompous, their interactions may become guarded, and they may not feel comfortable participating in group discussions.

The facilitator should follow the agenda as closely as possible, not abandon a good plan without a valid reason, or lose continuity by omitting part of the agenda. On the other hand, he or she should not be rigid and unable to modify plans when unexpected events dictate change. Experience with focus group facilitation and common sense may be the best combination for assessing the need for changing the agenda and selecting alternative procedures.

■ *Step 10: Explain the Procedures*

Before beginning an activity, the facilitator explains the procedure and gives brief examples of how the procedure works. Group members should know what to expect during the activity and, as individuals, what parts they play. Each should be aware of what other group members are doing and toward which objective the group is working. Knowing their exact roles in an activity will help build confidence in the process and encourage active participation.

■ *Step 11: Manage Input/Output Activities*

This is the most interactive phase of the focus group work. The facilitator directs the activities by:

- encouraging each member to contribute ideas
- giving positive feedback
- controlling the interactive climate
- helping to resolve conflicts
- requesting consensus when appropriate.

Group members will:

- generate and classify ideas
- discuss issues
- define concepts
- clarify terms
- negotiate support
- rank ideas
- consider alternative training solutions.

The facilitator establishes continuity between processes and provides quick visual referents by promptly displaying information using LCDs, flipcharts, display boards, or other presentation devices.

■ *Step 12: Record and Share Data*
The support team should record the products of the group work using mechanical or electronic means. The facilitator should arrange for the results of the work to be displayed or distributed when and where the group is meeting. This will allow participants to review, clarify, or discuss their work.

Other events may demand a long-term, accurate record of the focus group activities. Training assessments usually are not acted upon by focus group participants. Other groups or training personnel may find it necessary to examine the data and the basis for the assessments. An accurate record of all the activities is essential for reviewing, assessing, and resolving the training problem.

Documentation Activities

The last phase of focus group facilitation involves the following:

- creating a narrative of the activities

- analyzing the data

- disseminating the results of group work

- recommending training changes, modifications, and revisions.

■ *Step 13: Report the Results*
All stakeholders deserve a report of the group's assessment activities and recommendations. The recipients of the report include group members, the representative, and all other persons responsible for implementing solutions. The report should include a list of group members, a narrative of events, a copy of all electronic or paper-based materials that the group generated, and the recommendations they developed. The facilitator and representative should allow each group member to review a draft report, make revisions for accuracy, and add comments to the narrative before the support team assembles the final document.

■ *Step 14: Evaluate Group Performance*
The facilitator and the representative evaluate the outcomes of the group assessment. An experienced focus group facilitator will be able to determine if the assessment strategies were successful. The facilitator and the representative will determine if the results of the group assessment correspond to the goal. If the results of the group work do not completely satisfy the goal, the facilitator may suggest follow-up sessions using a different facilitator, different strategies with the same group, or different strategies with another group of stakeholders. If the goal is met, the facilitator recommends closure of this needs assessment activity.

The facilitator and the representative integrate this data into a larger needs assessment profile. The larger profile is a collection of data from other sources: surveys, observations, interviews, and reviews of existing training.

The framework for organizing and managing focus group assessment in training needs assessment consists of 14 steps within three skill areas: preparation, leadership, and documentation. This approach is not the same as directing a group toward a specific result.

Focus group assessment designed to uncover training problems can be an excellent interactive experience for all concerned if the facilitator has an effective plan and can put it into action smoothly. Conversely, if designed poorly, focus group work can be a noninteractive disaster. In many ways, conducting less complicated, directive work is easier. Of course, the assessment group will have little chance to learn about the problems, to uncover needs, or to become more skilled in assessing training or other problem areas.

Focus groups offer an approach that allows the people involved to uncover training needs and to become responsible for training solutions. In this way employees will have a vested interest in seeing their solutions succeed. Consequently, the organization has a better chance of seeing greater gains from new training initiatives.

Case Study: High Effort, Low Outcome

A corporate business unit was charged with producing advertising and informational in-house publications. The production team was experiencing problems meeting deadlines set by the corporate officer in charge of information distribution and by the publisher. The 26-member, year-old team was made up of a cross-section of special talents and specific expertise: writers, editors, artists, and design specialists. Individual efforts and skills were previously evaluated as positive contributions toward productivity. The overall efforts of the group, however, were below corporate standards and continually fell behind production schedules. In addition, the team's inability to meet deadlines in a cooperative manner seemed to be contributing to hostilities, frustrations, high turnover, and loss of revenue. The final products were costly and of poor quality.

Management decided that there was a need to identify and to address the team's problems. Management further speculated that training might be a way to improve team performance. Because individual effort and skills were not perceived as root problems, management felt the need to identify why team performance was poor and to generate ideas for its improvement. An employee focus group strategy was chosen to assess real and perceived training needs and to identify possible solutions. Working with two assistants, the facilitator provided an overall group process facilitation of this training needs analysis. The effort spanned four two-hour sessions on four consecutive days. Participants were selected by management to represent all production skills and tasks.

Session 1

Following preparation activities, the facilitator presented the problem statement, directed the group in the silent generation of ideas, and led a round robin to record its ideas. The facilitator asked the participants to identify the most important barriers to meeting production deadlines. The group identified 54 items that represented barriers to meeting those deadlines.

Session 2

Each contributor was asked to clarify, in turn, why his or her item was an important contribution toward identifying the problems of the group. Discussion was limited to item clarification and examples. Following clarification, each group member was asked to identify and prioritize seven of

the most important barriers. A final list of 11 high-priority barriers was developed.

Session 3

The facilitator divided the participant group into triads for the purpose of mapping the relationships among the 11 most important barriers. Lines and arrows were used to indicate the flow or direction of the item relationships. The triad selected one member to present their relationship map to the whole group. The triads generated the four maps that accompany this sidebar.

Session 4

After the presentation of the triads' relationship maps and a discussion of common problem factors, the participants brainstormed a list of solution statements for removing the most important barriers identified by the group. Each person generated 10 to 12 solution statements. Subsequent analysis of the solution statements revealed four core categories:

- ideas to improve general work-related attitudes

- ideas to encourage each person to take personal responsibility

- new strategies for team interactions

- suggestions for improving editor responsiveness.

By analyzing the relationship maps, the participants identified three root problems that served to aggravate other barriers. The root problems identified were assigned to the left side of the relationship maps. This indicated that the barrier item was of primary concern to the participants. The root problems were as follows:

- editors not specifying tasks
- lack of communication among staff
- lack of organization.

These primary barriers and their associated solution statements formed the basis for initial training recommendations. Because editors functioned as project managers, the participants suggested that the editors receive management

(continued on next page)

Case Study *(continued)*

skills training and the remainder of the production staff receive related management support training. Participants recommended that the staff receive training in interpersonal communication skills and work-schedule organization strategies for greater team productivity. Furthermore, participants suggested that concurrent editor and staff training would provide faster results from the recommended training.

Triad Map 1

Aggravates

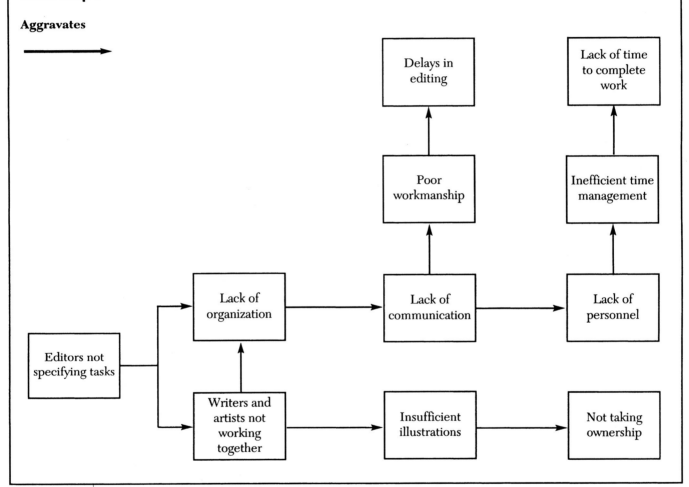

Triad Map 2

Aggravates

→

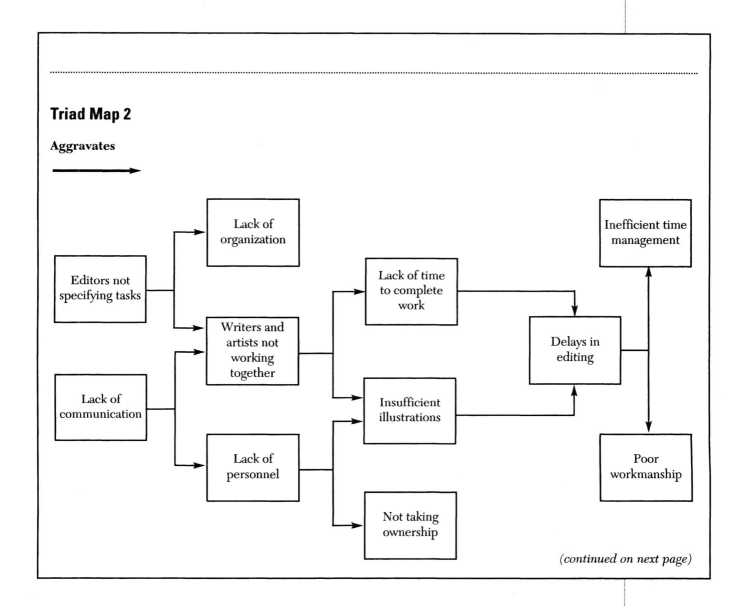

(continued on next page)

Case Study *(continued)*

Triad Map 3

Aggravates

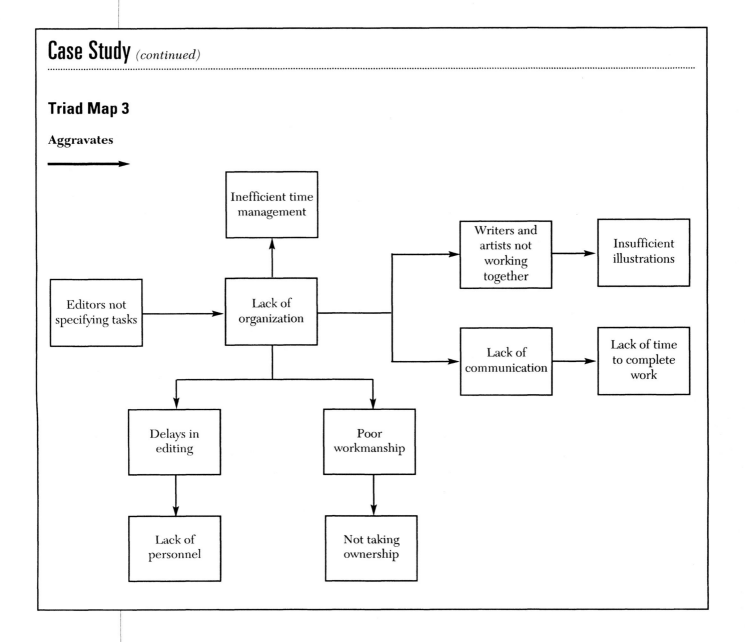

Triad Map 4

Aggravates

→

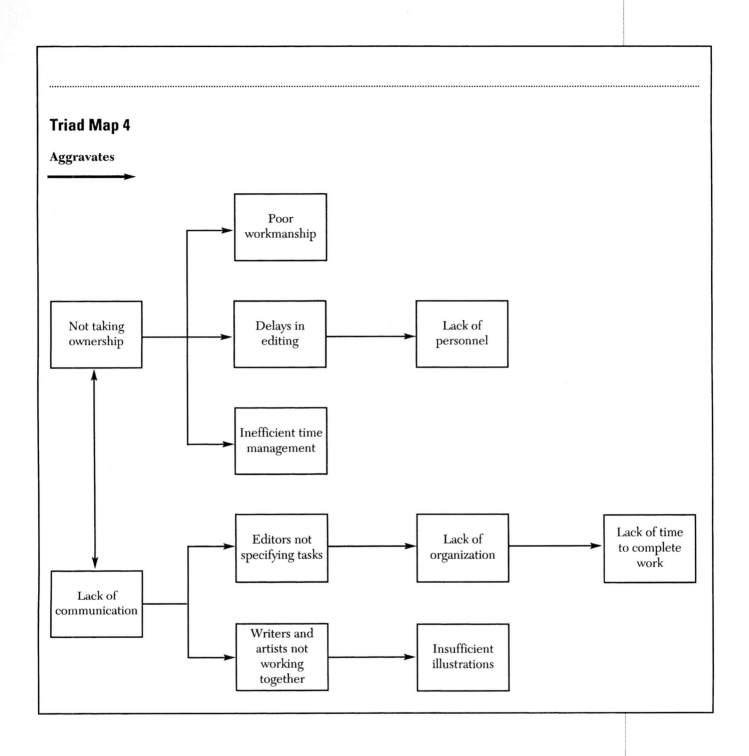

References & Resources

Articles

Buttram, Joan L. "Focus Groups: A Starting Point for Needs Assessment." *Evaluation Practice,* October 1990, pp. 207-212.

Chilambaram, L., et al. "Longitudinal Study of the Impact of Group Decision Support Systems on Group Development." *Journal of Management Information Systems,* Winter 1991, pp. 7-25.

Clark, Jim, and Richard Koonce. "Meetings Go High-Tech." *Training & Development,* November 1995, pp. 32-38.

Connaway, Lynn Silipigni. "Focus Group Interviews: A Data Collection Methodology." *Library Administration & Management,* Fall 1996, pp. 231-239.

Crane, Eric C., and Brenda M. Dillon. "Focus Visits: A Process Improvement Model for Technical College Program Evaluation." *Minnesota State Council on Vocational Technical Education,* November 1996, pp. 1-72.

Dennis, A.R., et al. "Bringing Automated Support to Large Groups: The Burr-Brown Experience." *Information and Management,* vol. 18 (1990), pp. 111-121.

Fulop, Mark P., et al. "Using the World Wide Web to Conduct a Needs Assessment." *Performance Improvement,* July 1997, pp. 22-27.

Graham, Ernie. "Focus Groups: Don't Plan Training Without Them!" *Technical & Skills Training,* January 1996, pp. 26-27.

Grohowski, R., et al. "Implementing Electronic Meeting Systems at IBM: Lessons Learned and Success Factors." *MIS Quarterly,* December 1990, pp. 368-383.

Hoffer, J.A., and J.S. Valacich. "Group Memory in Group Support Systems: A Foundation for Design." *Group Support Systems,* 1993.

Lange, Steven R., and Colleen M. Shanahan. "Designing Instructor-Led Schools with Rapid Prototyping." *Performance Improvement,* September 1996, pp. 26-29.

Martz, W.B. Jr., et al. "Electronic Meeting Systems: Results from the Field." *Decision Support Systems,* vol. 8 (1992), pp. 141-158.

McClelland, Samuel B. "Training Needs Assessment Data-Gathering Methods: Part 1, Survey Questionnaires." *Journal of European Industrial Training,* vol. 18, no. 1 (1994), pp. 22-26.

———. "Training Needs Assessment Data-Gathering Methods: Part 3, Focus Groups." *Journal of European Industrial Training,* vol. 18, no. 3 (1994), pp. 29-32.

Poole, M.S., and G. DeSanctis. "Understanding the Use of Group Decision Support Systems: The Theory of Adaptive Structuration." *Organizations and Communication Technology,* 1990.

Poole, M.S., and M.H. Jackson. "Communication Theory and Group Support Systems." *Group Support Systems,* 1993.

Preskill, Hallie. "A Comparison of Data Collection Methods for Assessing Training Needs." *Human Resource Development Quarterly,* Summer 1991, pp. 143-155.

Books

Arnold, C.A., and J.W. Bowers. *Handbook of Rhetorical and Communication Theory.* Newton, MA: Allyn & Bacon, 1984.

Delbecq, A.L., et al. *Group Techniques for Program Planning.* Glenview, IL: Scott, Foresman, 1976.

Gordon, W.J. *Synectics.* New York: Harper and Row, 1961.

Hersey, P., and K.H. Blanchard. *Management of Organizational Behavior: Utilizing Human Resources.* 5th edition. Englewood Cliffs, NJ: Prentice-Hall, 1988.

Littlejohn, S.W. *Theories of Human Communication.* 3rd edition. Belmont, CA: Wadsworth Publishing, 1989.

McClelland, Samuel B. *Organizational Needs Assessments: Design, Facilitation, and Analysis.* Westport, CT: Quorum Books, 1995.

Owens, R.G. *Organizational Behavior in Education.* 3rd edition. Englewood Cliffs, NJ: Prentice-Hall, 1987.

Warfield, J.N. *Societal Systems.* Salinas, CA: Intersystems Publications, 1989.

———. *A Science of Generic Design: Managing Complexity Through Systems Design (Vol. 1).* Salinas, CA: Intersystems Publications, 1990.

———. *A Science of Generic Design: Managing Complexity Through Systems Design (Vol. 2).* Salinas, CA: Intersystems Publications, 1990.

References & Resources

Papers

Broome, B.J. "Guidelines for Applying Computer-Assisted Methodologies for Managing Complex Problems in Group Work." Paper presented at the annual meeting of the Speech Communication Association, Applied Communication Division. Chicago, IL (1990).

Broome, B.J., and D.B. Keever. "Facilitating Group Communication: The Interactive Management Approach." Paper presented at the annual meeting of the Speech Communication Association. Chicago, IL (1986).

Gouran, D.S., and R.Y. Hirokawa. "Small Group Communication in the 1980s." Paper presented at the annual meeting of the Speech Communication Association. New Orleans, LA (1988).

Infolines

Gupta, Kavita. "Conducting a Mini Needs Assessment." No. 259611 (revised 1999).

Hodell, C. "Basics of Instructional Systems Development." No. 259706.

Sharpe, Cat., ed. "Be a Better Needs Analyst." No. 258502 (revised 1998).

Sparhawk, Sally, and Marian Schickling. "Strategic Needs Analysis." No. 259408 (revised 1999).

Waagen, Alice K. "Task Analysis." No. 259808.

Internet Sites

ASTD:
http://www.astd.org

Center on Education and Work:
http://www.cew.wisc.edu/

NY State Education Department: Workforce Preparation and Continuing Education
http://www.emsc.nysed.gov/workforce/home.html

Needs Assessment—Allison Rossett:
http://www.gwu.edu/~lto/rossett.html

Needs Assessment Tools:
http://www.nnlm.nlm.nih.gov/ner/nes1/9410/tol.html

Job Aid

Facilitation Checklist

Complete this checklist one month to one week prior to beginning the focus group session.

☐ Define objectives for session. _____

_____

_____

_____

☐ Identify participants. _____

_____

_____

_____

☐ Schedule an appropriate meeting room.

☐ Prepare participant materials.

    ☐ Name tags

    ☐ Background report

    ☐ Agenda

    ☐ Accommodations

☐ Assign support staff. _____

_____

_____

_____

☐ Locate support materials.

    ☐ Computer system(s)

    ☐ Graphics software

    ☐ Printer(s)

    ☐ Group decision support software

    ☐ Projection system(s)

    ☐ Participant recording device(s)

    ☐ Word-processing software

    ☐ Flipchart(s)

☐ Gather supplementary materials.

    ☐ Writing pads

    ☐ Scissors

    ☐ Pens and pencils

    ☐ Stapler

    ☐ Markers

    ☐ Tape-recording system

    ☐ 3 x 5 cards

    ☐ Power strip(s)

    ☐ Tape

    ☐ Printing papers

    ☐ Diskettes

Task Analysis

Issue 9808

Task Analysis

AUTHOR

Alice K. Waagen, Ph.D.
President
Workforce Learning
1557 Hiddenbrook Drive
Herndon, VA 20170-2817
Tel: 703.834.7580
Email: worklearn@aol.com
Web: www.workforcelearn-
ing.com

Alice Waagen is president and founder of Workforce Learning, a full-service training and development company. She has more than 18 years of experience in all facets of training program development and evaluation. Dr. Waagen holds MS and PhD degrees in education.

What Is Task Analysis? 93

    Jobs Versus Processes 94

    Undertaking a Task Analysis 94

    Data Collection Methodology 97

    Prioritizing and Classifying Tasks 99

    Collecting and Organizing Data 101

    Process Mapping 101

    Guidelines for Writing Task Analyses 102

Case Studies 103

    University Program Development 103

    Computer Training Support 103

    Law Enforcement Training 104

    Aviation Inspector Training 105

References & Resources 106

Job Aid

    Practice Task Analysis 107

Editor
Cat Sharpe

Associate Editor
Sabrina E. Hicks

Production Design
Anne Morgan

ASTD Internal Consultant
Phil Anderson

What Is Task Analysis?

Once, long ago, working for an organization was a marvelously predictable thing. People entered the workforce after they completed whatever level of schooling their aptitudes, inclinations, and finances dictated. They began at the bottom rung of the mythical career ladder, whether that was as a floor sweeper in a manufacturing plant or as a mailroom clerk in the service sector.

Jobs in those days were well defined and documented in formal job descriptions delineating those knowledge, skills, and abilities—or KSAs—required for success in the position. Well-defined career ladders meant you always knew your current place, future opportunities, and even where you would go if job performance or political mayhem required a backward step.

With jobs and job progression so well defined, the course developer's task was equally well structured. Different models for structured course development, like the instructional systems development (ISD) model, proliferated. Such ISD models as the ADDIE (that is, analysis, design, development, implementation, and evaluation) model offered a wonderfully concrete, step-by-step approach to developing training. The ADDIE model begins with front-end analysis and concludes with evaluation, with multiple steps and substeps in between. (See the model on the following page.) One of the critical front-end analysis steps is task analysis.

Task analysis is defined as the systematic identification of the following items, which are necessary to perform any job:

- specific skills
- knowledge tools
- conditions
- requirements.

In the past, instructional designers relied on formal job descriptions as the basis for beginning a task analysis. The job descriptions, which often were written after the completion of a job analysis, defined the specific tasks and duties of the position. The designer's job, in essence, was to translate the requirements of the job, as noted in the job analysis and job description documents, into training materials and then to train employees to successfully perform the job.

This process has no flaws in its logic. Indeed, it is still followed in many organizations as a way to develop the support materials and programs needed to ensure optimal job performance. But more and more, the business mantras of improved speed, performance, and process all but do away with the formal definitions of jobs and the rigidity of organizational job tables and progression steps.

Noticing this change, William Bridges, in his innovative book *JobShift*, writes, "There are no more jobs, only work to be done." The rigid job structures of the past have all but been eliminated from many of today's forward-thinking organizations. Employees are expected, indeed required, to perform multiple jobs, which are, in reality, tasks merged from many jobs into one. Few document these new "jobs," for when they put keystroke to paper, employees find that business exigencies require them to stop performing certain tasks and start performing all new ones.

Where in the chaos of fluid job roles and responsibilities does that leave task analysis? Is performing a task analysis a thing of the past, gone the way of the keypunch machine? No, task analysis still has an important place in the development of sound training programs. What has changed is not the need for documenting the required actions that ensure top job performance but the sources of information the developer examines to determine the job or tasks to be trained.

This chapter describes the value and utility of good task analysis—specifically how to analyze work and work processes using various task analysis methods. It will describe how to plan task analyses as well as provide guidelines to ensure that your research stays focused and produces results. Case studies are provided to illustrate how training practitioners apply the principles of analysis to create various training deliverables.

The ADDIE Model of ISD

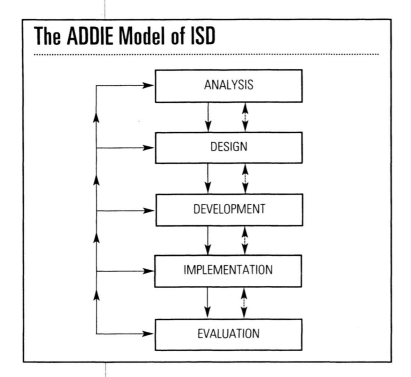

ANALYSIS

DESIGN

DEVELOPMENT

IMPLEMENTATION

EVALUATION

Jobs Versus Processes

The thrust of total quality management (TQM) and reengineering movements centers on improving processes to increase efficiency and effectiveness. Some organizations that adopted TQM define work totally in terms of processes, not jobs. TQM encourages all employees to understand their place in the total, end-to-end, process and to strive to continually improve the effectiveness of the process. In these quality-based organizations, an employee's job might entail performing one segment of a larger process or many segments of multiple processes.

The fundamental difference between job- and process-based work is the degree of change in process-based work. Continuous quality improvement requires employees and their work teams to constantly question the efficiency of how they perform and to correct their actions so that they can improve the overall process.

What does this mean to task analysts? Primarily, it means that they can be less reliant on printed documentation about jobs. In organizations, the formal job descriptions that once defined the duties of the job have all but been abandoned. Job duties are more often documented in process charts and

process descriptions. When functioning in a process-based work environment, trainers faced with developing task or process training should do the following things:

- Shift their orientation and language from *jobs* to *processes*.

- Search out all process documentation as the basis for development work.

- Ask to join process improvement teams early in their work to pinpoint the needed training.

- Be active participants in process improvement teams. (As teams redesign work, trainers can provide valuable input on how easy or difficult the new process will be to train and communicate.)

- Constantly think of speed—ways to shorten and improve the training development process itself. (For example, use existing documents, like process flowcharts, as job aids rather than create new ones.)

Undertaking a Task Analysis

To perform a useful and valid task analysis, you must know the basic steps to follow and what methods of gathering data are most effective and appropriate for your assignment. Once the upfront planning is completed, use the following guidelines to help you reach a successful conclusion to the task analysis process.

First Steps

Task analysis can differ in complexity and scope. For instance, you could accurately document a simple set of tasks by interviewing current employees, if they were performing the tasks successfully to performance standards. On the other hand, it could take many interview and data-gathering sessions to identify all the components of a complex job or a position that was undergoing change and did not currently exist in a well-understood manner.

Regardless of the level of complexity, task analyses share the following fundamental steps:

1. Identify the major or critical outputs of the job. This will help you identify the major tasks and task groupings.

2. Break down the major tasks into subtasks or steps. You have completed the task breakdown when you can achieve the goal or result of the task by completing all the steps or subtasks.

3. Determine the type of all tasks and subtasks:

   - Knowledge tasks—require the trainee to acquire knowledge, information, or understanding. These tasks are also known as cognitive tasks.

   - Skills tasks—require a change in behavior or an action on the part of the trainee. These tasks are also called action tasks or behavior tasks.

4. Collect all data necessary to document the tasks and subtasks. Using a variety of data sources increases the validity of the data. Make sure each task has a discernible output or result.

5. Validate the data. You can confirm information derived from interviews by direct observation. Likewise, you can validate observation logs by reviewing with subject matter experts (SMEs). Direct observation or employee reviews can verify formal job descriptions or job analyses.

6. Obtain review and approval of task analysis from client, training management, or other management in your organization. Provide management with the opportunity to modify the scope of the tasks, if needed.

7. Finalize the reporting of the task analysis. The format you choose depends on the end use of the data. For the final result, you can generate any tables, flowcharts, and narrative descriptions in the detail needed.

8. Distribute your findings to management for final approval. Once approved, your task analysis is complete.

Task Analysis Planning Checklist

The proper design of a training program depends on a comprehensive task analysis. The key to writing accurate learning objectives is to specify *what* is to be learned, based on identifying the individual tasks the learner needs to perform.

Careful up-front planning is critical to the success of the task analysis. Planning ensures that you are gathering the right amount of data: Too much data gathering results in redundant data sets and wasted time; too little, and you may lack the full picture of the job or process you are documenting. Use the following checklist to increase your chance of producing good results.

☐ What is the end result of the task analysis? Is it strictly training development, or will the data generated also be used for performance appraisal criteria or job description copy?

☐ Has anyone ever researched this job before? Has a job analysis been performed? Job aids developed? Any other documentation that will help in the analysis?

☐ What is the relationship you have with the client? Do you have a formal status-reporting agreement? Have you specified procedures for communicating project delays, problems, concerns, or issues?

☐ Who will be trained? How many? Where are they located? What are the timeframes and deadlines for the deliverables?

☐ What is the background knowledge or skill level of the audience? Are they complete novices to the tasks, or have they some experience to draw on for the learning?

☐ What is the nature of the tasks to be analyzed? Are they skill (behavior) based? Knowledge (cognitive) based? Both?

☐ How will you collect the data? Direct observation, interviews (individual or focus groups), review of existing documents, questionnaires, surveys?

☐ How will you verify the data for accuracy? Do you have subject matter experts (SMEs) who can help with this?

☐ How will you organize your results? For yourself? For your client?

Task Listings

Task listings or inventories are accurate task statements describing the work activities of employees in specific occupational areas. This format specifies the actual job tasks. It involves a process of organizing the tasks, determining their importance, detailing the steps, and putting them in proper sequence. Here is an example of a task listing:

Task Listing Sheet

Job: Receptionist

Tasks:
   (In order of importance)

1. Answers telephone.

2. Greets clients.

3. Receives mail.

4. Calls office personnel to inform them that their visitors have arrived.

5. Updates office telephone directory and receptionist relief schedule.

6. Assists with other departments' administrative duties.

When to Use Task Listings

You can use task listings when you need to accomplish the following things:

- discover different jobs and tasks, their relationships to each other, and the requirements for successful performance of the task

- develop task descriptions for all jobs in the occupational area

- identify training that should be modified or completely eliminated (outmoded or irrelevant information may be identified and cut from the curriculum)

- identify and structure jobs into career fields

- determine the tasks critical to sound vocational or technical education programs

- determine critical tasks for occupational competency and certification tests

- illustrate the range of activities to provide a basis for trainees and supervisors to form realistic perceptions of the job.

How to Prepare Task Listings

Prepare a form for the task listing; choose a simple, straightforward format for easy use in recording data. The form should provide space for the task description and any other information necessary for your analysis, such as level of difficulty, degree of importance, and frequency of performance. Then follow these guidelines:

1. If you are reporting the prevalence of tasks, indicate how often they are performed during the job performance. Focus only on frequency rather than on other factors, such as importance and level of difficulty.

2. Record the actual number of times the task is performed within a set period of time (per day, week, or month) or record general frequency (the task is performed frequently, occasionally, or rarely). Either approach will help you decide on the sequence of lessons, range of subject matter, and the amount and scope of practice exercises.

3. If time is the most important feature of your study, use a modified task-listing approach and arrange the information in a timeline format showing each task as it occurs during a performance.

4. Show that some tasks are more important than others by listing them in the order of their importance.

5. Research by looking at the job description, talking with employees, or observing employees as they perform actual work. This kind of investigation will help you select relevant content for your course.

6. List all the tasks that are part of the job.

Advantages

Task listings have a number of advantages. They are inexpensive; data can be quantified; and information regarding size of the workforce, numbers of employees performing specific tasks, and descriptions of work and workers is readily available. Finally, computers easily store, organize, analyze, and report quantifiable information.

Disadvantages

Disadvantages to this method of data gathering include the fact that task listing is very time consuming and can be tedious if the particular job is extremely detailed. The technique works most effectively when the job being studied is linear and requires the trainees to make only a few simple decisions.

Data Collection Methodology

How you collect data for a task analysis can vary widely depending upon the needs of the organization, the time allotted for the task, and the nature of the information to be identified. The following sections describe methods you can use to collect data for a task analysis.

Observations

When directly observing employees performing tasks in the work setting, do the following:

● Make sure that you explain to the employees, their supervisors, and union representatives the purpose of your observation.

● Explain that the work performed during the observation period must be done exactly as it is always done, not modified because of the observer.

● Take notes on each work task and element.

● Use the observation data to validate findings obtained through other data-gathering methods.

Individual Interviews

This method employs direct questioning of employees, their supervisors, and other employees with significant involvement in the task performance. Following are some useful points to remember:

● These interviews can be highly structured, using standard questions for each interview, or open ended, asking respondents to narrate how they perceive a task is performed.

● You may choose to ask questions about how employees currently accomplish the work, as well as gather information about improving the performance of the tasks.

● You can use interviews to clarify ambiguous or confusing information obtained from documents or observation.

Group Interviews

This method involves direct questioning of several individuals in the same position to acquire consensus data about how employees perform the tasks. You can also use it to interview a team that has more than one person responsible for completing a given task or series of tasks. These interview sessions are also called focus interviews and facilitated research sessions.

When using group interviews, remember the following guidelines:

- Encourage employees to analyze and discuss various aspects of the job, especially areas that are problematic or difficult to perform.

- Use group interviews to determine how cooperative and interdependent roles contribute to accomplishing goals.

Printed Materials

Many printed materials such as job analyses, university or technical training materials, job descriptions, and technical manuals include information about jobs or processes. When using them to collect data, follow these guidelines:

- Be aware that job descriptions may be written to justify pay levels or job titles and may not accurately reflect how employees perform the work.

- Look for rich sources of information outside of your organization—such as benchmarking studies, professional journals, or academic publications.

- Use printed information to supplement other methods. If using information from outside of the organization you are studying, verify that they follow similar job and task standards.

Sample Task Criticality Rating Form

Measure the importance of the specific task to the overall process or job by assigning ratings as shown in the form below.

Task	% of Total Job (All must add up to 100%)	Time (in minutes/day)	Relative Importance Scale (1 = low importance, 5 = high importance)				
Perform basic statistical calculations	5	10	1	2	3	4	5
Analyze data using statistical packages	5	15	1	2	3	4	5
Report results to management	5	5	1	2	3	4	5
Propose corrective action	2	5	1	2	3	4	5

Questionnaires

When using prepared question-and-answer formats (checklists, surveys, polls) that focus on detailed information about various work activities, perform the following:

- Design the questionnaire with the help of an SME to ensure that the questions are focused and accurate.

- Test the questionnaire with a sample group of employees to verify that its directions are clear and easy to understand.

- Use the questionnaire to gather data from large numbers of geographically dispersed employees or to add validity to data gathered from other methods.

Checklists

Checklists from which respondents choose the tasks they perform in their jobs can be useful tools, but they involve some precautions:

- Use of checklists requires extensive preliminary work involving questionnaires, interviews, or observations to identify tasks.

- The checklist method requires recognition rather than recall. This is simpler for respondents and less time consuming if used also as a questionnaire. The information gathered may be limited, however, particularly in relation to task sequencing, relationships between tasks, and employee-machine interactions.

Diaries

The diary method for collecting data requires participants to organize activity schedules and to follow schedules by keeping logs and records of their daily activities. When using this method, remember the following:

- This method may be time consuming and disruptive.

- You can use diaries to determine the frequency of task performance.

Prioritizing and Classifying Tasks

Often direct observation or interviews yield long lists of tasks being performed. You need to prioritize or classify these tasks to facilitate moving to the next step of the process—whether it be training design or job redesign. Prioritizing tasks also helps to indicate if you have overlooked any tasks or if the list is incomplete. Use the following factors to prioritize tasks:

- time spent completing task

- frequency of task execution

- importance of task to overall process or job (also known as a *task criticality rating*).

Use task criticality ratings to accomplish the following items:

- Capture critical behaviors that are required to perform the task.

- Develop criteria for designing a training program.

- Determine the parts of the training program that should be emphasized, further developed, shortened, or eliminated.

- Establish operating procedures and policies regarding specific behaviors (such as handling customer complaints).

- Generate helpful suggestions and recommendations for equipment design or modification.

You should take other factors into account when using criticality ratings. Ratings of importance are subjective and determined by the background experience or point of view of the rater, but using multiple raters can minimize the subjectivity factor.

The previous page has an example of a task criticality rating form that you can use to assess the importance of a task to the whole process.

Sample Process Flow

The following diagram depicts the tasks needed to be executed to begin the task analysis phase of a curriculum development project.

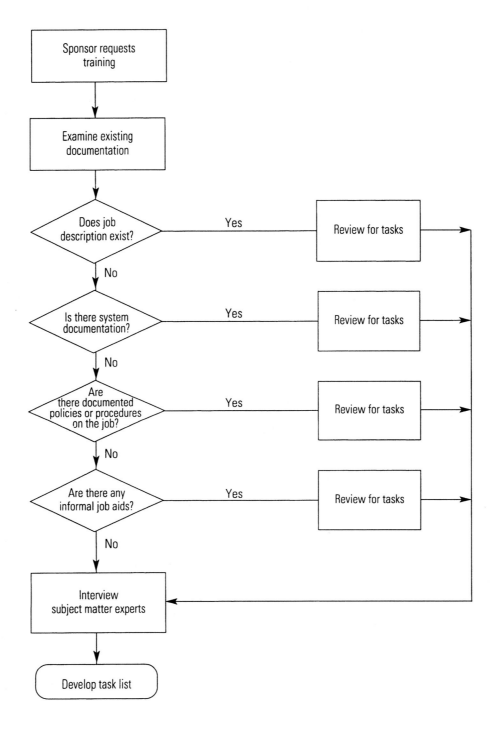

Collecting and Organizing Data

Two additional data-gathering techniques will be useful to you: critical incident technique and process mapping. You can use these methods to gather, organize, and display data as well as to indicate any data gaps or missing information.

Critical Incident Technique

Critical incident technique uses the individual or group interviews to document tasks surrounding a critical incident in the workplace. Most task analysts use this method of data collection after a perceived serious failure of job performance results in employee or customer injury, equipment malfunction or damage, or other event determined to be critical to the business.

Frequently, critical incident investigations appear on the news after air or rail transportation accidents. Once an accident occurs, federal agencies like the Federal Aviation Administration (FAA), Federal Rail Administration (FRA), or National Transportation Safety Board (NTSB) rush to the accident scene and sift through both physical and verbal evidence to determine the cause of the mishap. The focus of these investigations centers on two factors: human or mechanical error. The human errors are detected by interviews structured around questions like "What did you do? What next? When?"

If the source of the error is determined to be performance, employees require new or upgraded training to ensure that the performance shortfall is corrected. Task analysts can use the investigation documents as well as perform further critical incident interviews to determine the tasks needed to be trained.

Some considerations for using critical incident technique are as follows:

- Stress that respondents describe only actual events, not "What did they want to do?" but "What did they really do?" You are trying to document actual job performance and current techniques, not how people envision performing the task.

- Do extensive prework before the interviews to identify all possible critical incidents.

- Try to interview at least five different sources for each incident. Remember, you are recording their recollections of how they responded to circumstances at the time of an incident. With more sources, it is less likely that subjective information will sway you.

- As always, be extremely wary that the outcome of the investigation will be a recommendation for more training. Objective, unbiased research may indicate that mechanical failure or inefficient work processes caused the incident. Additional training will not "fix" these problems, and another accident may occur.

Process Mapping

Process mapping is a visual tool used to systematically describe actions and behaviors in a sequential flow. A process flow or map presents a clear and logical visual representation of all the tasks and steps involved in the execution of a particular process. Unlike a simple task list, process maps are beneficial in that they graphically demonstrate decision points and their multiple selections, thus allowing "branching" of the tasks into separate paths, depending upon the outcome of the decision (see the sample process flow on the following page). Process mapping allows the task analyst to record multiple outcomes of decisions and is an ideal technique for documenting knowledge or cognitive tasks.

The foundation of process mapping is the depiction of an *input,* the *process* or *action* taken on the input, and the *outcome* or *result* of the action. Information for the process map can come from direct observation of the tasks or from interviews with top performers.

You can create process maps by following these steps:

1. Assemble a group of top performers or employees who are experts in the process.

2. Use a meeting room with white boards, flipcharts, or large pieces of paper attached to the wall. Have chairs facing these media.

Process Mapping

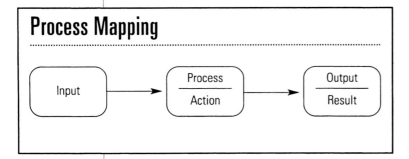

3. Brainstorm the inputs to the process—all people, materials, activities, or resources that are used in the process. Write each input on a separate note card.

4. Define the outputs from the process, including any financial, material, and people resources. Write each output on a separate note card.

5. Map the activity flow, including the "What happens?" and "Who does it?" Write each activity on a separate note card. Have participants arrange the note cards in sequential order and pencil in the direction of the flow between notes.

6. Use separate shapes to denote actions versus decisions. Usually, an action is depicted in a rectangle, while a decision is shown as a diamond.

7. Annotate each process step with who is responsible for the step, the time it takes to complete the step, where the step is performed, or any other relevant information.

8. Review with the team the final flow for any changes or adjustments.

Guidelines for Writing Task Analyses

Task analysis can require a considerable investment of time, energy, and resources. Get the most from your analysis project by following these suggestions.

For your first draft of the analysis, describe the tasks as they currently exist. Do not include any suggested improvements or "what if" proposed changes to the process. Annotate these items in an appendix or footnote and have SMEs or expert reviewers verify.

Include all elements or work activities that are the employee's responsibility regardless of how long or how often they are performed. Tasks that can take only minutes to perform can be as vital to the job as those that take months to complete.

Describe tasks according to the policies, procedures, and performance (output) standards of the company or organization.

Get management verification that employees are performing tasks according to standards. Be mindful of company policies, safety rules, or procedures as you document how employees perform the task. You may unearth some work practices that are actually in violation of these rules.

Study the task, not the employee. Characteristics of individuals, their education and background for example, are irrelevant to the analysis unless successful performance of the task requires knowledge or skills acquired from the education.

Distinguish between human activity and other kinds of work (such as machine operation). Employees manipulate controls—push buttons, turn dials, pull levers—so that machines will perform assorted tasks like drilling, sawing, photocopying, and so forth.

Distinguish between an employee's tasks and the team's tasks. If developing public relations materials is the objective of a group effort, consider the individual functions involved: Analyze tasks involved with individual production, research, visual art, marketing, and management positions.

Study all process flowcharts if your organization has undertaken any process reengineering work. They can be good high-level breakdowns of how work is accomplished.

Research any information systems projects that have been done to automate the function you are examining. Data flow diagrams and information flow diagrams document the flow of information and work and can contain valuable information.

Note the amount of action or behavior tasks. If the job is primarily physical, you can document it quickly and accurately by videotaping it. You can then translate the video into a text document or use it as a future training aid.

Case Studies

One serious consideration of any task analysis work is *time*. Traditional analysis work, based on multiple interviews and document analysis, takes considerable time and resources. As stated earlier, one of the real enemies of a lengthy analysis is the speed of change. In many organizations, training development cycles have shrunk from months to weeks to days.

When tasked with developing and delivering training within a day or week, an analyst can use various techniques to reduce analysis time without affecting the quality of the final piece. The following case studies are real-life examples of development efforts shortened by the use of creative analysis techniques.

University Program Development

Gloria Holland, PhD, of the Center for Instructional Advancement and Technology at Maryland's Towson University, was asked to develop new degree and certificate programs that epitomized academic excellence in research and theory and also provided students with the KSAs that would ensure them employment in their field upon graduation.

The **goal** was to design—from the bottom up—credit programs, which defined the end employers as key stakeholders in the development process, and to build strong ties between the university and its business partners.

Techniques

Local business organizations were contacted and asked to identify an internal SME in the specific field of study. This expert, collaborating with colleagues, described and prioritized specific workplace abilities graduates needed for success. The ability lists served as the first draft of the task listings.

Business experts then participated in a facilitated session during which participants consolidated and transferred the ability lists to note cards and grouped them under categories. Redundancies were eliminated, and dialogue began regarding

priorities or task descriptions. The business experts and their academic partners reached a final consensus on the task list and descriptions. Next, the academics used this guidance as the basis to develop the curriculum.

Rapid Analysis Tips

- Provide worksheet formats and guidance to individual experts.

- Use facilitated consensus techniques in group meetings to allow analysts to shorten the data-gathering phase.

- Identify redundant tasks easily by grouping under categories.

- Discuss and resolve priority conflicts quickly.

Using a facilitated meeting technique shortened the original process—based on individual interviews—from months to a half-day.

Computer Training Support

John Keim of Computer Learning Centers, was asked to design a curriculum to train non-computer users to staff computer help desks. The overall **goal** was to develop a seven-month-long curriculum of progressive courses supporting the KSAs required for an entry-level position at a computer help desk. For the graduates of this program to be placed in positions with area employers, Keim had to design the curriculum around the specific needs of these employers.

Techniques

To start, an analyst went to the Help Desk Institute to acquire names of experts in the field—actual practitioners able to describe all of the nuances of the job. These experts became the base team members. Because it was vital to have input from managers who hire program graduates, this team also included help desk supervisors from the local business community.

The Developing a Curriculum (DACUM) methodology of design analysis was employed to create the curriculum. During the DACUM session, a facilitator led the group through a series of brainstorming exercises to determine the exact tasks and duties required by a help desk individual.

The team stated the behavioral outcomes of the tasks as well as task frequency, criticality, and degree of difficulty. They then grouped similar tasks, wrote overall objectives, and organized the objectives into individual courses. The tasks and objective groupings were then handed off to the developer for lesson plan and course material development.

Rapid Analysis Tips

- The team followed DACUM task charts, which allowed them to be aware of what content preceded and followed their own content. This enabled the team to provide links between the classes, providing a cohesiveness to the curriculum.

- Industry experts used in the design work enabled the team to view course content from a customer's point of view. The importance of customer service skills, such as defusing anger, listening, and stress reduction, did not occur to the more technically focused team members but were clearly identified by the expert employees.

- Group-facilitated sessions to map the program's design, rather than build the curriculum course by course, reduced the course development time to two days.

Law Enforcement Training

Ken Hayes, of Wackenhut Services in Aiken, South Carolina, had the task of developing a basic skills and knowledge course for newly hired law enforcement state troopers that met both state and Department of Energy requirements.

Techniques

An initial draft of the task list was developed, based on reviewing existing documentation (for example, work orders and required regulations) and interviewing employees and management. In a facilitated session, Hayes asked SMEs to review the task list and determine whether the task was performance or knowledge based. Subtasks with related KSAs were also noted for every task.

Next, each main task was posted to a wall. Experts were grouped according to tasks that fit their backgrounds and experience. Then an analyst coached them on developing instructional objectives for each task. Once appropriately sequenced, the expert teams and training staff worked independently to develop lesson plans and training materials.

At one point, an older, obsolete course was examined for relevant content. When the experts matched objectives of this course against the final task/skill/knowledge matrix, they discovered that more than 30 percent of the existing course material was irrelevant.

Rapid Analysis Tips

- Using a facilitated session that paired the instructional design team with the appropriate SME enabled the team to move very quickly from initial task listing to training development.

- Using a structured approach to develop content and objectives, analysts were able to identify and eliminate the "nice to know" information from the curriculum and concentrate solely on what was needed to perform the job.

Aviation Inspector Training

Jennifer Guitard, of Tecsult Eduplus, Halifax, Nova Scotia, was tasked with developing competency profiles of skills, knowledge, and attributes of several types of Transport Canada inspectors. The overall **goal** of the analysis was to conduct an intensive and detailed competency inventory (a task list structured by skills and subskills that lists the knowledge and attribute components of each skill) of aviation transportation inspectors—identifying common elements in order to train them as a group. A follow-on activity was to employ competency inventories as a means of training in specific areas.

Techniques

The analysis team began by reviewing all known documentation on aviation inspection, which included the following items:

- current regulations
- past task analyses
- checklists
- job aids.

The team—usually in pairs, one representative from central headquarters and one from a regional office—then interviewed inspectors. Using this information, the team compiled a competency inventory. Once all task lists were compiled, the team performed an in-depth content analysis, looking for common elements. These elements formed the basic inspectors' course, followed up by courses specific to inspector type.

Rapid Analysis Tips

- Interviewing groups of inspectors concurrently provided richer material than from single or paired interviews.

- Interview location influenced the quality of the responses. Those conducted at headquarters had a more serious demeanor than those at the regional offices, where inspectors were in their own work environment and unable to mentally "escape" from their day-to-day tasks.

References & Resources

Articles

Ahlers, Robert. "Automated Task Analysis for Training Development." *Bulletin of ASIS,* August/September 1990, pp. 11-14.

Clifford, James P. "Manage Work Better to Better Manage Human Resources." *Public Personnel Management,* Spring 1996, pp. 89-102.

DeSalvo, Gerald L. "Write It Right." *Security Management,* May 1991, pp. 81-83.

Elliott, Paul. "Power-Charging People's Performance." *Training & Development,* December 1996, pp. 46-49.

Fetterman, Harry E. "Certifying Instructors In-house." *Technical & Skills Training,* August/September 1996, pp. 10-15.

Gayeski, Diane M., et al. "Getting Inside an Expert's Brain." *Training & Development,* August 1992, pp. 55-62.

Korotkin, Arthur L. "A Taxonomic Approach to Integrating Job Analysis with Training Front-end Analysis." *Performance Improvement Quarterly,* vol. 5, no. 3 (1992), pp. 26-34.

Miller, Janice A., and Diana M. Osinski. "Training Needs Assessment." *SHRM, White Paper,* 1997.

Reynolds, Angus. "The Basics: Job/Task Analysis." *Technical & Skills Training,* November/December 1994, pp. 5-6.

Rogers, James L. "Helping Clients Make Training Decisions." *Performance & Instruction,* July 1996, pp. 24-27.

Romano, Gerry. "Successful Task Analysis: All Questions Asked." *Technical & Skills Training,* October 1990, pp. 37-43.

Smith, Teresa L. "Job-related Materials Reinforce Basic Skills." *HRMagazine,* July 1995, pp. 84-90.

Still, Tim. "Training on a Tight Budget." *Technical & Skills Training,* February/March 1994, pp. 29-32.

Books

The Best of Needs Assessment. Alexandria, VA: ASTD, 1992.

Bridges, William. *JobShift: How to Prosper in a Workplace Without Jobs.* Reading, MA: Addison-Wesley, 1994.

Lock, Edwin A., and Gary P. Latham. *A Theory of Goal Setting & Task Performance.* Englewood Cliffs, NJ: Prentice-Hall, 1990.

Patrick, J. *Training: Research and Practice.* San Diego: Academic Press, 1992.

Rothwell, William. *Mastering the Instructional Design Process: A Systematic Approach.* San Francisco: Jossey-Bass, 1992.

Swanson, Richard A. *Analysis for Improving Performance: Tools for Diagnosing Organizations and Documenting Workplace Expertise.* San Francisco: Berrett-Koehler, 1994.

Zemke, Ron, and T. Kramlinger. *Figuring Things Out.* Reading, MA: Addison-Wesley, 1982.

Infolines

Austin, Mary. "Needs Assessment by Focus Group." No. 259401 (revised 1998).

Kirrane, Diane. "The Role of the Performance Needs Analyst." No. 259713.

Plattner, Francis. "Instructional Objectives." No. 259712.

Sharpe, Cat, ed. "Basic Training for Trainers." No. 258808 (revised 2003).

———. "Be a Better Needs Analyst." No. 258502 (revised 1998).

———. "Course Design and Development." No. 258905 (revised 1997).

———. "Write Better Behavioral Objectives." No. 258505 (revised 1998).

Practice Task Analysis

Task analysis is the systematic identification of all the elements necessary to perform a job. The work and work processes that make up your analysis will determine what training programs need development. Practice doing a task analysis by using the exercises and worksheet.

Task Analysis Exercises

Gaining real experience with analysis without having to worry about someone evaluating your performance is easy. Try performing some sample field exercises to get your analytical skills honed.

1. Complete a task analysis for a simple, everyday household job like loading the dishwasher or making a bed. Have a "top performer" in your home verify the accuracy of your analysis work by using the task list to perform the job.

_____

_____

_____

_____

_____

_____

_____

_____

_____

_____

2. Complete a task analysis for a more complex task for which you have no experience, like tuning a car or painting a house. Interview at least two or three subject matter experts (SMEs) to gather task data. Have these SMEs review your analysis work for accuracy (or, if possible, use your analysis work to train a new employee!). Now, take this approach into the workplace. Select a simple office task (like mail distribution) and analyze it.

_____

_____

_____

_____

_____

_____

_____

_____

_____

(continued on next page)

Job Aid

Task Analysis Worksheet

1. List the primary elements of the task or skill.

_____
_____
_____
_____
_____
_____
_____
_____

2. Sequence the tasks in performance order.

_____
_____
_____
_____
_____
_____
_____
_____

3. List any skills or knowledge needed to perform the tasks (prerequisites).

_____
_____
_____
_____
_____
_____
_____

4. Describe the desired outcome of performing this job. _Be specific. This information will be used to develop evaluation methods for your analysis._

_____
_____
_____
_____
_____
_____
_____
_____

INFORMATION
LINE
Tips, Tools, and Intelligence for Trainers

The material appearing on this page is not covered by copyright and may be reproduced at will.

Course Design and Development

Issue 8905

Course Design and Development

Course Design and Development 111

    Front-End Problem Analysis 112

Models for Design and Development 113

    Competency-Based Approach 113

    Functional-Context Learning 114

    Design Basics 115

    Strategies: Media and Methods 117

    Course Description 118

    Course Development Materials 120

References & Resources 123

Job Aid

    Course Design Quality Checklist 125

Editorial Staff for 8905

Editor
Susan G. Butruille

ASTD Internal Consultant
Greta Kotler

Production Assistant
Lee Allen

Revised 1997

Editor
Cat Sharpe

Designer
Steven M. Blackwood

Copy Editor
Kay Larson

Course Design and Development

So what do course *design* and *development* really mean? Webster says it as well as anyone:

Design: a preliminary sketch or outline showing the main features of something to be executed.

Development: to set forth or make clear by degrees or in detail.

Course design and development are phases of instructional systems development (ISD). In the design phase, the course director outlines the main features of the course and in the development phase, he or she makes the course content clear by increasing the level of detail.

The other major ISD phases are analysis, implementation, and evaluation. The illustration on the next page depicts the ISD phases. For a complete overview of ISD, refer to *Infoline* No. 259706, "Basics of Instructional Systems Development."

In the course design phase, the course designer or design team plans the course, while in the course development phase, the designer develops the actual training materials for the course. In both phases, the trainer makes increasingly precise decisions about what to include in a course and how to convey the content to learners. Several factors guide these decisions.

■ *What Participants Need to Know*
The analysis phase determines the knowledge, skills, and attitudes (KSAs) to be learned for satisfactory job or task performance. The KSAs to be learned are written in the form of objectives.

■ *A Focus on Learning Transfer*
By focusing on transferring participants' learning to job performance, the training ultimately must lead to better job performance. Otherwise, no matter how entertaining or enlightening, the training will fail.

■ *Impact on the Organization*
The design and development phases spell out the course's expected benefits and costs to the organization. The careful planner keeps costs proportionate to benefits.

Course design begins with broad planning or macro-level planning, moves toward midlevel planning for units or modules (also called mesolevel), and ends with detailed lesson or learning plans at the microlevel. For example, in the design or planning phase, a class designer may feel that a film offers the best overview for a course. In the development phase, he or she will select or create a particular film.

During both phases, the course designer considers:

Instructional objectives: What must the film show to introduce concepts that meet the stated learning objectives? Is the vocabulary level appropriate? How will learning be evaluated to ensure that learners have grasped the key concepts?

Available resources: Would a generic, commercially produced film serve the purpose? If so, should it be rented or bought? If not, how soon can a film be created and what will it cost? Are enough VCRs and televisions on hand?

Next, a lesson or learning plan specifies:

● how the film will be introduced

● what activity will monitor participants' learning

● how the film's information will link with the next training or learning activity.

Throughout design and development, the course designer constantly needs to assess the value of learning activities and the means for carrying them out by keeping in mind the following factors:

● Does the activity enhance participants' motivation to learn?

● How does this activity lead to the desired learning?

● What kind(s) of feedback will evaluate and validate participants' progress in meeting learning objectives?

● Do the activities promote learning retention and transfer of learning to the job?

An Instructional Systems Development Model

This ISD model, reprinted from *Infoline* No. 259706, "Basics of Instructional Systems Development," shows the basic phases of ISD and the relationship of the phases to one another.

The lines and arrows show that phases interrelate and may be changed during development. Lines and arrows leading back to each phase from the evaluation phase show that evaluation may turn up some problems that make it necessary to go back to a particular phase and make changes.

The ADDIE Model

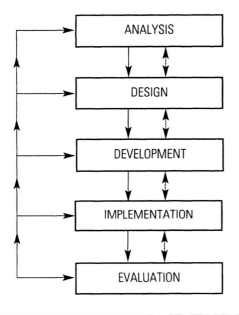

This *Infoline* focuses on the broad or macrolevel of course design and development and the midlevel (meso) of unit and module design and development. It describes the major terms associated with course design and development, the analyses that contribute information to course design, trends influencing course design and development, considerations that affect writing and sequencing objectives, contents of a course description, design strategies and development steps, and characteristics of a high-quality course design.

Infoline No. 258906, "Lesson Design and Development," concentrates on the microlevel of lesson or learning plan design and development.

Front-End Problem Analysis

Training design should begin only after a fundamental front-end problem analysis yields a "go" (as opposed to a "no-go") signal. Joe Harless, author of *Analyzing Human Performance: Tools for Achieving Business Results,* points out that when a performance problem is perceived—by trainers, managers, supervisors, or employees—training may be the solution, only part of the solution, or unrelated to the solution.

Because of this, several questions arise, such as:

- What indicators or symptoms suggest that change is needed?

- What is the root of the problem?

- What role, if any, can training play in remedying the problem?

- What is the monetary value of solving the problem?

- Would an improvement—but less-than-complete remedy—be acceptable?

Models for Design and Development

If training is needed, the analysis phase of ISD continues, and the training designer(s) may start roughing out a design according to such factors as current law, policies, procedures, and negotiated agreement clauses related to the proposed training; organizational relationships among and within divisions and departments; job duties and determined performance levels; as well as the following resources and constraints:

Time: How soon must training be accomplished? When will prospective training participants be available? When are heavy workload periods? Should instruction be carried out in one block of time or "paced" to alternate with time on the job?

Money: How much money will be available? When? All at once or over a span of time?

Culture—national, ethnic, and corporate: How are decision makers and prospective training participants used to doing things? What values, rituals, and shared or different points of view must be reflected and respected in the instructional design?

Training population characteristics: What related education, training, and experience do prospective training participants have? How have KSAs and on-the-job performance been assessed? Where are prospective participants? Are they close to one another or to other possible training sites?

Availability and location: Where and when can trainers, facilitators, subject matter experts (SMEs), design and development specialists, and others who will contribute to the ISD process be made available? Also to be considered is the availability, location, and cost of training facilities, equipment, and supplies.

ISD models dating back to World War II depict sequential but interactive phases. Recent models, however, emphasize interactivity and de-emphasize sequence, so that course design may begin before all analyses are complete; development may fill in completed parts of a design while other parts still are unfinished; and the trainer may improve a course—update its information content or refine its evaluation techniques—during any phase, or even after the course has begun.

Competency-Based Approach

A major trend in ISD is the competency-based, functional-context approach, described in the writings of Tom Sticht, Larry Mickulecky, and others. This approach focuses on the learner, with heavy emphasis on individual learning plans.

Features of the competency-based approach are:

- Occupational analysis identifies competencies (performance objectives) required for successful performance.

- The validity of competencies is verified through people who actually perform the job.

- Criteria (standards) for adequate or excellent performance, and the conditions under which the job is to be performed, are made known to learners from the beginning.

- The learner and trainer plan individual instruction and evaluation for each competency.

Although certain KSAs may be evaluated, the main measure of success is performance that integrates KSAs under job conditions.

For more than a decade, many trainers acknowledged the appeal of the competency-based approach. But they resisted it, believing they did not have the resources to use it. Individualized content and pacing were the key sticking points. But from the mid-1970s to the present, trainer resistance faded as business competition became global, pressure to prove training's value increased, and many organizations faced labor shortages. More important, trainers discovered that this approach worked, and could be managed incrementally in several ways:

- Occupational analyses could be initiated for particular organizational levels, divisions, or departments—or for selected jobs.

- Portions of existing and new courses could be individualized.

- Some new courses could be fully competency based.

Trainers also found that occupational analyses became quicker and easier once they fine-tuned the initial analytical process to organizational culture and built an updatable information base. The competency-based approach originally applied to relatively separate and sequential tasks. But now, training researchers are studying how the competency-based approach applies to complex skills such as those related to leadership and interpersonal relations.

Many training experts believe that the competency-based approach should replace the traditional approach to design and development. They disparage the conventional process of gathering and analyzing content information, listing topics, developing and sequencing course objectives, preparing a course description, and developing unit and lesson plans.

Many, however, see that it is not an either-or situation and understand the value of adapting competency-based principles to the traditional process. Most important, however, is the recognition that learning is what must be planned, not just instruction. This *Infoline,* like much training today, is based on the traditional process, while showing the strong influence of the competency-based approach.

It is essential that trainers within an organization share a common approach to training so that program planning, course evaluation procedures, and documentation can be coordinated and integrated.

Coming to Terms

Training experts vary in their use of the terms listed below. For instance, some trainers use the terms *program* and *course* interchangeably. For purposes of this *Infoline,* the following definitions will be used:

Course: a planned, organized series of learning experiences related to a particular topic or group of tasks. This term may be applied to trainer- or facilitator-led experiences, or self-instruction for training, education, or development.

Learning plan: a detailed plan of learning activities and experiences (describes what learners will do and use); associated with the competency-based approach to training and with self-instruction. (See *Infoline* No. 258906, "Lesson Design and Development.")

Lesson plan: a detailed plan of instructional activities (describes what trainers and facilitators will do and use).

Module: a unit, especially one that can stand alone, to be learned independent of other units.

Occupational analysis: a blanket term to cover analysis of jobs, tasks, and relationships among jobs, performance conditions, and standards.

Training program: an organization's overall training effort, or a group of related courses.

Unit: a major subtopic, task, or task cluster to be learned within a course.

Functional-Context Learning

The term functional context often crops up in discussions of the competency-based approach. It too describes training that relates to actual job circumstances, because training is successful only when learners can carry out learned tasks at their actual work stations. For example, a learner may be able to diagnose a mechanical problem and perform a series of repair steps in a logical, timely way during the training course. But if actual work conditions are noisy and chaotic, those conditions may need to be simulated during training.

Similarly, the materials, tools, and aids that learners use in training must match those available on the job. Conditions during training should increasingly approximate conditions on the job.

Advancing Technology

Advancing, affordable computer-based technology has changed many trainers' approaches to course design and development.

Technology offers these potential benefits:

- Data to be analyzed may be recorded on machine-readable forms, then scanned by an optical character reader and tabulated by off-the-shelf computer software.

- Training design and development print materials may be word processed, produced through desktop publishing, and easily adapted.

- The latest software allows for more individualized learning (interactive video, CBT, multimedia, Internet, intranets) and analysis of design alternatives and other design decision support (spreadsheet programs and expert systems).

- Databases store historical training information for flexible future reference.

Design and Development Teams

Sometimes a solo trainer is responsible for course design and development. Even so, the trainer will need to consult with other people and with information resources such as training services or materials directories. It is also desirable to involve training specialists in course design and development. So where budgets and time permit, design and development usually are carried out by a team headed by someone from the training department—a course designer.

Teams should consist of people knowledgeable or competent in one or more of the following areas:

- organizational culture and resources
- adult learning styles
- instructional technology
- matching strategies with course content
- job and occupational analysis
- skills needed for the job
- testing and evaluation.

The course designer often calls on consultants to work on specialized aspects of course design and development. The director may also consult informally with training media and materials suppliers during design and development, but the suppliers are not part of the design and development team—unless a course's primary goal is to acquaint learners with use of a supplier's product or service. In that case, a supplier representative will likely be on the team.

Design Basics

Various documents record decisions made during the design phase and note steps and decisions yet to be made in the development phase. A course design should consist of the following:

■ *A Budget Request*
Unless the course's funding is already set, a budget needs to be requested. If only the total budget allocation is known, the design still should specify funding categories (personnel, equipment and supplies, facilities). Some organizations demand a budget justification. This can provide an opportunity to justify, for example, using a conference center with the necessary equipment and supplies versus a less expensive site that will involve extra company time and expense to lease and ship equipment.

■ *A List of Objectives*
A sequenced list of objectives should be prepared along with any corresponding test items.

■ *A Course Description*
A course description records broad design considerations and decisions and supports a budget request (if made). A course description will vary in length, depending on organizational custom and the scope of the course.

■ *A Project or Administrative Plan*
A project or administrative plan will specify individual responsibilities and deadlines for course development.

■ *A List of Needed Equipment*
A tentative list of needed equipment, materials, and supplies. A final list will emerge with completed lesson and learning plans.

Objectives and Test Items

Throughout the sequence of instruction, learners will be working to meet objectives—and to prove through testing that objectives are met. Over the years trainers have defined many kinds of objectives. So many, in fact, that in his book *Making Instruction Work,* instructional design expert Robert F. Mager warned against "goofing off with objectives." Most, if not all, of the objectives to be determined and put into writing fall into one of the following categories:

Course objectives that state the general purpose(s) or benefit(s) of a course.

Subordinate or enabling objectives that describe the learning steps leading to terminal objectives.

Terminal learning objectives or performance objectives that state what a learner should be able to do after training, under what conditions, and to what standards or criteria.

Examples:

A *course objective* for editors might be: "Learners will become proficient in using a new word processing package."

An *enabling objective* might be: "Learners will be able to use the appropriate keys for moving, deleting, or copying text."

A *performance objective* might be: "Given access to a personal computer installed with XYZ software, an instructor-provided disk with unedited text and hard copy showing the text with 20 common proofreader's marks, the learner will produce edited text with no more than two errors within a pre-established time period." This objective assumes that all editors have proofreading and typing skills.

An enabling objective or terminal learning objective should be written in terms of observable behavior. For that reason, an action verb telling what the learner will do (list, repair, type, bake) is the heart of an objective. Even for learning that involves attitudes or knowledge, objectives should not contain verbs (such as "know") that describe a learner's internal state. Rather, the designer should use verbs that describe behavioral indicators of a person's internal state (knowledge, for example, is indicated by ability to list, classify, identify, and so on).

Each enabling or terminal objective should be measurable. Some measures of behavioral objectives are of a pass or fail nature; a learner either performs the required behavior or not. Other measures are gauged according to standards set, for instance, by an employer, a professional society, or the law.

The standards associated with an objective should be based on adequate performance, not best performance. Some learners may demonstrate excellent performance by the end of a course, while others will improve with subsequent practice, and some will plateau at the adequate level.

Writing objectives requires the following:

- distilling performance information to essentials

- grouping performance requirements into learning activities of similar scope

- standardizing the format that outlines performance requirements.

To help ensure the validity of performance objectives, designers may observe on-the-job performance, ask job holders or their supervisors to assess written objectives, or consult with curriculum experts or subject matter experts (SMEs).

Each objective should be testable and written in terms of what the learner will do. Well-stated, realistic, job-related objectives are a giant step toward the design of test items, but in themselves do not constitute test items.

The design of test items begins with general decisions about how a learner can demonstrate performance of an objective. If an objective requires a learner to list 10 items in order, that task might be demonstrated orally, on paper, or on a computer. If an objective requires a learner to identify five major parts of a machine, testing may be carried out with the actual equipment, a simulator, or a photograph or drawing.

In choosing how to test, the designer will look at the interplay between instructional considerations and resource limitations. Testing, especially of enabling objectives, may demand safety precautions. Many behaviors that are safe for job veterans are not safe for novices. As a rule, subject matter experts can alert a designer to errors—safety related and otherwise—that novices are likely to make. Instruction should include direct warnings or advice about avoiding such errors. When safety is not a concern, however, it may be better for learners to make a few minor errors, because that helps them open up to new ideas and procedures.

Learners commonly resist testing. But that resistance can be lessened by closely relating test items to objectives, and objectives to job performance requirements. For more information, see *Infolines* No. 259712, "Instructional Objectives"; No. 258502, "Be a Better Needs Analyst"; No. 259808, "Task Analysis"; No. 258505, "Write Better Behavioral Objectives"; and No. 259705, "Essentials for Evaluation."

Strategies: Media and Methods

Once objectives are refined and tests designed to validate learning, it's time to consider instructional strategies. To begin with, will the course be instructor led, on the job, machine mediated, peer learning, self-instruction, or a combination of these?

To make this and other strategic decisions, Leonard Nadler has noted that the "designer must know enough about learning theory to know what has been researched and theorized in the past. There are proponents and opponents for every learning theory.... The designer may not want to choose sides, but at times must make decisions as to which learning theory is most appropriate for a specific learning experience."

Training theorists and practitioners often advocate using strategies related to experiential, active, or discovery learning. This means that learners participate in activities—such as role play, discussion, and hands-on practice—that help them discover what to do for good job performance. In contrast, didactic strategies involve telling or showing learners what to do.

Active learning tends to be more meaningful and memorable than passive learning, but it isn't always appropriate or feasible. If there truly is only "one right way" to perform a task, learners may well resent spending time to discover it while a knowing trainer withholds "the answer." If time for learning is short or unskilled performance is dangerous, it's best to tell or show learners what to do.

In the early 1970s, Malcolm Knowles popularized the term *andragogy* to describe principles of adult learning and teaching (as distinguished from pedagogy, a term applied to children). Over the years, Knowles himself and other training experts downplayed several distinctions between how adults and children learn. But today, virtually all theorists and practitioners agree that instructors for adults must acknowledge that adults bring a wealth of experience to learning.

Past experiences make adults more diverse, but also equip them with information and coping strategies that must be taken into account. While some adults' current skills and knowledge may be a good foundation for learning, some of their prior learning may be outmoded. In such cases, an instructor may need to help a learner "unlearn," while still respecting his or her past learning.

Trust, respect, involvement, and collaboration are concepts that arise repeatedly in discussions of andragogy. An attitude of "we're all adults here"—with experience, skill, and knowledge to contribute—underlies modern course design.

One outgrowth of this trend toward team efforts is *synergogy*. The term, used by J.S. Mouton and R.R. Blake (best known as the developers of the "managerial grid"), describes learning in which a group of employees, regardless of organizational rank, suspend traditional competition and share knowledge, skills, and viewpoints. For more information on this, refer to *Infoline* No. 258804, "Training and Learning Styles."

Course Description

Putting a course description together is like doing a crossword puzzle: Some parts are easy to fill in; some are difficult; and later information may invalidate earlier choices. The final course description should tell you:

WHY the course is needed and should include the course objectives; the expected benefits—for the organization, learners and their supervisors, colleagues, and for organizational clients or customs; and the estimated dollar value of these benefits.

WHO is involved (job titles, number of people) in the course's analysis, design, development, implementation, and evaluation. The *who* should include:

- who is to receive training

- prerequisites or entry requirements, if any

- availability of learners for training

- whether trainers will be working with SMEs, facilitators, other trainers, training managers, consultants, suppliers, or other individuals

- staff trainers' special interests, knowledge, and skills

- availability of people involved in designing, developing, implementing, and evaluating the course.

WHAT aspects of their work must be coordinated and who will oversee coordination. This should include the following:

- general course content—major topics, tasks, and task clusters

- KSAs to be learned or improved

- approximate proportions of cognitive learning (knowledge), psychomotor learning (skill), and affective learning (attitude) the course will involve

- how topics, tasks, and KSAs have been identified and analyzed and their relevance to improved job performance

- how a participant demonstrates successful learning (for example, pencil and paper tests, oral presentations, construction of a model, a performance of activity).

HOW course content is sequenced and what strategies are employed to engage participants in learning. This includes:

- learning events and activities

- whether learning will be accomplished in a group or individually

- which portions of the course, if any, will be designed for self-instruction

- whether portions of the course allow a trainer or participants to choose among alternative activities.

You will also need to determine how much the course is expected to cost. This includes such factors as how it will be funded: through an organization-wide budget category or the HRD/ training department budget, by charging departments whose workers use the course, through grants from outside sources, by the participants, or through some combination of sources.

WHEN the course will take take place and how it will be run. This includes:

- whether it will be run once, several, or many times, and whether it will be on company time or on learners' time

- whether it must be run in a particular season, on particular days, or at particular times

- expected course completion date

- whether everyone will participate at the same time or at different times, according to such factors as available sites or organizational levels

- whether the course will run in segments, or as a whole

- whether there will be any pilot tests and, if so, whether alternative designs will be offered.

WHERE the course will be conducted. This should include:

- whether it will be at a central site, such as a corporate training center or at individual plants, offices, field sites, or any combination thereof

- special facilities requirements—electrical power, lighting, space, seating, and viewing arrangements

- whether, if all or part of the course is self-instruction, learners will perform this training at their regular work stations, at learning centers stocked with special equipment, or at home.

Sequence of Instruction

The analysis phase of ISD begins before the design phase and discloses various relationships among job tasks. Some tasks are subordinate to others, some are equal in importance but must be performed in a particular sequence, some tasks have a logical relationship but may be performed in any order, and some tasks within a job are unrelated to others.

A designer may notice that certain task clusters can be translated into training and learning units or modules. Also, it may be evident that performance of some tasks—especially those performed infrequently or those demanding strict adherence to a sequence—should be supported by job aids. Refer to *Infoline* No. 259711, "Create Effective Job Aids."

Typically, instruction is structured and sequenced according to tasks, topics, or problems. For example, training for a new salesperson might follow a task chronology (greet customer; determine needs; if appropriate, present merchandise and suggest accessories; close and record transaction; thank customer and invite him/her to visit store again).

Which Comes First: Budget or Design?

In an ideal world, budget allocation for a particular course follows the design phase. After this, each course would then receive funds according to anticipated costs and benefits.

Realistically, an organization's budget cycle and funding practices often dictate a course's budget, limiting design and development decisions. Gradually, organizational decision makers are becoming more aware of the value and utility of basing a course's budget on its design, rather than the reverse. However, there still is little logic to the funding of many courses.

Trainers need to seek information about budget cycles and funding practices. Besides making formal inquiries, a trainer who consults the organizational grapevine may discover which kinds of funding appeals—formal or informal, mostly prose or mostly statistics, early or late in the budget cycle—have been the most successful in the past.

Or, such training might group tasks by topics (customer service; demonstration and description of merchandise; mechanics of recording sales, returns, and other transactions).

The problem-solving approach is similar to the topical approach but emphasizes problem diagnosis and solution. This might be appropriate for a midlevel sales training workshop (how to determine customer priorities efficiently, handle difficult customers tactfully, complete complex transactions accurately).

Within a framework of tasks, topics, and problem solving, instruction usually is either sequenced step-by-step in job performance order, in order of priority or frequency of performance, or by moving from:

- simple to complex
- overview to detail
- specific to general
- known to unknown
- concrete to abstract
- practical to theoretical
- present to future
- observation to reasoning.

Media, Methods, and Materials

Decisions about media, methods, and materials involve trade-offs. For example, color print and film cost more than black and white. But color is attractive and may alert learners to key points or hazards, or help them distinguish parts of a whole.

When listing preliminary decisions about media, methods, and materials, it's a good idea to note those that require:

- a large sum of money to buy, rent, or create

- significant time to locate, adapt, or develop

- any needed help outside the training department or design team.

Simply jotting down symbols (say, a "$" by expensive items; "T" for time-consuming; and "O" for outside assistance) will help clarify how resources are allocated. And if the first, ideal design requires too much money, time, or staff, these symbols point out where to look first for design changes.

On the other hand, it is important to avoid the common mistake of choosing and using methods, media, and materials just because they are familiar and available, or because they seem entertaining.

Motivation to learn and remember is important, but sheer entertainment is not. Money and time are important, but value—successful learning that will improve productivity—is more important. The main concern is to choose strategies that will lead learners to pass tests related to validated performance objectives. Bearing all this in mind, a designer or design team selects media, methods, and materials. Design specialists define media as whatever transmits instruction. Among the choices to consider are:

- small or large group, or individual instruction

- structured on-the-job training, apprenticeship, formalized mentioning, coaching

- instruction at a field site, classroom, laboratory, or work station

- workshop, simulation, programmed instruction workbook, correspondence course, teleconference, videoconference, or outside source such as a training school or college

- instruction delivered by instructors, facilitators, managers acting as trainers, or self-instructional materials

- lecture, discussion, panel presentation, interviews, or debate

- modeling, demonstration, observation, field trip, or tour

- case study, role play, game, brainstorming, or buzz groups

- coaching and mentoring

- drill and practice

- work materials and tools

- mock-ups, models, and simulations

- print material such as texts, lists, or reference bibliographies

- films, tapes, records, transparencies, slides, charts, graphs, flipcharts, magnetic boards, or chalkboards

- interactive video, CBT programs, Internet, intranet, or other computer multimedia

- recorders, computers, projectors, cameras, and simulators.

Course Development Materials

Development should proceed according to some project planning and control method. The course director will need a record of who has responsibility for course development steps and will need to coordinate and monitor intermediate due dates to ensure that the course is ready on time.

Training Materials

During the development phase, media and materials will be located, selected, or created. Off-the-shelf materials can be used as is, or adapted when appropriate. Suppose, for example, that a video film contains an excellent illustration of a procedure, but uses many terms that don't fit the organizational culture. In this case, the film might be run with the sound shut off, and the instructor reading a script aloud. Or, the trainer could give a special pre-viewing explanation of the film.

Training materials to be gathered, created, or designed include the following:

- instructional guides such as lesson and learning plans that detail introductory material

- bridges that lead from one instructional activity to another

- integrators that tie course activities together and link them to participants' prior learning

- administrative aids such as participant rosters; maps; name tags; and material, equipment, or supplies checklists

- evaluation materials (see below)

- participant guides such as texts, workbooks, and job aids

- activity aids such as checklists, role-play scripts, case studies, and lab exercises

- actual equipment and supplies—paper, videotapes, VCRs, films, projectors, computers, charts, pointers, flipcharts, markers, and spare parts.

Evaluation Materials

Evaluation will be either formative or summative, and must be tied to objectives. Formative evaluation continues throughout the analysis, design, development, and implementation phases. Summative evaluation occurs after course completion.

Although, as baseball great Yogi Berra said, "You can observe a lot by watching," subjective impression should be only part of evaluation. Both formative and summative evaluation should be supported by a plan for objective measures of success and by written materials devised during the development phase.

A formative evaluation plan describes means for improving a course and for assessing learners' in-training progress and attitudes toward training. A summative evaluation plan describes such measures as posttraining employee performance, turnover, and customer comments. An overall evaluation plan should tell how and when, throughout the entire ISD process, information will be distributed and collected, and from and by whom.

Many organizations conduct one or more pilot tests of a course before carrying it out on a large scale. If a control group is used, or if more than one pilot test is conducted, designers may test alternative designs. But this is a luxury that many organizations cannot afford.

Evaluation techniques should cause as little disruption as possible. Forms should be clearly worded, quick and easy to fill out. Evaluation results can lead to design refinements by answering questions about:

■ *Tasks*
Do instructors and learners believe that tasks are sequenced properly for effective, efficient learning? Do they believe learning has been broken down into tasks that are not boringly easy or overwhelmingly difficult?

■ *Topics*
Do instructors or learners believe any information is missing? Do they find any information to be misleading or wrong?

■ *Learning Activities and Materials*
Do learners believe they get enough feedback and practice? Do they and their supervisors consider the course useful? Do they consider it interesting, difficult, or fun? Do learners and facilitators consider learning activities and materials worth the time (and money) invested in them?

■ *Tests*

Do tests call for participants to demonstrate (rather than describe) learning? Do participants consider tests fair? Do participants and their supervisors consider the tests reasonable indicators of ability to perform on the job?

■ *Productivity*

Have measures of productivity (absenteeism, turnover, rework, rates, and quality tests) improved for individuals or groups after their training?

For more information, refer to *Infoline* No. 259705, "Essentials for Evaluation."

Training Documentation Materials

During course development, a documentation plan will be created to tell what training records will be kept, how, by whom, and for how long. Training records may be kept on paper, file cards, microfilm, or computer files. Original or back-up records may be maintained in the training, information systems, planning, or legal department.

Original training records or copies may need to be forwarded to a government agency, private regulatory group, or to a professional agency that issues credentials. Record retention and destruction schedules may be established by law, organizational policy, or by the designer's recommendation.

During development, any needed documentation materials will be developed or copied. For example, the training department probably has a standard daily attendance form that needs only to be copied. But a new legally mandated safety course might require a form documenting employee's attendance according to specific units within the course.

Organizations typically save a course history showing who was responsible for various aspects of ISD; samples of forms; the course design document and lesson and learning plans; the course budget; attendance by learners, trainers, facilitators, and guests; evaluation records about individual participants, instructor performance, and course effectiveness and efficiency.

References & Resources

Articles

Chapman, Bryan L. "Accelerating the Design Process: A Tool for Instructional Designers." *Journal of Interactive Instruction Development,* Fall 1995, pp. 8-15.

Dixon, Daniele M. "Standardizing Craft Training," *Technical & Skills Training,* May/June 1995, pp. 10-13.

Friedlander, Philip. "Competency-driven, Component-based Curriculum Architecture." *Performance & Instruction,* February 1996, pp. 14-21.

Hites, Jeanne M. "Design and Delivery of Training for International Trainees: A Case Study." *Performance Improvement Quarterly,* vol. 9, no. 2 (1996), pp. 57-74.

Holton, Elwood F., and Curt Bailey. "Top-to-Bottom Curriculum Redesign." *Training & Development,* March 1995, pp. 40-44.

Murk, P.J., and J.H. Wells. "A Practical Guide to Program Planning." *Training & Development Journal,* October 1988, pp. 45-47.

Patrick, Eric. "Distributed Curriculum Development Environments: Techniques and Tools." *Journal of Interactive Instruction Development,* Spring 1996, pp. 26-34.

Rogers, James L. "Helping Clients Make Training Decisions." *Performance & Instruction,* July 1996, pp. 24-27.

Shaffer, Mary K., and Isobel L. Pfeiffer. "A Blueprint for Training." *Training & Development,* March 1995, pp. 31-33.

Shultz, Fred, and and Rick Sullivan. "A Model for Designing Training." *Technical & Skills Training,* January 1995, pp. 22-26.

Sullivan, Richard L. "Transferring Performance Skills: A Clinician's Case Study." *Technical & Skills Training,* January 1996, pp. 14-16.

Wedman, John, and Martin Tessmer. "Instructional Designers' Decisions and Priorities: A Survey of Design Practice." *Performance Improvement Quarterly,* vol. 6, no. 2 (1993), pp. 43-57.

Williams, Deborah, and Scott Stahl. "Ford's Lessons in Distance Learning." *Technical & Skills Training,* November/December 1996, pp. 10-13.

Wircenski, Michelle D., and Jerry L. Wircenski. "Greek to Me: Training Effectively with Unfamiliar Content." *Technical & Skills Training,* February/March 1997, pp. 28-30.

Zemke, Ron, and Judy Armstrong. "How Long Does It Take?" *Training,* May 1997, pp. 69-79.

Books

Kemp, Jerrold E., and George W. Cochern. *Planning for Effective Technical Training: A Guide for Instructors and Trainers.* Englewood Cliffs, NJ: Educational Technology Publications, 1994.

Knowles, Malcolm S. *Designs for Adult Learning: Practical Resources, Exercises, and Course Outlines from the Father of Adult Learning.* Alexandria, VA: ASTD, 1995.

Phillips, Jack J., and Donald J. Ford, eds. *In Action: Designing Training Programs.* Alexandria, VA: ASTD, 1996.

Piskurich, George M. *Self-Directed Learning: A Practical Guide to Design, Development, and Implementation.* San Francisco: Jossey-Bass, 1993.

Rothwell, William J., and H.C. Kazanas. *Mastering the Instructional Design Process: A Systematic Approach.* San Francisco: Jossey-Bass, 1992.

References & Resources

Infolines

Butruille, Susan G., ed. "Lesson Design and Development." No. 258906 (revised 1999).

Eline, Leanne. "How to Prepare and Use Effective Visual Aids." No. 258410 (revised 1997).

Hodell, Chuck. "Basics of Instructional Systems Development." No. 259706.

Kirrane, Diane. "Listening to Learn; Learning to Listen." No. 258806 (revised 1997).

Plattner, Francis. "Instructional Objectives." No. 259712.

Russell, Susan. "Create Effective Job Aids." No. 259711.

———. "Training and Learning Styles." No. 258804 (revised 1998).

Sharpe, Cat, ed. "Be a Better Needs Analyst." No. 258502 (revised 1998).

———. "Write Better Behavioral Objectives." No. 258505 (revised 1998).

Waagen, Alice. "Essentials for Evaluation." No. 259705.

———. "Task Analysis." No. 259808.

Course Design Quality Checklist

During the design phase of ISD, a course director must pay attention to innumerable details. Once a design is written, the director needs to step back and assess the quality of the overall scheme. The director may also ask design and development team members (or, if no team was formed, people with relevant knowledge and skills) to assess design quality.

The checklist below is admittedly subjective. Everyone will not necessarily agree, for example, about what equals "adequate" resources. But whenever someone who reviews the checklist believes that a course lacks one of the desired characteristics, that person should be asked for suggestions to improve the course design. This request often brings useful advice. Responses also help the course director recognize when reviewers have an overly ambitious idea of what's possible. In this case, the director may need to talk with reviewers to modify their expectations or to marshal their support for additional resources. Some public relations work may also be in order.

This checklist can be handed to a reviewer for use as a course design evaluation form, or the course designer can use it to evaluate his or her own design.

Instructions to reviewer:

Please review the attached design, then check as many of the descriptors below as you believe apply. For any descriptor that you do not check, please indicate in the space provided (use the back of the form, too, if necessary) what change(s) you recommend for improving the design. Or, use a question mark to indicate that you lack the information to assess the particular characteristic.

Please return this form in the enclosed envelope by
_____.

Thank you.

Signature Block
(Course Director)

Course Title: _____

Course Objective(s): _____
_____
_____

The Design

☐ Describes training, education, and development capable of solving all or part of a performance problem. _____
_____
_____

☐ Is systematic; offers orderly plans. _____
_____
_____

☐ Is valid; is based on analyses of training population and job tasks, topics, and problems. _____
_____
_____
_____

☐ Is efficient, uses least disruptive data collection methods and timing; uses appropriate technology for data collection and analyses, forms production, and so on. _____
_____
_____
_____

☐ Considers training participants' prior level of training.
_____
_____
_____

☐ Respects resource constraints, but provides adequate resources for meeting the course objective(s). _____
_____
_____
_____

☐ Appropriately involves training population representatives, their supervisors, and subject matter experts (SMEs). _____
_____
_____

(continued on next page)

Job Aid

☐ Is relevant and meaningful; focuses time on skills, knowledge, or attitudes that learners need on their jobs—and in which they need improvement. _____
_____
_____
_____

☐ Is comprehensive; covers all essential tasks, topics, and problems. _____
_____
_____

☐ Emphasizes "need to know" tasks and topics; avoids extraneous information or activities. _____
_____
_____

☐ Emphasizes active learning, except when safety or deadline considerations dictate otherwise. _____
_____
_____

☐ Includes written performance objectives that state what a learner ultimately is expected to do, under what conditions, and to what standard(s). _____
_____
_____

☐ Logically sequences subordinate and final learning and performance objectives. _____
_____
_____

☐ Maintains (through trainer, facilitator, or learning materials) appropriate degree of control over process—to ensure efficient use of time, learner safety, and so on.
_____
_____
_____

☐ Allows, to the extent possible, learners choices based on individual needs and control over their own rates of progress. _____
_____
_____

☐ Is internally consistent; matches test items to performance objectives. _____
_____
_____

☐ Is standardized; uses formats, forms, and data analysis categories in keeping with usual training and organizational requirements. _____
_____
_____

☐ Provides learners with adequate feedback on their progress. _____
_____
_____

☐ Offers learners adequate practice especially for difficult or important, but infrequently used, tasks. _____
_____
_____

☐ Includes job aids as necessary. _____
_____
_____

☐ Makes critical use of media, methods, and materials, avoids overly complex, expensive, or time-consuming strategies. _____
_____
_____

☐ Approximates or duplicates the context (physical surroundings, materials, tools, equipment, aids) in which learners must function after training. _____
_____
_____

☐ Clarifies roles and responsibilities of course developers, instructors, facilitators, and learners; incorporates plans to ensure accountability of achieving their responsibilities. _____
_____
_____

☐ Incorporates evaluation plans for individual learner's progress and for the course itself. _____
_____
_____

☐ Incorporates plans for training documentation, noting any related level or organizational policy requirements.
_____
_____

☐ Appears reliable; pending pilot testing or implementation, seems reasonable to expect design to produce good results for its target audience. _____
_____
_____

The material appearing on this page is not covered by copyright and may be reproduced at will.

Lesson Design and Development

Issue 8906

Lesson Design and Development

Lesson Design and Development 129

    Process and Structure 129

    Instructional Techniques and Materials 133

    Incorporating Evaluation 134

    Guidelines for Design and Development 136

    Individualized Instruction 138

    The "Instant" Lesson Plan 140

References & Resources 141

Job Aid

    Sample Lesson Plan 142

    Lesson Plan Checklist 144

Editorial Staff for 8906

Editor
Susan G. Butruille

Revised 1999

Editor
Cat Sharpe

Contributing Editor
Ann Bruen

Contributing Consultant
Chuck Hodell

Lesson Design and Development

In their book *Developing Vocational Instruction,* authors Robert F. Mager and Kenneth M. Beach once described a lesson plan as "the instructional prescription, the blueprint that describes the activities the student may engage in to reach the objectives of the course." Mager and Beach wrote the book for vocational teachers more than 40 years ago, but their description still applies. Then as now, it is as relevant for those in the training field as it is for educators.

In a training context, the trainer or facilitator follows lesson plans as a prescription or blueprint to guide learners in performing the "training objectives." David R. Torrence, in his article "Building a Lesson Plan," describes a lesson plan as both a *strategy* and a *ready reference:*

● As a *strategy,* the lesson plan is "a sequential set of events that leads to a desired goal."

● As a *ready reference,* the lesson plan is "a checklist of the necessary information to effect the set of events. A lesson plan summarizes who will conduct the instruction, to whom the instruction is directed, and what, where, when, why, and how instruction will take place."

Infoline No. 258905, "Course Design and Development," covers the overall design of a course—the big picture. This follow-on chapter narrows the focus to zoom in on the details of designing and developing the actual lesson plans within the course design.

Lesson design and development represent the final refinement of course design and development, contained within the design and development phases of instructional systems development (ISD). The five basic ISD phases, all of which interrelate, are:

1. Analysis.

2. Design.

3. Development.

4. Implementation.

5. Evaluation.

Lesson plans are developed within the conventional ISD model, in which the trainer or facilitator has a larger role. Learning plans are developed with the competency-based ISD model, which is more learner centered and individualized. This issue concerns mainly the conventional ISD model structure, which moves from courses to units to lesson plans to activities.

Refer to *Infoline* No. 259706, "Basics of Instructional Systems Development," for a complete examination of ISD principles and methods. For further information on the competency-based model, see *Infoline* No. 258905, "Course Design and Development," and the section of this chapter that provides information on individualized instruction and learning plans. For a discussion of the roles that designers and facilitators fill in lesson design and development, see the sidebar *Designers and Facilitators: Who Does What?*

Process and Structure

Lesson design, like any other element of ISD, is not static. Nor is there any one way to do it. But to produce a good lesson plan, you will generally do the following things:

1. Specify the title of the lesson and write a one-line description of the lesson.

2. Based on the course objectives, state the lesson objectives, specifying the following:

● the conditions under which the objectives will be achieved (equipment or material to be used)

● performance (observable behavior) expected

● criteria used to judge satisfactory performance.

3. For each objective, design a posttest, stating how the learner will be tested or evaluated for achievement of the objective. Each posttest should match the conditions of each objective and should contain instructions and specific items to be tested.

Designers and Facilitators: Who Does What?

The training designer and the instructor or facilitator often play different roles in lesson design and development. It is not unusual, however, for the same person to design and present the training program. This is especially true in organizations with small training departments.

It is important to know which person is responsible for certain decisions in the ISD process. In lesson design and development, the designer outlines the lesson, suggests approaches to topics, determines instructional periods and breaks, and selects and prepares major instructional material such as tests and guides.

The chart below, adapted from *Principles of Instructional Design,* shows how responsibility may be divided between designer and facilitator in lesson design and development.

General Division of Responsibility

Lesson Designer	Instructor/Facilitator
Chooses major strategies.	Selects details of strategies and implements presentation.
Selects major training aids.	Implements use of major training aids; chooses and implements use of minor training aids.
Designates number of instructional periods and break points.	Selects and implements structure and timing with instructional periods.
Selects and prepares participants' handouts, such as exercise sheets, data sheets, instructor and learner guides.	Implements use of materials—detailed selections and timing.
Selects principal components of content and evaluation.	Selects and implements ways to stimulate interest, motivate, and present material.

4. Outline how the performance objectives will be achieved in the following areas:

    - content
    - instructional methods, media, and techniques
    - student activities.

5. Build in evaluation to determine learners' progress during the course. Posttests will show whether or not the learner can perform the objective *after* the learning event (summative evaluation); while feedback during the learning event will check learners' progress *during* the learning event (formative evaluation).

6. Create the lesson plan (strategy), specifying learning activities, time allotted, and materials used.

    Not all lesson plans will look alike. For one thing, their design depends on whether learning will be:

    - cognitive (knowledge)
    - psychomotor (skills)
    - affective (attitudes or values).

Use the material presented in *Lesson Plan Variations* on the next page for a more complete understanding.

Once the designer goes through the design steps, he or she will have a lesson plan that includes the following components:

■ *Course and Lesson Title*
These should provide the purpose and conceptual framework of the lesson so that participants and their supervisors will be able to determine what will be taught and whether or not it is applicable to their learning needs.

■ *Time and Date*
This information must provide employees and managers sufficient lead time for planning purposes in the event that they need to make arrangements for their normal workload to be temporarily covered by someone else.

Lesson Plan Variations

The *Develop a Lesson Plan* module of the *Professional Teacher Education Module Series* shows model lesson plans based on whether learning objectives are informational (knowledge), manipulative (skills), or problem solving/managerial (attitudes).

The **informational (knowledge)** format has these components:

- unit title

- lesson topic

- objectives

- introduction

- method (technique)

- learning activity

- resources

- evaluation

- summary.

The **manipulative (skills)** format has the following components:

- unit

- lesson

- job

- aim (objective or purpose)

- tools and equipment

- materials

- teaching aids

- references

- four-step method (preparation, presentation, application, test)

- suggested reading for students.

The **problem-solving/managerial (attitude)** format has these components:

- unit

- lesson topic

- objective

- instruction

- introduction (identification of the problem—informal; statement of the objective—informal)

- method (key questions to ask to identify factors; factors to be identified)

- resources (list of resources for students to use in locating information needed to solve problem)

- summary (draw conclusions to the problem)

- evaluation.

For further information about the four-step method, see *Infoline* No. 258808, "Basic Training for Trainers."

■ *Objectives*

Develop the lesson objectives from the course and unit objectives. These are the most important elements in the lesson plan. Objectives should specify what the learner will do or know as a result of the lesson, the conditions under which the performance will be accomplished, and the criteria for judging performance or understanding of the skill or knowledge.

■ *Posttests*

List the posttests the learners will be expected to perform as a result of training. Tie each posttest to an objective. Examples of types of posttests include: true-false, essay, multiple choice, performance, demonstration, and standardized. (For more information on this topic, see *Infoline* No. 258907, "Testing for Learning Outcomes.")

■ *Materials and Media Lists*

Make a detailed checklist of supplies and equipment needed for conducting the lesson, such as projector, screen, tools, paper, pens, lights, outlets, extension cord, adapter, extra bulb, flipcharts, films, computers, and so forth. Include instructor and learner guides, texts, name tags, participant rosters, and job aids.

■ *Timeframes*

Somewhere in the lesson plan, often in the left-hand margin, list the expected duration of each activity within the lesson plan. Each activity should last not less than five minutes, or more than one hour. Plan for breaks, listing the duration of the break.

■ *Introduction*

The introduction orients learners by informing them of the following:

● lesson objectives

● content of posttests

● how the lesson relates to their jobs

● how the lesson relates to previous knowledge and present skills.

The introduction also motivates learners by arousing interest and attention through:

● a brief demonstration
● a funny story or interesting anecdote
● provocative questions
● background information.

■ *Content*

Based on the objectives, develop a list of topics and subtopics. Topics are arranged in the following sequence:

● known to unknown
● simple to complex
● concrete to abstract
● big picture to details.

Teaching or learning points to be covered during the lesson are then developed from the sequenced list of topics and subtopics.

■ *Trainer Activities*

This component lists the techniques used by the trainer or facilitator to guide the learner toward achieving the objectives. Examples of these techniques include: lectures, demonstrations, films, discussions, or records or tapes. For further information, see *Selecting Instructional Techniques and Materials* on the next page.

■ *Learner Activities*

This component lists what the learners will do to achieve the learning objectives. Examples include the following: practice, role play, fill out a form or worksheet, participate in a discussion, read out loud, demonstrate, brainstorm, debate, research, write.

■ *Summary*

The summary serves several purposes by doing the following:

● reinforcing major concepts
● relating themes
● drawing conclusions or generalizations
● clarifying or expanding major concepts.

■ *Evaluation and Feedback*
Summative evaluation takes place with some kind of posttest, while formative evaluation checks ongoing learning through periodic question-and-answer sessions, discussions, self-evaluations, and so forth. (See the job aid at the end of this chapter.)

Instructional Techniques and Materials

Before choosing techniques and training materials, the designer must consider many factors. These include the following items:

■ *Instructional Objectives*
Instructional techniques and activities must match the objectives—whether they involve cognitive learning (knowledge), psychomotor learning (skill), or affective learning (attitude):

- Cognitive learning involves mental processes and the acquisition of knowledge.

- Psychomotor skills involve manipulation of objects or machinery based on mental decisions. Training techniques include demonstration—practice, simulation, and mock-ups.

- Attitude involves motivation and perceptions. Training activities include role play, discussion, and brainstorming.

For a more complete discussion of how people learn, see the *Motivational Principles* sidebar.

■ *Cost or Budget*
Designers must always keep in mind cost benefit when determining training media and activities. Does the effectiveness of the activity in helping learners meet learning objectives justify the expense?

■ *Lesson Content*
Techniques and media must be consistent with the lesson content.

Selecting Instructional Techniques and Materials

The chart below matches some training techniques and instructional media with the three categories of learning (knowledge, skills, and attitudes—KSA). Use the chart only as a guide.

Technique/Activity	Knowledge	Skills	Attitudes
Assigned reading and research	X		X
Brainstorming	X		
Buzz group	X		X
CD-ROM	X	X	X
Computer-based instruction	X	X	X
Critical incident	X	X	X
Demonstration/practice		X	
Field project	X		X
Field trip	X		X
Flipcharts	X		X
Games	X	X	X
Guided discussion	X		X
Handouts	X	X	X
Job aids		X	
Lecture	X	X	X
Manuals	X	X	X
Panel	X		
Role play		X	X
Simulation		X	
Video	X	X	X
Web-based instruction	X	X	X

Motivational Principles

Understanding how people learn is an integral part of planning and writing a lesson plan. What motivates adults to learn? Six basic motivational principles apply within the context of planning and writing a lesson: relevance, conceptual framework, learning outcome, method, evaluation, and primacy or recency.

■ *Relevance*
This principle addresses the relevance of the lesson for the trainees. It is usually covered in the introduction part of the lesson plan and tells trainees what benefit they will derive from the lesson.

■ *Conceptual Framework*
This consists of the main ideas and secondary ideas of the lesson. It provides two important things. First, it tells trainees where they are going during the lesson. Second, it creates gaps in the trainees' minds that must be filled. When the instructor tells a trainee that he or she will talk about three things and then names those three things, he or she creates gaps, which can be powerful learning tools. By filling the gaps, the instructor provides closure in the trainees' minds, a subconscious force that can be used as part of the strategy for learning.

■ *Learning Outcome*
This principle tells trainees what they must be able to do at the end of the lesson, under what conditions, and how well. Knowing the expected outcome reduces trainees' anxiety.

■ *Method*
The method tells trainees how they will learn. It should cover all the methods that will be used in a particular class, such as lectures and demonstrations.

■ *Evaluation*
One of the most important things learners want to know is how they will be tested. When describing the evaluation of trainees' learning, the instructor should cover the method of evaluation and when it will occur. This also tends to decrease trainees' anxiety.

■ *Primacy or Recency*
Research shows that people tend to remember best the first and last things they see or hear. The course developer should keep this principle in mind when determining the sequence of teaching points and for planning reinforcement of what was taught in the middle of the lesson.

Adapted from "Lesson Plans—Strategies for Learning" by Michael R. Toney, Training & Development, June 1991.

■ *Learners' Knowledge and Expectations*
Learners will come from different ages and backgrounds as well as varying levels of experience and knowledge. Training activities must meet their needs while avoiding the extremes of being overly simple or too complicated. Trainers must consider the learners' level of comfort with different activities.

■ *Trainer's Experience and Capability*
The trainer should be comfortable and experienced with the training technique. If he or she has not tried a particular technique before, sharing that information with the learners can help enlist their support.

■ *Time Availability*
Expected duration of training activities must realistically fit within time constraints.

■ *Facilities, Equipment, and Material*
Even such constraints as fixed row seating can greatly affect the choice of training and learning activities, and the availability of equipment obviously affects the choice of training media.

See *Infoline* No. 258808, "Basic Training for Trainers" for listings and explanations of various training activities and techniques. See *Infoline* No. 258804, "Training and Learning Styles," for explanations of various training and learning styles.

Incorporating Evaluation

When building evaluation into a lesson plan, it is helpful for the designer to be familiar with the four classical steps in evaluation outlined by Donald L. Kirkpatrick in *Evaluating Training Programs*:

1. Reaction.

2. Learning.

3. Behavior.

4. Results.

Reaction, or Level 1, evaluation tests how well participants liked a training program. This is the easiest—and most common—form of evaluation, usually done by questionnaire. This type of evaluation focuses heavily on the trainer in terms of subject, techniques used, and performance. Here are some sample questions:

● Did the course, lesson, or session address your needs?

● How well did the trainer convey the objectives?

● Was the trainer well prepared?

● Did the trainer hold your interest?

● Did he or she adequately cover the subject?

● How well did the trainer summarize the subject?

● What was your most valuable experience during the session? The least valuable?

The evaluation form should be phrased to allow the respondent to answer as briefly as possible—for example, ask for a rating from 1 (poor) to 10 (excellent). The form should include space for additional comments.

Learning, or Level 2, evaluation is harder than Level 1. Evaluation of learning should, of course, be based on learning objectives. (See the sidebar *Choosing Evaluation Techniques* for a list of some common evaluation techniques used to measure learning.) Kirkpatrick emphasizes the importance of building in pretests and posttests when measuring learning, as well as using control groups and statistical analysis in analyzing and interpreting results.

Behavior, or Level 3, evaluation is harder yet to measure. One way to measure on-the-job behavior is by an attitude survey—getting feedback on the participant's behavior from the participant, that person's peers, supervisors, and subordinates.

Results, or Level 4, evaluations measure what happens because of training. Such results as reduction of costs, increase in production, and reduction of turnover often can be measured by a comparison of records. Other, more elusive effects, such as quality, can be assessed through interviews, questionnaires, and other techniques. For a thorough discussion of evaluations, refer to *Infoline*s No. 259813, "Level 1 Evaluation: Reaction and Planned Action"; No. 259814, "Level 2 Evaluation: Learning"; No. 259815, "Level 3 Evaluation: Application"; and No. 259816, Level 4 Evaluation: Business Results."

Evaluation Tips

When you are building evaluation into your lesson design and development, you may find it helpful to do the following:

● Allow enough time for participants to complete evaluation forms. Do not let the participants take the forms home; they are hardly ever returned.

● Build in "processing time"—time for participants to reflect on and discuss their own experience during the session.

● Try to include the same number of questions about strengths and weaknesses of the learning event.

● Allow for quick, on-the-spot evaluations throughout the course—even if it is simply asking the participants, "How are we doing?"

● Build in frequent written feedback. The trainer can prepare a written summary of evaluations and discuss them at the beginning of the next session.

Choosing Evaluation Techniques

The chart below matches some evaluation techniques with the three categories of learning (knowledge, skills, and attitudes).

Technique/Activity	Knowledge	Skills	Attitudes
Demonstration/performance test		X	
Essay	X		
Interview			X
On-the-job observation		X	
Oral presentation	X		
Paper and pencil test	X		
Questionnaire			X
Role play		X	X
Survey			X

- For written evaluations, give participants the option of remaining anonymous.

- Design written forms so that responses can be tabulated and quantified.

- Instead of having participants fill out the entire evaluation form at the end of the session, allow breaks after each topic to jot down reactions.

- Evaluations should be kept for future reference.

For further information, see *Infolines* No. 259705, "Essentials for Evaluation," and No. 258808, "Basic Training for Trainers."

Guidelines for Design and Development

When designing and developing lessons, you should focus on several broad areas of concern: the learning process, timing and flexibility, participant involvement, creative learning experiences, retention and transfer of knowledge, and automated instructional design.

The Learning Process

A basic understanding of the learning process will guide the designer in narrowing down lesson content and activities in the lesson plan. The learning process, as explained by Lawrence Munson in *How to Conduct Training Seminars,* can be described in six general phases.

1. Motivation.
Learners need to see "what's in it for them"—how they can benefit personally from the learning process.

2. Explanation.
Objectives and learning activities should be presented clearly and in a logical sequence.

3. Demonstration.
The trainer or subject matter expert demonstrates the skill to be learned, or, particularly in the knowledge or affective domain, provides an example or illustration.

4. Self-evaluation.
Learners should assess their own learning, both during the course (formative evaluation) and afterward (summative evaluation).

5. Application.
Learners must be able to apply ideas and skills learned when they return to their jobs.

6. Feedback.
Learners need to know how they are doing. The lesson design should provide for feedback during the course and at its conclusion.

Timing and Flexibility

Management of time must be built into the lesson plan, allowing flexibility for unforeseen circumstances, and for varying the pace according to participants' learning styles and speeds. Here are some tips for timing and flexibility:

- Training time should not exceed six to seven hours a day, excluding breaks. Generally allow for two 10-minute breaks before lunch and two after lunch. Each learning period should not exceed an hour.

- Be clear what the learning objectives are and plan time accordingly.

- Prioritize activities according to their importance: "A" for critical, "B" for should be done, "C" for nice to do. This way the trainer can add or subtract activities according to the learners' receptivity, pace, or such unexpected events as electrical failure or a class emergency.

- Allow enough time for learners to become proficient in each objective before moving on to the next.

- Keep in mind the attention span of learners; for example, attention span for a video will be much greater than for an audiotape. Lecture periods should not last more than 10 minutes at a time.

- Concentrate on techniques that allow the most time for learner participation; too much instructor-led "busy work" wastes the learners' time.

- Mix group activities with individual events for variety and maximum effectiveness.

- Allow for periodic transitions to summarize previous material and set the stage for what comes next.

- Consider individualizing instruction or inviting learner participation in designing some segments within the lesson.

Participant Involvement

The more participants are involved with their own learning, the faster and better they will learn. Here are some ways to increase their involvement:

- Punctuate lecture periods with question-and-answer sessions, quick quizzes, and other forms of feedback.

- Consider giving brief, learner-involved assignments, such as self-assessment quizzes, before the learning event. This allows for instant feedback from the beginning.

- Assign more advanced and time-consuming reading assignments before the learning event to allow more time for class discussion and group activity.

- Ask participants what their expectations are— either in writing or orally. This increases interest level while giving the trainer an indication of whether or not the learning event will meet expectations.

- Allow plenty of time for questions and build in opportunities to turn learners' questions into learning activities.

- Depending on the skill level of the trainer and the participants, share responsibility for lesson design. Working with the basic course or lesson design, participants may themselves fill in learning activities they feel will best help them to reach their learning goals.

Creative Learning Experiences

Involving participants in lesson design can lead to some creative learning experiences. The trainer and participants can negotiate all or part of a design as it relates to:

- goals
- objectives
- tasks
- timeframes
- values and norms
- evaluation.

Some creative teaching or learning activities to consider include the following:

- visualization
- guided imagery
- drawing
- journal keeping
- listening to music
- coaching.

For ideas on building creativity into lesson design, see *Infoline* No. 258902, "15 Activities to Discover and Develop Creativity."

Retention and Transfer of Knowledge

If participants cannot remember what they have learned in training and relate new skills and knowledge to the job, training has failed. Strategies for ensuring retention and transfer of knowledge to the job include building into the lesson plan ways to do these things:

Review material periodically. Using the new skill or knowledge periodically and relating it to something new enhances retention.

Generalize knowledge. Change the context in which the new skill or knowledge is applied; for example, use new computational skills in a different way.

Build in feedback. Getting feedback through games, role-playing, demonstration, and other techniques tests understanding as well as retention. Asking participants to critique or evaluate themselves periodically also ensures retention and tests understanding.

Ask questions. Build in question-and-answer sessions to get immediate feedback.

Automated Instructional Design

Do not overlook the ever-increasing advances in computer technology for designing and developing instructional materials. Examples of uses of automated systems include media selection, evaluation, materials design and development, flow charting, script writing, content development, simulation, testing, and front-end analysis.

Individualized Instruction

Individualized instruction can constitute a whole course or part of a course, depending on any number of factors. A program or lesson designer can use individualized instruction to complement group instruction by designing portions of the course or lesson for self-instruction. Individualized instruction is a key part of competency-based instruction (CBI).

When should the designer consider individualized instruction? Likely situations include the following:

Differences in learner needs or capabilities. Participants' work experience or skill levels may differ widely. Or learners may have vastly different learning styles or learning rates.

Budget considerations. Once materials are developed, the costs of implementing individualized instruction are generally lower than trainer-led instruction.

Schedules. Sometimes workers are on different shifts, which makes scheduling group instruction difficult.

Characteristics of individualized instruction include some distinguishing features:

- The course is divided into learning modules or units, with each module containing assigned reading, study guides, and possibly a programmed textbook. Learning plans are contained within each module and often worked out cooperatively between learner and instructor.

- Pretests are used for initial diagnosis of learner knowledge and skill to determine efficient use of time and resources.

- Lectures and demonstrations are used sparingly, if at all.

- Learners themselves control how quickly they master the program or module.

- Frequent self-assessment helps learners to assess what they have mastered and what they still need to know.

- Both summative and formative evaluations can be built into the program.

- The role of the instructor becomes that of a guide, rather than teacher.

- Records of the learners' progress can be recorded on computers to follow progress and for future reference.

There are more advantages of individualized instruction in addition to those outlined above, and they include:

- Participants take responsibility for their own learning.

- Individualized instruction focuses on mastering a task, rather than on instruction. Learners can test their mastery of a skill when they feel they are ready.

- Learners progress at their own speed without disrupting the pace of the class as a whole.

On the other hand, there are some disadvantages to individualized instruction:

- Learners may not be able or motivated enough to work through the program independently.

- Independent study can be lonely; it will not work with people who need the stimulus of others in order to learn.

- Evaluation can be more difficult because periodic oral feedback and other techniques are limited.

- There can be logistical problems, such as what to do with learners who complete the program way ahead of others, or those who cannot handle the material.

Learning Package Components

The designer, often in conjunction with the learner(s), develops learning packages for individualized instruction. Learning packages, or modules, generally consist of the following elements:

- a cover page
- an introduction
- directions
- performance objectives
- learning activities and materials
- a performance evaluation or assessment.

The learning plan generally consists of a description of the following:

- learning goal or objective
- skills to be developed
- proposed start date
- proposed completion date
- date(s) to be rated.

Both learner and instructor sign the learning plan.

The "Instant" Lesson Plan

When the time to create a lesson plan is limited, trainers can create an effective, complete, and internally consistent plan by including four basic elements:

- an introduction—consisting of the overview, the lesson objectives, the teaching methods to be used, and the evaluation

- the core of the training—essential course content, demonstration, practice, and feedback (in sufficient detail to enable a substitute trainer to give the class)

- an opportunity to ask questions—allowing the learners to ask questions and provide the trainer with immediate feedback on the effectiveness of the lesson

- a summary of what has been learned—a restatement of the main ideas, application to the work place, and testing to reveal learners' strengths and weaknesses.

This approach to lesson design and development addresses the few essential requirements that will create learning environments that benefit learners and save the trainer time. Ideally, however, the lesson plan developer will have sufficient lead time to carefully follow the conventional ISD structure outlined above in order to create the most effective learning experience for trainees.

References & Resources

Articles

Broadwell, Martin M., and Carol Broadwell Dietrich. "How to Get Trainees Into the Action." *Training,* February 1996, pp. 52-56.

Downs, Sylvia, and Patricia Perry. "Can Trainers Learn to Take a Back Seat?" *Personnel Management,* March 1986, pp. 42-45.

Eline, Leanne. "Choose the Right Tools to Reach Your Training Goals." *Technical & Skills Training,* April 1997, p. 4.

Mullaney, Carol Ann, and Linda D. Trask. "Show Them the Ropes." *Technical & Skills Training,* October 1992, pp. 8-11.

Quinlan, Laurie R. "The Digital Classroom." *Techtrends,* November/December 1996, pp. 6-8.

Tate, Ted. "Lesson Planning." *Successful Meetings,* March 1998, p. 118.

Toney, Michael R. "Lesson Plans—Strategies for Learning." *Training & Development,* June 1991, pp. 15-18.

Torrence, David R. "Building a Lesson Plan." *Training & Development Journal,* May 1987, pp. 91-94.

Wircenski, Jerry L. "Improving Your Questioning Skills." *Technical & Skills Training,* May/June 1996, pp. 25-27.

Yelon, Stephen, and Anne Wineman. "Efficient Lesson Development." *Performance & Instruction,* August 1987, pp. 1-6.

Yelon, Stephen, and Lorinda M. Sheppard. "Instant Lessons." *Performance Improvement,* January 1998, pp. 15-20.

Books

Briggs, Leslie J., editor. *Instructional Design: Principles and Applications.* 2nd edition. Englewood Cliffs, NJ: Educational Technology Publications, 1991.

Earl, Tony. *The Art and Craft of Course Design.* New York: Nichols, 1987.

Gagne, Robert M., and M. Driscoll. *Essentials of Learning for Instruction.* 2nd edition. Boston: Allyn and Bacon, 1988.

Hamilton, James B. *Develop a Course of Study.* Athens, GA: American Association of Vocational Instructional Materials, 1985.

———. *Develop a Lesson Plan.* 2nd edition. Athens, GA: American Association of Vocational Instructional Materials, 1984.

Kirkpatrick, Donald L. *Evaluating Training Programs.* San Francisco: Berrett-Koehler, 1994.

Lynton, Rolf P., and Udai Pareek. *Training for Development.* 2nd edition. West Hartford, CT: Kumarian Press, 1990.

Mager, Robert F. *Making Instruction Work.* 2nd edition. Atlanta: Center for Effective Performance, 1997.

Mager, Robert F., and Kenneth M. Beach Jr. *Developing Vocational Instruction.* Belmont, CA: Fearon Publishers, 1968.

Munson, Lawrence. *How to Conduct Training Seminars.* 2nd edition. New York: McGraw-Hill, 1992.

Nadler, Leonard. *Designing Training Programs.* 2nd edition. Houston: Gulf Publishing, 1994.

Yelon, Stephen. *Powerful Principles of Instruction.* White Plains, NY: Longman Publishers, 1996.

Infolines

Gryskiewicz, Stanley S. "15 Activities to Discover and Develop Creativity." No. 258902 (revised 1997).

Hacker, Deborah G. "Testing for Learning Outcomes." No. 258907 (revised 1998).

Hodell, Chuck. "Basics of Intructional Systems Development." No. 259706.

Phillips, Jack. "Level 1 Evaluation: Reaction and Planned Action." No. 259813.

———. "Level 2 Evaluation: Learning." No. 259814.

Phillips, Jack, and Ronnie D. Stone. "Level 4 Evaluation: Business Results." No. 259816.

Phillips, Jack, William Jones, and Connie Schmidt. "Level 3 Evaluation: Application." No. 259815.

Plattner, Francis. "Instructional Objectives." No. 259712.

Russell, Susan. "Training and Learning Styles." No. 258804 (revised 1998).

———. "Create Effective Job Aids." No. 259711.

Sharpe, Cat, ed., "Basic Training for Trainers." No. 258808 (revised 2003).

———. "Course Design and Development." No. 258905 (revised 1997).

Waagen, Alice. "Essentials for Evaluation." No. 259705.

Job Aid

Sample Lesson Plan

....

Course title: _____

Lesson title: _____

Time and date: _____

Objective(s):

_____
_____
_____
_____
_____
_____

Posttest(s):

_____
_____
_____
_____
_____
_____

Notes: time, transitions, key points	Introduction	Content/teaching points	Instructor activities	Learner activities	Summary

Materials:

_____

_____

_____

_____

_____

_____

Evaluation plan:

_____

_____

_____

_____

_____

_____

Notes/comments:

_____

_____

_____

_____

_____

_____

_____

_____

_____

_____

_____

_____

_____

_____

(continued on next page)

Job Aid

Lesson Plan Checklist

This checklist will help the lesson designer check for missing elements, relevance, and clarity:

☐ The lesson plan clearly states one or more learning objectives.

☐ Lesson objectives are based on the unit or course objectives.

☐ Objectives state conditions under which the objectives will be achieved, and criteria by which achievement of the objectives will be measured.

☐ Posttests are stated in terms of objectives.

☐ The introduction contains information that motivates participants and orients them to the lesson objectives.

☐ The number of teaching points is appropriate to meet the objectives within the allotted timeframe.

☐ Teaching and learning activities and techniques are based on learning objectives.

☐ The lesson plan employs a variety of teaching and learning activities.

☐ Teaching and learning techniques are relevant to learners' needs and learning domain (whether knowledge, skills, or attitudes).

☐ Learners are given ample opportunity to participate and to apply what they learn.

☐ Instructional media are appropriate for the learning domain, budget, and learner needs.

☐ The summary reinforces and pulls learning points together.

☐ Timeframes and transitions are noted.

☐ Both summative and formative evaluation are planned for each learning objective.

☐ Ample time is allowed for participants to process their own experiences.

☐ Segments within the lesson plan are long enough to accomplish the objective, and short enough to say within learners' attention span.

☐ Content is prioritized to provide flexibility.

☐ The lesson plan provides for individualized learning (if needed).

 The material appearing on this page is not covered by copyright and may be reproduced at will.

Instructional Objectives

Issue 9712

Instructional Objectives

AUTHOR

Francis Plattner
AARP
601 E Street, NW
Washington, DC 20049
Tel: 202.434.2995
Fax: 202.434.6490
Email: fplattner@aarp.org

Francis Plattner has more than 20 years' experience as a trainer and instructional systems designer. His career has spanned work specializing in law enforcement and intelligence for the U.S. Air Force, State Department, and as an independent contractor; presently he is the senior technical training specialist for the American Association of Retired Persons (AARP).

Instructional Objectives 147

    Why Use Objectives? 147

    The Basic Objective Statement 148

    Levels of Instructional Objectives 152

    Writing Instructional Objectives 154

References & Resources 155

Job Aid

    Objective Development Checklist 157

Editor
Cat Sharpe

Associate Editor
Patrick McHugh

Designer
Steven M. Blackwood

Copy Editor
Kay Larson

ASTD Internal Consultant
Phil Anderson

Instructional Objectives

Over the past four decades, instructional systems development (ISD) has proven itself as the vehicle for developing sound training programs. One of the most important parts of ISD is the creation of instructional objectives. Objectives describe what students should be able to do (student performance) and the conditions under which this should occur, and set acceptable performance standards. Written instructional objectives lead to consistent results across large training audiences, as well as providing measures against which your training's success can be benchmarked.

The three parts of an instructional objective—performance, condition, and standards—directly contribute to lesson plan design and development, selection of training aids, student measurement, and course evaluation. Preparing instructional objectives fits into the overall ISD process primarily as part of the design and development areas, but also assists trainers and course designers with implementation and evaluation.

Instructional objectives are typically written before courses are prepared, and are continually modified as time and experience reveal gaps, unrealistic expectations, or other ways they may be improved. Without clearly defined objectives, trainers and instructors cannot make informed decisions about selecting or designing training materials, instruments, or methods. Instructional objectives are the backbone of the curriculum.

Instructional objectives are created and developed as an organization determines that training is required. For example, company *XYZ* knows that it is about to launch a new product. The company also knows it needs to train its salespeople about the product so they can demonstrate its features to customers. With this in mind, company *XYZ* conducts a comprehensive front-end analysis that concentrates on accurate, focused, and job-based information. Because this type of analysis takes a specified period of time to complete, company *XYZ* has allotted sufficient time for the analysis, as well as the design, development, and implementation of the training.

Company *ABC* on the other hand, discovers its need for training through "trial and error." Through experience, the organization knows what it wants to teach when it has a new product to launch. The company adjusts its programs as necessary if the new product has significant changes

from a previous product, but all this adjusting takes a toll on trainers and product managers and does not always give salespeople the information they need to sell and demonstrate the product. At this point, the organization needs assistance to develop its existing training into a more structured program. This structure can be achieved through the use of instructional objectives.

However an organization identifies its formal training needs, the requirements can be expressed in broad statements and then broken down into specific parts that can be easily understood and used by instructional designers. Designers then take these broad statements and break them down into their component parts to create instructional objectives. These objectives can then be used to guide an organization toward its goal(s).

This *Infoline* presents the basic elements of instructional objectives, describes how to prepare each element and how they work together, and finally offers you the opportunity to practice writing instructional objectives as an exercise toward preparing objectives that meet your organization's needs.

Why Use Objectives?

Instructional objectives are a major component of any training curriculum. They can be used to develop or select training materials and to guide instructors, students, and test writers. Following are some of the more common ways instructional objectives are used in the workplace:

■ *Training Materials*
Because objectives are clear, precise statements of student goals, they provide guidance when developing or selecting training materials to support these goals.

■ *Instructors*
Instructional objectives offer specific directions for instructors who are developing lesson plans. The objectives can be grouped together to form complete lesson plans or broken into smaller segments that teach specific tasks. Objectives also guide instructors to the best methods that help students reach their goals by providing specific standards against which student performance can be measured. Because objectives are written in terms of demonstrable behaviors, instructors can

measure students' progress through question-and-answer discussions or through skills performance evaluations.

■ *Students*

Instructional objectives define for students the range of subject matter they will be tested on, how much they have learned, and how much more they still need to learn. This also allows them to prepare for testing.

■ *Test Writers*

Instructional objectives give test writers the details they need to select and construct items for written, oral, and performance tests. Results of these tests can identify learning objectives that have not been met and allow instructors, designers, and supervisors to identify and correct such problems.

The Basic Objective Statement

While there are different levels of objectives, which will be discussed later, they are all based on the basic form of performance, conditions, and standards.

Performance Statements

The performance statement tells—in precise words—what the student will be doing by specifying how he or she will demonstrate applied knowledge, skills, or behaviors. The main parts of a performance statement are the:

- subject
- performance-oriented verb
- object.

Of the three objective elements—performance, conditions, standards—the student performance statement is the least difficult to write. The objective's condition and standard—the other two parts of an objective—must also be related to the performance statement. Remember that the three parts of an objective must work together as a single statement to tell students what you want them to accomplish.

The student is always the implied subject so there is generally no need to include a subject. For example, in a statement such as "turn on the lathe," it is obvious that the student is the subject. If you have difficulty writing performance statements without a clearly defined subject, write something like this, "At the end of this training each student will be able to…" once and then list the verb(s) and object(s) for each performance statement.

A performance-oriented verb describes the action students will perform to demonstrate how they fulfill the performance statement and overall objective. You will want to avoid words that cannot easily be measured, are vague, or are open to misinterpretation. These include words such as:

- understand
- grasp
- believe
- internalize
- study
- familiarize.

Instead, use specific action words that describe what the student is doing, such as:

- write
- identify
- solve
- construct
- list
- conduct.

See the list at left for additional action verbs that are well suited for performance statements.

Suggested Action Verbs

Align	Identify	Program
Balance	Justify	Quote
Calibrate	List	Record
Demonstrate	Locate	Sanitize
Encode	Measure	Transmit
File	Name	Update
Gather	Notify	Validate
Hold	Obtain	Write

Two action verbs can be used when writing one performance statement, but keep in mind that all parts of the statement must be related; for example, "List and describe the basic steps for writing a background paper." A person performing the task would normally do both at the same time so it's appropriate to use both verbs in the same sentence.

The object of a performance statement is acted on by the verb. First identify an action verb, then ask yourself what the verb is acting on (the object). See the chart at right for some examples.

Condition Statements

The condition statement of an instructional objective defines the circumstances under which students will perform a task. Condition statements specify the tools students will be allowed to use as well as the environment in which they will work. The following types of questions help identify these conditions:

- Are students allowed to use reference books to perform the task?

- Can students ask for assistance from others?

- Are standard operating procedures or checklists available?

- What equipment will learners need?

- Are trainees allowed to use their notes?

- Where will students work? On the shop floor? At a desk? Outside?

By requiring students to perform a skill under specific conditions, you help ensure they will be able to accurately repeat their performance on the job. Below are several examples of condition statements:

Given classroom instructions, the required computer equipment and software, hands-on student exercises, a handwritten draft letter, and without instructor's assistance…

Given classroom training on note-taking skills and a student exercise document containing three lengthy written opinions on why three departments in the XYZ corporation should or should not merge into a single department…

Sample Performance Statements

Verb	Object
write	a report
grammar check	office letters
identify	steps in designing tables
clean	your work area
teach	basic HTML coding
demonstrate	professional email etiquette

Given classroom training on basic technical writing skills and a 10-page inventory report as a student exercise…

Given classroom instructions on HTML coding, an HTML editor, three student exercises, and without instructor's assistance…

Remember when you prepare condition statements that you are setting limits for the students. Tell them what references, job aids, tools, and other materials they can and cannot work with. If you fail to specify this, students can and will use any tool reasonably available to them—including asking the instructor for information—to complete their task.

Standards

Standards describe at what level students must perform a task to be acceptable. They often can be expressed incorrectly due to the limited language skills of the person writing the standards—illustrated in the common statement, "I know a passing effort when I see one, but I can't find the right words to express it," or a lack of awareness of the standards; that is, not being told what the standards or expectations actually are and what they mean.

Knowing the different types of performance standards will help the trainer formulate them. Commonly used standards include:

Sample Standard Statements

Example #1

Given classroom training on writing background papers, a writing style book, and a set of documents discussing various points on a specific topic, write a background paper containing the following elements:

1. A brief introductory paragraph that provides the reader with a clear statement of purpose and an outline or "road map" for the paper.

2. The basic discussion, which comprises the bulk of the paper (cohesive, single idea paragraphs).

3. The conclusion.

Example #2

Given classroom training on writing position papers, a writing style book, and a set of documents discussing various points on a specific topic, write a position paper containing the following elements:

1. An opening statement that clearly states your purpose in presenting the issue and your position on that issue.

2. Integrated paragraphs or statements that logically support or defend that position.

3. A conclusion paragraph containing specific recommendations or a clear restatement of your position.

Example #3

Given classroom training on painting and a student exercise consisting of a door that has already been prepared for painting, use the techniques taught to paint the door. Your door should:

1. Be completed within 20 minutes.

2. Be completely covered with paint.

3. Be uniformly coated.

4. Be free from imperfections such as fingerprints.

■ *Previously Prepared Standards*

Time and space may be saved by referring to an outside reference in instructional objectives. Other authors of course material often define qualitative and quantitative standards very well, so rephrasing them may be a waste of time. Referencing specific regulations, manuals, authors, checklists, or rating scales is appropriate and should be encouraged. Below is an example of an objective that uses an existing reference source as the standard:

Given classroom instruction, the required computer equipment and software, hands-on student exercises, a handwritten draft letter, and without instructor's assistance, create a word processing document. The completed document must be in accordance with the XYZ corporation basic business letter writing style standards checklist.

The already completed standard in this case is XYZ's style standards checklist, which follows:

Checklist:

- *no misspelled words*
- *1" top and bottom margins, 1.25" side margins*
- *header 0.5" from top of paper*
- *footer 0.5" from bottom of paper*
- *letter-size 8½" x 11" paper*
- *portrait orientation*
- *single line spacing*
- *tabs every 0.5"*
- *flush left text alignment.*

■ *Repetition or Redundancy*

Standards requiring "no errors" usually indicate a one-time test. That is, if the student does something without error once or locates two or three malfunctions in one inspection, the objective has been met. You may want the student to show mastery of the objective more than once to prove that learning has occurred. In these cases, you would add another statement such as "in two consecutive tests." For example:

- *Find 90 percent of the spelling errors in two consecutive business letters.*

- *Identify all paint defects in at least three out of five sample widgets.*

- *Find and replace all defective parts in two engines.*

Tips For Writing Better Objectives

- Specify actions that students must take.

- Specify the conditions under which the action must be performed.

- Specify the standards that students must meet to satisfy the objective.

- State objectives in measurable terms.

- Keep objectives simple.

- Use highly detailed objectives only when necessary and if their use will produce significantly enriched benefits.

- Avoid hidden descriptions of instruction such as, "Given two classroom training sessions and word processing trial exercises…"

- Use enough conditions.

- Implied conditions or standards should be understood by everyone.

- Terminal objectives and enabling objectives should be related.

- Be specific, but not excessively so. The narrower the focus on instructional content, the greater the scope and detail of the objective.

- Don't use objectives as a basis of discussion about instructors, trainers, the training process, or students.

- Understand that objectives define the outcomes of training—not the means to those outcomes.

- Specify the different types of performance and activities that characterize the objectives—intellectual (cognitive domain), physical (psychomotor domain), or attitude (affective domain).

■ *Physical Measurement*

Physical measurement—such as tolerance, weight, number of words, distance, degree, and rate—should be used wherever possible. Examples include:

- *no misspelled words*
- *with two errors on a noncritical task*
- *in correct HTML coding sequence.*

■ *Time*

You should define standards whenever time might affect student performance. If no time limit is included, some students will assume that they have as much time as they like. The limit should allow students who have mastered the skill to complete the task. Set the time limit according to how long it takes an experienced person to complete the task and then add whatever additional time is necessary to compensate for the inexperience. In a paper and pencil test, time limits may be set for each instructional objective tested or for the test in its entirety. Examples include *within 30 minutes* or *within five minutes after receiving each component of the task.*

■ *Degrees of Supervision or Assistance*

The degree of supervision or assistance during a test may affect results. Students require a much higher degree of skill and need a clearer understanding of how to perform a task without supervision or assistance. If no level of supervision or assistance is spelled out, it is assumed that the student must perform the assignment without supervision or assistance. For example, the standard can include the following:

- *with no supervision*
- *with instructor's assistance*
- *with no assistance from other team members*
- *without the manual*
- *only using the procedural checklist*
- *from your notes taken during today's class.*

See the box on the previous page for more examples of standard statements.

Levels of Instructional Objectives

Now that we have dealt with the basic form of objectives, we can move on to the four basic levels of instructional objectives: lesson, terminal, enabling, and interim. When used together, they guide the entire curriculum development process. Department heads, supervisors, and instructors should use them to:

- develop tests (written, oral, or performance)
- develop lesson plans and training aids
- sequence the course
- determine presentation methods
- develop internal and external course evaluations.

Lesson Objectives

Also known as course descriptions or goal statements, lesson objectives tell curriculum developers what students need to know, understand, or apply, as well as identify the target audience of the course. Lesson objectives are broad statements and do not have the three basic parts of an objective. Rather, they take the form of a written statement that guides development of terminal, enabling, and interim objectives.

Terminal Objectives

Terminal objectives describe students' expected level of performance by the end of a training program. They contain the three basic parts of an objective, but describe results rather than procedures. Terminal objectives:

- describe student competency upon completion of a training program

- state—in broad terms—tasks or jobs that the student must be capable of

- can be prerequisites of other courses

- provide the basis for enabling objectives.

An example of a terminal objective and its attendant enabling objectives appears in the box on the next page.

Enabling Objectives

Also known as subordinate objectives, enabling objectives define the skills, knowledge, or behaviors students must master to successfully complete terminal objectives. Enabling objectives contain all of the basic parts of an objective. They also:

- track students' competency during the training program

- are subordinate to terminal objectives

- must be related to terminal objectives

- lead up to achievement of terminal objectives

- are more detailed than terminal objectives

- address particular units or sessions rather than the entire course or training program

- are rarely tested or evaluated at the end of the training

- focus on short-term, specific results.

The three enabling objectives cited below describe an editing function that must be mastered before students can complete the terminal objective. While there are more enabling objectives to editing a document, these demonstrate the difference between enabling and terminal objectives.

Given classroom instruction on word processing and a 10-paragraph document, move the second paragraph to the end of the document.

Given classroom word processing instruction and a 10-paragraph document, cut the second sentence in the fifth paragraph and paste it at the beginning of the seventh paragraph.

Given classroom instructions on word processing and a 10-paragraph document, change the line spacing of the third paragraph to 1.5 lines.

Interim Objectives

Interim objectives, also known as sample of behavior statements, are the most basic form of objectives and are expressed in terms of student performance with an action verb and object. They define what

Sample Terminal and Enabling Objectives

The following objectives illustrate how enabling objectives support a terminal objective. In this case, the enabling objectives provide writing exercises for students to complete that will build the skills they need to complete the terminal objective—writing a technical paper for publication. Each enabling objective provides experience in an aspect of writing for publication: note taking, technical writing, and conforming to a particular style.

Terminal Objective

Given classroom training on note-taking skills and techniques, technical writing skills and techniques, word-processing skills and techniques, and six months of on-the-job experience, write a technical paper for publication for the XYZ corporation's monthly newsletter.

Enabling Objective

Given classroom training on note-taking skills and a student exercise document containing several lengthy written opinions on why three departments in the XYZ corporation should or should not merge into a single department, write a single paper combining the three opinions. Minimally, the paper must:

1. Be completed within 60 minutes.

2. Contain principal points the authors are trying to make.

3. Contain the most important details or examples the authors use to support their opinions.

4. Be written as a standard outline using Roman numerals, capital letters, Arabic numerals, lowercase letters, and indentations to show relationships.

Enabling Objective

Given classroom training on basic technical writing skills and a student exercise report, evaluate the report for technical writing techniques. At a minimum:

1. Underline the topic sentence of each paragraph.

2. Circle the noun and verb in the topic sentence.

3. Place a "(" by each paragraph where the sentences relate to one another.

4. Place an "X" by each paragraph where one or more sentences do not relate to the topic sentence of the paragraph.

Enabling Objective

Given classroom training on writing background papers, a writing style book, and a set of documents discussing various points on organizational development, write a background paper containing the following elements:

1. A brief introductory paragraph that provides the reader with a clear statement of purpose plus an outline or "road map" for the paper.

2. The basic discussion, which comprises the bulk of the paper (cohesive, single idea paragraphs).

3. The conclusion.

you want students to know, comprehend, or apply at the most basic level. Conditions and standards are not included in interim objectives, but they specify achievement as measured by test (oral, written, or performance) or demonstrated behavior. Interim objectives directly support the lesson objective by introducing the component skills students will need to successfully complete enabling and terminal objectives. For example, in the enabling objectives listed on the previous page, students are told to cut and paste sentences in a word processing document as well as adjust the line spacing. Interim

objectives supporting those enabling objectives would include:

-   *Cut a sentence from a given document.*

-   *Paste the sentence into another location on the same document.*

-   *Locate the "line spacing" window.*

-   *Change the line spacing of the document to 1.5 lines.*

As you can see, each objective level supports the next until the overall goal is reached. Interim objectives support enabling objectives, which support terminal objectives, which are created to fulfill the lesson objective. Working from a lesson objective back to interim objectives essentially allows you to map out the entire course as you think about what skills students need to successfully complete the training.

Writing Instructional Objectives

There are several ways to write instructional objectives. Their final form depends on the amount of information that will be included for the performance, conditions, and standards sections. How they will be finalized also depends on their readability and who will be using the objectives—instructors, students, or examination writers. Regardless of who uses them, objectives must be written clearly so that students know what they are required to accomplish. Below are three examples of instructional objective formats. Use a format, or combination of formats to clearly express the intention of the objective.

Example #1

Given classroom training on basic technical writing skills and a 10-page trip report as an exercise, evaluate the report for technical writing techniques. At a minimum:

1. *Underline the topic sentence of each paragraph or section.*

2. *Circle the noun and verb in the topic sentence.*

3. *Place a "(" by each paragraph where the sentences relate to one another.*

4. *Place an "X" by each paragraph where one or more sentences do not relate to the topic sentence of the paragraph.*

Example #2

Condition: Given classroom training on basic technical writing skills and a 10-page trip report as a student exercise,

Performance: evaluate the report for technical writing techniques.

Standard: At a minimum:

1. *Underline the topic sentence of each paragraph or section.*

2. *Circle the noun and verb in the topic sentence.*

3. *Place a "(" by each paragraph where the sentences relate to one another.*

4. *Place an "X" by each paragraph where one or more sentences do not relate to the topic sentence of the paragraph.*

Example #3

Evaluate a report for technical writing techniques.

Given classroom training on basic technical writing skills and a 10-page trip report as an exercise,

At a minimum:

1. *Underline the topic sentence of each paragraph or section.*

2. *Circle the subject noun and verb in the topic sentence.*

3. *Place a "(" by each paragraph where the sentences relate to one another.*

4. *Place an "X" by each paragraph where one or more sentences do not relate to the topic sentence of the paragraph.*

Instructional Objectives and ISD

If ISD is a road map to training, instructional objectives are the landmarks on that map. Once you identify what students need to know or be able to perform (the analysis phase), you can develop instructional objectives to get them there. Detailed and accurate objectives ensure that everyone—students, instructors, evaluators, and supervisors—will know what the training will accomplish and how they can get there. Detailed objectives also allow you to accurately evaluate student progress and the program's effectiveness by targeting which sections need to be redesigned.

References & Resources

Articles

Braden, R.A. "The Case for Linear Instructional Design and Development: A Commentary on Models, Challenges, and Myths." *Educational Technology,* March/April 1996, pp. 5-23.

Chapman, B.L. "Accelerating the Design Process: A Tool for Instructional Designers." *CBT Solutions,* August/September 1995, pp. 1-7, 22.

Coffey, D. "Are Performance Objectives Really Necessary?" *Technical & Skills Training,* October 1995, pp. 25-27.

Gagne, R.M., and M. David Merrill. "Integrative Goals for Instructional Design." *Educational Technology Research & Development,* vol. 38, no. 1 (1990), pp. 23-30.

Geber, B. "The Granddaddy: Bloom's Taxonomy." *Training,* March 1990, pp. 107-108.

Heideman, J. "Writing Performance Objectives: Simple as A-B-C (and D)." *Technical & Skills Training,* May/June 1996, pp. 5-7.

Madhumita, K.L. "Twenty-one Guidelines for Effective Instructional Design." *Educational Technology,* May/June 1995, pp. 58-61.

Martin, B.L. "A Checklist for Designing Instruction in the Affective Domain." *Educational Technology,* August 1989, pp. 7-15.

Nelson, H.G. "Learning Systems Design." *Educational Technology,* January 1994, pp. 51-54.

Overfield, K. "Easy-to-Use Instructional Systems Design Methodology." *Performance & Instruction,* April 1996, pp. 10-16.

————. "Non-Linear Approach to Training Program Development." *Performance & Instruction,* July 1994, pp. 26-35.

Piskurich, G.M. "Developing Self-Directed Learning." *Training & Development,* March 1994, pp. 30-36.

Reid, R. "On Target: Designing Training." *Technical & Skills Training,* January 1994, pp. 27-30.

Reynolds, A. "The Basics: Learning Objectives." *Technical & Skills Training,* February/March 1991, p. 15.

Shultz, F., and R. Sullivan. "A Model for Designing Training." *Technical & Skills Training,* January 1995, pp. 22-26.

Stoneall, L. "The Case for More Flexible Objectives." *Training & Development,* August 1992, pp. 67-69.

Varnadoe, S., and A.E. Barron. "Designing Electronic Performance Support Systems." *Journal of Interactive Instruction Development,* Winter 1994, pp. 12-17.

Books

Dillman, C.M. *Writing Instructional Objectives.* Belmont, CA: Lear Siegler, 1972.

Gronlund, N.E. *How to Write and Use Instructional Objectives.* New York: Macmillan, 1991.

Hackbarth, S. *The Educational Technology Handbook.* Englewood Cliffs, NJ: Educational Technology Publications, 1996.

Instructional Systems Development. Alexandria, VA: ASTD, 1994.

Leshin, C.B., et al. *Instructional Design Strategies and Tactics.* Englewood Cliffs, NJ: Educational Technology Publications, 1992.

Mager, R.F. *Goal Analysis.* Belmont, CA: David Lake Publishers, 1984.

————. *Measuring Instructional Results or Got a Match?* Belmont, CA: David Lake Publishers, 1984.

————. *Preparing Instructional Objectives.* Belmont, CA: David Lake Publishers, 1984.

Molenda, M., et al. "Designing Instructional Systems." In *The ASTD Training and Development Handbook: A Guide to Human Resource Development,* edited by R.L. Craig. New York: McGraw-Hill, 1996.

References & Resources

Phillips, J.J., and D.J. Ford, eds. *In Action: Designing Training Programs.* Alexandria, VA: ASTD, 1996.

Piskurich, G.M., ed. *The ASTD Handbook of Instructional Technology.* New York: McGraw-Hill, 1993.

————. "Self-Directed Learning." In *The ASTD Training and Development Handbook: A Guide to Human Resource Development,* edited by R.L. Craig. New York: McGraw-Hill, 1996.

Richey, R. *The Theoretical and Conceptual Bases of Instructional Design.* New York: Nichols Publishing, 1986.

Rogoff, R.L. *The Training Wheel.* New York: John Wiley & Sons, 1987.

Smith, P.L., and T.J. Ragan. *Instructional Design.* New York: Macmillan, 1993.

Wilson, B. *The Systematic Design of Training Courses.* Park Ridge, NJ: Parthenon Publishing Group, 1987.

Infolines

Butruille, S.G., ed. "Lesson Design and Development." No. 258906 (revised 1999).

Hodell, C. "Basics of Instructional Systems Development." No. 259706.

Sharpe, C., ed. "Course Design and Development." No. 258905 (revised 1997).

————. "Write Better Behavioral Objectives." No. 258505 (revised 1998).

Objective Development Checklist

Use this checklist as a guide to ensure your objectives are complete and accurate.

Performance Statement

☐ Does it have a subject, performance-oriented verb, and object?

☐ Is it related to the condition and standard?

☐ Does it use specific, measurable action words?

☐ If two or more verbs are used, do they relate to each other?

Condition Statement

☐ Does it specify what tools or reference sources students will and will not be allowed to use?

☐ Does it specify the environment in which they will perform the task?

Standard Statement

☐ Is it specific and measurable?

☐ Does it refer to any previously prepared standards? If so, are they specific and measurable?

☐ Does it specify how many times students will have to complete the task?

☐ Does it specify the amount of time students will have to complete the task?

☐ Does it spell out how much instructor assistance students can expect?

The material appearing on this page is not covered by copyright and may be reproduced at will.

Write Better Behavioral Objectives

Issue 8505

Write Better Behavioral Objectives

Why Have Behavioral Objectives? 161

Defining Behavioral Objectives 162

Types of Behavioral Objectives 164

Developing Behavioral Objectives 167

Components of Behavioral Objectives 168

Writing Effective Objectives 169

References & Resources 174

Job Aid

Objectives Checklist 175

Editorial Staff for 8505

Editor
Madelyn R. Callahan

ASTD Internal Consultant
Eileen West

Revised 1998

Editor
Cat Sharpe

Contributing Editor
Ann Bruen

Designer
Steven M. Blackwood

Why Have Behavioral Objectives?

Writing better behavioral objectives means knowing precisely where you want to go before you choose a way to get there. Simply stated, behavioral objectives are statements that describe the kind of performance learners should be capable of at the end of the training period. Objectives set the stage for the selection of training materials and approaches to training. They are guidelines for learners' courses of study and instruction, and they provide sound bases for developing tests and other means of evaluating performance.

Behavioral objectives—also referred to as *performance, training,* and *learning* objectives—are an integral part of the instructional design process. Instructors use objectives to plan their training programs and courses. Learners use them to help direct their learning behavior and activity more efficiently. Classification of objectives according to learning domain helps trainers and course designers understand and explain the objectives in greater detail. Objectives are classified under these domains:

- cognitive (knowledge)
- psychomotor (skills)
- affective (attitudes).

These categories are helpful in selecting the language for describing certain objectives.

Cognitive objectives, for example, may describe situations in which the employee would be *critiquing, analyzing,* or *evaluating* something.

Psychomotor objectives would describe *operating, painting,* or *coordinating.*

Affective objectives might involve employees' *showing, demonstrating,* or *exhibiting* a change of attitude or outlook through specific behaviors.

Needs Analysis

To begin developing objectives accurately, designers must first distinguish them from other design variables, such as needs. An effective needs analysis identifies a need by determining the discrepancy between the actual and expected, between what learners are presently capable of doing and what they *should be* capable of doing. For example, a person typing 60 words per minute may be expected to type 80 words in that period of time. After the identification process, needs are verified and put in priority order. The next step is to translate them into goal statements. For further information, see *Infoline* No. 258502, "Be a Better Needs Analyst," or No. 259611, "Conducting a Mini Needs Assessment."

Task Analysis

Another useful reference in developing and writing objectives is task analysis. Task listings and reports offer important information about the training, but again, it is important for designers to make distinctions between objectives and tasks early in the design process.

One outstanding difference is that task analyses of jobs are based on the best performances, while objectives state what will be expected from the learner at the end of the training program. In other words, the performance of a highly skilled worker during a task analysis will have much higher levels of competency than the performance of a recent training program graduate.

Whereas top performers may complete their jobs in record time without the assistance of job aids, entry-level employees cannot be expected to do as well. What is most important is that the employee successfully complete all phases of the job; increased competency will come with practice.

Another difference is the content of the task listings and reports as compared with objectives. Task analysis includes every step that must be taken to perform the job, including those that learners may know how to do before training. Objectives, on the other hand, do not include steps that learners know prior to training. For more information, see *Infoline* No. 259808, "Task Analysis."

Goals

The desired outcome of writing behavioral objectives is a successful training program. You must know your destination before you can figure out how to get there. Once designers understand how needs, tasks, and goals are instrumental in formulating objectives, they can begin to define the behaviors and performances in clear and precise verbal descriptions. Their aim is to describe specific, measurable, and observable behaviors that will communicate as completely as possible the designer's intent and the purpose of the instruction or training. By measuring and observing the behaviors, trainers can find out how well learners have met their instructional objectives—that they have learned what was required of them.

This chapter will review the classic approaches to writing behavioral objectives and introduce some ideas and suggestions to help you sharpen your skills in this area. The emphasis is on maintaining a clear, distinct, and sharply defined focus and communicating those qualities in your best, most effective objectives.

Defining Behavioral Objectives

Behavioral objectives state what the learner will be able to do at the end of the training program or at the end of a phase of training. They describe the planned outcome of the training rather than the training process—results rather than procedures. Objective statements range in specificity from highly to moderately detailed.

Primary or course objectives describe training outcomes. The prerequisite skills or knowledge needed to accomplish these objectives are specified in terminal or enabling objectives.

Terminal objectives describe students' expected level of performance by the conclusion of a training program.

Enabling objectives define the skills, knowledge, or behavior students must master to successfully complete terminal objectives.

Course objectives are comparatively much broader statements than enabling objectives. For example, the companion enabling objective to a course objective such as "Given classroom instruction on word processing, produce a document for publication" would specify, "Given classroom instruction on word processing and a 10-paragraph document, move the second paragraph to the end of the document and change the line spacing of the third paragraph to 1.5 lines." The course objective describes the general outcome of an entire instructional endeavor, while the enabling objective focuses on short-term, specific results of lessons, units, or modules of that larger instructional enterprise.

Why Use Behavioral Objectives?

Objectives are a major component of any training curriculum. They provide goals and guidance to instructors and students alike. Following are some essential reasons to use behavioral objectives:

- Describe competent performances that should be the result of training or instruction.

- Select and design training materials, content, or methods.

Case Study: ISI Robotech

ISI Robotech, a division of ISI Robotics in Detroit, Michigan, builds automated equipment to move sheet metal through stamping press lines. The ISI Robotech Technical Training and Development Center team designs training programs for the skilled trades that consist of a 50/50 combination of classroom theory and hands-on workshops.

In an effort to improve the results of their instruction, the training department established the following criteria for their course objectives:

● They must describe trainee performance after the completion of training.

● They must identify standard performance.

● They must describe the conditions under which the performance should be demonstrated.

The department manager then decided to examine the objectives of their mechanical maintenance course to see if they measured up to the new standards.

The first objective in the course stated:

Upon completion of this course students will be able to identify major components in the system.

This objective stated the desired performance, but it did not supply a condition or standard of performance.

In order to determine if the learner had successfully exhibited the performance described in the objective and to comply with their newly established criteria, the team rewrote the objective to read:

Given a written test, the student will identify major components in the ISI Automation System with a score of 80 percent or higher.

Next the team examined the second objective of the maintenance course, which stated:

Upon completion of this course, the student will be able to replace and adjust the x-axis and y-axis motors.

Again they developed a more comprehensive objective:

Given an ISI Pathfinder robot, the student will replace and adjust the x-axis and y-axis drive motors to ISI standards.

Later the training department team reviewed all of the behavioral objectives for each of their courses and rewrote them to include the performance, standard, and condition elements. In order to observe the performance of learners after training, the team created a performance demonstration checklist for supervisors to measure specific tasks learned in the classroom and workshops.

After improving their objectives and measuring them with their new assessment instruments, the company saw immediate results and benefits, especially in the preparation of training bids. Now, when clients ask for training on specific job tasks, the company's training bid quotation clearly identifies and describes objectives before the training is purchased. The quotation also describes the assessment instruments used to measure the objectives after training. This provides clients with a detailed list of job tasks and assessment tools in the quotation itself, enabling clients to know exactly what they are getting for their money.

Adapted from Technical & Skills Training, *October 1995.*

- Direct and organize the learner's course of study or training.

- Implement training.

- Stimulate in-depth review of the value and usefulness of the training.

- Communicate instructional intent.

- Design test items and procedures for performance appraisal.

- Provide a framework for developing ways to evaluate the success of the training.

Characteristics of Behavioral Objectives

Well-constructed behavioral objectives are clear descriptions of the learning expectations for students. They share the following characteristics:

- They are observable and measurable; that is, they describe behaviors that can be seen and evaluated.

- They are results oriented, clearly worded, and specific.

- They focus only on important aspects of the job.

- They can be measured with both qualitative and quantitative criteria.

- They are action-oriented statements outlining both specific activity and measurement of performance.

- They are written in terms of performance. Instructors and trainers are then able to select the most appropriate activities to help students achieve objectives.

- They communicate a picture of the successful learner in behavioral terms.

- They specify what the learner must do rather than describe the textbook, instructor, or experience of the training session.

- They talk about students' behavior or performance rather than that of the trainers. Objectives do not describe what students must know or understand, but rather what they must do to demonstrate their understanding, knowledge, or skill.

- They describe the learners' competency at the end of the training or a phase of training rather than the actual instruction used to make them competent.

- They talk about the conditions under which learners will be performing. For example, some situations may require the use of job aids such as a calculator to help solve problems; others will not provide such assistance.

- They indicate the minimum level of performance that is acceptable. Some objectives state a specific time limit or degree of accuracy.

- They can be separated into two categories: those that describe learners' actions and those that describe actions demonstrating attitudes.

Types of Behavioral Objectives

When you describe desired behaviors, it is important to select the appropriate language. Here are descriptions of the objectives that fall into the different learning domains.

Cognitive Objectives

Objectives in the cognitive domain include all task performances and behaviors that use knowledge of certain information—for example, the concepts, data, and research methods necessary for a needs assessment. This domain may involve knowledge of terminology, specific facts, conventions, trends, classifications, methodology, principles, generalizations, and theories. Use objectives in the cognitive domain to do the following:

- develop classroom instruction

- organize instructional content on the basis of increasing difficulty of subject matter

- describe intellectual aspects of learning, such as knowledge, information, thinking, naming, solving, analyzing, evaluating, and synthesizing.

Psychomotor Objectives

Objectives in the psychomotor domain focus on skills. Performance requires adept use of objects, tools, supplies, machinery, or equipment. State-ments of psychomotor performances include the following: "operate word processor, construct a scaled-down model of a bridge, develop black and white film, print photographs, style hair." Use objectives in the psychomotor domain to:

- focus on actual skill performance

- focus on the finish product

- specify accuracy with limits, level of excellence, and speed.

Enabling Objectives

Enabling objectives are related to the three primary types of behavioral objectives (cognitive, psychomotor, and affective). In order to perform the tasks of the course objectives, learners must have prerequisite skills, knowledge, and attitudes. Objectives that enable learners to perform the task are appropriately called enabling objectives. Here is an example of how enabling objectives are related to overall course objectives.

Course Objective

Given the required amount of copy for a monthly publication, prepare for print production meeting organization's standards for accuracy and speed.

Enabling Objectives

1. Learner will be able to write instructions for production specifying type size and leading of print style. Individual will make notations on the manuscript labeling titles, heads, subheads, sidebars, boxes, features, and page width and depth. Following three practice sessions, learners should be able to mark specifications at a rate of two minutes per page without errors.

2. Given a marked-up manuscript, learners should be able to proofread the final copy for spelling errors and for mistakes in the format and type specifications.

3. Given the final layout, learners will be able to proof for spacing, completeness, and organization.

4. Given a 30-page publication, learners will be able to specify print size and style, and proofread for content and visual appearance.

Enabling objectives have their own set of characteristics:

- Designers and trainers may develop them from behavioral objectives.

- They are more detailed than the course objectives, being addressed to particular units or sessions rather than to the entire course or training program.

- They are seldom tested or evaluated at the end of the training because their only purpose is to enable learners to do what is necessary to complete those tasks required by the course objectives.

- If learners are capable of satisfying behavioral objective criteria, they have been equally successful with criteria for enabling objectives.

Affective Objectives: A Special Case

Affective objectives require detailed preparation. Here are some suggestions for preparing this type of objective.

1. Indicate affective objectives by inferring from observations of what learners say or do as objective-related behavior. It is not possible to indicate these objectives in directly measurable terms.

2. Start writing affective objectives by answering questions such as, "Should I expect an entry-level employee or new graduate of the training program to have this particular feeling or attitude?" (Consider whether you are making unrealistic demands.) "What kind of behavior would I expect of someone with this particular feeling or attitude?" Think of behavior patterns you would expect in particular situations; for example, how does a cooperative employee behave on the job? Provide various scenarios for learners to show how they would possess the right attitudes in order to behave appropriately.

3. List relevant actions defining the performance of an objective. Though feelings are not measurable, you can, for example, measure a supervisor's attitude toward improving relationships with support staff. In checking behavioral clues, you would probably want to know if the supervisor:

   • is courteous and friendly, calling employees by name and not using a condescending tone when speaking with them

   • makes an effort to visit the different departments and work stations and talk to employees about their work

   • holds meetings with staff to find out if working conditions are satisfactory and to listen to employees' views

   • demonstrates interest in employees as individuals by talking with them about topics of interest that are unrelated to the job.

4. Describe performance in the affective domain as the demonstration of feelings and attitudes, for example:

   • show interest in safety of laboratory personnel

   • display concern for anxious patients

   • show improved relations with support staff.

5. Include conditions under which these attitudes are demonstrated, for example:

   • during every laboratory session

   • in situations that require it

   • after reading material on employee motivation.

6. Establish criteria for achievement of objectives by measuring behaviors that demonstrate feelings and attitudes. Similar to performance statements, the criteria contain action words or verbs. Examples of criteria are:

   • notifies proper authorities and anyone working in or near laboratory facilities of any danger

   • consoles and is supportive of anxious patients preparing for surgery.

7. Measure positive attitudes with related actions. For example, some indications of positive interest in an activity are the following:

   • Learners enthusiastically participate in the activity.

   • They say they like the activity.

   • They choose it instead of other activities.

   • They talk about the activity with others and invite them to participate.

8. Use the following verbs to state affective objectives:

- agrees

- attempts

- avoids

- cooperates

- defends

- disagrees

- helps

- is attentive to

- joins

- offers

- participates in

- resists.

There are some problems associated with using affective objectives. They are difficult to measure because learners may falsify the required behavior. They can pretend to act cooperatively toward coworkers, as their objective states, and then may change their behavior when not observed. In addition, feelings and attitudes are expressed in many different ways. People have different reactions to situations. For example, some choose to resolve teamwork problems by interviewing individuals, and others prefer to speak with the entire group. Still others arrange team building seminars and other diagnostic procedures that the group can work out by itself under a leader's direction.

Affective Objectives

Objectives in the affective domain require demonstrations of attitudes, feelings, and emotions. They enable trainers to identify aspects of training and instruction that can help learners on a personal or social level. One example is: "To increase confidence in negotiating abilities." These objectives involve paying attention to people and events, responding to them through participation, expressing values by showing either support or opposition, and acting according to those values. Use objectives in the affective domain to:

- demonstrate listening, perceiving, tolerating, and being sensitive to someone or something

- show a willingness to cooperate, follow along, reply, answer, approve, and obey

- select, decide, identify, and arrange values in order of importance as they relate to specific situations

- translate feelings and attitudes into observable behaviors.

Developing Behavioral Objectives

How you prepare and draft your objectives has as much effect on clarity as the language and form you use to present them. Follow these suggestions for setting and formulating objectives before and during the actual writing phase:

- Look at sources of objectives: needs and task analyses, position descriptions, earlier performance plans, other departments' objectives, surveys, documented interviews with supervisors, subordinates, clients.

- List the major objectives for the job or task.

- Distribute the list to supervisors, subordinates, and clients and request their comments on clarity and sequencing. Will the statements be understood, and are they in the proper order?

Checklist for Preparing Behavior Objectives

Without clearly defined objectives, trainers and instructors cannot make well-informed decisions about selecting or designing training materials, instruments, or methods. Answer the following questions before you proceed beyond the objectives phase of your instructional design process:

☐ Are your statements distinct though clearly derived from the needs, goals, and tasks that are part of this design process?

☐ What is the purpose of the objective? Is it to be used for designing training, performance appraisal, or program evaluation?

☐ Do you have a clear idea of what you expect your learners to be able to do at the end of the instruction or training?

☐ Will your learners be able to understand this idea once you have put it into words?

☐ Is the objective written to include a clearly measurable or observable outcome?

☐ What kinds of objectives will you be working with? How will they involve knowledge, skills, and attitudes of employees?

☐ What prerequisite capabilities must learners possess before they are able to meet the objectives satisfactorily?

☐ What is the educational background of your group? Is the concept or language of the statement too difficult or too easy for them?

☐ What is the level of experience of the group? Are you asking them to perform well above or below their capabilities?

☐ How specific should the statements be? How narrow or wide should your scope be to ensure that learners understand completely what is expected of them? Should you include *several* conditions and criteria, if appropriate, to clarify your statements?

☐ If learners accomplish all objectives, will they be able to perform the job?

- Draft objectives.

- Discuss differing opinions and reach consensus.

- Establish criteria and draft action plans for objectives.

- Delete or reword objectives for which criteria and action plans cannot be developed.

- Break objectives down into subobjectives or components, if necessary.

- Describe any conditions not under your control that may influence the accomplishment of objectives.

- Ascertain which objectives are critical to the performance of the job.

- Review objectives, criteria, and standards with managers and supervisors.

- Adjust and revise objectives as necessary.

Components of Behavioral Objectives

In order to develop clearly defined behavioral objectives, you must address the areas of performance, conditions, and standards.

■ *Performance*
The performance statement of an objective defines in precise terms what the learner will be doing. These statements contain statements with action verbs, such as the following:

- Repair the telecommunications equipment.

- Locate distributors of heat-sensitive shields.

- Identify cognitive, psychomotor, and affective objectives.

■ *Conditions*

This component explains the circumstances under which the learner will be performing the activity. It describes equipment, supplies, and job aids that may or may not be used on the job. It also describes the work setting and any information used to direct action. Add the following phrases to the above statements:

- given the technician's maintenance and installation guides

- using four telephone lines, a current telephone directory, and last year's listing of local vendors

- with the help of checklists and guidelines for each domain.

Some conditions restrict assistance, such as the following:

- without the aid of a repair manual
- by contacting the Chamber of Commerce only
- in a simulated laboratory situation.

Others guide the action in specific directions, for example:

- after reading all the assigned literature
- using provided resource materials
- using specific definitions and examples.

■ *Criteria (Standards)*

This part of the objective specifies the level or degree of proficiency that is necessary to successfully perform the job. The criterion indicates the quality of the performance required to achieve objectives. The information provided in the criterion is used to evaluate performance. Some of the criteria involve speed, accuracy with a margin of error, maximum amount of mistakes permitted, productivity level, and degree of excellence. Complete the statements with phrases such as these:

- according to the manufacturer's specifications
- at a rate of three per hour
- with a maximum of two mistakes.

Writing Effective Objectives

There are six basic steps that you should follow in order to write clear behavioral objectives.

1. Start by asking yourself every time you begin to write an objective, "What should the learner be able to do by the end of the training program?" Attempting to answer this question will direct your efforts.

2. Begin writing the objective by using a verb and an object (for example, "type a letter, write a report"). The subject "you" is understood.

3. Use *action verbs* describing what must be learned by the student population. Examples of these are: "operate, collect, organize, arrange." (See the sidebar list of suggested action verbs.)

Format

Objectives may be written in a variety of ways. They are sometimes one sentence or one paragraph long. Here are some examples of the different formats for writing objectives.

Using a jack, lug wrench, and tire iron, be able to correctly remove a damaged automobile tire and mount a new tire onto the hub. Performance will be judged as successful if tire change is accomplished according to trade standards and if wheel inspection indicates tire is accurately installed.

Provided with current tax rate schedules, taxpayer's gross income, withholding credits, and number of dependents, be able to compute the net tax due or refund within 2 percent. The learner must accurately complete 10 consecutive tests for this criterion.

Performance: Critique a videotaped presentation on needs assessment.
Condition: Use the format and checklists provided.
Criterion: The critique must fulfill the standards indicated on the checklists.

Goal: Be able to type lists of words.
Behavior: Type on standard keyboard.
Conditions: Learner must have access to typewriter and use words selected by the instructor.
Criterion: The learner must type at least 23 of 25 words correctly.
Criterion: The learner must type words in columns or lists.

4. Follow the verb with a description of what is being treated (for example, "operate a fork lift, collect data processing information, organize personnel and incentive award files"). The combination of the action verb and description state what the learner must accomplish.

5. Add conditions by answering questions such as the following: "Will special equipment be available? What are the time limits? What instruments will be used for testing? What resources may be used?" Some examples of this are as follows:

   Using standard directories, company reports, and Chamber of Commerce listings, survey the sales market of all major distributors in the Northwest region.

   With the use of a pencil, ruler, masking tape, and a single-edge razor, mount photographs for framing with a margin of 1/4 inch on all sides.

   With the aid of a building guide, master keys, and a flashlight, complete a security check of the main offices within 4 1/2 minutes.

6. If a training course has proficiency requirements, as in competency-based programs, build into the objective performance standards defining the minimum acceptable levels of achievement and the conditions under which performance will occur. To define achievement levels, answer such questions as: "How comprehensive? How accurate? What was the time frame? How well? How effective?" Some examples of answers to these questions are:

   Survey the sales market covering all the major distributors in the Northwest region.

   Mount photographs for framing with a margin of 1/4 inch on all sides.

   Complete a security check of the main offices within 4 1/2 minutes.

Sequencing Objectives

Logical sequencing of training objectives contributes to the successful completion of a performance and gives learners orderly guidelines for accomplishing activities. The value of the sequence is its effect on the development of the required skills, knowledge, and attitudes that the objectives describe. How you decide to sequence objectives depends on the purpose of your instruction or training. Here are some suggestions and examples to help you organize training objectives.

Put enabling objectives in a sequence that will be most helpful as a logical and orderly procedure for accomplishing the major task of the course or behavioral objective. For example, if the objective is to "write better behavioral objectives," the sequence for enabling objectives would be as follows:

- Develop objectives.

- For each objective, state the performance, condition, and criteria components. If necessary, rewrite objectives.

- Identify objectives as either cognitive, psychomotor, or affective.

- State objectives for each domain.

- Put objectives in logical sequence.

Use a sequence that best serves your purpose. If you want to catch the attention of the group early in the course or program, begin with an appropriate objective. If your group would benefit from an early success in the program, use some interesting but easily achieved objectives to start off, before you present the group with some of the more challenging objectives. If the students require a general overview, sequence a broad objective first and follow it with some specifics.

Action Verbs

Selecting the most suitable action verb to describe the behavior being taught to learners is a difficult but critical activity of writing objectives successfully. Helpful guidelines for choosing appropriate verbs are Benjamin Bloom's six intellectual levels of the cognitive domain. The lowest level is knowledge, and the five increasingly intellectual levels are comprehension, application, analysis, synthesis, and evaluation. Verbs to describe the mental abilities in these categories are as follows:

Knowledge	Application	Synthesis
arrange	apply	arrange
define	choose	assemble
list	demonstrate	construct
memorize	illustrate	create
name	interpret	design
organize	operate	formulate
relate	prepare	organize
recall	sketch	plan
	solve	prepare
	use	set up
		synthesize

Comprehension	Analysis	Evaluation
classify	analyze	appraise
describe	appraise	assess
explain	categorize	choose
identify	compare	compare
indicate	contrast	defend
locate	diagram	estimate
report	differentiate	evaluate
restate	distinguish	judge
review	examine	rate
select	inventory	select
sort	question	value
translate	test	

This sequence or taxonomy is particularly helpful for professionals working in instructional technology.

Use a common sense approach to sequencing—simple to complex or known to unknown represent some of the usual sequence patterns. Arrange the order of the objectives to provide learners the basic skills early in the training program. Program participants learn and accomplish objectives at different levels and speeds. The proper sequence will give some learners, at the very least, minimal skills.

Rules for Writing Objectives

To ensure success when writing behavioral objectives, there are a number of specific guidelines that you should follow.

Keep statements short and simple. Avoid excessive detail; lengthy descriptions of requirements are overwhelming.

Do not use objectives to describe instructors, trainers, materials, the training process, or the learner population. Instructional design information is useful in official descriptions of courses and training programs but is not usually stated in behavioral terms.

Differentiate activities and objectives. For example, "Read pages 40-65 of the operator's manual" is a learning activity that is part of the training, but "Operate the sorting machine" is the end result of the learning.

Differentiate descriptions and objectives. Descriptions explain course or program content, while objectives tell what will be accomplished. An example of a description is: "Discuss and provide practice of the first aid emergency procedure for cardiopulmonary resuscitation." A companion objective would specify: "Be able to alternately massage the heart and perform mouth-to-mouth breathing."

Know what training objectives do not do. Because these objectives talk about performance (the demonstration of knowledge, skills, and attitude), they define outcomes of training without describing the means to those outcomes.

Specify the action that must be taken for each objective, the conditions under which this action should be performed, and the criteria or standards that the performer must meet so that the objective is accomplished successfully. Keep in mind, the objectives you write must tell learners precisely what is expected of them. For the learners, such exact statements will let them know how much they have accomplished and how much more they are required to learn.

Be specific but not excessively so. The scope of what must be covered depends on the purpose or subject of that particular objective. Specificity varies at each stage of an instructional plan. For example, course, unit, and lesson objectives are each more specific than the previous objective. The narrower the focus on instructional content, the greater the scope and detail of the objective.

Specify the different types of performances and activities that characterize the objectives. Intellectual (knowing) activities are classified as the cognitive domain; physical activities as psychomotor; and demonstrations of personal qualities and attitudes as the affective domain.

Tips for Success

Objectives tell what the learner should be able to do, describe the important conditions under which this performance should occur, and set standards for acceptable performances. To accomplish this, use the following tips:

1. State objectives in measurable terms. Each statement should be written so that it describes the behaviors to be taught or trained.

2. Do not write more detailed objectives than necessary. Defining and writing highly detailed objectives involves a great deal of time and expense. Use these objectives when the situation demands them and when you are sure that their use will result in maximum benefits.

3. Use task analysis sheets to guide your preparation of objectives. Write a task at the top of a sheet and below it a detailed description of learners' task-related accomplishments expected at the end of the training.

4. Make a spreadsheet of your objectives. Divide the sheet into six columns. Begin at the left, labeling columns: Objectives, Performance, Condition I, Condition II, Criterion I, Criterion II. If you do not need the second column for conditions or criteria, leave it blank.

5. Watch out for hidden descriptions of instruction. A phrase such as "Given two classroom training sessions and on-the-job trial exercises" describes the instructional process. All components of objectives should describe outcomes.

6. Use a sufficient number of *suitable* conditions: "Be able to administer first aid accurately and thoroughly within the first 1 1/2 minutes following the crisis" states the performance and its standard, but it does not specify the recipient of the treatment. In this case, administering first aid to infants, adults, children, burn, shock, or bleeding victims will make a significant difference in the kind of treatment rendered.

7. Do not assume that implied conditions or criteria will be understood by everyone. Implications may be interpreted differently by different readers. If any part of an objective is vague, clarify it to reduce as much as possible the risk of misinterpretation. Suppose your objective reads: "Be able to explain six health and safety standards." If you add a criterion phrase such as "according to federal, state, and local codes," you can make the objective more clear and effective.

8. Analyze first drafts of objectives by focusing on the performance part of the statement before the condition and criterion parts. If the performance component is missing, you do not have an objective. For example, "Student will learn the difference between cognitive, psychomotor, and affective objectives" does not describe performance because *learn* is not an action. A better description is: "Be able to differentiate between...."

9. In analyzing your draft, be sure that course and enabling objectives are related. First ask *why* an employee should be able to do "X." Put your answer in the form of an objective. Continue asking and answering until you find out the main reason or objective for the training. Consider the following objective: "Employees must be able to find spelling mistakes." Why? So they can be good proofreaders. Why should they proofread well? So they can *produce quality publications*. Why should they produce such publications? Because publication production is part of their job description.

10. After checking the course objective, look at the enabling objectives to see if they are logically connected. Using the same example, ask what a person would need to know or do to produce quality publications. Some answers include: They would have to know how to proofread using specific symbols or notations for proofreaders; they would also have to know how to spell and use proper grammar.

11. In situations where evaluation will be particularly important, designers may write objectives with an emphasis on evaluation. When they prepare to write such objectives, they can start by asking themselves: "How will I ascertain whether or not this objective has been satisfied?"

In today's competitive business climate, all training must produce a positive return-on-investment. One way to ensure that training is cost effective is to provide demonstrable and measurable results. The best way to do that is to write good behavioral objectives for your training programs. As the saying goes: "If you don't know where you are going, how are you going to know when, or if, you get there?" If you employ precise objectives in your training courses, then you will know when you have achieved your training goals—you will have arrived at your destination.

References & Resources

Articles

Coffey, Dennis. "Are Performance Objectives Really Necessary?" *Technical & Skills Training,* October 1995, pp. 25-27.

Gagne, Robert M., and David M. Merrill. "Integrative Goals for Instructional Design." *Educational Technology Research and Development,* vol. 38, no. 1 (1990), pp. 23-30.

Geber, Beverly. "The Granddaddy: Bloom's Taxonomy." *Training,* March 1990, pp. 107-108.

Heideman, Jim. "Selecting Media for Training." *Technical & Skills Training,* August/September 1992, pp. 33-35.

————. "Writing Performance Objectives: Simple as A-B-C (and D)." *Technical & Skills Training,* May/June 1996, pp. 5-7.

Langdon, Danny. "Are Objectives Passé?" *Performance Improvement,* October 1997, pp. 12-16.

Martin, Barbara L. "A Checklist for Designing Instruction in the Affective Domain." *Educational Technology,* August 1989, pp. 7-15.

Reynolds, Angus. "The Basics: Learning Objectives." *Technical & Skills Training,* February/March 1991, p. 15.

Stoneall, Linda. "The Case for More Flexible Objectives." *Training & Development,* August 1992, pp. 67-69.

Books

Baird, L.S., et al. *The Performance Appraisal Sourcebook.* Amherst, Massachusetts: HRD Press, 1982.

Bloom, B.S., et al. *A Taxonomy of Educational Objectives. Handbook I: The Cognitive Domain.* New York: Longman, 1977.

Davies, I.K. *Objectives in Curriculum Design.* London: McGraw-Hill, 1976.

Dillman, Caroline M. *Writing Instructional Objectives.* Belmont, California: Lear Siegler, 1972.

Gagne, R.M. "Analysis of Objectives." In *Instructional Design: Principles and Applications,* edited by L.J. Briggs. Englewood Cliffs, New Jersey: Educational Technologies Publications, 1977.

Gronlund, Norman E. *How to Write and Use Instructional Objectives.* New York: Macmillan, 1991.

Kemp, J.E. *The Instructional Design Process.* New York: Harper & Row, 1985.

Mager, Robert F. *Goal Analysis.* (3d edition). Atlanta: Center for Effective Performance, 1997.

————. *Preparing Instructional Objectives.* (3d edition). Atlanta: Center for Effective Performance, 1997.

Mager, Robert F., and K.M. Beach Jr. *Developing Vocational Instruction.* Belmont, California: Fearon Publishers, 1968.

Michalak, D.F., and E.G. Yager. *Making the Training Process Work.* New York: Harper & Row, 1979.

Nadler, L. *Designing Training Programs.* (2d edition). Houston: Gulf Publishing, 1994.

National Center for Research in Vocational Education. *Develop Student Performance Objectives.* Athens, Georgia: American Association for Vocational Instructional Materials, 1983.

Ribler, R.I. *Training Development Guide.* Reston, Virginia: Reston Publishing, 1983.

Infolines

Gupta, Kavita. "Conducting a Mini Needs Assessment." No. 259611 (revised 1999).

Sharpe, C., ed. "Be a Better Needs Analyst." No. 258502 (revised 1998).

Waagen, Alice. "Task Analysis." No. 259808.

Objectives Checklist

In order to be effective, behavioral objectives must meet criteria in each of the learning domains: cognitive, psychomotor, and affective. Check each objective that you write to make sure you have complied with the following principles:

Cognitive Objectives

Comments

☐ Specify performance.

☐ State performance in action-oriented terms.

☐ Ensure primary performance relates to the demonstration of knowledge.

☐ Specify condition.

☐ Ensure that condition is realistic.

☐ Specify criterion.

☐ Ensure that criterion is realistic.

Psychomotor Objectives

☐ Specify performance.

☐ State performance in action-oriented terms.

☐ Ensure primary performance relates to the demonstration of skill.

☐ Specify condition.

☐ Ensure that condition is realistic.

☐ Specify criterion.

☐ Ensure that criterion is realistic.

Affective Objectives

☐ Specify performance.

☐ State performance in action-oriented terms.

☐ Ensure primary performance relates to the demonstration of attitudes or feelings.

☐ Specify condition.

☐ Ensure that condition is realistic.

☐ Specify criterion.

☐ Ensure that criterion is realistic.

☐ Ensure that feelings and attitudes are realistic according to entry-level requirements of the industry.

Teach SMEs to Design Training

Issue 0106

CONTRIBUTING AUTHOR

Linda J. Elengold
5268 Bright Dawn Court
Columbia, MD 21045
Tel: 301.596.5591
Fax: 410.997.7946
Email: linda-e@home.com

Linda J. Elengold specializes in the application of adult learning theory, user-centered design, and business process reengineering. She has used instructional systems design methodology to analyze, design, develop, and evaluate interactive multimedia, computer-based and Web-based training, instructor-led training, online help systems, job aids, and electronic performance support systems.

Teach SMEs to Design Training

Design Training 101 179

Adult Learning Theory 180

Analysis 183

Design 183

Development 185

Implementation 187

Evaluation 190

References & Resources 192

Job Aid

Course Evaluation 193

Editor
Cat Sharpe Russo

Managing Editor
Stephanie Sussan

Production Design
Kathleen Schaner

***Infoline* Consultant**
Phil Anderson

Design Training 101

Designing a training class can be a daunting task for anyone, especially someone who is not an experienced course designer. While some employers spend millions of dollars each year on training, not every company has the funds to maintain such a substantial program. And in today's era of budget cuts and belt tightening, employers are more and more often calling on internal subject matter experts (SMEs) to train their employees. A subject matter expert is someone with more qualified expertise in performing a specific job, task, or skill than anyone else in an organization.

From the employer's perspective, SMEs have both the technical expertise and a familiarity with the organization's politics and history. Because SMEs understand the inner workings of the organization, they can use familiar lingo and relate to the students on a comfortable level. Current trends indicate that effective learning environments are ones that closely duplicate the day-to-day job. SMEs already understand the workplace environment, and therefore can easily relate to it in the training room. This, in turn, can reduce anxiety among the students and help establish the credibility of the SME.

It can take the generic trainer weeks, if not months, to get up to speed on a specific process or skill. An SME, however, already has mastered this information and can provide real-world examples on how to use these new skills.

On the other hand, SMEs usually are unfamiliar with adult learning theory and the steps necessary to design a class with the adult audience in mind. However, many employers believe that it is harder to turn a professional trainer into a technically savvy trainer than it is to turn an SME into a trainer.

One of the biggest challenges for the SME designing a training class is finding the time. Training is not the SME's main responsibility, and many other things can take priority. Because of this time constraint and because they likely already know all the information backward and forward, SMEs often think they can short-circuit the design-and-development process and "wing it." But, it is important to ensure the quality and effectiveness of the program. While training may look deceptively easy, there is a great amount of preparation involved. If SMEs take that time up front, they will gain new insights into their workplace and co-workers during the analysis period.

Using the ADDIE Model

A series of simple processes will help SMEs develop effective ways to determine what is needed to create a lesson plan and present the material. Many experienced trainers develop their programs using an instructional systems development (ISD) approach. The ISD approach is a behavior-oriented model that emphasizes the specific skills to be learned and the learners' abilities to demonstrate these skills. The ISD method outlined in this *Infoline* is referred to as the ADDIE (analysis, design, development, implementation, and evaluation) model.

This *Infoline* guides the subject matter expert through the adult learning theories and the essential steps to design and develop a successful training program. The five basics steps of the ADDIE model, all of which interrelate, are:

1. Analysis. During this step, the SME defines his or her target audience and determines the expected outcome of the training session.

2. Design. At this stage, the SME develops the training goals.

3. Development. This is the point when an SME determines the best instructional method and creates the training materials.

4. Implementation. At this point, the SME will make all logistical arrangements, work on his or her delivery skills, practice the presentation, and then present the material.

5. Evaluation. This essential step provides the necessary feedback to determine whether the training was effective.

These five steps are part of an iterative process that the SME trainer must constantly revisit and revise.

The ADDIE Model

This ISD model shows the basic phases of ISD and the relationship of the phases to one another.

The lines and arrows show that the phases interrelate and may be changed during development. Lines and arrows leading back to each phase from the evaluation phase show that evaluation may turn up some problems that make it necessary to go back to a particular phase and make changes.

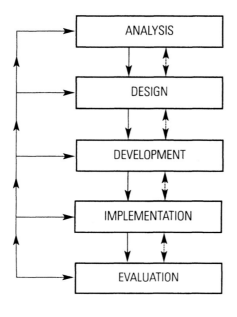

Adult Learning Theory

A key part to delivering a successful training program is understanding how adults learn and retain information. Generally adult learners need active involvement and need to understand the relevance of the information to their job or organization in order for them to retain the information presented.

Furthermore, adults tend to retain information better if it is built on prior knowledge and experience. Adults generally are goal oriented, organized, and resistant to change. In addition, most adults fear failure. Adult-learning theorist Malcolm S. Knowles determined that adult learners:

- need to see the relevance of the training to their own life experience

- learn best when they have a measure of control over their learning experience

- like to apply their own experience and knowledge to the learning

- are actively involved in the learning process

- benefit from task- or experience-oriented learning situations

- learn best in cooperative climates that encourage risk taking and experimentation.

How adults learn is equally important, especially to the SME who has been tasked with training the adult learner. Each person has a preferred learning style. Some people learn best by seeing information, some by hearing, and other by hands-on experience. Some learners need time to reflect on the material, while others like to dive right in and try things themselves. Often, adults are influenced by their backgrounds—their cultural legacies, their adult experiences, their perceptions, and their skills.

So what can an SME do to accommodate different learning styles? Chances are you will not be able to make every person happy, but the SME can help accommodate a variety of learning styles by:

- asking the learners to share their related experiences

- including group activities, such as brainstorming, role playing, and games

- supplementing written information with illustrations (graphs, charts, and so forth) wherever possible

- including the complete course content in a participant guide for learners to reread after the course

- leaving space in handouts for the students to take notes

- repeating and summarizing information using auditory, visual, and hands-on methods.

See the *Types of Adult Learners* sidebar at the right for more information.

Participant Involvement

The more learners are involved with their own learning, the faster and better they will learn. Here are some ways to increase their involvement.

- End training sessions with question-and-answer sessions, quick quizzes, and other forms of feedback.

- Give brief, learner-involved assignments, such as self-assessment quizzes before the learning begins. This allows for instant feedback from the beginning.

- Ask participants what their expectations are. This increases their interest level, while giving the SME trainer an indication of whether the training will meet expectations.

Types of Adult Learners

Geri E. McArdle outlines several types of adult learners in her book *Training Design and Delivery*. If the SME trainer is aware of the types of personalities, he or she can adapt the lesson to the personalities that are in the classroom. The types of learners include:

1. Confident: These learners want to know *why* they are assigned a specific task. They like to be involved and may be irritated by slow progress of other learners.

2. Affective: These learners like to be reassured that they are doing OK. They are very influenced by feelings and want to feel a connection to the trainer. They want to be invited to participate.

3. Transitional: This involves those being promoted or moving horizontally to a new job. These learners focus on the type of information they are learning and how it will apply to new situations. They are hesitant and want to share their work experiences. They need reassurance that they are capable of learning.

4. Integrated: These learners establish a peer-like relationship with the trainer. They know what they want and want the freedom to accomplish the assignments without much guidance. They are self-directed and demand quality from themselves and from others.

5. Risk-Taking: These learners thrive on new skills and information. They like to deviate from traditional course content. They will work hard, but will stray from course guidelines if it will give them more information.

Learner comprehension and retention increases dramatically when you use visual aids and other materials in training programs. Adult students also need time to absorb the information presented. Give the learners the opportunity to get up and move. Include frequent stretch breaks (brain breaks).

In addition to adult learning theories, familiarize yourself with the 10 learning principles to designing and developing a training program, as outlined in Geri E. McArdle's book *Training Design and Delivery*. It is important to include as many of these principles as possible. Check off a topic when you have included it.

☐ Part Learning: This is when the lesson is divided into small learning segments. This helps compartmentalize the information and makes it easier for the learner to remember the new skills.

☐ Spaced Learning: This type of learning spaces out the instruction over a period of time, giving the learner time to process the new information. These breaks present the perfect opportunity for review.

☐ Active Learning: This keeps the learners active and encourages self-motivation. Active learning also enhances retention.

☐ Feedback: There are two types of feedback. The first is feedback given to trainees about their progress. It is important for the SME trainer to let the learners know if they are on the right track. The second type of feedback is given to the SME trainer about his or her performance. This lets you know if the learners are getting it, if the session is boring, and if the trainees have any questions.

☐ Overlearning: This is learning until the trainees have a near-perfect recall, and then learning the material some more. This increases retention of the material. It is important to note that the trainer's repetition of information does not maximize retention; rather, active involvement by the trainees does.

☐ Reinforcement: Positive reinforcement encourages learners to respond and facilitates active learning. Negative reinforcement, which is when the trainer tells the learners they are wrong without giving guidelines to improve, can discourage learners.

☐ Primacy and Recency: This is when information is presented in a sequence. Adult learners tend to remember the first and last things that were said. To compensate for this, you should emphasize the middle portion of material, or present all critical information at the beginning or the end.

☐ Meaningful Material: When planning the training session, make sure it is valid and useful to the audience. If adult learners do not think the information will benefit themselves, they likely will tune out the lesson and not get anything out of the training program.

☐ Multiple-Sense Learning: People absorb information in a variety of ways. Studies indicate that 80 percent of adult learners absorb information when it is presented visually, 11 percent through hearing, and 9 percent when all other senses are combined. To compensate for this, design your session using methods that use two or more of the senses.

☐ Transfer of Learning: The amount of information that is transferred from the training session to the workplace depends on the similarity between what is learned and what happens in the workplace, and how well the learners can integrate the skills they learned.

The SME trainer should consider all of the above items when planning a training session. It is likely that a program will use more than one method.

Once you have a greater knowledge of adult-learning theory, you are ready to begin the five steps to preparing a training program.

Analysis

Chances are the SME knows much more than a training class can absorb in a single training program. The SME must whittle down what is essential for the audience to retain and understand. The SME trainer can find out exactly what the learners need to know by talking with the learners' supervisors and with the students themselves.

The purpose of the analysis phase is to identify the desired performance and compare it with the current level of performance. You will want to answer these questions:

- Who are the learners?
- Where are the gaps in performance?
- What will be the outcome of the training?
- How will you know if the training is a success?

Once you have determined what information the learners need to understand, you need to assess the learners themselves.

- What is their proficiency?

- What type of attitude do they have?

- What is the work environment they are accustomed to?

- How are they used to doing things?

- What shared or different points of view must be reflected and respected in the course?

It also is important to consider the differences among the participants and how they may react to certain situations. For example, if a group is composed of independent workers who rarely work with others, how will they feel about being put into teams? Likewise, if you are working with a group of people who tend to work in groups, independent learning may not be effective for them. Much of this information can be obtained by talking with the students before training begins. A simple five-minute conversation could help you understand what the audience needs. This will help you select the appropriate tone and level for the course.

Budget

Part of finalizing the program is including the direct and indirect costs involved. The direct costs include the operating costs, such as salaries, travel, lodging, supplies, and materials. The indirect costs include secretarial help, use of phone and audiovisual equipment, and the cost of lower productivity because the workers are at training.

If funding has not been set, the SME trainer needs to request a budget. Your organization's training manager or department should be responsible for setting and allocating appropriate resources for course design and development.

Design

Now that you have determined what to teach and the type of students you will be working with, you need to develop objectives for the course, which are the building blocks for the entire training session.

Developing Objectives

The results of the analysis will translate into specific learning objectives. The objectives must contain observable and measurable outcomes and should state in detail what the learners will be able to accomplish once the training session is over.

There are two types of objectives: terminal and enabling.

1. The terminal objective clearly states the tasks the students need to perform by the end of the training.

2. The enabling objective lists the knowledge and skills needed to meet the terminal objective. Usually there are several enabling objectives for each terminal objective. Be careful not to impart too much information at once, as information overload can cause the learners to tune out and miss essential details.

Design Checklist

Below you will find a list that will help organize the design phase of your training planning. Check the appropriate box once you have completed the step.

- ☐ Secure needs analysis data.

- ☐ Consider culture of audience.

- ☐ Identify target audience.

- ☐ Determine class size.

- ☐ Align course content with needs analysis.

- ☐ Develop course theme.

- ☐ Develop course goals.

- ☐ Develop outline.

- ☐ Consider format and flow for course.

- ☐ Identify instructional methods.

- ☐ Determine prerequisites.

- ☐ Consider media to use.

- ☐ Consider evaluation.

- ☐ Pilot test course for other SMEs.

Adapted with permission from *Creating Training Courses (When You're Not a Trainer)* by Donald V. McCain. © ASTD 1999.

The learning objectives will provide the framework for the development phase. They provide a focus for the learners so they know what is expected from them. They also provide a focus for the SME trainer so you can ensure the presentation is on target.

According to McArdle's book *Training Design and Delivery*, there are three characteristics of objectives.

1. Performance. This explains what the learners will be able to accomplish when the training is complete. For example: *Write a training needs analysis report.*

2. Condition. This is the condition that the learners will be able to perform. Using the above example: *Given the formal training report format, write a training needs analysis report.*

3. Criterion. This is how well the learner must perform. Again, using the above example: *Given the formal training report format, write a needs analysis report covering all the components that meet the trainer's specifications.*

The objectives also should include the:

- amount of information the program will cover
- desired results
- necessary conditions to carry out the session
- minimum acceptable performance
- any restrictions or limitations.

The objectives should be very specific and should be put into practice. The practices should occur in a concentrated time period to increase efficiency; over a period of time to boost retention; and in a variety of settings. See the *Design Checklist* sidebar to the left to learn how to organize the design segment.

For more information on objectives, refer to the following *Infolines*: No. 259712, "Instructional Objectives"; No. 259706, "Basics of Instructional Systems Development"; No. 258905, "Course Design and Development"; and No. 258906, "Lesson Design and Development."

Development

The development step is the longest and most labor-intensive part of the process. During this stage, you will actually create, test, and produce the training materials; structure the lesson; and create exercises. You should already understand what the appropriate level of challenge for this audience is and which media would be most effective to drive the content and facilitate learning. Things to consider in this process are:

- audience preferences
- available equipment
- time and budget constraints
- your skill level.

There are different instructional strategies that can motivate, prepare, and aid retention. Some of the strategies include:

The lecture. This is the most frequently used method for training. Good presentation skills are a must for a productive lecture, but even then it can lack interactivity between the lecturer and the audience. One note of caution: Often SMEs know so much that they lecture and answer all questions rather than act as a facilitator who draws on the expertise of the group. See *Infoline* No. 259409, "Improve Your Communication and Speaking Skills," for more information.

A demonstration. This is best used if the SME needs to show how to accomplish a step-by-step process. Typically, you use demonstrations to present skills and techniques in action. For example, this is an ideal method for teaching employees how to use a new computer software program.

A discussion group. In this method, groups explore specific topics by analyzing, evaluating, or reviewing the subject matter. This method is highly participatory and relies heavily on involvement from the learners.

On-the-job training. Most SMEs are familiar with this method because, as an organization's SME, they have most likely been asked to help their co-workers acquire or fine-tune a skill. Using this method simply means having an expert teach another employee how to perform a task. Please see *Infoline* No. 259708, "On-the-Job Training," for more information.

Programmed instruction. In this method, printed, video, audio, or computer-based programs allow learners to follow a sequence of planned instructions.

Role play. During this method, SME trainers assign learners roles to act out in scenarios. This shows how to solve problems and encourages understanding. Adults, however, often resist this method because they feel self-conscious or silly. Please see *Infoline* No. 258412, "Simulation and Role Play," for more information.

Games. Trainers can use competitive activities with preset outcomes to motivate learners. This motivational teaching method facilitates active learning. To learn more about the types of games instructors can use to facilitate learning, see *Infoline*s No. 250105, "Fun in the Workplace," and No. 258411, "10 Great Games and How to Use Them," for more information.

Case study. In this method, the SME trainer explains a problem case, and the group discusses the situation to help find a solution. Although the outcome often is hard to control, this flexible format can stimulate and involve participants.

When choosing instructional methods (usually more than one method is used), it is important to keep the topic, acceptability of the audience, demographic information, learning styles, budget for the training, the audience size, and the available resources in mind. For example, the lecture method most likely would be ineffective for a group of three people, and role playing probably would not work in a large group that has only a short amount of time to spend in the training session. Responding to the learners' preferences for an instructional method can improve their motivation. More details on these methods can be found in *Infoline* No. 259911, "Teaching SMEs to Train."

Once the SME trainer has chosen the methods he or she will use to teach the training program, it is time to start creating the actual lesson.

Media and Materials

Media and materials are the measures to deliver the training content. Some of the more common media and materials the SME trainer will need include:

- written or electronic instructional guides providing introductory or background information

- administrative aids (such as participant rosters, maps, equipment, supplies checklists, and name tags)

- evaluation materials

- participant guides (such as texts, workbooks, job aids, pretests, and posttests)

- activity aids (such as texts, role-play scripts, case studies, and exercises)

- actual equipment and visual aids (such as video equipment, VCRs, film, computers, Internet access, flipcharts, PowerPoint documents, whiteboards, overheads, videos, and slides).

It is not always necessary to reinvent the wheel. Often there is material already out there that you can use for your class. Make sure this material meets your objectives, is appropriate for your target audience, and still is accurate. Also, beware of copyright laws. Trainers often duplicate magazine articles, display cartoons on overheads, and play musical selections without permission of the copyright holders. Generally copyright holders will be happy to grant you permission to use their material for training if you credit them. But, you must ask first!

Once you have figured out the best media and materials to use for your training program, go back to your original objectives and link supportive information to each one. This information should include teaching points, the instructional method you will use, the media you will use to deliver the content, and the testing requirements. See the *Selecting Instructional Techniques and Materials* sidebar on the opposite page for more information.

Organize a Lesson Plan

Adults learn best when things are organized and clearly stated. The lesson plan will include the content to be delivered and the method of delivery.

The following checklist of items will help structure your lesson plan in an organized fashion. Make sure you have fully worked through all these items:

- ☐ the objectives

- ☐ the class size

- ☐ the course materials

- ☐ your delivery strategy

- ☐ the audience's experience

- ☐ the relationship of the course to the job conditions

- ☐ the learners' motivation

The lesson plan should include:

- ☐ session title

- ☐ learning objectives

- ☐ timing

- ☐ key points

- ☐ synopsis of the content

- ☐ delivery methods

- ☐ definitions of terms

- ☐ key questions

- ☐ resource needs

- ☐ learner activities

- ☐ review

See the *Sample Lesson Plan* sidebar for an example.

The suggested format for an outline is to begin with a warm-up introduction that briefly outlines what the class will accomplish. Then you should delve into the actual delivery of information.

Following the content delivery, it is important to present a way for the learners to apply the information. Finally, the SME should close the session with a reinforcement stage. This goes over everything that should have been learned and reinforces it for the students.

The last step in the lesson plan should be the evaluation. Details about what an evaluation should include are outlined in the "Evaluation" section of this *Infoline*.

The lesson plan lets you see if the sequence is correct, if the content is relevant, and if the design is appropriate. It also acts as a checklist for the SME trainer. (See the *Ten Tips for SME Trainers* sidebar.)

Pilot/Beta Test

The last step is to practice your presentation in front of other SMEs and colleagues. They can validate the direction of the objectives, goals, and design of the course. Listen to their suggestions and modify the course if necessary. See the *Trainer Competencies* sidebar.

Implementation

There are three main steps to the implementation process. They are:

1. Making all logistical arrangements.

2. Practicing your delivery skills.

3. Conducting a pilot test.

Selecting Techniques and Materials

The chart below matches some training techniques and instructional media with the three categories of learning (knowledge, skills, and attitudes—KSAs). Use the chart as a guide.

Technique/Activity	Knowledge	Skills	Attitudes
Assigned reading and research	X		X
Brainstorming	X		
CD-ROM	X	X	X
Computer-based instruction	X	X	X
Demonstration/practice		X	
Field project	X		X
Field trip	X		X
Flipcharts	X		X
Games	X	X	X
Guided discussion	X		X
Handouts	X	X	X
Job aids		X	
Lecture	X	X	X
Manuals	X	X	X
Panel discussion	X		
Role play		X	X
Simulation		X	
Video	X	X	X
Web-based instruction	X	X	X

Sample Lesson Plan

Title:

Written by: (author's name)

Date: (date written)

Objectives: At the end of the session, the trainees will be able to:

1. _____

2. _____

3. _____

Session Time: (amount of time sessions will take)

Number of Participants:

Equipment:

1. _____

2. _____

3. _____

Potential Faults:
_____
_____

Methods Used:
_____
_____

Introduction—Day 1:
_____
_____

Body—Day 1:
_____
_____

Conclusion—Day 1:
_____
_____

Introduction—Day 2:
_____
_____

Body—Day 2:
_____
_____

Conclusion—Day 2:
_____
_____

Logistical Arrangements

Announce the session. Contact the responsible parties to ensure the announcements about the training program have been made.

Arrange for the room. Make whatever arrangements are necessary to have the proper size room.

Organize the room. Prepare the appropriate seating arrangements. Move the chairs and tables around so no view is obstructed and everyone can hear the session. Test the acoustics and the lighting. Finally, set up all necessary equipment, including audiovisual equipment, televisions, VCRs, whiteboards, overhead projection machines, and computers. See *Infoline* No. 258504, "Facilities Planning," for more information.

Delivery Skills

The above guidelines for design and development help the SME trainer prepare a course program, but actually conducting the session is an entirely different situation. Making effective oral presentations, whether speaking to an individual or a group, is one of the most important skills a trainer can have. It helps establish credibility and confidence.

SMEs should keep their verbal skills in mind, as they can dramatically influence a training program. These include volume of their voice, enunciation, and the pace, variety, and pitch of their delivery.

Your ability to convey information to your audience is also affected by what you communicate nonverbally. For example, your appearance (how you dress) can influence how the audience perceives you and your presentation style. As a general rule, trainers should dress in the most formal clothes they expect to see in the audience. Your expressions—whether you make eye contact, your posture, and your gestures—also send clear signals. Smiling, nodding your head, making eye contact, and generally seeming interested have enormous positive effects on your training program.

Ten Tips for SME Trainers

1. Plan. Provide a concise project plan.

2. Set reasonable expectations. Understand the responsibilities and expectations, including quality, quantity, and scope of work.

3. Communicate. Regularly check with learners and learners' supervisors during the development phase to make sure each task is on track.

4. Provide guidance. Provide examples and templates of each lesson given.

5. Be flexible. Just as you have other responsibilities, so do the learners and supervisors. Whenever possible, work around their schedules. They will be appreciative and will make a much greater effort to meet deadlines when they feel that their other responsibilities are respected.

6. Be available. The learners should know how to reach you if they have questions. You don't want to hold up their end of the work when they have unanswered questions.

7. Be responsive. Be responsive to the learners' concerns.

8. Provide feedback. Provide constructive feedback and praise their sincere efforts. Schedule an individual session with each learner, if possible, to assess needs, give feedback, discuss problems, and just keep in touch. If the learners are not in your location, communicate by telephone and email.

9. Recognize accomplishments. Provide rewards when possible. Taking a small group or the entire group to lunch after working particularly hard fosters team work and work satisfaction. In sessions, acknowledge ideas, creative efforts, and contributions.

10. Provide necessary resources. If the students are to perform to the best of their ability, make sure they have access to the Internet, or whatever tools they need. Make sure they have computers, software, telephones, and email at their disposal, particularly if they are working in a location other than their regular workplace.

Trainer Competencies

Based on work done by the International Board of Standards for Training, Performance and Instruction (IBSTPI), whose goal is to "promote high standards of professional practice in the areas of training, performance, and instruction," following is a summary list of 14 essential competencies or standards that every trainer should master:

1. Have the ability to analyze course materials and learner information.

2. Ensure the preparation of the instructional site.

3. Establish and maintain credibility.

4. Manage the learning environment.

5. Demonstrate effective communication skills.

6. Demonstrate effective presentation skills.

7. Demonstrate effective questioning skills.

8. Respond to learners' needs for clarification or feedback.

9. Provide positive reinforcement and motivational incentives.

10. Use instructional methods appropriately.

11. Use media effectively.

12. Evaluate learner performance.

13. Evaluate delivery of instruction.

14. Report evaluation information.

While public speaking can cause many people to become anxious and nervous, the following hints should help alleviate uneasiness:

● Don't let your audience intimidate you. They are there to learn from you, not judge you.

● Do not rush to begin speaking.

● Use nervous energy to your advantage.

● Rehearse your presentation in front of a small group and accept constructive criticism.

● Be enthusiastic about the material you present.

● Use humor when appropriate and as an ice-breaker.

It is important to be warm, yet businesslike. If you follow your lesson plan, be yourself, and speak to the audience's interest and concerns, the session will go well. See *Infoline* No. 259409, "Improve Your Communication and Speaking Skills," for more information.

Evaluation

This stage provides feedback and lets you assess whether the training objectives were met. There are several types of evaluations. They include:

Reaction evaluation. This measures the trainees' attitude about the training. It does not measure learning. This evaluation can be accomplished with a questionnaire or a follow-up interview.

Learning evaluation. This measures the level of learning that took place. This is done with written tests. In order to measure the amount of learning that took place due to the training, it is useful to have a pre-session test and a post-session test. Types of tests include:

● A quiz. This requires the learners to recall facts, rules, and procedures.

● Skill drills. This requires the learners to use facts, rules, and procedures to complete simple tasks.

- Case study. This requires the learners to apply facts, rules, and procedures to complex job scenarios.

- Interactive simulation. This requires learners to perform complex skills or procedures under simulated job conditions.

- Laboratory. This requires learners to complete a task using what is being taught.

On-the-job performance evaluation. This measures the changes in the on-the-job behavior, and is usually measured by observation.

Return-on-investment (ROI) evaluation. This evaluation method compares the monetary benefits resulting from the training program with the cost of developing and delivering the course. Look to see if the training has brought about a cost savings, improved productivity, increased customer satisfaction, and decreased turnover. ROI can be difficult to assess, as it includes trying to quantify soft training impacts, such as attitudes.

The SME trainer needs to decide which outcome to measure and select the appropriate measurement method. Then you need to decide what you will do with the results.

For more information on evaluations, check out these *Infolines:* No. 259705, "Essentials for Evaluation"; No. 259805, "Level 5 Evaluation: Mastering ROI"; No. 259813, "Level 1 Evaluation: Reaction and Planned Action"; No. 259814, "Level 2 Evaluation: Learning"; No. 259815, "Level 3 Evaluation: Application"; and No. 259816, "Level 4 Evaluation: Business Results."

The Final Steps

There is no question that developing a training seminar is not an easy task—even for those trained to do so. Therefore, do not hesitate to call on professional trainers for guidance. Use this *Infoline* to help guide you through the process and help you figure out the best method to conduct your particular class.

References & Resources

Articles

Dumas, Marie A., and David E. Wile. "The Accidental Trainer: Helping Design Instruction." *Personnel Journal*, June 1992, pp. 106-110.

Hudspeth, Lauren, and Rick Sullivan. "Teaming to Design Interactive Media." *Technical Training.* August/September 1997, pp. 22-28.

Kiser, Kim. "When Those Who 'Do,' Teach." *Training*, April 1999, pp. 42-48.

Leininger, Robert A., et al. "Transforming Technical Experts to Technical Trainers." *Performance & Instruction*, January 1992, pp. 21-28.

Marsh, P.J. "Training Trainers." *Technical & Skills Training*, October 1995, pp. 10-13.

Mueller, Nancy. "Using SMEs to Design Training." *Technical Training*, November/December 1997, pp. 14-19.

Mullaney, Carol Anne, and Linda D. Trask. "Show Them the Ropes." *Technical & Skills Training*, October 1992, pp. 8-11.

Norton, James R. "Designing and Evaluating Product Training Presentations." *Performance & Instruction*, April 1994, pp. 33-37.

Reiss, Charlene J. "Turning Technicians into Trainers." *Training*, July 1991, pp. 47-50.

"Shh! You're a Facilitator!" *Training Directors' Forum Newsletter*, June 1999, p. 7.

Smith, Katlin. "Teaching Operators to Write Training Manuals." *Technical & Skills Training*, January 1992, pp. 8-13.

Tessmer, Martin. "Meeting with the SME to Design Multimedia Exploration Systems." *Educational Technology Research & Development*, vol. 46, no. 2 (1998), pp. 79-85.

Wein, Gerald J. "Experts As Trainers." *Training & Development*, July 1990, pp. 29-30.

Books

Bullard, Rebecca, et al. *The Occasional Trainer's Handbook.* Englewood Cliffs, NJ: Educational Technology Publications, 1994.

Goad, Tom W. *The First-Time Trainer: A Step-by-Step Quick Guide for Managers, Supervisors, and New Training Professionals.* New York: AMACOM, 1997.

Knowles, Malcolm S. *Designs for Adult Learning: Practical Resources, Exercises, and Course Outlines from the Father of Adult Learning.* Alexandria, VA: ASTD, 1995.

McArdle, Geri E. *Training Design and Delivery.* Alexandria, VA: ASTD, 1999.

McCain, Donald V. *Creating Training Courses (When You're Not a Trainer).* Alexandria, VA: ASTD, 1999.

McCoy, Carol Prescott, ed. *In Action: Managing the Small Training Staff.* Alexandria, VA: ASTD, 1998.

Weiss, Elaine. *The Accidental Trainer: You Know Computers, So They Want You to Teach Everyone Else.* San Francisco: Jossey-Bass, 1997.

Infolines

Buckner, Marilyn. "Simulation and Role Play." No. 258412 (revised 1999).

Butruille, Susan G. "Lesson Design and Development." No. 258906 (revised 1999).

Dent, Janice, and Debra Weber. "Technical Training." No. 259909.

Finkel, Coleman, and Andrew D. Finkel. "Facilities Planning." No. 258504 (revised 2000).

Hodell, Chuck. "Basics of Instructional Systems Development." No. 259706.

Levine, Charles L. "On-the-Job Training." No. 259708.

Phillips, Jack. "Level 1 Evaluation: Reaction and Planned Action." No. 259813.

———. "Level 2 Evaluation: Learning." No. 259814.

Phillips, Jack, and Ronnie D. Stone. "Level 4 Evaluation: Business Results." No. 259816.

Phillips, Jack, William Jones, and Connie Schmidt. "Level 3 Evaluation: Application." No. 259815.

Phillips, Jack, Patricia F. Pulliam, and William "Bud" Wurtz. "Level 5 Evaluation: ROI." No. 259805.

Plattner, Francis. "Improve Your Communication and Speaking Skills." No. 259409 (revised 1997).

———. "Instructional Objectives." No. 259712.

Russo, Cat Sharpe, ed. "Teaching SMEs to Train." No. 259911.

Sharpe, Cat, ed. "Basic Training for Trainers." No. 258808 (revised 2003).

———. "Course Design and Development." No. 258905 (revised 1997).

———. "10 Great Games and How to Use Them." No. 258411 (revised 1999).

Thiagarajan, Sivasailam ("Thiagi"). "Fun in the Workplace." No. 250105.

Waagen, Alice K. "Essentials for Evaluation." No. 259705.

Course Evaluation

Course Title: _____ Date(s):_____

Instructor: _____ Location: _____

Job Title:_____

The statements below concern specific aspects of the course. Please indicate the extent you agree or disagree with each statement.

Not Applicable = N/A   Strongly Disagree = 1   Disagree = 2   Agree = 3   Strongly Agree = 4

Course Content

1. Objectives were clearly explained.	NA	1	2	3	4
2. Participant ideas were relevant to content and incorporated.	NA	1	2	3	4
3. Stated objectives were met (write in objectives):					
• Objective #1	NA	1	2	3	4
• Objective #2	NA	1	2	3	4
4. Content is relevant to my job (if disagree, please explain).	NA	1	2	3	4

Comments:

_____

_____

Course Methodology

5. The following activities and materials helped me understand the content and achieve the objectives:

Case Study	NA	1	2	3	4
Audiovisual (flipcharts, videos, tapes)	NA	1	2	3	4
Exercises and Activities	NA	1	2	3	4
Written Assignments	NA	1	2	3	4
Facilitated Discussions	NA	1	2	3	4

Comments:

_____

_____

(continued on next page)

Job Aid

Instructor

6.	Promoted an environment of learning.	NA	1	2	3	4
7.	Presented clearly to assist my understanding.	NA	1	2	3	4
8.	Appeared knowledgeable about the subject matter.	NA	1	2	3	4
9.	Provided feedback effectively to participants.	NA	1	2	3	4
10.	Presented content in an appropriate sequence.	NA	1	2	3	4
11.	Promoted participant discussion and involvement.	NA	1	2	3	4
12.	Demonstrated an understanding of the organization.	NA	1	2	3	4
13.	Demonstrated and referenced personal experience.	NA	1	2	3	4

Comments:

_____

_____

Administrative Support

14.	Registration process was effective.	NA	1	2	3	4
15.	Course materials were received in a timely manner.	NA	1	2	3	4
16.	Training room was appropriate in size and arrangement.	NA	1	2	3	4
17.	Training room was well lit, clean, and ventilated.	NA	1	2	3	4
18.	Meals and breaks were on time and appetizing.	NA	1	2	3	4
19.	Promotional material was accurate and informative.	NA	1	2	3	4

Comments:

_____

_____

Summary

	Poor	**Fair**	**Good**	**Excellent**
20. Overall rating for the course.	1	2	3	4

21. Would you recommend the course to your peers? ☐ Yes ☐ No

Comments:

_____

_____

Please share any information you believe would help us to improve this course:

_____

_____

Briefly describe any training areas you would like addressed in the next few months:

_____

_____

Thank you for taking the time to share your comments and your reactions!

■■**INFO**RMATION
■**LINE**■
TIPS, TOOLS, AND INTELLIGENCE FOR TRAINERS

Adapted with permission from Training Design and Delivery *by Geri E. McArdle. ASTD 1999.*

Create Effective Job Aids

Issue 9711

Create Effective Job Aids

AUTHOR

Susan Russell
Micros Systems
1200 Baltimore Avenue
Beltsville, MD 20705
Tel: 301.210.8000 ext. 2701
Fax: 301.210.3427
Email: susanrussell
@micros.com

Susan Russell is a practitioner in the training and development field specializing in analysis and evaluation of training interventions. She holds a Masters Degree in Business from Johns Hopkins University and is completing a second Masters in Instructional Systems Development through the University of Maryland Baltimore County.

Create Effective Job Aids 197
   Advantages of Job Aids 197
   Types of Job Aids 199

Putting Together a Job Aid 202
   Analyzing a Job Aid's Function 202
   Designing a Job Aid 205
   Developing a Job Aid 206
   Implementing Job Aids 207
   Evaluating Job Aids 208

References & Resources 210

Job Aid
   Checklist for Creating Effective Job Aids 212

Editor
Cat Sharpe

Associate Editor
Patrick McHugh

Designer
Steven M. Blackwood

Copy Editor
Kay Larson

ASTD Internal Consultant
Phil Anderson

Create Effective Job Aids

How many times have you had to reset your VCR or reprogram your answering machine? How many times have you baked a cake from scratch? Chances are that you have performed at least one of these tasks at some point. When it comes to these common but infrequent tasks, most of us need a reminder of sorts to help us complete them. We usually pull out the reference guide that came with the VCR if we need to reset it or a cake recipe when we bake a cake from scratch. If we have to reprogram the answering machine, we usually look for a little sticker with the instructions taped to the back. These quick reference guides are all types of job aids. We can't always be expected to remember the specific steps necessary to complete a task when the task is not performed frequently or is very complex; we need a reminder.

Organizations are asking employees to do more, to perform a variety of tasks. Some are simple. Some are complex. Some are performed on a routine basis. Some are performed infrequently. Sometimes, employees are asked to perform these tasks with little or no training. Job aids can fill an important gap in education and training. When people use machines or procedures infrequently, they often forget how to use them. Or, when they perform a complicated procedure as part of their routine, they may get careless and need a reminder to perform all of the necessary steps. In these situations a job aid is a useful tool to bridge the gap.

What Is a Job Aid?

You may be thinking that anything that helps a person do his or her job is a job aid. Well, that's not quite true. Although it is difficult to find a universally accepted definition, there are three primary components of a job aid:

1. A job aid stores information or instruction external to the user.

2. A job aid guides the user to perform the task correctly.

3. A job aid is used during the actual performance of the task when the user needs to know the information or procedure.

A job aid may be a sign, checklist, or chart placed in or near the work area to remind users of specific actions to take when performing a task. It may be a tent card, flowchart, poster, sticker, or small card. It can sit on a desk, be attached to a computer, stuck on a bulletin board, or taped to the overhang in a cubicle. A job aid is something that may be consulted quickly, when needed. It provides specific, concise information to the user.

It may be helpful at this point to define what is not a job aid. A job aid is not the tool used to perform the task. It is not the remote control used to reset the VCR, the answering machine itself, or the measuring cup or blender used to make the cake. Although these items are external to the user, they do not store information or instruction. They may be used during the actual performance but do not serve as a guide for the user while performing the task.

Advantages of Job Aids

There will always be a need for formal training, but job aids offer several benefits. Below are a few of the major advantages of using job aids.

■ *Timeliness*
Job aids are designed to be used when the need to know arises. They can be effective in increasing employee productivity and in reducing error rates. Employees can access a job aid in real time versus fumbling around for 15 minutes looking for information, giving up when they can't find it, continuing with the task, and then making a mistake.

■ *Cost-Effectiveness*
Job aids are less expensive to produce than formal training classes. They can also, in some instances, reduce the amount of time employees spend in training, which means less time away from the job. Therefore, job aids are a cost-effective intervention to help employees perform their jobs more effectively and efficiently.

■ *Transferability*
Job aids help employees transfer new skills and knowledge from a training class to their job. You have probably heard, "I know they told us how to do that in training, but I can't recall what they said" or received a call from a trainee asking a

Sample Flowchart

This flowchart is an example of a job aid used when a performance problem is identified. Notice that the answer the user provides to the *yes* or *no* questions directs him or her to the correct path to follow in order to complete the task.

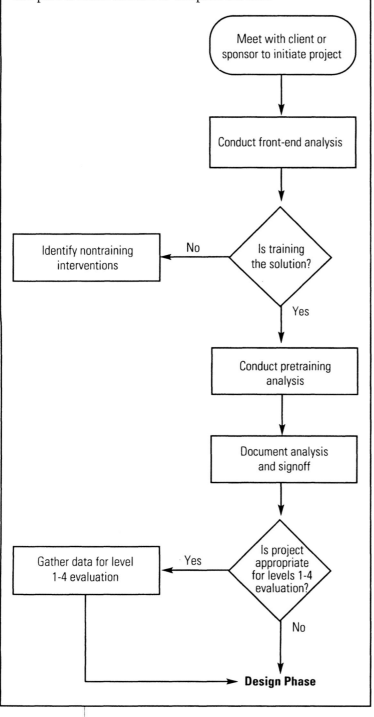

question about a procedure covered in class. Used to supplement material from a training class, job aids can bridge the gap between class content and on-the-job performance.

■ *Maintenance*
Job aids are easier to revise and update than training classes. This is not to say job aids are always easy to revise and update, but it is easier to update a job aid than a training course. Not only are more labor hours required to update a training class, but consider the training time required to update all of the former class participants.

■ *Reduction in Recall*
Job aids reduce the need for individuals to remember so much information. Memorizing tedious and complex processes and procedures takes time and practice. Relying on memorization may lead to costly errors because retention rates decrease as the period between learning and actual performance increases. Job aids are an efficient method to reduce problems associated with relying strictly on recall to perform in certain situations.

When Is a Job Aid Appropriate?

Wouldn't it be great if we could use a job aid to solve all performance problems? We could give employees a tool to use on the job that would reduce errors and improve productivity. This could reduce the time employees are away from their jobs for training and, therefore, reduce the cost of training. As the training industry moves toward improving performance using appropriate cost-effective interventions, clients are beginning to realize that formal training is not always the answer. Sometimes, the most appropriate and effective intervention will be a job aid.

Joe Harless, author of "Guiding Performance with Job Aids" in *Introduction to Performance Technology*, gave us cause to think when he wrote, "The relevant question is not 'Can the task be job aided?' but 'Should the task be job aided?'" Consider the answers to the following questions when deciding if a job aid is appropriate.

■ *How Frequently Is the Task Performed?*
Job aids should be used when an employee does not perform the task frequently or on a regular basis. No one can be expected to remember how to do something that is done infrequently.

■ *How Complex Is the Task?*
Tasks with multiple steps or those with elaborate, lengthy decisions that are difficult to remember may lend themselves to job aids.

■ *What Are the Consequences of Errors?*
Here we are concerned with tasks that if not performed correctly cause high costs, may endanger life, or produce a similar negative effect. Examples of this may include tasks where errors may cause damage to costly equipment, harm the operator, or result in the loss of a major customer or contract.

■ *How Frequently Does the Task Change?*
Job aids are easier to update and revise than traditional training. If a task changes frequently, it probably is not cost-effective to revise the training curriculum and materials and retrain employees with each change. Also, asking employees to constantly learn new tasks is not only time consuming, but also can result in high task error rates.

■ *Where Will the Task Be Performed?*
Remember that job aids are external to the user and are accessed during the actual performance. This means we need to know something about the physical and social environment where the task is completed. You are not deciding on a form for the job aid yet, but determining if the environment will support the use of a job aid. Consider whether employees will be able to physically access a job aid or if there are any psychological reasons for not using the job aid. For example, do employees feel that their credibility will be compromised if they use a job aid when performing a task?

Each situation and each task should be considered on an individual basis when deciding if the job aid is an appropriate tool. Job aids can be used in situations that call for following detailed, linear, step-by-step procedures or those that involve complicated multifaceted decision making.

Types of Job Aids

Job aids can be as small as a template on an answering machine or as large as a procedural manual. Allison Rossett and Jeannette Gautier-Downes, authors of *A Handbook of Job Aids*, maintain that job aids serve to provide information, support procedures, as well as coach perspectives, decisions, and self-evaluation. Most tasks entail either decision making, following procedures or linear sequences, or a combination of the two. Some of the more common job aid formats are listed on the next page and samples appear throughout this issue.

Sample Reference Job Aid

Reference job aids contain information users may need to perform a task. Below is an example that provides a listing of light bulbs for salespeople to refer to for part numbers, order numbers, and prices.

Part No.	Description	Order No.	Quantity	Price
100253-4	Incandescent 80 watt bulb	5002	Doz.	$27.50
100253-5	Incandescent 150 watt bulb	5003	Doz.	$56.45
100254-10	Soft brite 75 watt fluorescent bulb	5004	Each	$21.23
100254-22	Soft brite 95 watt fluorescent bulb	5005	Each	$35.97

■ *Steps*

This format presents information and directions in a specific sequence. The step format is most appropriate when the user must complete a series of linear procedures in which detail and sequence are critical to completing the task.

■ *Forms and Worksheets*

Forms and worksheets are similar to the step format in that they guide the user through a process in a specific sequence. They require user participation, however, and include blanks or spaces for the user to record responses. Forms and worksheets are most appropriate when calculations must be performed or when information is stored for future reference (see the next page).

■ *Checklists*

Checklists are groups of items to be considered when planning or evaluating. They present guidelines for completing a task and are most commonly used to ensure consistency. Items are presented in a logical order but are not necessarily followed in that order by the user (see *Sample Checklist*).

■ *Decision Tables*

Decision tables allow the user to make decisions and complete tasks based on a set of conditions. They are usually composed of "if-then" statements that guide users to appropriate decisions. Decision tables are most appropriate when tasks or decisions are dependent on conditions that may vary (see below).

■ *Flowcharts*

Flowchart job aids are similar to decision tables in that completing the task or deciding on a course of action is dependent on conditions that may vary. Unlike the decision table, however, questions in a flowchart can be answered with a "yes" or "no." Each answer the user provides leads to another decision point, which again is answered by a "yes" or "no." The user follows the flowchart until enough questions have been answered for an accurate decision to be made or until a task is completed (see sample flowchart depicted earlier).

What Type of Job Aid Should You Use?

If...	Then Consider a...
• The task consists of steps that must be completed in a specific sequence. • The user does not need to make decisions regarding the task. • The task or procedure is linear and there is only one path for the user to follow.	Step-by-Step Job Aid
• The task consists of steps that must be completed in a specific sequence. • The user needs to document information to be used to complete the task. • The task consists of performing calculations. • Information that is used to complete the task will be referenced at a later time.	Form or Worksheet Job Aid
• The task does not consist of steps that must be completed in a specific sequence. • The task involves inspecting, observing, or planning. • Consistency is an important factor.	Checklist Job Aid
• The task does not consist of steps that must be completed in a specific sequence. • Several conditions or variables may exist. • There are limited options associated with each decision variable.	Decision Table Job Aid
• There are several *yes* or *no* decisions that must be made. • The decisions must be made in a specific order. • Completion of the task is dependent on the answer given at each decision point.	Flowchart Job Aid
• The task does not consist of steps that must be completed in a specific sequence. • The task requires reference to data versus performing a process or procedure.	Reference Source Job Aid

Sample Worksheet Format

The worksheet format below includes space for the user to record information about the instructional strategy used for each lesson objective in a training course. The user can refer back to this information as the project progresses.

Instructional Strategy Form

The instructional strategy form should document the instructional strategy plan to be used for each objective. The strategy used should be determined by the lesson objective.

I. Overall Course Description

Course Title: _____

Course Description: _____

Terminal Objective(s): _____

_____

Team Information:

● sponsor_____

● subject matter experts_____

● other individual(s) involved in the ISD process _____

II. Instructional Plan Description

The instructional plan description should be completed for each course objective.

Objective #1: _____

_____

_____

Lesson Objective:_____

_____

_____

Description of instructional method(s) to be used: _____

_____

Include conventional lecture, demonstration, individual study, programmed instructions, case studies, simulations, team teaching, and so forth.

Description of media devices to be used: _____

_____

Include audiovisual aids, television, computers, and so forth.

■ *Reference Sources*

Reference sources primarily provide information required for completing a task. Unlike the other types of job aids, they do not provide information to be followed in a step-by-step manner nor do they coach the user in a decision-making process. Examples of reference sources include telephone books and parts catalogs containing detailed information such as product and price data.

A job aid can also be a combination of two or more of the formats listed above. The type of job aid that is designed should be contingent on the type of task being performed. For example, using a decision table job aid when the task entails completing specific steps without decision dependencies would not be the most effective type of job aid, just as using a step format job aid would not support a highly complex decision-making task.

Job Aid Mediums

Usually, people think of paper-based job aids: posters hung at eye level in an assembly line, laminated cards perched atop PCs, or flowchart diagrams stuck to cubicle walls. Job aids are not always paper-based, however. They can be audio, visual, a combination of the two, or even in an electronic format such as electronic performance support systems (EPSS), which can be quite elaborate. For more information on EPSS, see *Infoline* No. 259806, "EPSS and Your Organization."

For example, many restaurants employ several types of job aid mediums. There may be a poster hanging in the kitchen reminding employees of acceptable hygiene practices and posters hanging above the food preparation area with a picture of each main dish. The chef may even have a display that will run a short video providing instructions on how to prepare a dish, just in case that special secret ingredient slipped his or her mind.

Putting Together a Job Aid

Another benefit of job aids is that almost anyone can create an effective one without extensive training. This does not mean, however, that a systematic process shouldn't be followed when creating a job aid. Following a systematic process ensures the following:

- appropriate content is included in the job aid
- an appropriate format is used
- an appropriate medium is used
- the effectiveness of the job aid is measured.

Below are steps to follow when creating a job aid. These steps follow an instructional systems development (ISD) approach. You may find another process that works equally well for your situation but following an ISD approach helps ensure that the job aid is based on a real performance need and includes observable, measurable elements. For additional information on ISD, see *Infoline* No. 259706, "Basics of Instructional Systems Development."

Analyzing a Job Aid's Function

The first step in the analysis phase is to determine if the job aid is an appropriate intervention by answering the questions found under the section "Advantages of Job Aids." Remember that it is not *can* the task be job aided, but *should* the task be job aided. Assuming that you have already determined that a job aid is an appropriate intervention, you need to gather specific data on the three Ws: the work, the worker, and the workplace. Use observations and interviews to collect your data.

■ *The Work*

When possible, observe both novice and expert individuals perform the task. This will allow you to determine differences in the way the task is performed at various levels of expertise. As you observe each individual, take explicit notes and document every step the individual takes and any references or external materials the individual uses to perform the task.

Observe the task being performed from start to finish and collect enough information so you can break the task or decision-making process down into small "chunks" of information. Consider the following questions as you gather information about the work itself:

Sample Checklist

The checklist below includes guidelines for developing a training course. Though the checklist format is frequently used when step-by-step procedures are not required, this particular example does dictate the order of the guidelines. For example, the user would not develop a course before an analysis was complete.

Instructional Systems Development (ISD) Checklist

Project Name: _____

Analysis

- ☐ Complete TNA Proposal.
- ☐ Receive signoff.
- ☐ Conduct needs assessment.
- ☐ Receive signoff.

Design

- ☐ Develop a topic list and topic map.
- ☐ Complete course syllabus.
- ☐ Complete instructional strategy form.
- ☐ Receive signoff.
- ☐ Create assessment items.
- ☐ Receive signoff.

Development

- ☐ Develop instructor guide.
- ☐ Receive signoff.
- ☐ Develop participant guide.
- ☐ Receive signoff.
- ☐ Develop media.
- ☐ Receive signoff.
- ☐ Develop pre- and posttests.
- ☐ Receive signoff.

Implementation

- ☐ Select and prepare appropriate facility.
- ☐ Prepare and gather materials.

Evaluation

- ☐ Collect and summarize Level 1 and Level 2 data.
- ☐ Distribute Level 3 action plans.

- What is typically done to complete the task?

- What is the order of steps, process, or decision making?

- What tools are used to perform the task?

- Are the same steps followed in the same order each time the task is performed?

- Are there times when the task is performed in a different order?

■ *The Worker*

After you observe individuals performing the task, ask them about their thought processes while performing the task. It is important to identify any unobserved processes that the individual performs. This is especially critical when developing a job aid for decision making or coaching. In many cases, these thought processes would not be observable.

Keep in mind who will be using the job aid as you proceed with your analysis. Consider the following questions:

- What is the user's experience level? If the user is new or has limited experience, you will need to include more detail in the job aid.

- What is the user's experience with job aids? Are they commonplace? Will a job aid be a new tool for the users?

- What is the demographic makeup of the user audience? What is its primary language? What is its reading level? What is its education level?

■ *The Workplace*

Collecting accurate information on the work environment during the analysis phase is key to selecting an appropriate medium to use during the design phase. As you conduct your analysis, be sure to collect any information regarding the physical surroundings where the task is performed.

Ask yourself where the job aid will be used. Is the task performed at an employee's desk, on a shop floor, or on the top of a telephone pole? Consider psychological factors in the workplace as well. Does the employee perform the task in view of a supervisor, peers, or customers? Will the individual be likely to consult the job aid only when others are not around? These issues are important to note as they dictate the type of medium used and how to effectively implement the job aid in the environment.

Conducting a needs analysis for a job aid is just like conducting a needs analysis for a training class. Without performing a complete analysis up front, you run the risk of creating a job aid that will not produce the desired results. If observations are not possible, use a more in-depth interview process. Have the users talk you through the process in an unstructured format, then follow up with more direct questions, just as you would after an observation.

Sample Step-by-Step Job Aid

The step-by-step format is used when the task must be completed in a specific sequence. This example provides additional information under some steps for the benefit of more novice users, making the job aid appropriate for employees of various skill levels.

1. Use the TNA Proposal template to plan your analysis.

   - identify sponsor
   - determine the information to be gathered
   - determine the sources of data
   - access the TNA Proposal template
   - complete items 1 through 7 on the template
   - obtain signoff from the instructional designer.

2. Gather the data.

3. Analyze the data to identify needs.

4. Use the TNA Summary template to report your findings.

   - complete items 8 through 10 on the template.

5. Obtain signoff from the instructional designer.

6. Save the report in the project directory.

Designing a Job Aid

Once you have completed the needs and task analysis, you should have a complete representation of the user and the task. You are now ready to map out the structure and background of the job aid.

■ *Determine the Job Aid Format*
Decide what part of the task is being supported by the job aid. Will it provide the step-by-step procedures, guidelines to follow, or reference information? Visualize how the job aid will be consulted and how it should be structured. Consider the characteristics of the task and the user as you select the format to use. See the samples of various job aid formats included throughout this issue.

■ *Determine the Medium*
Design the job aid for use where and when the task is completed. Now is the time to consult all of that data you collected about the workplace. Decide how best to convey the information. You can develop the most complete job aid ever, but if the medium used is not conducive to the actual work environment, it will not be effective.

■ *Cost*
Stay within resource allocation. Cost is an important factor to consider when determining which medium to use. For example, paper-based job aids are less costly to produce and maintain than electronic job aids. Black and white drawings are cheaper to reproduce than color photographs. As you design the job aid, factor in the resources that are available to produce, distribute, and maintain it.

■ *Storyboard the Job Aid*
Graphically lay out the job aid. Diagram the steps to complete the task. Indicate where visual elements and words will be placed.

In "How I Created the Award-Winning Job Aid," author Susan Zagorski explained some of her own techniques for designing a job aid:

Sample Decision Table

This decision table for customer service representatives covers several variables or conditions that may exist when a representative answers a call. In this example, there are actually nine possible conditions that have been identified. Each probable condition is listed so representatives need only identify the condition and follow the chart to find the appropriate action.

If	And	Then
The caller is employed	The employer has an account with us	Refer the caller to customer service employer accounts at ext. 5641
The caller is employed	The employer does not have an account with us	Refer the caller to broker sales at ext. 5487
The caller is self employed	Has an account with us	Refer the caller to customer service small groups at ext. 8745
The caller is self employed	Does not have an account with us	Refer the caller to small group sales at ext. 8692
The caller is not employed	Has an account with us	Refer the caller to customer service individual accounts at ext. 9632
The caller is not employed	Does not have an account with us	Refer the caller to individual accounts sales at ext. 9832

Eight Ways to Foil Job Aids

Jeffery J. Nelson listed "eight time-tested techniques…to sabotage the use of job aids" in his article of this title in *Performance & Instruction Journal:*

1. When preparing a job aid for a person's job, emphasize to him or her how the job aid will capture his or her twenty years of job experience—in only two pages!

2. Be sure that the job aid does not reflect how the task is actually done on the job. In fact, the more creative and bizarre you can make the job aid, the sillier the person will look when using it.

3. Don't include any instruction in the actual job jargon, theory, or background. This will make the user sound totally naïve about the job. It will also stifle communications among the user, his or her peers, and the supervisor and make the user sound like he or she just beamed down to earth.

4. Be sure to job aid everything. The best technique is to turn even simple prose statements into decision tables and algorithms. The more complex, the better.

5. Make people memorize all job aids. Acknowledge and reward those employees who have all the information in their heads. Also, practice scowling at anyone who has to use props such as job aids. Tell them that if they really knew the job, they'd have it memorized.

6. The most insidious and perhaps delightful technique is to build errors into the job aid. You've got an advantage because the user probably thinks the thing will really work and won't expect errors. But, just in case, camouflage the errors in the most complex part of the job aid.

7. Refer the user to another page or to a job aid that doesn't exist. I've seen this work and it's really fun.

8. Don't brief supervisors or peers about job aids. Tell them that those "funny little books" are only for people who don't know their jobs. Again, combining this technique with all of those previously mentioned will insure the elimination of all job aids from the workplace.

Reprinted with permission from Performance & Instruction
Journal, *July 1985. Copyright National Society for
Performance and Instruction, 1985.*

When I sit down to actually, physically design the job aid, I make a rough sketch that includes everything—all the facts and minute details I might possibly want to include. I can always throw something out later, but I might forget a detail that is not in the original rough draft.

This is an unusual method. Putting everything down on paper, barely legible, pages taped together, arrows and marginal notes everywhere. But this method works very well when I have no clear beginning or end in mind, just the stuff that goes somewhere in the middle. It allows me to naturally discover the best sequence and flow of information.

She then does three or four rough drafts, eliminating extra words, combining ideas and eliminating some, working toward "a niftier arrangement."

Developing a Job Aid

During the development phase you will actually produce the job aid. Consider the following as you work on your job aid:

■ *Content*
Include only the necessary steps or information required by the user. Ask yourself if the step or content is relevant to the task at hand.

Keep the information as simple and concise as possible. Present the information in small pieces. Write short sentences and use short words to describe or list the steps, processes, calculations, or decisions that need to be made.

Leave out "nice-to-know" tidbits of information; they only serve to clutter the job aid. Remember that the job aid should be a quick reference for the user. Place critical information in the first and last parts of sentences or sections of the job aid.

■ *Language*
Use language that the user will understand. Avoid long, unfamiliar words and jargon unless appropriate to the task and the user. Use verbs and actions words at the beginning of sentences wherever possible.

■ *Visual Elements*

Use drawings or graphics when appropriate to clarify information or provide more detail than words would allow. Graphics and illustrations should be clear and simple. Be consistent in the type of visual that is used. If you use a drawing in one step, use one in any subsequent steps.

Highlight critical points or steps by using bold or italicized text. Colors can also be used to highlight and code items or sections of the task. For example, suppose you are developing a paper-based job aid to be used by sales associates at a local insurance company. You may use color codes to differentiate the tasks that are job aided. A blue card may be used for the steps to open a customer account and a red card for the steps to close a customer account. This way associates can easily locate the appropriate job aid by color.

■ *Accessibility and Usability*

Be sure the job aid is accessible and convenient to use. Employees are not likely to search for a job aid while in the middle of performing a task. Size and shape of the job aid play a critical role in how effective the job aid will be. For example, if a task requires an individual to use both hands, reaching for a bulky manual or flimsy paper job aid is not possible. A laminated card or poster hung where it can be consulted quickly may be a better choice.

Implementing Job Aids

During the implementation phase you will present the job aid to users in the workplace, preferably before final production and distribution take place. In *A Handbook of Job Aids,* Rossett and Gautier-Downes provide a comprehensive checklist to use when piloting a job aid.

Ask users:

☐ Do you have any questions?

☐ Were you unsure of what to do at any time?

☐ Which steps were hardest to follow?

☐ Was the job aid difficult to use?

☐ Were the instructions clear?

Measuring the Effectiveness of Job Aids

One of the advantages of job aids is that the results of their use can be measured or evaluated. Below are examples of two types of measurement.

Non-Dollar Value

Situation:
The central air conditioning unit of the plant is only started two or three times per year. Similarly, it is turned off only at the end of the season or in an emergency. The plan operations director knows how to do the job. But because the unit is turned on or off infrequently, employees forget how to do the job. In an emergency, someone has to call the operations director in to turn the unit on or off, no matter what the hour.

Intervention:
A job aid was developed and placed at the air conditioner control. At an on-site staff meeting, the problem and its solution were explained to all employees.

Result:
Dollar and cents were not measured. However, there were no more emergency calls.

Value:
No measure of dollar and cents value; no further emergency calls were reported. Personal satisfaction reported.

Dollar Value Estimated

Situation:
New time card machines were to be installed. Executives did not feel the need for training until they tested a unit in the remote data processing building. The supervisor there spent a great deal of time correcting employees' mistakes with the new machine. She made a list of the problems and called the training department.

Intervention:
A job aid was placed over each time card machine.

Result:
Fifteen minutes training time saved per employee. 15 minutes x 2,000 employees x $8.00 per hour = $4,000 saved.

Value:
Training time saved. Cost of training reduced.

☐ Were the steps ordered correctly?

☐ Did you need more information?

☐ Was there was too much information?

☐ Was the wording clear?

☐ Were the diagrams or graphs helpful?

☐ Were there any typographical errors?

☐ Were all circumstances covered in the job aid?

☐ Should any special circumstances be covered?

☐ Was the format appropriate for your work area?

☐ Was it easy to use?

☐ Will you use it again?

Once you have piloted the job aid and made any necessary revisions, you are ready to fully implement it in the workplace. Job aids are independent and although they generally need no formal introduction to the user, there are some circumstances that may warrant an introduction:

● Users may be unfamiliar with the concept of job aids.

● Users may be intent on some form of training.

● Users might need some type of explanation for complicated job aids.

Tips for Measuring Job Aid Results

■ *Results Don't Always Have to Be Measured in Dollars*
Increased user satisfaction is important and can become a basis for developing new clients and increasing the training department's impact.

■ *Don't Make Up Dollar Figures*
If you're estimating, say so, and show how you reached your estimate. Making up numbers can breed skepticism.

■ *Find Organizational Problems*
Then fix them and report the results.

A formal presentation should follow this sequence:

1. Explain the performance problem, its impact on the organization, and how the job aid addresses the problem.

2. Explain how the job aid will make the users' job easier.

3. Show how to use the job aid by talking users through the steps.

4. Have an influential performer demonstrate the job aid, followed by as many performers as possible.

5. Conclude by telling the users when the job aid will be put into use, how you will monitor its use, and when and how you will report the results back to them.

6. Tell users how it will be maintained.

Evaluating Job Aids

Similar to developing an instructor-led class, computer-based training course, or any type of performance improvement intervention, job aids should be evaluated at each phase of the process including implementation. A plan for final evaluation should include maintenance of the job aid and a system for measuring its effectiveness. For further information on evaluation, see *Infoline* No. 259705, "Essentials for Evaluation."

Job aids, just like policy manuals, training classes, and organization charts need to be updated and revised. They will lose their effectiveness if not revised to reflect changes in the job itself, changes in the work environment, and changes in the employee profile. Consider buying a new personal computer and then noticing a newer one on the market just three months later. Job tasks also change, although thankfully not usually as quickly as PCs, but we need to be prepared to revise job aids to reflect any changes that do take place.

Consider the following as you plan for maintaining a job aid:

- Who will be responsible for making sure new employees have access to existing job aids?

- Who will be responsible for making revisions to existing job aids?

- How frequently will job aids be revised?

- How will changes in the job aid be communicated to the employees?

- How will you ensure that employees are using the most up-to-date version of the job aid?

- How will outdated job aids be collected?

The second component in the evaluation phase is measuring the effectiveness of the job aid after it has been implemented. Effectiveness can be measured in terms of dollars saved, reduced error rates, and increased productivity. Or, there may be other specific criteria your organization uses to evaluate the benefits derived from using a job aid. The criteria used to evaluate the job aid should be tied to the original performance problem that the job aid was developed to correct. See the sidebars *Measuring the Effectiveness of Job Aids* and *Tips for Measuring Job Aid Results* for more information on evaluating job aids.

Systematic Job Aid Creation

Job aids have been around for many years. Recently, we have seen them evolve to play an important part in filling the gap between training and on-the-job performance. People are asking, "Is formal training the answer?" The next time you find yourself considering interventions to a performance problem, ask yourself if the task or process should be job aided.

If the answer is yes, then follow a systematic approach to creating the job aid. Ensure that the job aid is task or process focused and consider the medium as well. Measure the effectiveness of the job aid. Create a job aid when it is appropriate for the situation at hand, making sure to conduct an analysis first. By following these steps, you can correct many performance problems without resorting to more expensive forms of training and still ensure employees will perform at their peak.

References & Resources

Articles

Carr, C. "PSS! Help When You Need It." *Training & Development*, June 1992, pp. 31-38.

Clark, R.C. "EPSS—Look Before You Leap: Some Cautions About Applications of Electronic Performance Support Systems." *Performance & Instruction*, May/June 1992, pp. 22-25.

Dumas, M.A., and D.E. Wile. "The Accidental Trainer: Helping Design Instruction." *Personnel Journal*, June 1992, pp. 106-110.

Geber, B. "Help! The Rise of Performance Support Systems." *Training*, December 1991, pp. 23-29.

Hequet, M. "Should Every Worker Have a Line in the Information Stream?" *Training*, May 1994, pp. 99-102.

Hubler, M. "Technical Writing Requires Clarity over Poetry." *Technical & Skills Training*, February/March 1992, pp. 29-30.

Kribs, H., et al. "The Impacts of Interactive Electronic Technical Manuals: Issues, Lessons Learned, and Trends in Training and Education." *Journal of Instruction Delivery Systems*, Fall 1995, pp. 17-23.

Laabs, J.J. "Electronic Campus Captures Apple's Corporate Memory." *Personnel Journal*, November 1993, pp. 104-110.

Ladd, C. "Should Performance Support Be in Your Computer?" *Training & Development*, August 1993, pp. 22-26.

Lemmons, L.J. "PSS Design: Getting Past that First Step." *CBT Directions*, February 1991, pp. 32-35.

Marsh, P., and D. Pigott. "Turning a New Page in OJT." *Technical & Skills Training*, May/June 1992, pp. 13-16.

Moseley, J.L., and S. Larson. "A Job Performance Aid Evaluation Tool." *Performance & Instruction*, September 1992, pp. 24-26.

Reynolds, A. "The Basics: Job Aids." *Technical & Skills Training*, August/September 1992, pp. 20-21.

———. "The Top Five Questions About Performance Support Systems." *Technical & Skills Training*, January 1993, pp. 8-11.

Plummer, K.H., et al. "Development and Evaluation of a Job Aid to Support Mobile Subscriber Radio-Telephone Terminal (MSRT)." *Performance Improvement Quarterly*, January 1992, pp. 90-105.

Rossett, A. "Electronic Job Aids." *Data Training*, June 1991, pp. 24-29.

———. "Job Aids in a Performance Technology World." *Performance & Instruction*, May/June 1991, pp. 1-6.

Ruyle, K.E. "Developing Intelligent Job Aids (Intelligently)." *Technical & Skills Training*, February/March 1991, pp. 9-14.

Still, T. "Training on a Tight Budget." *Technical & Skills Training*, February/March 1994, pp. 29-32.

Taylor, D. "Job Aids at QVC." *Technical & Skills Training*, April 1994, pp. 27-31.

White, F.J., and B. Centner. "Designing Effective Job Aids." *Technical & Skills Training*, October 1993, pp. 17-20.

References & Resources

Books

Craig, R.L., ed. *The ASTD Training and Development Handbook: A Guide to Human Resource Development.* New York: McGraw-Hill, 1996.

Reynolds, A., and R.H. Anderson. *Selecting and Developing Media for Instruction.* New York: Van Nostrand Reinhold, 1992.

Rossett, A., and J. Gautier-Downes. *A Handbook of Job Aids.* San Diego: Pfeiffer, 1991.

Wilcox, J., ed. *ASTD Trainer's Toolkit: Job Aids.* Alexandria, VA: ASTD, 1992.

Wurman, R.S. *Follow the Yellow Brick Road: Learning to Give, Take, and Use Instructions.* New York: Bantam Books, 1992.

Infolines

Hodell, C. "Basics of Instructional Systems Development." No. 259706.

Raybould, B. "EPSS and Your Organization." No. 259806.

Waagen, A. "Essentials for Evaluation." No. 259705.

Job Aid

Checklist for Creating Effective Job Aids

Use this checklist as a guide as you design job aids. The set of questions will help you plan, develop, and evaluate job aids.

1. Determine If the Task Should Be Job Aided.

☐ Is the task performed infrequently?

☐ What are the repercussions for error?

☐ How complex is the task?

☐ How frequently does the task change?

☐ What are the characteristics of the user?

☐ What is the environment like where the task is performed?

2. Design the Job Aid.

☐ What part of the task will the job aid support?

☐ What format will you use?

☐ Will the job aid support step-by-step procedures or decision-making tasks?

☐ Will the job aid be used to reference information only?

☐ What medium will the job aid take?

☐ In what type of environment is the task completed?

☐ What resources are available to develop the job aid?

☐ Is the medium easy to use while performing the task?

☐ Should the job aid be audio, visual, or electronic?

3. Develop the Job Aid.

☐ Is the job aid clear and understandable?

☐ Are the instructions free of unnecessary detail?

☐ Are the instructions clearly and correctly sequenced?

☐ Are examples used when appropriate?

☐ Does the job aid avoid confusing terms or jargon?

☐ Are words and sentences short?

☐ Does the job aid use visuals well?

☐ Are critical words highlighted?

4. Implement the Job Aid.

☐ Who will introduce the job aid?

☐ Is the job aid's importance evident to the user?

☐ Who will demonstrate how to use the job aid?

5. Determine How to Measure Job Aid Effectiveness.

☐ Who will maintain the job aid?

☐ How will revisions be distributed?

☐ What type of results will be measured: dollar value or nondollar value?

☐ How will the results be reported?

☐ Who will receive reports of the results?

INFORMATION
LINE
TIPS, TOOLS, AND INTELLIGENCE FOR TRAINERS

Effective Classroom
Training Techniques

Issue 0108

Effective Classroom Training Techniques

AUTHORS

Rick Sullivan
JHPIEGO Corporation
1615 Thames Street
Baltimore, MD 21231-3492
Tel: 410.614.3551
Fax: 410.614.9191
Email: rsullivan@jhpiego.org

Jerry L. Wircenski
University of North Texas
PO Box 311337
Denton, TX 76203-1337
Tel: 940.565.2714
Fax: 940.565.2185
Email: akadrj@unt.edu

Rick Sullivan is the director of learning and performance improvement support for the JHPIEGO Corporation, an affiliate of Johns Hopkins University. He oversees the design and delivery of training and improvement interventions for medical professionals throughout the world.

Jerry L. Wircenski is a professor and program coordinator in the Applied Technology, Training and Development program at the University of North Texas.

Editor
Cat Sharpe Russo

Managing Editor
Stephanie Sussan

Production Design
Kathleen Schaner

***Infoline* Consultant**
Phil Anderson

Training Techniques 215
Icebreakers and Energizers 216
Effective Presentations 217
Questioning and Reinforcement 219
Brainstorming 219
Group Discussion 221
Case Studies 221
Role Playing 223
Demonstrations 224
Simulations 224
Games 225

References & Resources 226

Job Aid
Assessment: Effective Classroom Training 228

Training Techniques

Think about your best classroom training experience. It most likely was interactive, participatory, and included a variety of engaging activities. Effective classroom training does not happen by accident—it requires a great deal of planning and preparation.

Variety is a key factor to successful classroom training. We all have attended courses when the trainer uses only one training method—usually a lecture. After a short period of time, the participants begin to drift away. Sadly, much of the hard work and preparation that went into that training course has fallen on deaf ears.

To avoid this predicament, each segment of your training should employ one or more training techniques. Use the techniques in a variety of combinations. For example, you may begin a session with brainstorming solutions for a specific problem and then move into a brief presentation. Following the presentation, the participants work in small groups on a case study focusing on the same problem as the brainstorming topic and presentation. Upon completion of the case study, facilitate a discussion of the answers to the case study questions.

Some of the most effective techniques include:

- icebreakers and energizers
- interactive presentations
- questioning
- brainstorming
- group discussions
- case studies
- role playing
- demonstrations and coaching
- simulations
- games.

These are several classroom-training techniques that can motivate and involve the learners, and thereby enhance the learning experience. These techniques are identified during the development phase of course design. Designing a course—known as instructional systems development (ISD)— generally has five phases: analysis, design, development, implementation, and evaluation.

During the development phase, you select the actual training materials for the course—including the training techniques.

Prior to this stage, you need to conduct a thorough needs analysis to determine what the participants need to know. This will help define the appropriate training techniques. You also need to complete a series of design and planning activities. These activities include:

☐ Conduct an analysis to determine the need.

☐ Analyze the target audience to determine any special needs.

☐ Create the course objectives.

☐ Select classroom training techniques that best meet the audience's needs while at the same time help accomplish the objectives.

☐ Determine what audiovisuals will help support the objectives.

Once you've completed the above tasks, begin to develop the training techniques that will best suit your particular training session. This *Infoline* introduces you to some very effective classroom training techniques and gives clear guidelines on how to develop them. The issue also delineates which techniques are appropriate, or inappropriate, for certain situations. Trainers can use this chapter as a guide when developing and planning all their training courses.

Selecting Techniques

There are countless classroom training techniques you will come across as a trainer. How do you decide which ones to use for a specific training session? Here are some questions to help you select effective classroom training techniques.

- Is this technique appropriate for the objectives?

- Are there sufficient trainers available to use this training technique? Some techniques may require more than one trainer.

- Are the resources available to use this training technique? Some techniques may require additional materials, supplies, and equipment.

- Are additional facilities required? Some techniques may require breakout rooms or rooms for hands-on activities.

- What is the projected size of the group? Some techniques are more appropriate for a small group than for a larger group.

- Is a special classroom arrangement required?

- What is the background of the learners? Some techniques work better with new employees who do not know each other, while others work better when you have a group of seasoned veterans.

Icebreakers and Energizers

Key to the success of any course is what happens in the first few moments. Once the participants enter the classroom, initiate an introductory activity. Start the course on a positive note by ensuring all of the learners feel comfortable and get to know one another as soon as possible.

Icebreakers and energizers accomplish many goals, including:

- reveal the group personality

- build group identity

- build or maintains participant self-esteem

- develop trust among participants

- establish a baseline on the group—how comfortable they feel with the level of participation

- let participants know their trainer

- set program tone

- open communication.

They also can serve as a source of additional data about the learners. For example, you can find out:

- how well the group is getting along
- supplementary personal information
- learner reaction to material
- the extent to which the group is bonding
- if any cliques are forming
- the energy level of the group
- if people like to have fun in training.

There are several icebreakers that can help facilitate your course:

■ *Divide the Group Into Pairs*
Give the participants a few minutes to interview each other. The participants then have a minute to introduce their partners to the group and share at least two unique characteristics about them.

■ *Write Three Questions*
Participants find someone in the room they do not know well. Each participant addresses his or her questions to the other person. The participants then introduce their partners to the group by sharing both the questions and the answers.

■ *Write Four Personal Facts*
One of these facts is not true. Each person takes turns reading their list aloud, and the rest of the group writes down the one they think is not true. When everyone is finished reading the lists, the first person reads their list again and identifies the fact that is not true.

These types of interactive activities are not only useful for starting a training course. *Energizers,* similar to icebreakers, are activities you can use throughout the course to encourage participant involvement and interaction. Here are several energizers you might want to try:

■ *Write Three Things You Want to Learn*

The participants attach their lists to a poster board or piece of flipchart paper, which is posted in the classroom. Review these expectations with the group. This activity also helps you focus the course on individual or group learning needs and interests.

■ *Create a Long List*

Ask teams to list things that are square, things associated with a holiday, things that are red, things you can make out of a paper towel tube, and so forth. There is no discussion; just list as many items as possible. The team with the most items wins. This activity stimulates group interaction and gets people talking. This can be especially helpful when groups are particularly reticent.

■ *Form Small Groups*

Write the word *interactive* on a flipchart. The groups have five minutes to create as many words (two or more letters) as possible from the word *interactive*. The group with the most words wins. This activity also fosters interaction among quieter classmates.

See the *Effective Introductions* sidebar on the next page for more information.

Effective Presentations

The most common training technique is the presentation. While most presenters feel they do well, many participants will tell you this often is not the case. A presentation can be an effective method for delivering information, but the key is to deliver an energetic, interactive presentation—and that is not as easy as it seems. Some suggestions for delivering interactive presentations include:

Project your voice. Periodically change the pitch, volume, and rate of your delivery. Nothing will put participants to sleep faster than someone speaking in a monotone voice.

Maintain an appropriate pace. If you move through the presentation content too rapidly, participants may have a difficult time following. If you move too slowly, participants may disconnect and drift away from your presentation.

Avoid using fillers. Fillers are expressions such as uh, um, you know, ok, and er. We all have sat in presentations where we started to count the number of times the presenter repeated the same filler. Having notes on paper or key points on a flipchart or projection screen will help prevent these fillers.

Enunciate clearly and distinctly. It is distracting and frustrating to listen to a presenter and not be able to understand what is being said.

Use participant names. People like to hear their name. Using participant names also keeps the learners focused on the presentation (in other words, they don't doze off).

Use familiar terms and expressions. Many presenters feel they need to impress the participants with their vocabulary. Your job is to inform—not impress. If you introduce an unfamiliar term or expression, define it.

Use lots of examples. Examples include personal experiences, facts, figures, illustrations, anecdotes, quotes, photographs, slides, real objects, and video examples. Participants want and need examples. An appropriate visual or story will make your point more clear. Examples also should be pulled from the participants.

Praise participants. Positive reinforcement increases the participants' interest level, keeps them focused on the topic, and improves the climate of your presentation.

Use appropriate humor. Periodic and suitable humor helps maintain participant interest and attention. See the *Adding Humor* sidebar for more information.

Maintain eye contact. Look at your participants and watch for questioning looks, confusion, boredom, agreement, and disagreement. Based on what you see, make adjustments to your content, questions, or schedule (maybe it's time for a break). In terms of your notes, glance at them to see the next point, but then return your eye contact immediately to your participants.

Effective Introductions

The first few moments of a presentation are critical. The introduction is the technique you will use to grab the attention of your participants as you move into a presentation. There are a number of techniques you can use to begin a presentation.

Review your presentation objectives. The introduction for every presentation should include the objectives.

Ask a series of questions. Take advantage of the fact that many of your participants probably have some background knowledge. Asking a series of questions immediately brings them into the presentation. This immediate interaction also will help you to relax.

Ask for a show of hands. This is another technique that involves everyone in the presentation from the start. When using this approach, encourage participants to look around the room to see that they are not the only ones familiar with the topic you are about to discuss.

Relate the topic to previously covered information. This technique is used quite often and works well when you are making several related presentations to the same participants. This technique also is useful during a course that spans several days.

Relate the topic to work experiences. This technique is used when you can link your presentation to the participants' work activities.

Use an interesting quotation. This can pique the interest of your participants.

Share a personal experience. Everyone likes to hear a good story. Be sure that when using personal experiences that they are interesting, relevant, and brief enough that your participants do not lose track of the purpose of the story.

Relate the content to a real-life experience. A real-life experience is something your participants can relate to, is topic related, but may or may not have happened to you. The intent is to help them see the connection between the presentation content and a real-life situation.

Use a case study or problem-solving activity. Participants enjoy working in small groups to solve a problem or tackle a case study. This technique can work well to introduce just about any presentation where the audience can be divided into small groups of four to eight participants.

Use videotape. All or part of a videotape may be an excellent technique for capturing the interest of your participants and then moving into your presentation topic. As this is the presentation introduction, keep the video brief.

Share an appropriate cartoon. Everyone enjoys a good laugh and most trainers keep a file of appropriate cartoons. Make sure the cartoon is topic related, not offensive to anyone, and that you are not violating copyright laws.

Give a unique demonstration. Some presentation topics lend themselves to a demonstration. This could be a demonstration of a concept or a hands-on skill. Participants not only enjoy watching a demonstration; for some this is consistent with their learning style and will help them understand information delivered during the classroom presentations.

Use a game or role-play activity. This is a good technique to start a presentation when you want lots of interaction and discussion on the topic.

Keep positive facial expressions. If you look stressed, participants will get the feeling that your heart is not in your presentation. Smile, look relaxed (even if you're not), and project expressions that are enthusiastic and say that you are enjoying the presentation.

Gesture with your hands and arms. Appropriate gestures help emphasize key points and maintain the interest of your participants.

Move about the room with energy. Moving around naturally and with confidence helps maintain the attention of the participants. Avoid the use of a lectern, desk, or table, as these often create a barrier that prevents movement. Tables arranged in a U-shape offer you plenty of space to move within the group.

Questioning and Reinforcement

Which classroom training technique do the best trainers employ? Which technique will make your classroom training more interactive? Which technique can be used with almost any other training method? The answer to all of these questions is effective questioning and reinforcement.

The primary purpose of questioning is to encourage the participants to think about the training topic. Participants often say they understand the content, but a knowledge or skills assessment proves otherwise. Effective questioning gives participants an opportunity to think through the content and gain a better understanding of the concepts being presented.

See the *Questioning Tips* sidebar on the next page for more information.

Brainstorming

Brainstorming is a training technique that stimulates creativity and often is used in conjunction with a group discussion. Brainstorming generates a list of ideas, suggestions, or potential solutions focusing on a specific topic, issue, or problem. This list can be used as the introduction to a presentation or form the basis of a group discussion. Brainstorming requires that participants have some background information related to the topic.

Adding Humor

Appropriate humor and laughter bring a wonderful energy into classroom training. This is especially critical when training courses are scheduled all day for several days at a time. Humor can help maintain interest, keep participants focused, and make learning more fun for everyone. Here are some suggestions for adding a touch of humor to your classroom training:

- Humor must always be appropriate and never offensive.

- Use topic-related anecdotes, puns, and stories at appropriate points in your presentations. These can be presented orally or visually using the flipchart or a projected image.

- Avoid telling jokes. This can open the door for participants wanting to tell jokes, and that can be a disaster.

- Use topic-related cartoons or drawings shown on a projection screen.

- When you make a mistake, turn it into an opportunity for laughter. For example, you realize that during brainstorming you have misspelled a word on the flipchart. Step back, look at all sides of the flipchart, and ask, "Does anyone know how to run spell check on one of these?"

- Interject topic-related trivia or brainteasers.

- Give participants working in small groups a topic-related cartoon with no caption and ask them to create a caption of their own. After the groups have shared their caption, share the original. This activity creates a great deal of laughter, as many are better than the original.

- Use your facial expressions, gestures, and body language to create humor.

- Don't joke about a person's name or nationality. As a trainer, you will run across some very unusual names. However, resist the temptation to remark about it.

- Use topic-related quotes and sayings. You can use the original quote or modify one to fit your specific needs. Be sure to credit your source.

- Never tell a funny story about a previous trainee or course. You never know who knows whom.

- Collect books, articles, cartoons, images, stories, and bookmark humor sites on the Internet to build you own humor library.

- Avoid trying to impersonate someone else. Develop your own approach.

Questioning Tips

Questioning is not an easy skill. However, there are techniques that can simplify the task. Some tips to developing effective questioning techniques include:

- Develop questions when you develop your presentation notes. Review your content and identify points where you will want to ask questions.

- Design questions to be brief. If you ask a question that is too long, you will hear that age-old response: "Could you repeat the question?"

- Ask questions at different difficulty levels. Some questions should require only a yes or no answer. Others should require that the participant explain a point in detail.

- Ask questions of the entire group. These are referred to as group or open questions, and anyone can respond.

- Target questions to individual participants. This allows you to include those who do not respond to the group questions. This also is an opportunity to use participant names.

- Attempt to involve all participants. While some participants may not want to get involved, most welcome the opportunity.

- Repeat participant responses so others can hear. This also is a form of positive feedback because you are accepting their answers. Plus this is another opportunity to use names.

- Respond to participant questions by repeating the question and either answering the question, opening the question up to other participants, or asking the originator another question to help the participant figure out the answer. If you don't know the answer, admit it. Find out the answer and share this with the participants during the next session

Here are some guidelines for facilitating a brainstorming session:

Announce the brainstorming ground rules. There are three basic rules.

1. All ideas will be accepted.

2. There will be no discussion of suggestions until later.

3. There will be no criticism of suggestions.

Announce the topic or problem. Clearly state the focus of the brainstorming session. For example: "During the next few minutes we will be brainstorming and will follow our usual rules. Our topic is 'Improving the performance of our supervisors.' I would like each of you to think of at least one idea. Sarah will write these on the flipchart so that we can discuss them later. Who would like to be first?"

Maintain a written record of the ideas. This will prevent repetition, keep participants focused on the topic, and will be useful when it is time to discuss each item. Ask someone to record the responses on a flipchart, as it is difficult to simultaneously pull ideas from the participants and clearly record them.

Involve participants and provide feedback. Avoid allowing a few of the participants to monopolize the brainstorming session and encourage those not offering suggestions to do so. When time permits, divide the participants into small groups allowing each group to generate a list of ideas. The reporter from each group can share the results of their brainstorming. When using the small-group approach to brainstorming, provide each group with a flipchart and markers.

Review the ideas periodically. This will help stimulate additional ideas. When you notice a pause in the flow of ideas, quickly run down the list to allow the participants to generate some more ideas. The key is to know when enough ideas have been developed.

Review all the suggestions. Post the flipchart page(s) on the wall for reference during any subsequent discussions or presentations.

What occurs after brainstorming depends on the purpose of the session. For example, brainstorming the characteristics of an effective trainer at the beginning of a train-the-trainer course may result in the list being posted on the wall for reference throughout the course. On the other hand, identifying potential solutions to a problem is likely to be followed by a discussion of each proposed solution.

Group Discussion

The group discussion is a training technique during which the participants develop most of their ideas, thoughts, questions, and answers. Your role is to guide the participants as the discussion develops. Group discussion is useful after a brainstorming session, at the conclusion of a presentation, after a case study or role-play activity, following a guest speaker, after watching a video, or at any other time when participants have prior knowledge or experience.

Conducting a group discussion when participants have limited knowledge of the topic often results in little or no interaction and thus an ineffective discussion. When participants are familiar with the topic, the ensuing discussion is likely to arouse participant interest, stimulate thinking, and encourage active participation. This interaction affords you opportunities to provide positive feedback, emphasize key points, and create a positive learning climate.

Follow these suggestions to ensure successful group discussions:

Arrange seating to encourage interaction. Set up tables and chairs in a U-shape, square, or circle so the participants face one another. Group discussions work best for groups of no more than 15-20 participants. See the *Tips for Arranging Your Classroom* sidebar on the next page for more information.

State the topic as part of the introduction. For example, "To conclude this presentation on management styles, let's take a few minutes to discuss the importance of human relations and staff supervision."

Shift the conversation to the participants. At this point you should take a seat, becoming an unobtrusive observer.

Enter the discussion only when necessary. For example, if two participants begin to monopolize the discussion you might say: "It is obvious that Mike and Kelly are taking opposite sides in this discussion. Mike, let me see if I can clarify your position. You seem to feel that…"

Summarize the key points. This allows the participants to reflect and affords you an opportunity to redirect the discussion, if necessary.

Keep the discussion on the topic. If a participant begins to move the discussion away from the topic, you might say, "Kay, can you explain a little more clearly how that situation relates to our topic?" Following the participant's point, move the discussion back to the topic.

Use the contributions of each participant. Provide positive reinforcement and encourage all participants to get involved.

Ensure that no one dominates the discussion. When this occurs, you might say: "John, you have contributed a great deal to our discussion. Would someone like to offer his or her view?"

Conclude the discussion with a summary. Relate the summary to the objective presented during the introduction.

Case Studies

A case study is a real-life situation presented to participants who are asked to react to the situation. Participant reaction may be given verbally or in writing. Case studies are especially helpful when there is a need to focus on real-life problems or situations. You also can use case studies when you want to ensure participants understand and can apply information.

Tips for Arranging Your Classroom

How your classroom is set up can have a significant impact on the result of your training. The following tips can help you in this process:

- Arrange for a room that adequately accommodates the number of participants. A room that is too large is just as bad as a room that is too small.

- Use a room that is free of distractions and noise.

- Arrange for a room that is accessible to all participants—including those with limited mobility.

- Arrange for breakout areas or rooms, if necessary.

- Locate the restrooms and telephones, and set up a message center for your participants. Announce these locations at the start of training.

- Select a seating arrangement with chairs that comfortably accommodate your audience.

- Specify your lighting requirements, locations of controls, and so forth. Be sure you can turn the lights up or down when needed.

- Specify your climate control requirements—a room that is too hot or too cold will leave a negative impression on your participants.

- Determine the types of audiovisuals you will need, including the size of the projection screen, computer projection equipment, number of flipcharts.

- Select a good location for refreshments to be placed and serviced throughout the day.

- Remind participants to turn off their cell phones and pagers. These are disruptive.

- Circulate a sign-up sheet for participant names, addresses, phone numbers, and email addresses. Use this list for follow-up purposes.

- Arrange for a table up front for your computer, projector, handouts, and so forth.

- Arrange for a microphone, if necessary—the wireless type works best.

- Make arrangements for distributing your handouts—before, during, or at the end of your presentations.

Case studies, like brainstorming, can be highly participatory, enjoyable, and interesting. Reacting to case studies can be a very motivational activity. However, case studies are not very effective if participants do not have some background related to the topic.

Case studies should be developed prior to the presentation. Situations for case studies can be developed from personal experiences, company records, and experiences from participants who have attended your training. Development of a case study typically involves the following steps:

1. Identify a situation, problem, or issue. Examples of case study topics include human relations issues, management concerns, and equipment problems.

2. Ensure your case study represents a real-life situation. The focus must relate directly to the background, experiences, and interests of your participants.

3. Determine whether individuals will complete the case study or whether the participants will tackle it in small groups.

4. Provide questions or activities that encourage participants to focus on the problem presented.

5. Determine whether participants will report the results of their work on the case study in writing or orally to the entire group.

6. Highlight key points on a flipchart.

When participants will be working in small groups, suggest that each group select a recorder. The recorder is responsible for taking notes and preparing the group's reaction to the case study. Selecting a recorder in advance prevents confusion and panic among group members when it is time to report their reactions.

When using this technique, the room must be flexible. Make sure that tables can be moved easily so the participants can form their groups. While participants are working on the case study, you should be able to move around the room to observe, check progress, and answer questions.

After the participants have read the case study, they should be given the opportunity to react to the case study. Typical reaction exercises include:

- reports about the problem being analyzed

- responses to the case-study questions

- recommendations on how to solve the problem

- suggestions on how the problem could have been prevented

- discussion of the responses

- summary of the key points.

Role Playing

A role-play activity is a spontaneous acting out of a situation or an incident by participants. The situation may be developed based on your background, participant experiences, or organizational records. Ensure that the situation is relevant and is similar to situations that participants attending your presentation will face. This is an excellent training technique for developing insights and reactions of participants in a situation. A well-planned role-play activity can enable participants to experience the complexities of the skills they will perform on the job. Role playing can be highly motivational and lead to experiences that will be recalled long after they have happened.

When conducting a role-play activity, always start with ideal physical surroundings. Choose a room that is large enough to accommodate role playing comfortably.

Avoid noisy locations that are open to distraction. No one should be able to enter the room, observe through the windows, or eavesdrop on the session. Restrict telephone or visitor interruptions. Try to find a location with an adjacent breakout room, or use available partitions, blackboards, or large plants for privacy.

Other suggestions to ensure successful role-play activities include:

- Choose an appropriate situation or problem.

- Brief participants on their roles.

- Set the stage for the role-play activity.

- Ask observers to record their observations.

- Give some insight to your participants as to what to look for—use of specific principles or skills, verbal communication skills, and so forth.

- Be ready to handle any unexpected situations that might arise—arguments or discussions that get a little out of hand.

- Prepare a set of discussion questions to follow up the role-play activity.

- Engage participants in a follow-up discussion.

- Summarize key points on a flipchart.

Role playing can accomplish many training goals, including:

- maximize participation and stimulate thinking

- promote learning through imitation, observation, feedback, analysis, and conceptualization

- inform and train participants, evaluate their performance, and improve their skills

- test and practice new behaviors participants can use in their jobs

- develop skills for implementing solutions and decisions

- develop interpersonal and practical skills

- experience and understand a variety of problem situations from other points of view and learn how to empathize with people

- generate feedback that will give participants insight into their behavior, and help them understand how others view them.

Demonstrations

From time to time you will face the challenge of presenting a demonstration. For example, you have been asked to demonstrate a new portable exhaust-sampling system. This is not a presentation on the importance of exhaust sampling or on the international environmental regulations and certification associated with meeting exhaust particulate standards. It is a demonstration of the steps involved in setting up the testing equipment, taking samples, recording the data, and disassembling the equipment. This type of presentation is different from providing information about exhaust-sampling systems.

The primary difference between an interactive presentation and a demonstration is that your participants will be expected to be able to perform the steps you are demonstrating, as opposed to only having background knowledge about the procedures.

Here are some suggestions for delivering an effective demonstration:

Plan for your demonstration. Analyze your audience, determine how many people will attend, arrange the facilities, and do the same type of planning you would do for any presentation.

Begin with an introduction. Quickly move into the body of your demonstration showing the participants each step.

Check whether your participants understand. Ask questions and provide feedback.

Explain new terms. Stress safety principles, when applicable.

Ensure that each participant can see. Walk around the room whenever possible. This is especially helpful when the items being demonstrated are difficult to see.

Avoid passing items among participants. This may be distracting. If appropriate, ask participants to gather around the demonstration area for a better view.

Provide notes on the steps. Walk the participants through the process.

Perform demonstration one way. Often a procedure can be performed several ways; demonstrate only one, preferably the most common one. Trying to remember different ways to perform a procedure can confuse your participants.

Reinforce your demonstration. Conclude with an effective summary.

Practice. Immediately following your demonstration is an ideal time for your participants to practice the procedures you have demonstrated. Your role then becomes one of facilitating, observing, and coaching.

Coach your participants during practice. Resist the temptation to do it for them the first time they falter. Answer questions and give prompts, but keep your hands off unless you really need to step in.

Simulations

Simulations enable participants to engage in learning activities that may be too complex, dangerous, or expensive to do with the actual equipment, people, or processes. Using a computer software program that creates a scenario surrounding the operation of a nuclear power plant teaches reactor operators about the plant's power-generation systems by imitating or replicating them. Participants learn by interacting with the simulation activity in a manner similar to the way they would react in a real-life situation. During the simulation, the trainer's role is to facilitate, observe, and answer questions.

Simulations are based on the premise that effective training requires a balance of three factors:

Content: the dissemination of new ideas, principles, or concepts.

Experience: the opportunity to apply content in an experiential environment.

Feedback: responses on actions taken and the relationship between performance and the subsequent result.

The two most important steps to take before designing or implementing a simulation are:

1. Review your objectives.

2. Determine group needs.

Once you have reviewed your organization's issues and expectations, set your goals and give some thought to how you are going to achieve them.

Remember, there are variations within the audience. Tailor the simulation to your participants. Are they executive, middle management, or supervisory? What problem-solving and interpersonal behavior techniques are required for different job functions? Some guidelines for facilitating simulations include:

• Determine the purpose of the simulation—is it designed to guide the participants in acquiring information and skills?

• Select a simulation to match the designed purpose.

• Set up the parameters of the simulation—start and stop time, the type of intervention you will make. As the facilitator, you need to be vigilant, patient, and available.

• Facilitate the simulation activity.

• Actively engage participants in the feedback or review process.

• Summarize the key points on a flipchart.

For more information on simulations, see *Infoline* No. 258412, "Simulation and Role Play."

Games

Why do people play sports, computer games, or board games? Because they are enjoyable. Games also make excellent learning tools. With games the problem at hand is the most important element. There is no sense in playing unless it is worth the effort. Games can be challenging and stimulating, exploiting the most natural and effective process of learning through personal experience and experimentation. They enable participants to quickly assess their strengths and weaknesses in a relatively safe environment. Participants become motivated to learn specific knowledge and skills through games and then apply them back in the workplace.

Games encourage participants to take risks. These experiences help them build confidence in their ability to correct their mistakes and improve their performance. They stimulate participants to ask more penetrating questions about themselves, their colleagues, and their actions. Some guidelines for using games as a training tool include:

• Identify a problem or situation related to your learning goals and objectives.

• Select an appropriate game that will be fun and enjoyable for your participants.

• Explain the rules of the game to your participants.

• Facilitate the activity—award points, keep score, and resolve any disputes.

• Engage all participants in a follow-up discussion.

• Summarize the key points on a flipchart.

For more information on using games, see *Infolines* No. 258411, "10 Great Games and How to Use Them"; No. 259106, "More Great Games"; and No. 250105, "Fun in the Workplace."

Keep It Active

When sitting in a classroom passively listening to a lesson, adults likely will forget the information delivered to them. One study concluded that within one year, adults are likely to forget 50 percent of what the have learned through passive methods. Another study indicated that approximately half of one day's learning may be lost during the ensuing 24 hours. In two weeks, an additional 25 percent may be lost.

When a trainer uses active training techniques, the learners take part in the lesson and are able to construct personal meaning from the presentation. When used correctly, the active classroom training techniques discussed in this issue will increase the longevity and relevance of your presentation.

References & Resources

Books

Biech, Elaine. *The 2000 Annual: Training*. Volume 1. San Francisco: Jossey-Bass, 2000.

Biech, Elaine, and Daniel P. Biebuyck. *Creativity and Innovation: The ASTD Trainers Sourcebook*. New York: McGraw-Hill, 1996.

Booth, Nan. *75 Icebreakers for Great Gatherings: Everything You Need to Bring People Together*. St. Paul, MN: Brighton Publications, 2000.

Brody, Marjorie. *Speaking Is an Audience-Centered Sport*. Jenkintown, PA: Career Skills Press, 1998.

Burn, Bonnie E. *Flip Chart Power*. San Francisco: Pfeiffer, 1996.

Caroselli, Marlene. *Great Session Openers, Closers, and Energizers: Quick Activities for Warming Up Your Audience and Ending on a High Note*. New York: McGraw-Hill, 1998.

Cherniss, Cary, et al. *Promoting Emotional Intelligence in Organizations*. Alexandria, VA: ASTD, 2000.

Fox, William M. *Effective Group Problem Solving*. San Francisco: Jossey-Bass, 1987.

Fuller, Jim. *Managing Performance Improvement Projects: Preparing, Planning, and Implementing*. San Francisco: Pfeiffer, 1997.

Fuller, Jim, and Jeanne Farrington. *From Training to Performance Improvement: Navigating the Transition*. San Francisco: Pfeiffer, 1999.

Hale, Judith. *The Performance Consultant's Fieldbook*. San Francisco: Jossey-Bass, 1998.

Hodgin, Michael. *1001 More Humorous Illustrations for Public Speaking*. Grand Rapids, MI: Zondervan, 1998.

Hunter, Dale, et al. *Zen of Groups: A Handbook for People Meeting with a Purpose*. Tucson, AZ: Fisher Books, 1995.

Justice, Thomas, and David W. Jamieson. *The Facilitator's Fieldbook: Step-by-Step Procedures, Checklists and Guidelines, Samples and Templates*. New York: AMACOM, 1999.

Kelly, Leslie, ed. *The ASTD Technical and Skills Training Handbook*. New York: McGraw-Hill, 1995.

Kelly, Mark. *The Adventures of a Self-Managing Team*. U.K.: Mark Kelly Books, 1991.

Kinlaw, Dennis C., and Richard L. Roe. *Facilitation Skills: The ASTD Trainer's Sourcebook*. New York: McGraw-Hill, 1996.

Kline, Theresa. *Remaking Teams: The Revolutionary Research-Based Guide that Puts Theory into Practice*. San Francisco: Jossey-Bass, 1999.

Knowles, Malcolm, et al. *The Adult Learner: The Definitive Classic in Adult Education and Human Resource Development*. Houston: Gulf Publishing, 1998.

Leonard, Dorothy, and Walter Swap. *When Sparks Fly: Igniting Creativity in Groups*. Cambridge, MA: Harvard Business School Press, 1999.

McArdle, Geri E. *Training Design & Delivery*. Alexandria, VA: ASTD, 1999.

Newstrom, John, and Edward Scannell. *The Big Book of Team Building Games*. New York: McGraw-Hill, 1997.

Nilson, Carolyn. *Team Games for Trainers Set*. San Francisco: John Wiley & Sons, 1998.

O'Neill, Mary Beth. *Executive Coaching with Backbone and Heart*. San Francisco: Jossey-Bass, 2000.

Pike, Robert, and Phillip Jones. *Creative Training Techniques Handbook: Tips Tactics, and How-to's for Delivering Effective Training*. 2nd edition. Minneapolis, MN: Lakewood Publications, 1994.

Pike, Robert, and David Arch. *Dealing with Difficult Participants: 127 Practical Strategies for Minimizing Resistance and Maximizing Results in Your Presentations*. San Francisco: Jossey-Bass, 1997.

Pohlman, Randolph, A., and Gareth S. Gardiner. *Value Driven Management: How to Create and Maximize Value Over Time for Organizational Success*. New York: AMACOM, 2000.

Putz, Gregory B. *Facilitation Skills: Helping Groups Make Decisions*. Bountiful, UT: Deep Space Technology, 1999.

Rees, Fran, and Arlette C. Ballew. *25 Activities for Teams*. San Francisco: Pfeiffer, 1993.

Robinson, Dana Gaines, and James C. Robinson. *Moving from Training to Performance*, San Francisco: Berrett-Koehler, 1998.

———. *Training for Impact: How to Link Training to Business Needs and Measure the Results*. San Francisco: Jossey Bass, 1989.

Schrage, Michael. *Serious Play: How the World's Best Companies Simulate to Innovate.* Cambridge, MA: Harvard Business School Press, 1999.

Silberman, Mel. *101 Ways to Make Meetings Active: Surefire Ideas to Engage Your Group.* San Francisco: Pfeiffer, 1999.

Stoll, Clifford, and Siobhan Adcock. *High Tech Heretic: Relections of a Computer Contrarian.* New York: Anchor Books, 2000.

Sullivan, Richard, et al. *Clinical Training Skills for Reproductive Health Professionals.* Baltimore, MD: JHPIEGO, 1998.

Tague, Nancy R. *The Quality Toolbox #H0861.* Milwaukee, WI: American Society for Quality, 1995.

Tesoro, Ferdinand, and Jack Tootson. *Implementing Global Performance Measurement Systems.* San Francisco: Jossey-Bass, 2000.

Thiagarajan, Sivasailam, and Glenn M. Parker. *Teamwork and Teamplay: Games and Activities for Building and Training Teams.* San Francisco: Jossey-Bass, 1999.

Torres, Cresencio, et al. *Teambuilding: The ASTD Trainer's Sourcebook.* New York: McGraw-Hill, 1996.

Ukens, Lorraine L. *Working Together.* San Francisco: Jossey-Bass, 1996.

Wilder, Claudyne, and David Fine. *Point, Click, and Wow!: A Quick Guide to Brilliant Laptop Presentations.* San Francisco: Pfeiffer, 1996.

Infolines

Buckner, Marilyn. "Simulation and Role Play." No. 258412 (revised 1999).

Sharpe, Cat, ed. "10 Great Games and How to Use Them." No. 258411 (revised 1999).

Sugar, Steve. "More Great Games." No. 259106 (revised 2000).

Thiagarajan, Sivasailam. "Fun in the Workplace." No. 250105.

Job Aid

Assessment: Effective Classroom Training

The following checklist will help you assess the effectiveness of your classroom training techniques.

Directions: Complete the checklist by checking yes or no next to each item. "No" answers indicate areas where you may need to improve the effectiveness of your classroom training. Record possible solutions and ways to improve your classroom training in the section for comments.

Icebreakers and Energizers	Yes	No	Comments
1. Planned icebreakers and introductions for the first day of the course.			
2. Prepared energizers for use at appropriate times during the course.			

Interactive Presentations

1. Projected voice and periodically changed pitch, tone, and volume.			
2. Maintained an appropriate pace.			
3. Avoided the use of fillers.			
4. Enunciated clearly and distinctly.			
5. Used participant names.			
6. Used familiar terms and expressions.			
7. Used numerous examples.			
8. Praised participants.			
9. Used appropriate humor.			
10. Maintained eye contact.			
11. Maintained positive facial expressions.			
12. Gestured using hands and arms.			
13. Moved about the room with energy.			

Questioning Techniques

1. Developed some questions in advance.			
2. Designed questions to be brief.			
3. Asked questions at varying levels of difficulty.			
4. Asked questions of the entire group.			
5. Targeted questions to individual participants.			
6. Attempted to involve all participants through questioning.			
7. Repeated participant responses and questions.			
8. Provided positive reinforcement after participant responses.			
9. Responded to participant questions.			

The material appearing on this page is not covered by copyright and may be reproduced at will.

	Yes	No	Comments

Brainstorming

1. Announced brainstorming rules.
2. Announced the topic or problem.
3. Maintained a written record of ideas and suggestions.
4. Involved the participants and provided positive feedback.
5. Reviewed ideas and suggestions periodically to stimulate additional ideas.
6. Concluded brainstorming by reviewing all suggestions.

Group Discussion

1. Arranged seating to encourage interaction.
2. Stated the topic as part of the introduction.
3. Shifted the conversation from the facilitator to the participants.
4. Entered the discussion only when necessary.
5. Summarized the key points of the discussion periodically.
6. Kept the discussion on topic.
7. Used the contributions of each participant and provided positive feedback.
8. Ensured no one participant dominated the discussion.
9. Concluded the discussion with a summary of the main ideas.

Case Studies

1. Identified a situation, problem, or issue on which participants were to focus.
2. Ensured that the case study represented a real-life situation.
3. Determined whether the case study was to be completed individually or in small groups.
4. Provided questions that encouraged participants to focus on problem presented.
5. Determined whether participants would report results in writing or orally.
6. Highlighted key points on the flipchart.

Role Playing

1. Selected an appropriate situation or problem.
2. Briefed participants on their roles.
3. Briefed participants on background information.
4. Asked observers to record their observations.
5. Gave some insight as to what to look for.

(continued on next page)

Job Aid

	Yes	No	Comments

6. Handled unexpected situations.

7. Created a set of discussion questions for the follow-up discussion.

8. Engaged all participants in discussion activity.

9. Summarized key points on the flipchart.

Demonstration

1. Planned for the demonstration—analyzed audience and arranged facilities.

2. Kicked off the demonstration with an effective introduction.

3. Asked questions.

4. Explained new terms and stressed safety principles.

5. Walked around.

6. Concluded with an effective summary.

7. Allowed participants time to practice.

8. Coached participants during practice session.

Simulation

1. Determined purpose of simulation.

2. Selected a simulation to match purpose.

3. Established parameters for simulation.

4. Facilitated simulation activity.

5. Engaged participants in feedback process.

6. Summarized key points or steps on the flipchart.

Games

1. Selected a game that was fun and enjoyable.

2. Selected a problem or situation that was related to the learning objectives.

3. Explained rules.

4. Facilitated activity.

5. Engaged participants in follow-up discussion.

6. Summarized key points on the flipchart.

INFORMATION LINE

Tips, Tools, and Intelligence for Trainers

 The material appearing on this page is not covered by copyright and may be reproduced at will.

Enhance Learning Retention

Issue 0302

Enhance Learning Retention

AUTHOR

Judith Gillespie Myers, PhD
10405 Gary Road
Potomac, MD 20854
Tel: 301.983.8513
Email: jgmyers64@aol.com

Judy is an experienced instructional designer, trainer, educator, writer, and editor. She has more than a decade of experience in teaching adults how to write and has published a writing guide for government employees and a textbook for educational administrators.

Make Learning Stick 233
   Five Steps to Learning Retention 233
   Applying the Five Steps 246

References & Resources 247

Job Aid
   Using the Nine Events of Instruction 248

Managing Editor
Mark Morrow

Editor
Stephanie Sussan

Associate Editor
Tora Estep

Copy Editor
Ann Bruen

Production Design
Kathleen Schaner

Make Learning Stick

Perhaps this has happened to you: You attend a class, participate enthusiastically, and even enjoy it a bit. However, a month later you barely remember a thing you learned.

What happened?

As trainers, you need to know the answer to this question. You might put in hours and hours of preparation for a class, but you will fail if your learners do not retain what you planned to teach them. You need to know *why* people tend to forget and *how* to encourage learning retention. The sidebar *Glossary* on the next page defines some basic terminology of learning and retention that may be helpful to you.

People often do not retain information because:

They don't pay attention. Competing stimuli constantly bombard the senses. For stimuli to register, learners must focus their attention on it and block out background noise.

They receive too much information. Even if people pay attention, they can become overwhelmed. This is especially true if the information is not well organized.

They do not have a context for the information. This is why nonsense words are so difficult to remember.

They experience interference. For example, suppose that on Monday John learns the Spanish word for receive, *recibir*, and on Wednesday he learns the French verb for receive, *recevoir*. During a Spanish test taken on Thursday, he writes the French verb instead of the Spanish. The memories of Spanish are competing with memories of French.

They cannot transfer the learning to the workplace. If there is no workplace relevance, learners will not use the information and soon will forget it.

In this chapter, you will find five steps that will ensure that your students retain the information you teach.

Five Steps to Learning Retention

You have your lesson plans, your agenda, and your students. Now, you're ready to ensure that they remember what you teach them. The five essential steps to ensuring learning retention are as follows:

1. Capture your learners' attention.

2. Organize and chunk information.

3. Use mnemonic devices.

4. Rehearse.

5. Transfer the information to the workplace.

Step 1: Capture Learners' Attention

Most people normally ignore much of what takes place around them. They do this through a mechanism called *perceptual filtering*, which allows them to block out huge amounts of irrelevant information to focus on what is important. Think about the child who is oblivious to a blaring television and burning toast because she is completely enthralled with the *Adventures of Harry Potter*. Or consider the birdwatcher, totally unaware of his wet feet or the biting mosquitoes, who focuses enthusiastically on the purple tanager.

The bookworm and the birdwatcher focus on certain information because it interests them. As trainers, you need to win and maintain that interest.

You can capture learners' attention through several strategies.

- **Introduce the lesson with an attention-getting activity,** such as a skit, case study, or short self-assessment.

- **Inform learners of the objective.** When learners understand the purpose of instruction, their expectations carry them through the learning process.

- **Match the instructional objective with the** learners' motivation. Suppose Andy decides to take a class so he can sharpen his word-processing skills and help improve his chances

Glossary

Following are terms that relate to learning and retention and types of memory.

Learning and Retention Terms

Encoding is the mental process that changes physical stimuli into a format that can be placed in memory, just as material must be typed before it can be saved in a computer's memory.

Storage, also called **retention,** is the process of holding or maintaining information in memory, just as a disk stores information for a computer.

Retrieval is when stored information is brought back to your consciousness. In the same way, you can retrieve a computer file from a disk.

Types of Memory

Declarative memory is what helps people recall facts and events, such as dates, historical facts, and telephone numbers.

Procedural memory refers to procedures and abilities, such as driving a car, playing tennis, or using a copy machine.

Episodic memory is long-term memory for events or episodes personally experienced.

---

of a promotion. If your objective is to increase typing speed to 120 words per minute and decrease errors by 60 percent, the instructional objective matches Andy's motivation.

- **Put the learning in context.** Learners retain information by integrating it with what they already know. You can help learners form these associations by building a context for them. You can provide learners with advance organizers: short introductory information packages that set up an expectation or build a vision. For example, an instructor of a presentation skills class might explain that learners will learn how to (1) prepare presentations, (2) give presentations, and (3) evaluate presentations.

- **Review prior knowledge, skills, rules, or** concepts. An explanation of how the new content will fit into this prior learning will help learners. For example, an instructor teaching equal employment opportunity law would review the relevant history that led to the legislation.

- **Arouse learners' curiosity.** Learners become curious when they need to solve a problem. For example, an instructor of an introductory management class presents a case study about an employee with body odor and asks the class how they, as managers, would deal with the problem.

- **Vary the stimulus.** You should change the stimulus frequently and unexpectedly. You can do this by interspersing lectures with group exercises or other activities. You also can maintain the learners' attention by gesturing or by varying the volume, pitch, and tone of your voice.

Step 2: Organize and Chunk Information

The way that information is organized has a lot to do with how well we remember it. To illustrate, here's a three-part exercise for you.

Exercise A:

1. Examine the following numbers for 15 seconds. Ready? Go!

    51066149216201776I929

Now cover up the numbers and write them in the same order below.

How many of the 21 numbers were you able to remember?

2. Now examine the following array for 15 seconds.

510-661-492-162-017-761-929

Now, without looking, write the numbers in the same order below.

Did you improve your score?

It is difficult for most people to remember 21 numbers if they are not grouped. In fact, one reason that telephone numbers have seven digits is that seven is the approximate limit of the average brain's capacity for recall. People do not like nine-digit zip codes because they exceed short-term memory capacity.

Grouping letters, digits, or words into units that are easy to remember is called *chunking*.

3. Finally, examine the following array for 15 seconds and try to reproduce the numbers without looking.

5-1066-1492-1620-1776-1929

You probably did a lot better on the third try because we organized the numbers in a *meaningful* way. We grouped the numbers into five memorable dates and put them in chronological order. You can associate the number five at the beginning with the number of dates. In this case, you were able to take advantage of both *chunking* and *meaning*.

Exercise B:

Consider another example.

Suppose you have the following 10 items to buy at the store:

1. Chocolate milk.

2. Green beans.

3. Whole-wheat bread.

4. Pineapple.

5. Cheddar cheese.

6. Tomatoes.

7. Pound cake.

8. Canned cherries.

9. Beets.

10. Pea soup.

Take a minute to think about how you would categorize these items. Write your categories below, then think of a way to remember each of the categories:

Categories:

You probably used one of the following three ways to categorize the items:

1. Food type:

- Bakery (whole-wheat bread, pound cake)

- Canned goods (pea soup, canned cherries)

- Produce (beets, tomatoes, green beans, pineapple)

- Dairy (cheddar cheese, chocolate milk).

And, to remember the categories, you might have used a mnemonic message, such as: *Bakeries Can't Produce Dairies.*

2. Color:

- Red (beets, tomatoes, canned cherries)

- Green (pea soup, parsley)

- Yellow (cheddar cheese, fresh pineapple, pound cake)

- Brown (chocolate milk, whole-wheat bread).

To remember the colors, visualize a *green* Christmas tree with a *brown* trunk with *red* bulbs and a *yellow* star.

3. First letters:

- B: beets, beans, bread
- C: cheese, chocolate milk, cherries
- P: pound cake, pineapple, pea soup, parsley
- T: tomatoes.

Then, to remember the letter categories, you can memorize: *Burly Chefs Pound Tomatoes.*

Spatial Organization

Information presented in a table, chart, or map is easier to remember than information presented in paragraph form. Use the principles of organizing and chunking illustrated by the previous examples to ensure that the information you present to learners is easier to remember.

Step 3: Use Mnemonic Devices

The three fundamental principles underlying the use of mnemonics are:

1. Association.

2. Imagination.

3. Location.

When designing your course, incorporate these three fundamental principles to improve your learners' memorization of the content you provide.

Association

Association is the method by which you link a new piece of information to information you already have stored in memory. For example, someone introduces you to a new client, Frank Mitchell. You associate his first name with the idea that he is frank, or candid, and his last name with the name of your brother-in-law, Mitchell. This type of association is called *verbalization.*

If you are a verbalizer, you probably outline and organize information according to meaning or according to the first letters of words. For example, you may have used the first letters of grocery items to remember their names.

Another type of association is called *visualization.* If you are a visualizer, you use mental pictures to recall names, numbers, or other information. For example, you may have remembered the grocery list by forming a mental picture of a green Christmas tree with a brown trunk with red bulbs and a yellow star, which helped you recall the four colors of the items.

Although someone can suggest associations to you, your own associations are much better, as they reflect the way in which your mind works. Generally, the gaudier and more dramatic the picture, the better. Encourage your learners to develop their own associations.

Imagination

Imagination is the way in which you use your mind to create the links that have the most meaning for you. Images that others create will have less power and impact for you, because they do not reflect the way in which you think.

The more strongly you imagine and visualize a situation, the more effectively it will stick in your mind. Mnemonic imagination can be as vivid and outrageous as you like, as long as it helps you to remember what needs to be remembered.

Look at the following numbers for 60 seconds:

9121310177631788812020259

Now cover them up for 30 seconds and see how many you can recall.

```
┌──────────────────────────────────────────┐
│                                            │
│                                            │
└──────────────────────────────────────────┘
```

How did you do?

Here again is the number:

9121310177631788812020259

Try memorizing the number again. This time, see if you can improve your recall by making up a story in which you associate words or ideas with the numbers. Take no more than two minutes to write down your story.

```
┌──────────────────────────────────────────┐
│ Story:                                     │
│                                            │
│                                            │
│                                            │
│                                            │
│                                            │
│                                            │
│                                            │
│                                            │
│                                            │
│                                            │
│                                            │
│                                            │
│                                            │
│                                            │
└──────────────────────────────────────────┘
```

Now, without looking at the numbers, write down as many as you can remember.

```
┌──────────────────────────────────────────┐
│                                            │
│                                            │
└──────────────────────────────────────────┘
```

Here's an example of a story: *The nine (9) members of a baseball team went to town to buy a dozen (12) eggs. But, before they left the house, they realized that it was Friday, the 13th. They were afraid to go, even though they had learned in their Logic 101 class not to believe in superstitions. So, they waited another week (7 days) to go. When they arrived in town the following week, they heard a parade coming, with 76 trombones, and they noticed that Baskin' Robbins was having a sale on all 31 flavors. Seven of the players ate and ate ice cream. However, one of the baseball players couldn't read the names of the flavors, so he went to get his eyes checked. When the doctor told him his vision was 20-20, the other players gave him the high five (5) and all nine (9) members in the group returned home.*

We created this story by using associations for numbers. Here are some general associations:

0 nothing, love (tennis)
1 won, wan
2 too, to
3 free, fee
4 for, fore
5 thrive, nickel
6 sex, sax, sacks
7 servin', Steven, lucky
8 ate
9 nein (German for no)
10 tan, tin, dime
12 months
13 unlucky
16 sweet
19 last year of teens
20 20-20 vision
21 age of consent
24 hours in a day
25 quarter
29 hard year
30 (don't trust anyone) more than 30
31 flavors

Location

When Mark Twain went on speaking tours throughout the country, he routinely would visit the local park and spend some time organizing his thoughts for his upcoming performance. He would do this by associating each idea with a park feature. For example, he might rehearse one idea while sitting on a park bench, the next idea while leaning against a Civil War monument, and the third perched atop a bandstand. He moved through the park mentally while delivering the speech, recalling each associated idea.

This is called the *method of loci* and is the most ancient mnemonic system, dating back to about 500 B.C. Greek and Roman orators used it to remember long speeches without notes. Effective speakers still use this technique to help them recall their ideas.

Using the three fundamentals of association, imagination, and location, you can encourage your learners to form visual or verbal links that help them retain information better.

The important thing is that the mnemonic should clearly relate to the things to remember, and it should be vivid enough for them to clearly remember it whenever they think about it.

Step 4: Rehearse

A final way to help retain information is to repeat it or rehearse it. If your learners only need to remember the information for a short time, you might recommend or use *maintenance rehearsal,* also called *shallow processing.* However, if your learners need to remember the information for a long period of time, they may need a more elaborate rehearsal, or *deep processing.* Use these and other methods of rehearsal, including overlearning, the SQ3R system of rehearsal, and games, when designing your course.

Consider the case study presented in the sidebar *How to Ensure Your Learners Will Forget* opposite, in which the co-facilitators John and Mary could clearly use an understanding of the keys to learning retention.

Types of Rehearsal

An example of *maintenance rehearsal* is when someone gives you a sales figure to include in a report and all you have to do is walk to your office and write it down without ever using it again. Your best bet is to repeat that number to yourself a few times as you walk down the hall. You recite the information until you no longer needed it.

If you know that you will need to remember the sales figure in the future, use an *elaborate rehearsal.* The repeated exposure to a stimulus or the rehearsal of a piece of information transfers it into long-term memory. You form associations between the new information and information already in your long-term memory. Once you have formed these associations, you use them whenever you rehearse the sales figure. Experiments suggest that an elaborate rehearsal is most effective if you distribute it over time.

The Importance of Serial Position

Go back and look at your responses to Exercise A. Which of the numbers did you remember? Chances are, you recalled the numbers in the beginning and the numbers at the end, but had the most difficulty with those in the middle. This tendency is called the *serial position phenomenon.* Psychologists believe that the interaction between short- and long-term memory causes this phenomenon.

The greater ability to remember items in the beginning of a list is called the *primacy effect.* When an item is at the beginning of a list, you will probably rehearse it; this causes you to transfer it to long-term memory. Items located in the middle of the list enter short-term memory while this rehearsal is going on and therefore you are likely to ignore them. The tendency to remember items at the end of a list is called the *recency effect.* These items are still in short-term memory and are readily available for retrieval.

How can you use the principle of serial position in the classroom? You can make a conscious effort to review information presented in the *middle* of a learning session.

How to Ensure Learners Will Forget

John and Mary were co-facilitators for a three-day grammar review class. Because of their busy schedules, they did not do much preparation. However, they both had several years of training experience and knew that they could "wing it."

Mary started out the class by answering a question that one trainee had asked about use of commas. It was difficult for the class to hear Mary because she has a soft voice and because there was a lot of noise from the open classroom door. Although the man who had asked the questions tried to listen, most of the other trainees spent the time talking among themselves.

John then explained the definition of a noun and gave several examples. Then he asked the class to give some examples.

"Excuse me," interrupted one of the trainees. "What is the purpose of this class? My boss told me I needed to take it, but I'm not sure why."

Before John could explain to the class *why* they were there, Mary suggested that they finish the lesson on nouns and then discuss the purpose of the class. Unfortunately, John forgot, and the class objectives were never discussed.

The following day, John presented 27 rules for pronoun use.

"That's a lot of rules to remember," remarked one trainee. Is there some way for us to group the rules together?"

"Well, not really," said John, "unless you want to look at each *type* of pronoun. I realize that the rules are kind of scrambled up, but just memorize them."

The trainees looked very discouraged.

"What are we doing tomorrow?" asked one class member at the end of the second day.

"We're not sure," said John. "We'll surprise you tomorrow. Any questions about what we've done so far?"

"If I could remember what we've done, I'd know what to ask," responded one trainee.

The facilitators decided to start out the last day with verb use, which Mary presented. When she was halfway through explaining passive voice, she realized that the class did not understand either verb tense or voice. Therefore, she finished up the lesson quickly and moved on to the next topic.

"Well, that's about it," said John, at the end of the day. "Make sure you use good grammar in your job."

"I'm not sure I know how to use this in my workplace," muttered one trainee.

The following week, one of the trainees was asked by his boss what he had learned in the grammar review class.

"What grammar review class?" asked the trainee.

What would you do differently if you were the facilitator?

Classify

This game was adapted from Steve Sugar's "More Great Games," *Infoline* No. 259106.

Purpose: This game demonstrates differences among similar items or processes and creates a dynamic exercise that requires players to sort items correctly.

Time: 15 to 30 minutes.

Number of participants: 10 or more.

Supplies needed:

☐ Newsprint flipcharts and felt-tipped markers

☐ One newsprint flipchart game sheet for each team, prepared in advance by the facilitator

☐ One or more sets of 3-by-5 inch item cards for each team, prepared in advance by the facilitator

☐ Masking tape or thumbtacks

☐ A stopwatch or other timing device

Preparing for the activity:

☐ Select your topic, determine the number of categories (usually two or three), and then determine the number of items to be categorized.

☐ Determine the duration of the game by allowing one minute for every 12 to 15 item cards.

☐ Prepare one set of item cards for each team.

☐ Prepare one newsprint game sheet for each team. If creating two choices, draw a vertical line down the middle of the sheet and then write the two choices at the top of the sheet. If creating three choices, draw two vertical lines down the sheet.

☐ Place each game sheet near a conference table to serve as a team's "base of operations" during play.

☐ Distribute masking tape or thumbtacks for affixing the items onto the game sheet.

Overview of player activity:

☐ Divide the group into teams of five to ten players.

☐ Place one prepared game sheet on the wall.

☐ Place one set of item cards face down and masking tape or thumbtacks by each team's game sheet.

☐ Have each team meet at one game sheet.

☐ Tell players this is a "relay" exercise, in which each team will be given one minute to attach all their item cards to the game sheet.

☐ Allow each team to prepare its item cards to be affixed to the game sheet on the wall.

☐ Tell the first player to turn over the first item card and place it into one of the categories. Warn players that some item cards may fit more than one category. In that case, they will want to place their card on the line dividing the two categories.

☐ Once a card is turned over, it must be played. Once a card has been placed, it cannot be moved. Only after the first card is placed may the second player turn over the second card.

☐ Play will continue until the team has placed all of its cards on the game sheet or time has expired.

☐ Call time at the end of one minute.

☐ Award one point for each correctly categorized item card. For item cards that can be placed in more than one category, award a three-point bonus for any card correctly placed on the line between the two categories. The team with the most points wins.

☐ Debrief and discuss the activity, as required.

Overlearning

What about continued repetition after you have learned something? If you memorize a speech and can recite it without a mistake, you may decide to stop working on it because further repetition would be inefficient. This is not true. *Overlearning*—continued learning beyond the point of mastery—strengthens learning and improves retrieval speed.

The SQ3R System of Rehearsal

The most effective method of rehearsal, which was developed in the late 1930s and early 1940s, is called the *SQ3R:* Survey, Question, Read, Review, Recite. Have your learners follow these steps:

■ *Survey*
Get an overview of the material. Quickly read the table of contents, headings, and any summaries.

■ *Question*
Skim the material again and ask yourself questions based on the headings.

■ *Read*
Read the material and take notes. Answer the questions you have asked. If you wish, underline carefully after you have read, marking only the most important points.

■ *Recite*
State or repeat the main ideas. Spend about half your time reciting, spending more time on meaningless, disconnected ideas.

■ *Review*
Survey the material again, reviewing what you could recite and noting what you could not. Question yourself again. The best times to recite are during study, immediately after studying, and before you must use the material (for speech, interview, exam, for example).

Other Rehearsal Techniques

Well-known training experts Harold Stolovitch and Erica Keeps suggest the following rehearsal techniques and give examples of their application. Ask learners to do the following:

- Repeat the words or steps. Give them a rhyme or a beat. Rap it.

- Read or listen to content. Take notes. Convert each point to a question. Keep on asking the questions until you get them all right (can be done in teams).

- Make up test questions (or have learners make up test questions) for a body of material. Test until perfect.

- Create notetaking guides. These can be lists with keywords that require explanations or elaborations, unlabeled diagrams or matrixes, or flow diagrams with empty boxes. Learners fill in as content is provided then compare with models. Study. Repeat until perfect.

Games

You also can help learners review material and maintain attention with games and other creative activities. An example of a game is presented in the sidebar *Classify* opposite; other games include, for example:

■ *Jeopardy*
Like the television show, you present answers, solutions, or output (good and bad) and the players must respond with the appropriate question. You could develop flash cards for this activity.

■ *Concentration*
Place a term or picture on one card and a definition on another. Shuffle the cards and place them face down. Players take turns turning over two cards. If they turn up a matching pair, they collect the cards and take another turn.

■ *Quiz Game*
Each participant develops a specific question and writes it anonymously on a card. The question should cover an important point. Collect the questions, shuffle them, and pass them out. Learners read and answer the questions on the cards they receive. This can be an open- or closed-book exercise, and you should debrief participants to ensure that all major points were covered.

Reinforcement

Suppose you were throwing darts blindfolded and had no idea how close you were coming to the target. How long would you stay interested in this activity? How much improvement do you think you would make? Taking off the blindfold would not only help maintain your interest but also gives you information about how you were doing so you could stay interested in the task.

Feedback helps maintain motivation and also increases learning retention. Positive feedback is especially effective. When you reward successful responses during practice sessions, participants gain confidence, feel more positive toward the content, and remember more. Creating a relaxed, positive atmosphere for learning leads to increased motivation and retention.

Distributed Rehearsal

Suppose you must give a presentation and you know you will need to spend two hours preparing for it. Would you be better off rehearsing the presentation for two hours the night before, or practicing for a four half-hour sessions spaced out over two or three days before the presentation?

Research shows that spaced reviews are more effective than continuous reviews.

1. You can concentrate for only so long before your attention wanders. You may not be able to maintain your attention for the entire two hours.

2. Consciously or unconsciously, you review the material in your mind between rehearsals.

3. Each time you approach a new rehearsal session, you have some information saved or retained from the last session. In the second session, you *overlearn* the information retained from the first session.

Some psychologists believe that you must retrieve information occasionally or it you will forget it, as if through a process of atrophy. Therefore, periodic rehearsal—every few months or years—will help you retain the information.

Step 5: Transfer Information to Workplace

The focus so far has been on the importance of retention—storage of knowledge and skills in long-term memory so that learners can retrieve the information when needed. As trainers, you need to ensure that learners can effectively and continually apply the knowledge and skills on the job. This application is referred to as *transfer.*

Types of Transfer

Some types of training are more easily transferred than others. For example, suppose you are teaching a group of computer technicians how to use diagnostic software. Both the computers and the software are identical to what they will use on the job. In this case, you and the manager easily can assess whether the training improves the workers' performance on the job. This is referred to as *near transfer.* The only problem with this training is that it is so specific that if a trainee's job changes, the training may not apply.

Far transfer occurs when the trainee learns theoretical principles, general information, or soft skills—so-called *declarative knowledge.* An example is when you teach team building to a group of employees from various departments in an organization, or even from different organizations. Because the backgrounds of the individuals are different, you must teach general principles and soft skills. The trainees need to apply the training in different contexts from the training environment. The benefit is that the trainees will gain flexibility. They can learn to be effective members of teams in many different situations and settings.

Ability, Prior Knowledge, and Motivation

Ability, prior knowledge, and motivation are three critical ingredients for learning. Brief descriptions of these factors follow, as well as tips for adapting to these differences.

Ability

As trainers, you need to recognize that differences exist in people's capacity to learn. Some learn quickly, while others have greater difficulties. This difference in general learning ability is both genetically endowed, as are height and musculature, and developed as a result of varying methods of fostering throughout a person's lifetime.

Although you can't change people's abilities, you can observe their differences and adapt your training by:

- adjusting the amount of time for learning

- providing more practice for those who require it

- simplifying and breaking learning into smaller chunks for those who are experiencing learning difficulties

- providing additional support for those who need it

- including activities with greater challenge for those who learn more quickly.

Prior Knowledge

The more background knowledge a person has, the easier it is for that person to learn more about the subject. Consider an example of giving someone directions to a train station. If the person trying to get to the train station is familiar with the city and knows the names of nearby roads and landmarks, he or she will be able to understand where the train station is in relation to that background knowledge. However, if the person is from out of town, much more background information in terms of street names and landmark descriptions will be required.

To adapt to differences in prerequisite knowledge and skills, you can:

- create prelearning session materials to close the gaps

- build supplementary learning events prior to or concurrent with the learning sessions

- create peer tutoring pairs and teams to provide mutual support for overcoming gaps

- provide overviews and summaries of prerequisite content in outline or summary form

- direct learners to online sites that can fill knowledge or skill gaps.

Motivation

Three major factors influence motivation: value, confidence, and mood. The first is obvious: The higher the value attributed to what is to be learned, the greater the motivation to learn about it. Similarly, people's confidence with respect to their ability to learn affects their motivation. Confidence levels that are low or too high are demotivating. Finally, a positive mood enhances motivation.

Based on these three factors, you can overcome deficiencies in motivation by doing the following things:

- Enhance the value of what is to be learned. Show the learners what's in it for them. Provide examples of benefits. Show them admired role models valuing what is to be learned.

- Adjust the learners' confidence levels with respect to the learning content. Be supportive to build their confidence that they can learn but provide sufficient challenge so that they don't become overconfident.

- Create a positive learning atmosphere and work climate. The more open and optimistic the context you build, the more open and positive the learners will be, which leads to greater motivation...and to learning.

Adapted from Telling Ain't Training *by Harold D. Stolovitch and Erica J. Keeps*

Cooperation in Transfer Maintenance System

Regardless of the type of training, the trainer, trainees, and manager all need to be involved in setting up a transfer maintenance system. The *trainer* must make sure that the design and delivery of training address the need to improve performance and meet organizational goals. The *trainee* must be willing to learn and use the new skills and knowledge in the workplace. And the *manager* must make sure that the people and systems in the organization are willing to support a trainee in applying these new skills and knowledge.

Activities to Ensure Transfer of Training

Effective transfer comes from good training. The training techniques discussed in this *Infoline,* including mnemonics, chunking, and rehearsal, all help enhance learning transfer. The sidebar *Ability, Prior Knowledge, and Motivation* on the previous page discusses three critical factors for learning transfer. In addition to these, training expert Paul Garavaglia offers the following tips to trainers for promoting transfer of training:

- Know your audience. Make sure trainees have the prerequisite skills and knowledge for training.

- Give advance notice. Transfer increases when trainees have time before class to study the concepts they will learn.

- Use examples and analogies. Numerous examples in different contexts help reinforce and broaden trainees' understanding. Analogies show how students can apply the general principles in different contexts.

- Create identical elements. Increase the number of cues common to both the learning situation and the job setting.

- Leave the classroom. Vary the settings for training.

- Use computer simulations. These give trainees hands-on practice and help them apply general principles to real-life situations.

- Use problem-centered training. Transfer increases when trainees produce real outcomes. This brings the job into the classroom.

- Make training fit. Make sure the training fits the organization's culture.

- Use job aids. These can include everything from performance support systems to posters that remind workers about their new skills or behaviors. The best job aids help workers track their progress.

- Follow up. Trainers can ask workers to describe how they used their new skills and how well they completed their action plans.

Measuring Transfer

Measuring transfer of training helps justify training programs. It also helps training designers overhaul their programs and helps the organization find performance shortfalls. Trainers typically wait about six months after training ends to take the first measurements, then follow up at six-month or 12-month intervals. The measurement can be done by the HRD staff, the trainers, the trainees, the line manager, an external contractor, or—best of all—by a combination of these. Some common techniques used are managers' reports; surveys of trainees, managers, or trainees' peers; trainee action plans; interviews with trainees, managers, or trainees' peers; and observation of trainees on the job.

Events of Learning: Three Examples

The chart below shows how to apply each event to three categories of learning: intellectual skills, motor skills, and attitudes.

Events	Categories of Instruction		
	Intellectual Skills	Motor Skills	Attitudes
Topic	**Using the Government Purchase Card**	**Carrying a loaded tray (waitpersons)**	**Preventing and managing sexual harassment**
1. Gaining attention (reception).	Hold up a huge cardboard model of the Government Purchase Card.	Using plastic dishes, show in a humorous way how not to carry a tray (and drop it).	Show a short video in which employees harass co-workers.
2. Informing learners of the objective (expectancy).	Explain the purposes of learning how to use the Government Purchase Card: convenience, avoidance of misuse, and so on.	Demonstrate the correct way to carry a tray, providing tips to trainees.	Describe the reasons for preventing and managing sexual harassment.
3. Stimulating recall of prior learning (retrieval).	Review with trainees the guidelines for using a commercial ("regular") credit card.	Ask trainees to review the steps leading up to the loading and carrying of the tray.	Ask trainees to describe situations in which they have experienced or witnessed sexual harassment.
4. Presenting the stimulus (selective perception).	Explain how to use the Purchase Card, contrasting it with commercial credit cards.	Describe in detail and demonstrate how to load and carry the tray.	Define sexual harassment. Give examples and describe how each situation should be handled and how it could have been prevented.
5. Providing learning guidance (semantic encoding).	Give examples of situations when the Purchase Card should and should not be used.	Display diagram showing waitress holding loaded tray correctly.	Give trainees a chart showing the steps to take in reporting sexual harassment.
6. Eliciting performance (responding).	Give trainees a list of items and services to be purchased and the prices. Ask trainees when the card could be used.	Ask each trainee to practice loading and carrying a tray.	Divide class into groups. Ask each group to read a different case and make recommendations.
7. Providing feedback (reinforcement).	Ask the trainees to provide feedback on classmates' responses to the exercise. Add to or revise feedback as needed.	Critique each trainee.	Ask each group to present its case study and recommendations. Ask for feedback from the class. Add to or revise feedback as needed.
8. Assessing performance (retrieval).	Give multiple-choice test on use of the Purchase Card. Correct in class.	Test each trainee on loading and carrying a tray.	Give a test on the definition of sexual harassment and how to prevent and manage it.
9. Enhancing retention and transfer (generalization).	Give learners some unusual problems or situations for use of Purchase Card. Ask how they would handle them.	Demonstrate how to carry drinks or plates correctly without trays.	Give examples of how procedures for handling sexual harassment may vary from one workplace to another (for example, in schools vs. offices).

Applying the Five Steps

In summary, nine events activate processes needed for effective learning. These nine events correspond to the processes of human memory and the keys to learning retention discussed in this *Infoline*.

1. Gain attention (stimuli activates receptors).

2. Inform learners of the objective (creates level of expectancy for learning).

3. Stimulate recall of prior learning (retrieval to short-term memory).

4. Present the stimulus (emphasizes features for selective perception).

5. Provide learning guidance—through examples, case studies, graphics, mnemonics, and analogies (semantic encoding for long-term memory).

6. Elicit performance—requiring learner to practice (activates response to enhance encoding).

7. Provide feedback (provides reinforcement of correct performance).

8. Assess performance (activates retrieval and reinforcement of correct performance).

9. Enhance retention and transfer (provides cues for retrieval and application of learned skill to new situations).

The sidebar *Events of Learning: Three Examples* on the previous page provides examples of how these events could play out in various classroom settings. If your training includes these nine events, you will be well on your way to ensuring that your learners learn.

References & Resources

Articles

Atkinson, R. C., and R. M. Shiffrin. "Human Memory: A Proposed System and Its Control Processes." *The Journal of Educational Psychology,* vol. 2. K. W. Spence & J. T. Spence, eds.

Laker, D. R. "Dual Dimensionality of Training Transfer." *Human Resource Development Quarterly,* Fall 1990, pp. 202-209.

Nutting, Robert. "20 Teaching Tips to Make Your Training Lessons Stick." *HRfocus,* October 2000, p. 13.

Ullius, Diane. "ART: Acronyms Reinforce Training." *Training & Development,* February 1997, pp. 9-10.

Werner, John, et al. "Augmenting Behavior-Modeling Training: Testing the Effects of Pre- and Post-Training Interventions." *Human Resource Development Quarterly,* Summer 1994, pp. 169-183.

Books

Anderson, J. R. *Learning and Memory: An Integrated Approach.* New York: John Wiley & Sons, 1994.

Driscoll, M. P. *Psychology of Learning for Instruction.* Boston: Allyn & Bacon, 1994.

Gagné, R. M. *The Conditions of Learning and Theory of Instruction.* New York: Holt, Rinehart, and Winston, 1977.

Gagné, Robert M., and Marcy P. Driscoll. *Essentials of Learning for Instruction.* 2nd edition. Englewood Cliffs, NJ: Prentice-Hall, 1988.

Gagné, R. M., and K. L. Medsker. *The Conditions of Learning.* New York: Harcourt Brace, 1996.

Higbee, K. L. Your Memory: *How It Works and How to Improve It.* New York: Marlowe & Co., 1996.

Hilton, H. *The Executive Memory Guide.* New York: Simon and Schuster, 1986.

Pinker, Steven. *How the Mind Works.* New York: W.W. Norton & Co., 1999.

Rupp, Rebecca. *Committed to Memory: How We Remember.* New York: Crown Publications, 1998.

Stolovitch, Harold D., and Erica J. Keeps. *Telling Ain't Training.* Alexandria, VA: ASTD, 2002.

Infolines

Butruille, Susan G., ed. "Lesson Design and Development." No. 258906 (revised 1999).

Elengold, Linda J. "Teach SMEs to Design Training." No. 250106.

Garavaglia, Paul L. "Transfer of Training." No. 259512 (revised 2000).

Meyer, Kathy. "How to Train Managers to Train." No. 259003 (revised 1997).

O'Neill, Mary. "Do's and Don'ts for New Trainers." No. 259608 (revised 1998).

Russell, Susan. "Training and Learning Styles." No. 258804 (revised 1998).

Sharpe, Cat, ed. "Course Design and Development." No. 258905 (revised 1997).

———. "10 Great Games and How to Use Them." No. 258411 (revised 1999).

———. "How to Create a Good Learning Environment." No. 258506 (revised 1997).

———. "Teaching SMEs to Train." No. 259911.

Sugar, Steve. "More Great Games." No. 259106 (revised 2000).

Sullivan, Rick, and Jerry L. Wircenski. "Effective Classroom Training Techniques." No. 250108.

Job Aid

Using the Nine Events of Instruction

Think about the training you will lead. In the chart below, describe how you will apply each event of instruction.

Events	Application of This Event
1. Gain attention (reception).	
2. Inform learners of the objective (expectancy).	
3. Stimulate recall of prior learning (retrieval).	
4. Present the stimulus (selective perception).	
5. Provide guidance (semantic encoding).	
6. Elicit performance (responding).	
7. Provide feedback (reinforcement).	
8. Assess performance (retrieval).	
9. Enhance retention and transfer (generalization).	

The material appearing on this page is not covered by copyright and may be reproduced at will.

Essentials for Evaluation

Issue 9705

Essentials for Evaluation

AUTHOR

Alice K. Waagen, PhD
Workforce Learning
1557 Hiddenbrook Drive
Herndon, VA 20170-2817
Tel: 703.834.7580
Email: WorkLearn@aol.com

Alice Waagen has more than 18 years of experience in designing and implementing corporate training. She has developed full systems of training measurement and evaluation, including cost of training, training volume and activity, training customer satisfaction, and ROI. She holds MS and PhD degrees in education.

Essentials for Evaluation 251

    Benefits of Evaluation 251

Evaluation of Training 252

    Participant Reaction Surveys 252

    What Have Participants Learned? 253

    On-the-Job Behavior Evaluation 255

    Evaluation of Organizational Results 257

    Testing Methods 259

    Evaluation Tips 260

    Follow-Up Evaluations 261

    Essential Corporate Partners 263

References & Resources 264

Job Aid

    Evaluation Guide 266

Editor
Cat Sharpe

Associate Editor
Patrick McHugh

Designer
Steven M. Blackwood

Copy Editor
Kay Larson

ASTD Internal Consultant
Dr. Walter Gray

Essentials for Evaluation

We all know the lingo: reengineering, downsizing, rightsizing, competition, globalization—the list seems endless. What all the "ations" and "isms" represent is the accelerated climate of change in corporate organizations today. Faced with maturing markets and global competition, corporate leadership has become extremely critical in its analysis of existing business processes and procedures.

One aspect of this introspection is the desire to eliminate waste and redundancy. Corporate overhead—or those support functions not directly responsible for generating revenue—has come under great scrutiny. The support functions that have survived this scrutiny best are those that, early on, learned how to operate like independent businesses themselves—providing optimal customer service while emphasizing value for the dollars spent.

Leading-edge training and development organizations, whether internal staff or contractors providing services to many corporations, know that the success of their businesses depends on demonstrating the value of training investment. The simplest way to prove training's value to a client is to document that the training has achieved its desired outcome.

Herein lies the fundamental secret to evaluating training: The evaluation process and procedure must be incorporated at the start; it must be an integral part of any program development process. If program development follows the classic steps of assessing needs and generating objectives, the evaluation criteria that follow are then based on measuring how well the program components—students, instructors, and materials—have met these objectives and answered the needs.

For more information on needs analysis and objectives refer to the following *Infoline*s: No. 258502, "Be a Better Needs Analyst"; No. 259808, "Task Analysis"; No. 258505, "Write Better Behavioral Objectives"; No. 259611, "Conducting a Mini Needs Assessment"; No. 259401, "Needs Assessment by Focus Group"; No. 259712, "Instructional Objectives"; and No. 259713, "The Role of the Performance Needs Analyst."

A broad range of methods and tools is available for every evaluation approach. Options include direct observation, comparisons of tests taken before and after training, interviews, reports, follow-up testing, questionnaires, and surveys. The most effective approach includes combinations of the aforementioned methods. Depending on your objectives, the nature of the training, and focus of the evaluation, some methods are more appropriate than others. For example, the best choice for measuring machine repair skills is direct observation, the worst evaluation tool is a survey.

This chapter outlines the basics of training program evaluation. Different methods of evaluation will be discussed and matched to assorted training program designs. You will learn the advantages and disadvantages of the various types of evaluation. And finally, the emphasis on reporting results to management will be discussed, as well as keeping the evaluation process *client focused* and closely tied to business results.

Benefits of Evaluation

Evaluation methods help determine whether training achieves its objectives. Programs that are structured and designed properly have objectives or elements that specify what the training must accomplish and in what time period these accomplishments must be realized.

A sound system of evaluating training provides valuable information for the client, training management, and senior corporate management. The information elicited from training evaluations should be the final instrument upon which training decisions such as program additions, changes, or deletions should be made. Good evaluations document results of training programs, which subsequently can be used to prioritize training needs at the corporate level. Then, financial and other resources can be shifted from training that has less impact on corporate goals to those objectives that have the most favorable cost-benefit ratio.

Some specific benefits of evaluation are:

- a tool to assess the value of courses, seminars, and workshops

- built-in quality control of training programs that documents whether or not course objectives have been met

- a method for identifying programs that need improvement

- a basis upon which decisions to continue or eliminate a program can be made

- a way to identify the proper audience for future programs

- a method for managing training programs

- a mechanism to review and reinforce essential program points

- a way to get top management and participants to buy in to the program.

When structured to elicit open-ended comments, training evaluations can serve two purposes: first, as a demonstrator of present-day benefits, and second, as an indicator of future training program needs.

Finally, summary or "macro" evaluation information can be proffered to senior management or key clients on a regular basis. This educates them as to the value of the training enterprise. Good evaluation reports should also document, in both statistical and qualitative terms, how training has helped the organization meet its goals.

Evaluation of Training

There are a number of ways to evaluate training and each method is designed to elicit different information. These various methodologies are often described as "levels" of information, from the simplest that obtain and quantify (reaction surveys), to the more complex and detailed (corporate results).

There are several levels of program evaluation criteria based on participants' reactions: what they've learned, their skills performance, their on-the-job behavior, and the effects and results the training has had on the entire organization.

The main evaluation methods will be discussed in terms of their strengths and weaknesses. Rather than thinking of these methods as a hierarchy from least valuable to most valuable, think of them all as useful tools in your training tool kit. If your client is most interested in seeing reaction data, this is a perfectly acceptable and useful form of evaluation; it should not be passed over for something more complex.

Following is a breakdown of how each level can be applied to help you develop a systematic approach to evaluating what your programs have accomplished.

Participant Reaction Surveys

Participant reaction surveys or "smile sheets" are questionnaires that are typically distributed at the end of each training program. They ask students to rate their perceptions about the quality and impact of the specific program. These questionnaires can range from a simple handful of questions regarding program design, instruction methods, and facilities to elaborate multipage forms for students to rate all facets of the program and provide input on future programs. This evaluation tool can serve as a valuable measure of attendee satisfaction and is relatively easy to administer, tabulate, and summarize in a results report.

Guidelines for Designing Reaction Surveys

Reaction surveys can provide quantifiable customer service data, giving you direct information from your program consumers. When designed with uniform overall questions, these surveys produce data that can be used to make comparisons between courses and participants. This allows program design decisions to be based on a broad range of perceptions, not just the responses of a few disappointed or disgruntled participants.

Reaction surveys provide the following results:

● Protection against making decisions based on a limited number of either satisfied or disappointed participants.

● Clues for improving programs, but no indication of how the training will affect job performance or organizational results.

Steps for Evaluating Reactions

The best instruments for reaction evaluations focus on points that are most important to the evaluator. They are straightforward and simple to fill out.

Evaluate reactions by using the following steps:

1. Determine what you want to know. Concentrate on specific areas such as methods, facilities, materials, and so on.

2. Design a comment sheet for tabulating and quantifying reactions. Experts suggest using a form designed for the particular program rather than a standardized or generic form.

3. Include sufficient space for questions and comments that cannot be quantified or tabulated.

4. Do not require participants to sign their evaluation forms. If participants are forced to identify themselves, they may feel obligated to be overly positive.

5. Keep the form simple and make sure it takes only a short time to complete. If you are interested in reactions, design sheets focusing on program content, not administration, for example.

6. Use a final comment sheet to gather additional or follow-up information. If you have already collected two or more previous evaluations, use a final one to clarify and complete information.

7. Establish standards of performance by converting reactions to numerical ratings. An example of this is a scale with numbers representing grades of quality: 1 = poor, 2 = adequate, 3 = good, 4 = very good, 5 = excellent.

What Have Participants Learned?

A number of different tools can be designed to measure what participants have learned in the training program. Paper and pencil tests, administered before and after training, can be used to measure acquisition of knowledge and information. Skills can be evaluated concurrently with the training through simulations or in-class activities, which allow students to demonstrate instructed skills. Regardless of the assessment method used, all of these tests must be designed to relate directly to the course objectives.

Participant learning evaluations are difficult and more time consuming to develop and administer, but they are essential if the nature of the training requires that the learning be demonstrated and documented. Learning assessments are most commonly used in training programs that lead to licensing, certification, or involve skills that contain elements of risk. Computerized simulators, used for airplane pilot and locomotive engineer training, are examples of learning assessment tools. One reason learning evaluations are difficult to design is that they must be customized for every instructional program and *must* reflect the conditions of the specific job.

It is important to remember that learning evaluations accurately measure the amount of knowledge and skills acquired *at the time the test is administered*. In no way do these tests indicate long-term knowledge or skill retention, nor are they an indicator of how knowledge and skills are applied to the job. They simply serve as a snapshot in time denoting that students have mastered the course objectives at the time the instruction was offered.

Components of Learning Evaluations

Effective tests must be thoroughly and thoughtfully designed. Most course developers will design questions as they author the course rather than wait until they are done. All evaluation instruments must be "dry run" on subject experts as well as sample student audiences. Be especially watchful for unclear or ambiguous wording in questions and instructions.

Paper and pencil tests and performance tests are the standard methods for measuring knowledge and skills. The first type measures knowledge, the second measures skills. The material in these tests relates directly to program objectives and the specific knowledge and skills learners work to acquire during training.

Evaluation tests may be based on standardized tests, but the ones that yield the best results are custom written for each specific program.

Designing Paper and Pencil Evaluations

You may want to use the following suggestions for designing and administering effective tests:

Increase your research resources by drafting sample questions before and during program development. Use these questions to make sure you have touched on all program areas; delete the ones pertaining to areas you could not cover during the session.

Plan thoroughly. Tests must be planned out in complete detail. Pay close attention to every part of the test including the schedule, timing breaks, review of instructions, administration, and scoring.

Give participants the opportunity to show what they have learned. Tests should be representative of the training, allowing learners to demonstrate their new knowledge. Relevant tests are more meaningful to learners and yield more valid results to instructors.

Use objective questions such as multiple-choice and true or false instead of open-ended essays.

Present only one correct answer. More than one right answer confuses test-takers, makes scoring more difficult, and reduces the validity of the test.

Never present misleading information. Trick questions invariably result in wrong answers, and are a waste of time for you and your learners. If trainees will be faced with difficult on-the-job decisions, represent these situations with challenging but fair questions.

Write questions for easy comprehension. Remember, your objective is to test participants' knowledge of the training material, not their reading skills.

Write questions to reveal how well the participants understand the material, not how well they can memorize it.

Use a random arrangement of answers to keep test-takers from guessing the pattern of correct responses (two false, three true).

Use multiple-choice items that do not allude to answers of subsequent questions. A block of answers that are tied together seriously affects a participant's score if he or she incorrectly answers the first question. Again, this kind of situation can affect the results and validity of your test.

Vary the level of difficulty throughout the test. Use a mixture of challenging, relatively difficult, and comparatively easy questions.

Try not to cue or signal the correct answer by varying the size of fill-in spaces or by letting one multiple-choice item stand out from the rest of the list as the only reasonable possibility.

Make the mechanics of test-taking simple. Remember, your objective is to measure participants' knowledge, not their ability to follow complex test instructions.

Review the test before you administer it. Is it valid? Does it meet the objectives of both the program and the evaluation process? Ask training colleagues to review the test and make suggestions for improving it.

Provide thorough and consistent directions. All learners must receive identical, clear, and concise instructions. Poor instructions can influence the outcome of the evaluation. When administering tests, be sure to provide whatever information is necessary such as blueprints, tables, charts, diagrams, reference books, and so on. If possible, the instructor should use a beta test to present samples of how trainees are expected to answer evaluation questions.

Use procedures for objective evaluations. Determine standards in advance and prepare learners so they will understand the requirements for satisfactory test performance.

Evaluating Skills Performance

Follow these suggestions to evaluate how well new skills have been learned:

- Design performance tests to objectively measure skills in quantifiable terms.

- Ensure that tests cover key requirements of the skills performance specified during training.

- Present the test to participants by clearly and simply explaining instructions, tabulation methods, and performance standards. Tell trainees precisely what they are expected to accomplish.

- Concentrate on improving participants' job performance rather than giving them more training material or information.

- Be sure evaluations reflect how the training has changed skill levels. To do so, carefully prepare and design evaluations. Research your procedures during program pilots and use "control" as well as "experimental" groups to gather data.

- Consult with design experts and other resource people to check the validity and value of your design methodology.

If the test is to be used to qualify a person for a specific job, use outside expertise to evaluate the test for validity and fairness. If test scores can be used to deny employment or promotion opportunities, they must be demonstrably sound or you will open your employer to discrimination charges. If you do not have the expertise yourself or in your staff to validate tests, seek validation from an industrial psychologist or other professional possessing this expertise.

A final note on testing: Be cautious of managers who ask for test results on individual students. Some managers may want to use learning evaluation scores as grounds for discipline, termination, or even promotion. Remember, these tests document a snapshot view of knowledge and skill acquisition. By no means do they accurately reflect on a person's job performance. Using test results as performance indicators can be misleading and even illegal. When in doubt, consult with your human resource or legal department.

On-the-Job Behavior Evaluation

The ultimate goal of any training program is to improve job performance. Often, training clients want to know more than "has the student acquired new knowledge and skills by the end of the program?" They also want to know if the student can apply the knowledge and skills on the job. Behavior evaluations are designed to measure changes in on-the-job behavior and document improved performance directly related to training.

Job performance evaluations measure whether or not the trainee can accomplish program objectives. These evaluations must be based on the actual task or job performance. This can be documented by observing on-the-job behavior; managers, peers, or subordinates can serve as observers, plus offer oral and written reports regarding performance changes.

If available, performance data can also be gathered and analyzed. For instance, most manufacturing facilities have detailed records of work units produced by employees. In the "soft skills" training programs, action plans can be developed based on observable results. Again, co-workers can be used to record the presence of these observable behaviors.

Evaluation Checklist

Training evaluations can make the difference between a company's losses and gains. Accurate methods and tools for measuring training outcomes can mean significant improvement in organizational performance—increased productivity and savings, decreased costs and personnel problems. To get valuable data from an evaluation, plan your approach by thinking through the following checklist:

☐ What questions do you want to answer? How did participants feel about the training? What did they learn? How did the training affect their attitudes and behavior? What were the organizational results?

☐ How will you measure the items addressed in your questions? Will you administer paper and pencil tests, questionnaires, or surveys? Will you require participants to demonstrate their new knowledge and skills in a role play or simulation?

☐ What are the objectives of your training program? Are your evaluation criteria based on these objectives?

☐ Do the criteria indicate improvement between expected and actual performance when measured against the results of your needs analysis?

☐ What data sources are already available to help you measure results (productivity reports, sales and revenue analyses, and so on)?

☐ Are there alternative methods for gathering this data such as interviews and on-site observations?

☐ What are the best and most cost-effective methods for measuring the results of training? Can you think of less costly, more efficient ways of administering the evaluation?

Components of Behavior Evaluations

The key to developing effective behavior change evaluations is to have clear, observable objectives. These objectives must be based on a systematic appraisal of on-the-job performance as well as interviews with employees and management about requisite levels of the task's performance. Essentially, the difference between current performance and desired performance should correlate to the content of the training.

Methods for gathering this kind of information include:

● on-site observations of performance by trained observers (supervisors, co-workers, or professional observers)

● analyses of individual performance records

● observable results of action plans developed during training to improve specific performance areas

● comments from managers, employees, or subordinates, describing behavior changes of their supervisors, co-workers, or support staff.

Steps for Data Collection

To determine the effectiveness of a program in behavioral terms, follow these steps and be sure measurements are objective and quantifiable:

1. Make a systematic appraisal of on-the-job performance both before and after the training.

2. Collect comments and performance appraisals from trainees, superiors, subordinates, and co-workers.

3. Compare pre- and posttraining performances and how they relate to the program's instruction.

4. Conduct posttraining evaluations at least three months after program completion to allow trainees sufficient time to practice and test their new skills and knowledge. Additional appraisals will add to the validity of your evaluation.

5. Use control groups that do not receive training to compare against those that do receive training. This helps you measure the effectiveness of your program and its impact on job performance.

One note of caution: In addition to skills or knowledge, behavior change is based on many factors. Training programs can be successful in knowledge and skill transfer yet not result in changed behavior on the job. Participants may choose not to change their behavior due to various reasons: lack of management support for the new behavior, lack of sufficient rewards to motivate change, or perhaps the workplace itself may not be conducive to change.

Because the cause-and-effect relationship between training and behavior change is complex, one should elicit more than just performance observations to have an accurate evaluation system. Posttraining interviews with employees can be used to discover why there has been a behavior change or resistance to change. If there has been no change, ask employees why they have not used the new skill or knowledge on the job. Keep this information confidential. The answers may reveal significant environmental barriers to the change. Until these barriers are identified and eliminated, performance measures will fail to produce positive results. Once the barriers are removed, training can more effectively produce the desired performance objectives.

Evaluation of Organizational Results

Evaluating organizational results measures and documents the effects of training interventions as they relate to the achievement of corporate goals and objectives. Essentially, this documents the overall "macro" result of training programs and is frequently sought when senior managers ask the question: "What real difference does training make? If we stopped training tomorrow, what effect would I see on my bottom line?"

Trainers who need to document their program's impact on the corporation should first look at the corporation's annual goals and strategic direction. They also need to examine any measures that are currently used at divisional or departmental levels to support these goals. Some of these metrics might include the following: new or existing reports and records covering profits and production, quality, sales, customer service, costs, waste, defects and efforts, efficiency, employee absenteeism, turnover, and so on.

After determining corporate objectives, trainers can relate the evaluation of results to organizational gains and improvements. The benefits of training can include:

- increased productivity
- increased savings
- better quality
- decreased absenteeism
- fewer errors, grievances, and safety problems.

To analyze the effects of the training program on the organization, practitioners compare pre- and posttraining data. Results evaluation measures the fiscal or financial impact of a program and is much more difficult than the simple reaction measurement, but possesses the highest value for an organization.

There is an inherent difficulty when measuring training in terms of results. This is because training is only one of many variables that affect organizational performance. In addition, because many corporate performance metrics are developed irrespective of the training, they can measure factors that may not directly relate to employee performance. These include things such as stock prices or equipment efficiency. Trainers must be cautious when stating that training affects a measure not directly linked to the objectives of the program. For this reason, many organizations opt only for reaction, learning, and behavior evaluations.

Choosing the Right Format for Questions

Selecting the right kind of questions for your particular program evaluation is essential for obtaining good results. Tests may consist of one or all of the following types of questions:

Multiple-choice. This format provides a selection of possible responses; the trainee is told to choose the most accurate one.

Open-ended. These tests offer unlimited responses. Learners write lengthy answers in blank spaces following each question. For example: "An angry customer arrives at your office complaining about your delivery service. How would you calm the customer down and resolve the situation?"

Checklist. This type of test presents the learner with a situation and a list of items which may or may not apply. The trainee must choose those items most applicable to the given situation. For example:

"Match the proofreader's symbols to their proper use."
  a. paragraph
  b. insert comma
  c. let it stand
  d. capital letter
  e. lower case letter

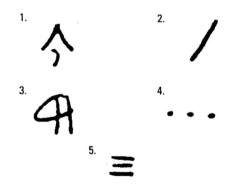

Two-way. This format poses alternate answers. Learners choose *yes* or *no* or else *true* or *false* responses. For example:

"Adult learners are mainly interested in highly job-relevant training."
  a. True
  b. False

Rating scale. This type of test asks learners to rank lists of items according to particular scale.

Guidelines for Measuring Results

Evaluations measuring the impact of training on the organization require hard data—new or existing reports and records covering profits and production, quality, sales, customer service, costs, waste, defects and efforts, efficiency, employee absenteeism and turnover, and so on.

Use the following guidelines to assist you when gathering evaluation material:

1. Gather accurate data from results evaluations; isolate the effects of the program in order to evaluate them objectively.

2. Be aware of external factors that are not related to training. Some of these include:

   • changes in procedures, processes, and new technology

   • the job experience and maturity of trainees

   • the trainee recruitment method; volunteer participation usually results in more positive performance than mandatory attendance.

3. Ensure validity by using the following methods:

   Control groups. These are employees who have not received training. Check organizational gains, such as increased productivity and decreased errors, against a performance comparison of trained and untrained employees. Note differences in on-the-job behavior and whether they are related to training or other factors.

   Sampling. This is a representative selection of the entire trainee population. Choose a sample that represents different backgrounds and levels of experience.

4. Analyze evaluation data carefully before making connections between training and organizational achievements. Review the data to make sure it is consistent and accurate. Scan reports and studies for excessive and unrealistic values and eliminate incorrect or incomplete items.

5. Never exclude relevant data. Valid, though often negative, information that does not support the desired outcome must be included with the positive data.

6. Keep your statistical and data analyses as simple as possible. Limit your methods and interpretations to a particular focus for drawing accurate conclusions.

7. Focus on bottom-line results directly related to organizational goals. Increased production or sales, for example, are frequently essential objectives for many companies. Calculate changes by comparing totals before and after the training program.

8. Determine the benefits of reducing time in production, processing, and construction. The valuable and visible result is improved service, or a decrease in the amount of time it takes to deliver products and services to customers.

9. Calculate the value of improved quality by comparing pre- and posttraining reports on the numbers of mistakes and necessary corrections, client dissatisfaction, and product liability.

Be sure to evaluate results in quantifiable and accountable terms. For example, assign a dollar value to cost savings, remembering to adjust costs experienced over time because they are likely to increase beyond the value of actual savings. Assign dollar values to the time saved by employees trained to perform their jobs faster and more efficiently. To calculate time savings, multiply the labor costs per hour by the amount of hours saved.

A final note on results evaluation: Many training managers have concluded in recent years that there is "no return-on-investment (ROI) when measuring the ROI of training." Results measurement is by far the most difficult, complex, and costly evaluation methodology. Be cautious of building elaborate systems of measurement and reporting unless your clients and management have specifically requested them.

If management requests that you demonstrate training's impact on corporate goals, research thoroughly the resources you will need, in staffing, computer power, statistical and analytical support, and so on. Prepare a cost analysis of the results evaluation project and present it to management before you begin.

Testing Methods

Comparisons of pre- and posttest scores are very good indicators of program effectiveness. Higher test scores show that the program has improved and strengthened trainees' skills, knowledge, and abilities. Following are types of tests used in human resource departments:

■ *Norm-Referenced*
Rather than rate learners according to program objectives, these tests compare individuals or groups to the norm, the average trainee performance. This kind of test identifies the best and weakest performers, the class rank of each person, the median score for the group, and the percentile standing of each participant. Norm-referenced tests are most useful in a program with a large learner population where score average and individual ranking are significant.

■ *Criterion-Referenced*
These are objective tests that require specific and precise responses based on program objectives. Criterion-referenced tests (CRTs) have predetermined cut-off scores and measure according to precisely defined program objectives. Rather than analyze how learners rank among one another, the CRT focuses on assessing, analyzing, and reporting what learners have achieved based on the combination of performance standards and program objectives. For example, the criteria for a typing test would follow from a program objective such as: "At the end of training, learner will be able to type 60 words per minute with no more than two errors." If the learner successfully meets this standard and accomplishes the objectives, he or she will have mastered the typing skills as specified in the training program.

■ *Performance or Simulations*

These tests permit the learner to physically demonstrate skills or the uses of knowledge in a program. Some types of skills exhibited may include analytical, manual, interpersonal, verbal, or any combination of the aforementioned. Most often, practitioners use performance tests to demonstrate activities in specific job-related training; for example, "Demonstrate the correct procedures for coding an HTML document for a Web page."

Supervisory and management training involves performance testing as role plays and skill practice exercises. Learners may be asked to demonstrate problem-solving or communications skills by acting out scenarios with each other.

Evaluation Tips

1. The basic steps for evaluation can be used in any kind of organization. The techniques and procedures have broad application, but never try to overlay evaluation results from one department or organization onto another department or organization.

2. Always give your participants enough time to complete evaluation forms in class. Experts agree that "take-home" forms usually stay at home. If you save only the last few minutes of the session for evaluations, the forms will show tell-tale signs of the time crunch—hurried and incomplete responses. Before the wrap-up segment of the program, put aside some time to review the program and answer questions about the evaluation forms.

3. To get a comprehensive picture of your program, try to ask the same number of questions about strengths and weaknesses. A "mixed review" can be more accurate and helpful than overly positive or negative responses.

4. Share responses with the group. Express your interest in their opinions and ideas by preparing a summary of the written evaluations and discussing the issues that seem most important. This gives individuals a sense of how others responded as well as how their own reactions compare with the group's response.

5. Conduct evaluations more than once during the training no matter how long or short the program. An eight-hour workshop can be evaluated at midpoint and improved for the remaining half. If you evaluate only at the end, you will not be able to share comments, use suggestions, or follow up for additional information.

6. When it is not feasible to stop and evaluate the program at different points, use a method of ongoing evaluation. Instead of evaluating only at the end of the program (during long programs it can be difficult to remember important details), hand out evaluation forms at the beginning and instruct learners when and how to fill them out. Give them a few minutes after each topic to evaluate the material, presentation, and presenter.

7. Review your evaluation methodology with your human resources and legal professionals to ensure that your tests are valid and nondiscriminatory. This is especially important if the test results are used to qualify a person for hiring, promotion, or to serve in a specific job. An invalid or discriminatory test can create a legal risk for the corporation. Also, determine with your legal partners how long test results must be stored for future reference.

8. Legal departments also use training attendance and completion records to demonstrate "due diligence" effort of corporations in sexual harassment or Equal Employment Opportunity (EEO) types of litigation. If a corporation can demonstrate that it takes an active role training its employees on appropriate behavior in the workplace, the organization can shift responsibility for subsequent misbehavior from the corporation to the individual. Partner with your legal staff to determine how training results need to be documented.

9. Keep all employee test results confidential and secured. Misuse of this information, especially low or failing scores, can be devastating to the employee and to the credibility of your entire training effort. Again, seek legal counsel as to the length of retention for this type of information and destroy it once obsolete. Keep all paper records locked and secured; password protect all electronic files.

Follow-Up Evaluations

After the last program evaluation, conduct a related follow-up evaluation that involves feedback questionnaires, interviews, and observations.

Use follow-up evaluations to:

- measure lasting results of training

- identify areas where learners show the greatest and the least improvement

- compare follow-up and end-of-program evaluation responses.

Guidelines for Follow-Up Evaluations

To find out the degree of improvement since the program, measure the success of the training according to participants' on-the-job accomplishments and how they are using the training to improve performance.

- Make sure learners are prepared for the follow-up. At the end of the program, announce your intention to conduct a follow-up evaluation and explain what kind of information you need. Providing this type of explanation will increase your response rates.

- Explain that the follow-up is mandatory, not optional; the evaluation is crucial in determining the effect and value of the program.

- Pose questions that are the same or similar to those that appeared on the end-of-program evaluation forms.

- Find out if the training worked.

- Share follow-up data with all managers and supervisors.

- The kinds of questions you ask will give you a reliable basis for accurate data comparison and analysis. For example, if learners were asked to estimate their increase in productivity resulting from the training, follow up by asking about their actual rate of increase.

- Encourage participants to identify reasons why they have or have not improved and what factors obstructed their progress. Isolating the negative effects can be as useful as identifying the positive ones.

- It is vitally important to share follow-up evaluations with participants' managers or supervisors. These individuals need to know the program results and follow-up information and should also be involved with the participants' practice and application of the training.

- As a final effort, assign follow-up activities when and if appropriate. For example, if a learner needs clarification in some aspect of the training, practitioners can instruct them to complete a task or achieve a goal related to the program's content. This helps learners to better evaluate the program.

Reporting Results to Management

At a minimum, training evaluation data should be reported to the training manager and on up to the senior level. At each level, the data should be increasingly summarized and extracted. No manager wants to wade through tomes of data, so reports should be condensed to provide the most relevant information for each level.

The fundamental question to ask in reporting any data is, "What business decision will the reader make after reading this information?" To answer this question, you need to determine the decision-making authority and span of control belonging to the reader. If the manager cannot use the report to assist in his or her decisions, it is "nice to know" information and will probably end up discarded and unread.

Evaluation Methods

Paper and Pencil Test. This method measures how well trainees learn program content. An instructor administers paper and pencil tests in class to measure participants' progress.

Attitude Surveys. These question-and-answer surveys determine what changes in attitude have occurred as a result of training. Practitioners use these surveys to gather information about employees' perceptions, work habits, motivation, value beliefs, working relations, and so on. Attitude surveys also reveal respondees' opinions about their jobs, the workplace, co-workers, supervisors, policies, procedures, and the organization. If you conduct a program to change attitudes, before and after surveys can assess improvement.

Simulation and On-Site Observation. Instructors' or managers' observations of on-the-job performance in a work simulation indicate whether a learner's skills have improved as a result of the training.

Productivity Reports. Hard production data such as sales reports and manufacturing totals can help managers and instructors determine *actual* performance improvement on the job.

Posttraining Surveys. Progress and proficiency assessments by both managers and participants indicate perceived performance improvement on the job.

Needs/Objectives/Content Comparison. Training managers, participants, and supervisors compare needs analysis results with course objectives and content to determine whether the program was relevant to participants' needs. Relevancy ratings at the end of the program also contribute to the comparison.

Evaluation Forms. Participants' responses on end-of-program evaluation forms indicate what they liked and disliked about the training.

Professional Opinion. Instructional designers critique and assess the quality of the program design.

Instructor Evaluation. Professional trainers administer assessment sheets and evaluation forms to measure the instructor's competence, effectiveness, and instructional skills.

Cost Analysis. The training manager compares costs of instructor's fees, materials, facilities, travel, training time, and the number of trainees to determine the hourly cost of training for each participant.

Consider using these suggestions for including management in the evaluation process:

- Involve line managers in developing evaluation objectives and determining criteria.

- Explain the process to managers and use their input to develop data collection methods and techniques that focus on the criteria and indicate the effects of training.

- Include managers in identifying significant results. They also can help determine the best ways to report results.

- Reach agreement on a reporting method—written, formal presentation, or informal discussion.

- Decide who should receive the reports (participants, administrators, department managers, supervisors), as well as the best times for distributing or presenting the reports.

Essential Corporate Partners

To the new trainer, developing good training evaluations can be a daunting task. But there are many skilled professionals within a corporation who can help you with this task. In return, you can make them special clients of training, offering them your training counsel and expertise. Actively seek out partners in the following departments:

■ *Information Systems Specialists*
These are the computer hardware and software gurus who can help you automate all your record-keeping and reporting. And no, there is no one miracle computer program out there that will do it all. Once you get into the intricacy of data collection and retrieval, you will need expert help in setting up programs to manage it.

■ *Human Resources*
Talk regularly with your corporation's recruiters. Ask them what positions are difficult or costly to fill. Then talk to the organizational development (OD) staffing experts about the possibility of retraining existing staff for these positions. OD, leadership, and executive development professionals can also provide you with keen insight about organizational difficulties that might be addressed through training.

Inquire from the compensation staff whether there are any requirements for training in the performance review process. If so, this will affect your training volume shortly before review time. The words trainers hate to hear are: "My performance review is next week and I have to take Course XYZ before then. Why aren't you offering it?"

Likewise, talk frequently with the employee relations and EEO people. They hear a lot of the negative stories about management and employee behavior; sometimes training can raise awareness and alleviate some of these problems.

■ *Legal*
Partner with the legal department to obtain help regarding the legal side of testing, surveying, record retention, and reporting.

■ *Finance/Accounting*
Somewhere in every finance department are people with expertise on statistics and modeling. They also are well versed on reporting complex statistical information in ways that are easy for management to comprehend. Get their advice to fine-tune your data reporting.

Financial experts can also provide you with models that determine the cost of training. Many corporations use standard algorithms to compute average employee salary costs. You need to use the same calculation for your reports.

■ *Employee and Corporate Communications*
These people not only have vehicles (email lists and newsletters) to reach all employees, they are often the consummate wordsmiths. They can help you with the appearance and readability of your reports.

This is but a small sampling of the corporate staff that can help you with training evaluation and reporting. Network frequently with these people, and they will help ease your reporting burden.

References & Resources

Articles

Barron, Tom. "Is There an ROI in ROI?" *Technical & Skills Training,* January 1997, pp. 21-26.

Benabou, Charles. "Assessing the Impact of Training Programs on the Bottom Line." *National Productivity Review,* Summer 1996, pp. 91-99.

Bernthal, Paul R. "Evaluation That Goes the Distance." *Training & Development,* September 1995, pp. 41-45.

Birnbrauer, Herman. "Improving Evaluation Forms to Produce Better Course Design." *Performance & Instruction,* January 1996, pp. 14-17.

Blickstein, Steve. "Does Training Pay Off?" *Across the Board,* June 1996, pp. 16-20.

Bushnell, David S. "Input, Process, Output: A Model for Evaluating Training." *Training & Development Journal,* March 1990, pp. 41-43.

Dixon, Nancy M. "New Routes to Evaluation." *Training & Development,* May 1996, pp. 82-85.

Dust, Bob. "Understanding Financial Terminology." *Training & Development,* May 1996, pp. 99-100.

Geber, Beverly. "Prove It! (Does Your Training Make a Difference?)" *Training,* March 1995, pp. 27-34.

Jedrziewski, David R. "Putting Methods to the Madness of Evaluating Training Effectiveness." *Performance & Instruction,* January 1995, pp. 23-31.

Lapp, H.J. "Rate Your Testing Program." *Performance & Instruction,* September 1995, pp. 36-38.

Lewis, Theodore. "A Model for Thinking About the Evaluation of Training." *Performance Improvement Quarterly,* vol. 9, no. 1 (1996), pp. 3-22.

McLinden, Daniel J. "Proof, Evidence, and Complexity: Understanding the Impact of Training and Development." *Performance Improvement Quarterly,* vol. 8, no. 3 (1995), pp. 3-18.

Phillips, Jack J. "How Much Is the Training Worth?" *Training & Development,* April 1996, pp. 20-24.

———. "ROI: The Search for Best Practices." *Training & Development,* February 1996, pp. 42-47.

———. "Was It the Training?" *Training & Development,* March 1996, pp. 28-32.

Pulley, Mary Lynn. "Navigating the Evaluation Rapids." *Training & Development,* September 1994, pp. 19-24.

Shelton, Sandra, and George Alliger. "Who's Afraid of Level 4 Evaluation?" *Training & Development,* June 1993, pp. 43-46.

Smith, Jack E., and Sharon Merchant. "Using Competency Exams for Evaluating Training." *Training & Development Journal,* August 1990, pp. 65-71.

Williams, Leigh Ann. "Measurement Made Simple." *Training & Development,* July 1996, pp. 43-45.

Willyerd, Karie A. "Balancing Your Evaluation Act." *Training,* March 1997, pp. 52-58.

Books

ASTD. *The Best of the Evaluation of Training.* Alexandria, VA: ASTD, 1991.

———. *The Best of the Return on Training Investment.* Alexandria, VA: ASTD, 1991.

Basarab, David J., and Darrel K. Root. *The Training Evaluation Process: A Practical Approach to Evaluating Corporate Training Programs.* Norwell, MA: Kluwer Academic, 1992.

Bassi, Laurie J., et al. *The ASTD Training Data Book.* Alexandria, VA: ASTD, 1996.

Dixon, Nancy M. *Evaluation: A Tool for Improving HRD Quality.* Alexandria, VA: ASTD, 1991.

Fisk, Catherine N., ed. *ASTD Trainer's Toolkit: Evaluation Instruments.* Alexandria, VA: ASTD, 1991.

Head, Glenn E. *Training Cost Analysis: The How-To Guide for Trainers and Managers.* Alexandria, VA: ASTD, 1994.

Kirkpatrick, Donald L. *Evaluating Training Programs: The Four Levels.* San Francisco: Berrett-Kohler, 1994.

References & Resources

Medsker, Karen L., and Donald G. Roberts, eds. *ASTD Trainer's Toolkit: Evaluating the Results of Training.* Alexandria, VA: ASTD, 1992.

Phillips, Jack J. *Handbook of Training Evaluation and Measurement Methods.* Houston: Gulf Publishing, 1997.

Rae, Leslie. *How to Measure Training Effectiveness.* Brookfield, VT: Gower Publishing, 1991.

Robinson, Dana G., and James C. Robinson. *Training for Impact.* San Francisco: Jossey-Bass, 1989.

Infolines

Austin, Mary. "Needs Assessment by Focus Group." No. 259401 (revised 1998).

Cheney, Scott. "Benchmarking." No. 259801.

Gupta, Kavita. "Conducting a Mini Needs Assessment." No. 259611 (revised 1999).

Hacker, Deborah Grafinger. "Testing for Learning Outcomes." No. 258907 (revised 1998).

Kirrane, Diane. "The Role of the Performance Needs Analyst." No. 259713.

Long, Lori. "Surveys From Start to Finish." No. 258612 (revised 1998).

Plattner, Francis. "Instructional Objectives." No. 259712.

Robinson, Dana Gaines, and James C. Robinson. "Measuring Affective and Behavioral Change." No. 259110 (revised 1997).

Sharpe, Cat, ed. "Be A Better Needs Analyst." No. 258502 (revised 1998).

———. "Write Better Behavioral Objectives." No. 258505 (revised 1998).

Waagen, Alice K. "Task Analysis." No. 259808.

Internet Sites

ASTD:
http://www.astd.org

Evaluation and Training Institute (ETI):
http://www.otan.dni.us/webfarm/eti/

Job Aid

Evaluation Guide

I. Client Needs

A. State the objectives of the program.

B. Describe evaluation criteria based on these objectives.

II. Participant Reaction

A. How will participants' reactions during and after the program be measured? State what methods will be used: questionnaires, surveys, interviews, observations.

B. Describe what measurement standards will be used. Examples of these are relevance ("Was the program relevant to your specific job needs?") and ease of learning ("Were you able to complete the activities and exercises with relative ease, or were they too difficult?").

C. List specific issues to be addressed. Some examples include program design, class size and arrangement, and the value of program's content.

D. How will the information be collected and tabulated?

E. State and describe back-up sources for information. These may include participants' remarks to the trainer, and their questions concerning program exercises and content.

III. Performance Skills and On-the-Job Behavior

A. List the methods for evaluating learning during and at the end of the training. Examples include tests, questionnaires, and company documents.

B. Describe the measurement standards. Use these questions to help establish standards. How much of the material do the participants understand? How well do they understand it and apply it?

C. List specific program areas that will be questioned. Focus on program structure, presentation, activities, and examples.

D. How will the information be collected and tabulated?

E. List and describe back-up sources. Look at the amount of time the training program required and note whether all or some of the content was covered. Check trainee performance on exercises, during demonstrations, and on the job. (Are trainees using the new skills and information successfully?)

IV. Organizational Results

A. How did the training affect the organization. Did it have a positive impact on organizational performance?

B. Using annual reports, corporate, strategic, and annual plans, list the organization's goals or objectives against which you will measure the training's impact.

C. Describe the measurement standards that will be used to evaluate organizational results.

D. How will the information be collected and tabulated?

E. List back-up data sources. Some of these may be interviews and discussions with management, personnel, and clients.

F. Include observations of procedures and processes.

Managing Evaluation Shortcuts

Issue 0111

Managing Evaluation Shortcuts

AUTHORS

Patricia Pulliam Phillips
The Chelsea Group
P.O. Box 380637
Birmingham, AL 35238
Tel: 205.678.9700
Fax: 205.678.8070
Email:
TheChelseaGroup@aol.com

Patricia Pulliam Philips is chairman and CEO of The Chelsea Group, a consulting company focusing on accountability and performance improvement issues. Certified in ROI evaluation, Patricia assists clients around the world in ROI implementation.

Holly Burkett, MA
Apple Computer
2911 Laguna Boulevard, MS B-11
Elk Grove, CA 95758
Tel: 916.394.5019
Fax: 916.394.5504
Email: burkett@apple.com

Holly Burkett, is a certified ROI professional and a senior training consultant at Apple Computer. She manages cost-effective evaluation of diverse operation initiatives.

Managing Editor
Stephanie Sussan
ssussan@astd.org

Production Design
Kathleen Schaner

The Bottom Line................................269
    Item 1: Plan Early 270
    Item 2: Integrate Evaluation into Training 271
    Item 3: Share the Responsibilities 272
    Item 4: Involve Participants 274
    Item 5: Use Shortcut Methods 274
    Item 6: Use Data Samples 275
    Item 7: Use Estimates 276
    Item 8: Use Internal Resources 278
    Item 9: Streamline Reporting Process 279
    Item 10: Use Technology 281

References & Resources.........................282

Job Aid
    Case Study: Just-in-Time Gap Analysis 283

The Bottom Line

The world economy is unpredictable, and every department in every company feels vulnerable. Companies are increasingly tightening their budget belts, and now it is more important than ever to prove the value of your training programs. Without some bottom-line information, training and development programs may fall to the budget ax. Evaluations prove the value of training and provide a means to align programs with corporate goals for improved individual and organizational performance.

Even if your organization has not asked for this information, now is the time to begin gathering and formatting the data. A proactive, comprehensive evaluation takes time to implement and perfect. The end result is worth the effort.

An in-depth evaluation often requires a generous amount of resources. Given the growing pressures for proving bottom-line value in just-in-time environments, human resource development (HRD) professionals must develop rapid response strategies for streamlining evaluation efforts. For a one-person training department or a department with limited time and resources, using shortcut methods for major steps in the evaluation provides a means for conducting an effective evaluation.

With careful planning, and with the use of proven shortcuts, a cost-effective, credible evaluation analysis can be implemented by training departments of all sizes and budgets. This chapter will explain in detail a 10-point system for managing evaluation shortcuts. This system has been proven to significantly decrease resource requirements while still providing sound, credible data. The 10 points are:

1. Plan for evaluation early in the process.

2. Integrate evaluation into the training process.

3. Share the responsibilities for evaluation.

4. Require participants to conduct major steps.

5. Use shortcut methods for major steps.

6. Use data samples to select the most appropriate programs for evaluation analysis.

7. Use estimates for isolating the program's effects and converting data to monetary value.

8. Have internal resources implement the evaluation process.

9. Streamline reporting.

10. Use technology.

Evaluation Timing

In addition to adopting the 10-point system, you must determine when is the best time in the process to conduct your particular evaluation. There are five commonly accepted types of evaluation. (See the sidebar *Evaluation Levels* on the next page for more information.) The type of evaluation determines when the evaluation is conducted. For example, Level 1 evaluations are conducted immediately following a program. Level 2 evaluations take place when the knowledge and skills are being applied. Once the Level 4 measures have been determined, the data is converted to monetary value and compared with the fully loaded costs to calculate the Level 5 measure, return-on-investment (ROI). Regardless of the type of evaluation, planning should begin early in the process.

Evaluation Levels

More than 40 years ago, Donald Kirkpatrick developed the four levels of evaluation that have become the framework for training practitioners. More recently, to meet the demand of expenditures and accountability, Jack Phillips added the fifth level, ROI. An explanation of the five levels of evaluation follows.

Level 1: Reaction and Planned Action. This measures the participants' immediate response and satisfaction. Participants usually identify the program's strengths and weaknesses with a generic end-of-program questionnaire.

Level 2: Learning. This measures the transfer of knowledge or skills. A variety of methods are available to assess learning gains, including self-assessments, facilitator assessments, simulations, case studies, and exercises.

Level 3: Application. This determines the extent to which the training accomplishes its performance objectives. A Level 3 evaluation takes time, adds costs, and can be disruptive. However, these evaluations can be conducted in many ways. The challenge is to select the method that best fits your culture, budget, and time constraints.

Level 4: Business Impact. This measures how training affects the bottom line in such areas as increased revenues, improved quality, reduced response times, or enhanced efficiency.

Level 5: ROI. ROI compares the monetary benefits with the program's costs.

Item 1: Plan Early

One of the most critical cost-saving steps to evaluation is to develop clear program objectives and plan early for the evaluation. Preliminary planning includes:

- clarifying evaluation purposes
- developing program objectives
- determining evaluation timing.

Evaluations succeed because of proper planning; the best way to conserve time and resources is to know what you are doing and where you are going.

What Is the Purpose of Your Evaluation?

Although an evaluation usually is undertaken to improve program implementation and success, there are several distinct purposes. The purpose often determines the scope of the evaluation, the type of data collected, and the analysis. For example, when an ROI calculation is planned, one of the purposes is to compare the costs and benefits of the program. This purpose has implications for the type of data collected, the data collection method, the detail of analysis, and the communication medium for results. For most projects, multiple evaluation purposes are pursued. Some of the key purposes include:

- to determine whether a solution is accomplishing its objectives

- to identify strengths and weaknesses

- to determine the cost-benefit ratio of a solution

- to decide who should participate in future initiatives

- to identify who benefited the most or the least from the solution

- to reinforce major points made to the target population

- to gather data to assist in marketing future initiatives.

Data Collection

By planning early for data collection, there is clear direction as to what type of data will be collected, how it will be collected, when it will be collected, and who will collect it. Ideally, the data-collection plan should be completed prior to the launch of a new training program, immediately after the preliminary information is gathered and the program's evaluation targets are selected.

Analysis

Another critical step in the planning process is planning the actual analysis. For example, planning the ROI analysis provides guidelines for isolating the effects of the program, converting business impact measures to monetary value, identifying intangible benefits, and considering other issues that may influence program success.

The Trainer's Role

The role of the training and development staff in planning the evaluation is to:

- communicate best practices in a results-based evaluation process

- provide a framework for evaluation

- assist in developing evaluation targets for each level of evaluation

- serve as technical assistant in developing instruments for data collection, analysis, and reporting

- provide evaluation guidelines, policies, and procedures for the entire organization

- ensure that evaluation processes are linked to other business processes.

For actions trainers should take, see the *Actions and Outcomes* sidebar to the right.

Actions and Outcomes

Listed below are several steps trainers should to take to ensure successful evaluations. The actions will result in the outcomes listed to the right of the action.

Action	Outcome
• communication about evaluation strategy, purpose, policies, and procedures	• education and increased awareness
• assign and share responsibilities for training evaluation efforts	• demonstrated commitment
• develop internal skills in training measurement and evaluation	• enhanced individual and organizational capabilities
• implement specific impact studies and establish guidelines for reporting and aligning results.	• training and development function linked as strategic business partner.

Item 2: Integrate Evaluation into Training

There is a saying: "Everything is connected to everything." By connecting the needs assessment to evaluation, the evaluation automatically becomes a part of, instead of apart from, the overall training process.

While a comprehensive needs analysis typically consists of numerous steps, a condensed, shorter version can be conducted by compressing common steps. Needs assessments traditionally focus on three levels of analysis:

1. Organizational needs.

2. Job needs.

3. Individual needs.

Program objectives are derived from the needs assessment process. For example, the specific business needs uncovered during the needs assessment will drive the impact objectives and identify the business impact. The job needs assessment will uncover gaps in tasks, job performance, and processes and procedures. These gaps will determine specific application objectives for the program. The skills, knowledge, and attitude deficiencies will determine specific learning gaps, which will appear as learning objectives in the program. Finally, preferences for learning in terms of type of program, location, specific instructor, media, timing, delivery, and content will drive satisfaction objectives.

With a clear linkage of needs and objectives, cost and time can be saved when conducting an ROI evaluation. The training process has built-in evaluation components, and programs are developed with job performance and business impact in mind.

Once you have integrated evaluation as an integral part of training, evaluation becomes a common component, thus saving time and money. As part of the integration, you need to establish policies, procedures, and guidelines. Policies and procedures provide guidance and direction for those who work closely with the evaluation process. They keep the process focused and enable the group to establish goals for evaluation. Policies and procedures also provide an opportunity to communicate basic requirements and fundamental issues regarding performance and accountability. Guidelines show how to use the tools and techniques, provide consistency, ensure that proper methods are used, and place proper emphasis on each area. They often include specific forms, instruments, and tools.

The policy statement contains information developed specifically for the measurement and evaluation process, with the input of the training staff and key managers or clients. Critical issues are addressed that will influence the effectiveness of the evaluation process.

Item 3: Share the Responsibilities

Defining the specific responsibilities for all of the stakeholders is critical to successful streamlining of the evaluation process. Many individuals should play a role. These include:

- performance consultants
- instructional designers and developers
- facilitators
- participants
- participants' managers
- internal subject matter experts.

There are many evaluation responsibilities. First, you need to ensure that the needs assessment includes specific business impact measures. For example, if you are running a training session on how to generate sales, you want to evaluate the various effects of boosted sales. While profits may increase, you should consider whether you have enough manpower to handle additional work or if any other changes are necessary to implement this successfully.

You also need to develop specific application objectives. Using the above example, an objective could read: Following this training seminar, employees will have increased knowledge of sales philosophy. Each sales manager should be able to increase their client list by 25 percent.

Focus the content of the program on performance improvement, ensuring that exercises, case studies, and skill practices relate to the desired objectives.

The sidebar, *Share Responsibilities*, on the next page illustrates a case study model for including participants, managers, and the training and development staff in the evaluation process. The *before, during, after* matrix in the sidebar shows how specific responsibilities were assigned to promote shared accountability and ownership before, during, and after the delivery of an actual continuous improvement training initiative. This approach also helps promote development and evaluation planning as a process, as opposed to an isolated event.

Share Responsibilities

Following is a matrix for how to spread out the responsibilities for evaluation. Everyone from participants to managers should be involved in the process.

	Before	During	After
Managers	• Participate in assessing training needs. • Establish performance standards. • Co-facilitate meetings and briefings to demonstrate support. • Require attendance at scheduled briefings. • Approve training time for target audience. • Approve control group for pilot offering. • Participate in establishing evaluation plan.	• Demonstrate commitment and support for training initiative by attending training sessions. • Co-facilitate meetings and briefings to demonstrate support. • Communicate the importance and relevance of training objectives to operation and organizational goals. • Discuss action plan.	• Participate in reviewing evaluation plan. • Reinforce follow-up and application of action plans. • Recognize individuals for successful completions of competentcy qualifications. • Support training in continuous improvement efforts with curriculum design, delivery. • Provide incentives. • Co-facilitate 30-day follow-up session. • Assist with final reporting and communication of results.
Supervisors	• Participate in needs assessment focus groups. • Attend briefing sessions. • Reinforce trainee participation.	• Remove barriers to trainees' attendance. • Attend sessions as available. • Ask trainees about training progress.	• Reinforce follow-up and application of action plans. • Assist in removing barriers. • Monitor performance.
Training and HRD	• Conduct needs assessment. • Develop job/task analysis. • Establish learning, performance, and impact objectives. • Design curriculum to meet desired objectives. • Incorporate benchmarked transfer strategies into course design. • Prepare training materials and job aids. • Deliver briefings. • Design evaluation plan. • Perform training administration duties.	• Communicate the importance and relevance of training objectives. • Assess trainees for reaction, learning, and skill/knowledge transfer. • Facilitate pre- and post-assessment process. • Introduce an action plan. • Facilitate skill building to support trainees' successful completion of the qualification. • Deliver training. • Discuss the action plan.	• Implement evaluation plan. • Conduct competency qualification and action planning sessions with individual trainees. • Enter qualifications in database. • Facilitate 30-day follow-up session and impact questionnaire. • Report results. • Work with management to continuously improve quality of training service and product.
Trainees	• Help establish incentives. • Participate in needs assessment focus groups. • Assist training in job analysis.	• Complete pre- and post-assessment. • Attend full program. • Demonstrate active participation in skill practices.	• Demonstrate proficiency with learned skill sets by completing qualification with 100 percent accuracy. • Apply training on the job. • Implement an action plan. • Identify barriers to application. • Complete 30-day impact questionnaire.

Item 4: Involve Participants

Another cost-saving approach to evaluation includes having participants conduct major steps in the evaluation process. Participants are the primary source of understanding the degree to which learning is applied. So, when collecting data for evaluations, participants are a logical source. This is especially useful when the evaluation is being conducted on a limited budget, because participants do not require payment.

Participants always should provide feedback as to their reaction and planned actions following a program (Level 1). The reaction data is good feedback for facilitators, and planned actions data provides information regarding the participants' intent to apply the learning received from the program. (While ROI data can be derived using the Level 1 feedback, it is not the most accurate estimate and often is unreliable.)

If the evaluation must stop due to resource constraints, such as a budget shortfall or time constraint, this approach provides valuable insight into the program and is better than the basic data from a typical end-of-course questionnaire. The data forms a basis for comparison of different presentations of the same program. Participants of the first presentation of the program may have more confidence in the planned application of the program material than participants in a second presentation of the same program.

Side note: Collecting this type of data causes increased attention to program outcomes. Participants leave the program with an understanding that specific behavior change is expected, which produces results for the organization.

Participants are the most reliable source that can provide learning data. Pre- and post-tests are the normal methods to collect Level 2 data. While there are other methods, such as role plays and performance monitoring, the easiest, most cost-effective way to collect data on learning is through these tests.

Participants also are a good source for Level 3 and Level 4 data, especially when conserving resources. If the budget and timeframe allow, participants are the most logical source to gather more comprehensive post-program data through questionnaires, surveys, interviews, focus groups, and follow-up sessions. By going to the participants only, you save time and money.

Item 5: Use Shortcut Methods

One area where shortcuts are feasible is in the needs assessment stage. A traditional needs assessment answers what your project needs. While it does not necessarily provide the means to the end, a needs assessment outlines your goals. If a comprehensive needs assessment for the evaluation has not been conducted or is not feasible, anticipate the needs and routinely examine existing documents. Proactively anticipate the demands of emerging trends, changing technologies, and new skill and knowledge requirements rather than waiting for customer requests to initiate performance improvement programs to address those needs.

Data Collection

If practitioners continuously collect formal and informal data from key sources during the course of normal business, when a need arises, existing baseline data is confirmed or extended instead of being generated anew. Examples of existing data sources include:

- goal or mission statements
- marketing plans
- budgets
- production volume, run rates, cycle times
- benchmarking studies
- process diagrams
- performance records, exit interviews
- organizational metrics
- quality reports.

An additional way to save time during a needs assessment is to make assumptions about gaps and check them out with reliable sources. For example, use existing data to hypothesize about perceived or identified needs, and possible solutions, and then convene a focus group of subject matter experts to critique your assumptions. The job aid at the end of the chapter, *Just-in-Time Gap Analysis,* depicts an analysis tool used to facilitate this process. Targeted questions to these reliable sources should include:

- Which part of the assumption is agreeable to you?

- Which part of the assumption may be faulty?

- What are some other assumptions we can make about this issue?

- What other information is needed to tell a better story or give a bigger picture?

- What are the driving and restraining forces with the proposed solution?

- Can the gaps be closed by redesigning a training process rather than creating a new training solution?

- Have we covered all bases?

During this continual process, it is important to

- know your sources
- continually observe work patterns
- know how to analyze root causes
- use your internal experts to explain data.

This approach also can be used to check out assumptions or interpretations in the data analysis step of ROI calculations. The more you use the right measurements and resources, the more expedient, more credible, and less expensive the ROI calculation process will be.

Provide Just-in-Time Solutions

Many just-in-time solutions enhance internal capability with evaluation knowledge and skill sets. These include:

- online needs assessment, self-assessments, surveys, and evaluations

- internal listservs to exchange information about training needs, business issues, and evaluation trends

- ongoing, periodic briefings

- train-the-trainer sessions

- online discussion groups

- published testimonials in newsletters, emails, and on Web pages.

Remember to integrate just-in-time solutions with existing systems and to caution against an over-reliance on a "quick fix" mentality. Most complex performance efforts involve systemic solutions implemented consistently over time. While just-in-time solutions are a practical way to shave time and provide direction, they are most effective when provided in the context of an established client relationship based on trust and support. In other words, short-term techniques are no substitute for long-term business partnerships, which ultimately drive the evaluation purpose, scope, and process.

Item 6: Use Data Samples

Not all programs require comprehensive evaluation. In determining which programs are appropriate for analysis, several issues should be considered.

■ *Determine the Available Resources*
A comprehensive evaluation process should only involve 3 percent to 5 percent of the total training budget. By conducting a thorough front-end analysis that complements the evaluation process, this funding can be found within the existing budget.

■ *Establish Criteria for Selecting Training*

Developing specific criteria by which to compare programs for evaluation will help conserve resources. Programs that generally call for a comprehensive evaluation:

- target a large audience
- have high visibility within an organization
- link to the organization's strategic objectives
- have a long life cycle
- are expensive.

The process of comparing programs based on these criteria is quite simple. Refer to the *Selecting Programs* sidebar on the next page, which provides a sample matrix listing specific selection criteria.

■ *Select Programs and Review with Managers*

Following the program selection process, consult with the managers or advisers to get concurrence. This step is critical in that their understanding of the overall evaluation strategy will pave the way and remove any initial barriers to implementation.

■ *Use Samplings to Evaluate Programs*

After determining the programs to be evaluated, evaluate one or two classes from a given program. For instance, if one leadership development course is being targeted for all managers with 10 separate delivery dates and times, there is no need to conduct a comprehensive evaluation all 10 times. All available resources would be consumed with the evaluation of that one program. Pick one class, preferably the first class, to conduct the comprehensive evaluation. Make adjustments to the program based on that evaluation, then use shortcut methods to gather similar data from participants in the remaining offerings.

When you take advantage of these cost-saving approaches, more evaluations can be conducted, thereby providing greater evidence of the impact of the training and development function.

Item 7: Use Estimates

Estimating for ROI cuts the costs of data collection, program isolation, and data conversion. Estimates use an approximate measure of bottom-line figures rather than specific figures. Estimating can reduce the credibility of the results if it is not properly handled. Credibility is influenced by the following factors:

Reputation of the data source. The actual source of the data is a major credibility issue. The most reliable sources of information are the participants and their managers. Participants are most aware of the degree to which skills learned through training are actually applied on the job and influence key performance measures. Because managers work closely with budgets, they can provide meaningful estimates for both the costs incurred for workers to participate and the estimates of the benefits received.

Reputation of the source of the study. Readers will scrutinize the reputation of the individual, group, or organization presenting the data.

Motives of the evaluators. Readers will examine the report for any hidden agendas that may be involved.

Study methodology. Readers will want to know how the study was conducted. Explain the estimation process to enhance the credibility of the data. If a clear, methodical approach is taken, the estimates have more credibility.

Analysis assumptions. Readers will look for an outline of any assumptions made in the study.

Realistic outcomes. Unrealistic outcomes may cause the entire process to be questioned and, possibly, rejected. Exclude any statistical outliers — values that are either very high or very low—that can skew the data. If a conservative approach is taken, ROI results will be more acceptable.

Selecting Programs

The process used to compare programs is simple. Following is a sample listing of specific criteria. Each program should be based on these criteria. The programs with the highest numbers are those that should be evaluated with ROI. Rate 1, 2, 3, 4, or 5 in each block below for each program you are considering evaluating.

Programs

Criteria	#1	#2	#3	#4	#5
1. Life Cycle					
2. Company Objectives					
3. Costs					
4. Audience Size					
5. Visibility					
6. Management Interest					
Total					

Rating Scale

1. Life Cycle	5 = Long life cycle 1 = Very short life cycle
2. Company Objectives	5 = Closely related to company objectives 1 = Not directly related to company objectives
3. Costs	5 = Very expensive 1 = Very inexpensive
4. Audience Size	5 = Very large audience 1 = Very small audience
5. Visibility	5 = High visibility 1 = Low visibility
6. Management Interest	5 = High level of interest in evaluation 1 = Low level of interest in evaluation

Using Estimates

Follow these guidelines when using estimates to isolate the effects of training:

- Describe the task and the process.

- Explain why the information is needed and how it will be used.

- Discuss the link between each factor and the specific output measure with employees.

- Provide employees with any additional information needed to estimate the contribution of each factor.

- Ask employees to identify any other factors that may contribute to a performance increase.

- Obtain an estimate of the contribution of each factor. The total must equal 100 percent.

Types of data. Hard data—information related to output quantity, cost, and time—is easily understood and closely related to organizational performance. Soft data, however, often is viewed with suspicion.

Scope of analysis. Limiting the study to a small group or series of groups makes the process more accurate. Conduct impact studies with one or more groups of participants, instead of all the participants. This will help manage the data-collection process and help eliminate unrealistic data.

Estimating often is used in the isolation and data-conversion steps. Participant estimates are both relatively easy to collect and relatively accurate. Because the application of their new skills will produce improvements, participants are in the best position to report the effects of training. In addition to the participants themselves, their supervisors and managers also are well placed to provide valuable information. The *Using Estimates* sidebar above provides guidelines to using estimates to isolate the effects training.

Estimates also can be used to convert data to monetary values. For example, participants can estimate the value of soft data. Participants should be provided with clear instructions, along with examples of the types of data needed.

In some situations, participants may be unable to place a value on an improvement. In these cases, supervisors or managers may be able to help. Training staff also may be able to provide value estimates. However, using estimates from the training staff may look biased.

To ensure that the estimation process will be accepted in an organization:

- Develop a comprehensive approach to increasing the credibility of estimates. Ensure that estimates are adjusted for the level of confidence of the participant and that extreme values are removed from the analysis.

- Develop a culture for accepting and appreciating the estimation process by using estimates even when more research-based methods are used.

- Build acceptance with additional validation data by comparing the estimated results with the results of the more research-based methodologies.

Item 8: Use Internal Resources

Despite increased interest in ROI, many myths exist about the complexity of conducting such an analysis. Brief mid- and senior-level managers on the importance of ROI. Establish an advisory committee to discuss the relevant issues and consistently boost your own knowledge.

Establish an Advisory Committee

An advisory committee can help establish evaluation targets as well as provide help in data collection and conversion. The team should have six to 12 members from all levels and functions in the organization.

The following activities are essential to convening this group:

- Clarify the group's purpose and scope.
- Identify what needs to be accomplished.
- Define roles and responsibilities.
- Establish ground rules and commitments.
- Define how to engage the whole organization.

Enhance Your Own Capability

Credible work-system diagnosis and effective analysis in today's training and performance improvement work requires capability in evaluation. The following competencies and skill requirements have been identified as critical for practitioners tasked with an evaluator role:

- measure performance gaps
- evaluate results against organizational goals
- establish standards
- assess organizational culture effects
- review interventions
- provide feedback.

Routinely assess your own competencies in each of these areas. Build credibility by continually developing your own knowledge, skills, and abilities. The reality is that the message of a technically sound evaluation report is never good enough unless people believe the messenger. Recognize that your ability to increase organizational confidence and competence with evaluation practices is directly correlated to your own level of confidence and competence with evaluation strategies. Knowing a process well also offers the opportunity to understand cost and timesaving approaches without losing the effectiveness and credibility of the process.

Finally, understand the measurement systems of your business. If you don't understand what management is measuring, how can you expect to affect it? Consistently measure the effectiveness of your training efforts against business measures.

Item 9: Streamline Reporting Process

Communicating the results of an evaluation analysis is vital, but it often is the most neglected step in the process. For an evaluation to be effective and efficient, there should be a plan for the intentional use of the findings; otherwise, investing the resources in an evaluation is questionable. The investment in developing a communication strategy for all evaluation results will serve the organization well and will save time and money often expended on digging up evaluations from past programs.

When communicating the results of an evaluation, two key questions must be answered:

1. Will the target audience believe the results?

2. How will the target audience react to a negative or less than desirable ROI?

Timing, as well as presentation format, are critical considerations.

The first time an evaluation study is presented, the complete report should be given in a face-to-face environment. The report itself, as well as the presentation, should begin with an overview, describe the methodology, and present the results beginning with Level 1 through ROI. The presentation also should include barriers and enablers to the transfer of learning to the job. Transfer of training is a critical issue, and barriers to its taking place can significantly inhibit program outcomes. A comprehensive report can be 100 to 250 pages long.

Once management is comfortable with the evaluation process, a shoestring approach may be more appropriate and less time consuming to develop and present. The streamlined report is a high-level summary covering the results of the training at the various levels.

The *Sample Streamlined Report* sidebar on the next page provides an example of this type of report.

Sample Streamlined Report

Following is a sample that you can use as a model to develop your own report.

ROI Impact Study

Program Title: Preventing Sexual Harassment at Healthcare, Inc.

Target Audience: First & Second Level Managers (655); Secondary: All employees through group meetings (6,844).

Duration: 1 day, 17 sessions.

Technique to Isolate Effects of Program: Trend analysis; participant estimation.

Technique to Convert Data to Monetary Value: Historical costs; internal experts.

Fully-loaded Program Costs: $277,987.

Results

Level 1: Reaction	Level 2: Learning	Level 3: Application	Level 4: Impact	Level 5: ROI	Intangible Benefits
93% provided action items	65% increase posttest vs. pretest skill practice demonstration	96% conducted meetings and completed meeting record 4.1 out of 5 on behavior change survey 68% report all action items complete 92% report some action items complete	turnover reduction: $2,840,632 complaint reduction: $360,276 total improvement: $3,200,908	1,051%	job satisfaction reduced absenteeism stress reduction better recruiting

To take the streamlined reporting process a step further, PowerPoint slides—each one representing the results of one level of evaluation—are printed on a single sheet of paper. This page often is mailed, faxed, or emailed to the target audience. It is recommended, however, that the streamlined reporting process not be used until the ROI evaluation process has become an accepted, routine process.

Item 10: Use Technology

There is much written on the advantages of technology in delivery training programs. There are similar advantages of using technology to conduct evaluations. Data collection is becoming much easier and less time consuming with the advancement of new software. Surveys can be launched online, either through email or on a Website. Also, analysis is much easier than it was before. Some of these software packages conduct the level of analysis necessary to provide credible information.

An important point to remember is that while technology is making it easier to collect data, it often takes more effort to encourage participants to participate in the follow-up when technology is used. Therefore, develop a data-collection strategy that includes a plan to enhance response rates to e-based surveys and questionnaires.

Finally, stay in tune with the many listservs and Websites focused on evaluation. A lot of good information on technology and its use is offered through these forums.

Keep It Simple

Evaluations provide essential facts about what is really going on in your company. Analyzing statistics can be a daunting prospect, especially when the future of your training program depends on hard numbers. They key is to keep it simple. If necessary, call on outside help. Statisticians, researchers, and consultants can expedite and improve the process. Produce only what your stakeholders need; otherwise you will be watching your hard work collect dust.

References & Resources

Articles

Bae, E.K., and R.L. Jacobs. "Three Perspectives of Training Evaluation Based on Organizational Needs." *Academy of Human Resource Development Conference*, 2001, pp. 712-717.

Barron, T. "Is There an ROI in ROI?" *Technnical & Skills Training*, January 1997, pp. 21-26.

Benabou, C. "Assessing the Impact of Training Programs on the bottom Line." *National Productivity Review*, Summer, 1996, pp. 91-99.

Bober, C.F. "Utilization of Corporate University Training Program Evaluation." *Academy of Human Resource Development*, 2001, pp. 696-703.

Chase, N. "Raise Your Training ROI." *Quality*, September 1997, pp. 28-41.

Phillips, J.J. "How Much Is the Training Really Worth?" *Training & Development*, April 1996, pp. 20-24.

Sibbett, D. "75 Years of Management Ideas and Practice 1922-1977." *Harvard Business Review*, 1997.

Books

Bartel, A.P. "Return-on-Investment." In *What Works: Assessment, Development, and Measurement*, L.J. Bassi and D. Russ-Eft, eds. Alexandria, VA: ASTD, 1997.

Broad, M.L., and J.W. Newstrom. *Transfer of Training*. Boston: Addison-Wesley Publishing, 1992.

Holton III, E. F. "A Snapshot of Needs Assessment." In *In Action: Conducting Needs Assessment*, J.J. Phillips and E.F. Holton, III, eds. Alexandria, VA: ASTD, 1995.

Hornegren, C.T. *Cost Accounting*. Englewood Cliffs, NJ: Prentice Hall, 1982.

Kirkpatrick, D.L. "Techniques for Evaluating Training Programs." In *Evaluating Training Programs*. Alexandria, VA: ASTD, 1975.

————. *Evaluating Training Programs: The Four Levels*. San Francisco: Berrett-Koehler, 1994.

Parry, Scott B. *Evaluating the Impact of Training*. Alexandria, VA: ASTD, 1997.

Phillips, J.J. *Return on Investment in Training and Performance Improvement Programs*. Houston: Gulf Publishing, 1997.

————. *Handbook of Training Evaluation and Measurement Methods*. 3rd edition. Houston: Gulf Publishing, 1997.

————. *Measuring Return on Investment*, Vol. 1. Alexandria, VA: ASTD, 1994.

————. *Measuring Return on Investment*, Vol. 2. Alexandria, VA: ASTD, 1997.

Phillips, J. J., R.D. Stone, and P.P. Phillips. *The Human Resources Scorecard: Measuring the Return on Investment*. Boston: Butterworth-Heinemann, 2001.

Phillips, P.P. *Measuring Return on Investment, Vol.3*. Alexandria, VA: ASTD, 2001.

Rossett, A. *First Things Fast*. San Francisco: Jossey-Bass, 1999.

Rothwell, W.J. *Models for Human Performance Improvement, Roles, Competencies, and Outputs*. Alexandria, VA: ASTD, 1996.

Wallace, D. "Partnering to Achieve Measurable Business Results in a New Economy." In *In Action: Return on Investment*, Vol. 3, P.P. Phillips (ed.). Alexandria, VA: ASTD, 2001.

Infolines

Hodell, Chuck. "Basics of Instructional Systems Development." No. 259706.

Phillips, Jack. "Level 1 Evaluation: Reaction and Planned Action." No. 259813.

————. "Level 2 Evaluation: Learning." No. 259814.

Phillips, Jack, and Ronnie D. Stone. "Level 4 Evaluation: Business Results." No. 259816.

Phillips, Jack, William Jones, and Connie Schmidt. "Level 3: Application." No. 259815.

Phillips, Jack, Patricia F. Pulliam, and William "Bud" Wurtz. "Level 5 Evaluation: Mastering ROI." No. 259805.

Waagen, Alice K. "Essentials for Evaluation." No. 259705.

Case Study: Just-in-Time Gap Analysis

Following is a real-world example of an identified performance gap and a just-in-time gap analysis worksheet capturing subject matter experts' assumptions and hypotheses about the problem. Hypothesis 1 represents the initial view that the downtime problem was performer based and that only a training solution was required. A blank worksheet follows for your use.

Hypothesis 1	**Sub-hypothesis**	**Key Findings**
The downtime on sub-assembly station 2 is due to operator error.	Operators do not get timely documentation about process changes.	Process deviations need to be communicated across all shifts. Address conflicting messages about this work process in next whiteboard meeting.
	Operators are placed at the station without adequate time or experience to gain task proficiency.	This is an intermediate task requiring high-level decision making and repetitive practice and experience. Errors have major risk potential. Suggestions include: • no new hires at this station • develop training plan and qualification to measure proficiency needs and gaps.
	Operators have to wait for parts or materials to complete the sub-assembly in this station.	The downtime is due to parts shortage not being properly captured/documented by line supervisors. Suggestions include: • implement training on downtime recorder • monitor through daily production checklist.
	Operators at the previous station do not consistently perform an outgoing inspection.	There is no evidence for this assumption.

(continued on next page)

INFOLINE

Job Aid

Following is a just-in-time gap analysis form for you to fill in.

Hypothesis 1   **Sub-hypothesis**   **Key Findings**

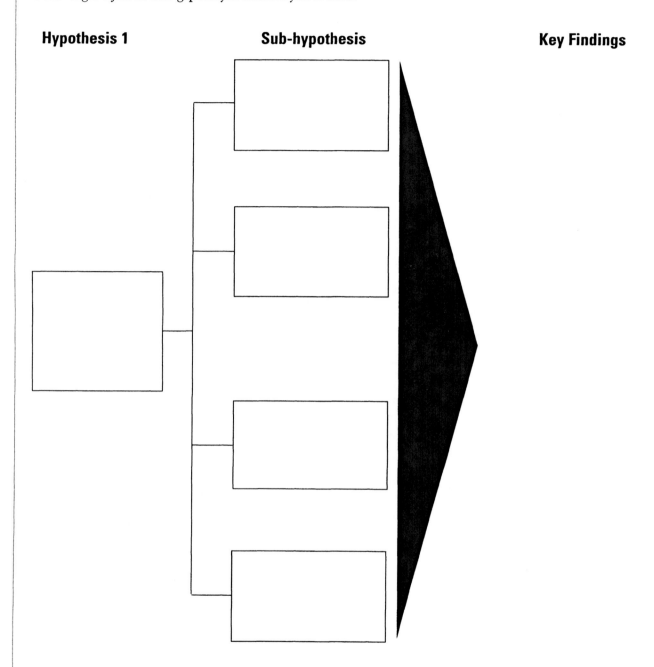

The material appearing on this page is not covered by copyright and may be reproduced at will.

Evaluation Data:
Planning and Use

Issue 0304

Evaluation Data: Planning and Use

AUTHORS

Patricia Pulliam Phillips
The Chelsea Group
350 Crossbrook Drive
Chelsea, AL 35043
Tel: 205.678.0176
Fax: 205.678.0177
Email: thechelseagroup@aol.com

Cyndi Gaudet, PhD
The University of Southern
   Mississippi
School of Engineering Technology
Box 5137
Hattiesburg, MS 39406-5137
Tel: 601.266.6181
Fax: 601.266.5717
Email: cyndi.gaudet@usm.edu

Jack J. Phillips
The Jack Phillips Center for
   Research, a division of
   Franklin Covey Company
350 Crossbrook Drive
Chelsea, AL 35043
Tel: 205.678.0176
Fax: 205.678.0177
Email:
roiresearch@mindspring.com

Managing Editor
Mark Morrow

Editor
Tora Estep

Copy Editor
Ann Bruen

Production Design
Kathleen Schaner

Planning Is Key 287
   Eight-Step Planning Model 287
   Evaluation Implementation 298

References & Resources 300

Job Aid
   Communication Planning Tools 301

Planning Is Key

Training and development professionals use evaluation data to ensure that their training or performance improvement programs meet the needs of learners and client organizations. Yet much of this valuable evaluation data is never used in any significant way to enhance the performance of learners or organizations. Focusing attention on the planning phase of the evaluation process and defining the future use of the data you collect will prevent this oversight and yield significant training and organizational benefits.

The expression, "plan your work, work your plan," is appropriate for evaluating training. A comprehensive plan defines the what, why, how, and who of the evaluation planning and implementation process. You can count on the following four outcomes if you develop a comprehensive evaluation plan. You will:

■ Save Money and Time
Make final decisions up front about data collection methods, sources of data, and timing of data collection to save yourself costly and time-wasting headaches. A complete plan of the data collection process enables you to easily implement data collection once the data collection instrument has been designed and tested, while early planning of data analysis allows immediate analysis and report development. In planning data analysis, choose from the outset statistical procedures, methods to isolate the effects of the program, and methods to convert data to a monetary value. Finally, having a plan for the client to sign off on further reduces problems after data collection begins.

■ Improve the Quality and Quantity of Data
Unnecessary, inappropriate, or insufficient data is useless and ultimately tarnishes the credibility of your evaluation efforts. Identifying the quantity and quality of data that is sufficient to describe the outcomes of your program is critical to evaluation success and further reduces costs and time.

■ Ensure Stakeholders Needs Are Addressed
Planning allows you to carry out your evaluation with the right end in mind. Stakeholder needs typically determine the end: Executive management may be interested in cost-benefit comparisons to determine the organizational benefit of the program; training staff may need participant reaction and learning data to know how to improve the program; and line management may want to know the extent to which learning has transferred to the job and, more important, whether or not the training improved the intended key measures.

■ Prioritize Budgeting
Planning enables you to fine-tune your project budgeting. Specify methods of data collection, sources of data, responsibilities for data collection, and timing of data collection to streamline allocation of the project budget. Improve management of the budget by itemizing costs for conducting the evaluation.

This *Infoline* presents an eight-step model as well as tips and tools to help you create a comprehensive evaluation plan. The last section of this chapter will show you how to plan the implementation of your evaluation. Use of the planning guidelines laid out in this *Infoline* will enable you to:

- develop comprehensive data collection and analysis plans

- develop a detailed communication strategy

- implement a comprehensive training evaluation without missing a step.

Eight-Step Planning Model

Evaluation planning delineates the parameters of data collection and lays out a clear path to data analysis and reporting. Ideally, you should carry out the evaluation planning process prior to the launch of a new training or performance improvement program to ensure that the need for the program, the objectives of the program, and the evaluation are in alignment. However, barring an ideal situation, develop the evaluation plan long before the evaluation actually begins.

Step 1: Determine Purpose

In a broad sense, evaluation is undertaken to improve training and development processes. However, specific purposes for evaluating training programs often define the scope of the evaluation process, including the type of data collected and the method of data analysis. Identify specific purposes for every level of evaluation. For example, when evaluation of the return-on-investment (ROI)

Why Evaluate Training?

The following list presents some specific purposes of training evaluation. Use training evaluations to:

- determine if the program accomplished its objectives

- determine the cost-benefit ratio of the program

- establish greater credibility for training practices

- identify future program participants

- demonstrate value

- track participant progress in applying skills or knowledge learned

- determine the strengths and weaknesses of the training process overall

- improve accountability and efficiency

- gain stronger commitment to the training function from key stakeholders

- gather data to assist in marketing new programs.

of the program is planned, one of the purposes is to compare the costs and benefits of the program. This has implications for the type of data collected, the data collection method, the details of analysis, and the medium used to communicate results. The sidebar *Why Evaluate Training?* at left presents some common reasons to evaluate training.

Remember that evaluations may have multiple purposes. As noted before, line managers may be interested to know the extent to which learning has transferred to the workplace and improved key measures, while different data necessary for improving the program is important to other stakeholders. Pinpoint the objectives of the evaluation to choose the right data to collect and to identify the right audience for the final report.

Step 2: Determine Stakeholders

The needs of critical stakeholders typically drive the purpose of the evaluation. Consider the following definitions of four stakeholder groups to identify important stakeholders in the evaluation process. These definitions describe the specific needs of each group and indicate how you may need to adjust the design of your evaluation to account for these needs.

■ *Decision Makers*
Decision makers are responsible for deciding whether a training or performance program will be implemented, continued, discontinued, or restructured. They include a wide variety of individuals in executive management or even the board of directors. For this group of stakeholders, evaluation results must demonstrate a contribution to the organization's overall goals and its key business measures. This group of stakeholders will be most interested in ROI evaluation results.

■ *Program Sponsors or Clients*
Sponsor and clients initiate and fund programs and are often decision makers also. Generally, program sponsors are line managers with budgetary discretion who are interested not only in issues such as teamwork, morale, and job skill development, but also in ensuring that changes in these areas lead to greater productivity, increased customer satisfaction, reduced turnover, and so forth. They also want to know if the benefits of sending their employees to training outweigh the costs. They want to see data on learning, application, and business impact.

■ *Program Participants*

Participants are the target of training and a critical source of data. They provide immediate feedback on the program. They also provide data on the extent to which newly acquired skills and knowledge are applied on the job, and they can elucidate the degree to which the program affects critical business measures. Participants are typically interested in the immediate results of the program, including the group's general reaction and level of learning, as well as the longer-term effects on the entire organization. To account for this stakeholder group's needs, gather reaction, satisfaction, and planned action data. These stakeholders also would be interested to see data on business impact.

■ *Training Providers*

Training providers include the training manager overseeing the entire training process as well as training facilitators, designers, and developers. This group also includes external training providers. Training providers want to know how well the program works. These stakeholders make the improvements in programs; thus, immediate feedback from participants on how well the program works, including its relevance and importance to the job and whether participants learn and apply the intended skills and knowledge, is critical. For this reason, keep training providers in the communication loop at all times during the evaluation. Training providers also are responsible for justifying existing programs, gaining funding for new programs, and marketing programs to future participants. Therefore, training providers need to understand the effect a program has on the organization, including the ROI. They are interested in all levels of evaluation.

Step 3: Determine Level

The sidebar *Evaluation Levels* at right briefly describes five levels of evaluation. Nearly all training programs are evaluated at Level 1, which addresses reaction, satisfaction, and planned action. At this level, the degree to which program objectives were met is measured, which is critical baseline data for all other levels of evaluation. Use this level of evaluation to gain immediate feedback on changes that may need to be made to the design and delivery of the program. Level 1 data is easy to collect, and, in many cases, program participants anticipate an end-of-course questionnaire; thus, resistance to providing data is minimal.

Evaluation Levels

Five levels of evaluation are described below. They follow the four levels of evaluation described by Donald Kirkpatrick, with the addition of a fifth level that measures ROI.

Level 1: Reaction, Satisfaction, and Planned Action

This level of measurement captures the participants' immediate response and satisfaction with the program and identifies actions planned as a result of participating in the program. Participants usually indicate the program's strengths and weaknesses with a generic end-of-program questionnaire.

Level 2: Learning

At this level, practitioners collect data on improvement in knowledge and skills, as well as confidence in using them on the job. You can use a variety of methods to assess learning gains, which include self-assessments, facilitator assessments, simulations, case studies, and exercises.

Level 3: Application

At this level, the extent to which participants actually apply what they learned on the job is measured. A Level 3 evaluation takes additional time, adds costs, and can be disruptive. However, you can conduct this level of evaluation in many ways, including follow-up questionnaires, interviews, and focus groups. The challenge is to select the method that best fits your culture, budget, and time constraints.

Level 4: Business Impact

This measures the consequences of the application of skills and knowledge in terms of increased revenues, improved quality, reduced response times, or enhanced efficiency.

Level 5: ROI

ROI compares monetary benefits of the program with its costs.

Level 2 evaluations focus on knowledge acquired and skills learned. Gathering Level 2 data entails only limited difficulty. However, not all programs are evaluated at this level because many programs are meant to be informative only, such as briefings; announcements of a new policy; and overviews of organizational mission, vision, and values. Therefore, the finding that only 60 percent of organizations' training programs are evaluated at Level 2 is not surprising.

Level 3 evaluations focus on behavior change and the application of skills and knowledge after the program. Collecting Level 3 data is a more comprehensive process than collecting Levels 1 and 2 data; therefore, it is not uncommon for only 30 to 40 percent of all training programs to be evaluated at this level.

Level 4 evaluations measure business impact. Evaluation at this level is attractive in relation to only 10 to 20 percent of all training programs, because this data is difficult to capture. Furthermore, to ensure the data collected represents only the impact of training on business measures, a step to isolate the effects of the program is required, which makes the evaluation process even more comprehensive.

Evaluation at Level 5, which measures ROI, is reserved for specific programs; only 5 to 10 percent of all training programs are evaluated at this level. Level 5 evaluations provide key stakeholders with a measure of the contribution of training that they can compare with other operational functions in the organization. By converting the benefits of training as defined in the Level 4 evaluation to monetary value, the benefits can be compared to the fully loaded cost of the program. This level also accounts for intangible benefits of the program. Intangible benefits are benefits that have not been converted to monetary value.

To select the appropriate level of evaluation, consider first the needs of the stakeholders, which will be defined in the program objectives if you have carried out a thorough front-end analysis. Remember that when stakeholder needs dictate a higher level of evaluation, the evaluation also should include lower levels of data. Presenting the full chain of impact is necessary to tell the complete story of program success. Use the simple tool presented in the sidebar *Evaluation Decision Tree* at right to select levels of evaluation to pursue.

Another way to determine the level of evaluation is to compare the program with a set of criteria. The closer the program comes to meeting the criteria, the higher the level of evaluation to pursue. Criteria may include:

- costs

- life cycle of the program

- level of linkage of the program to organizational objectives

- management interest

- program visibility

- target audience.

Many organizations make evaluation decisions at the beginning of the budget cycle. By reviewing all programs against the above criteria, an organization can decide how many and what programs to evaluate at the various levels. This enables the organization to allocate resources in advance so that budget constraints do not interfere with the evaluation process.

Step 4: Identify Program Objectives

Program objectives drive the evaluation planning process. Identify program objectives to ensure that evaluation measures reflect those objectives. Ideally, program objectives reflect the needs of the stakeholders and are based on a thorough needs assessment. However, research indicates that organizations conduct formal needs assessments only an average of 65 percent of the time. Even in cases where front-end analyses are conducted, program objectives often do not reflect stakeholder needs identified in the assessment. Barring the use of a needs assessment process to identify stakeholder needs, you can take a number of other avenues to identify program objectives.

Evaluation Decision Tree

To determine the level of evaluation, consider the requirements of stakeholders listed below. These will lead you to the appropriate level of evaluation.

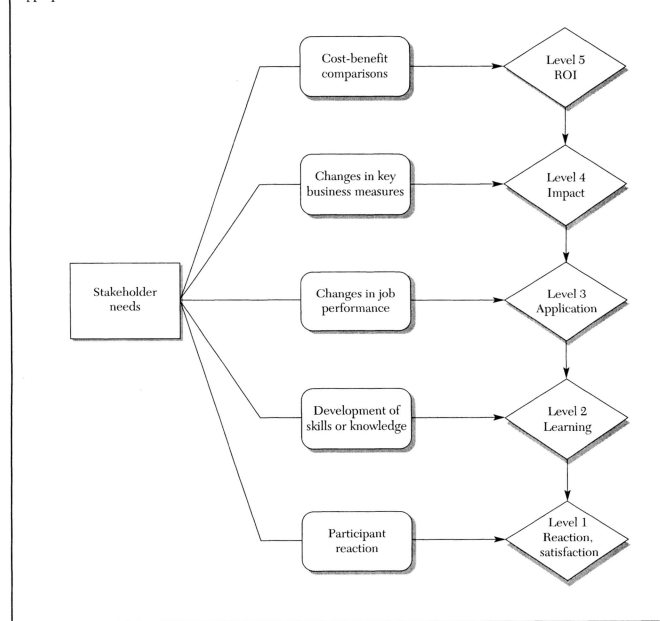

One method of determining program objectives is to refer to objectives in existing documents. A review of the documents that led to the program will identify objectives by which to measure program success. When external training suppliers provide programs, review their documentation; these materials often outline some objectives. While the use of existing documents is a relatively simple way to identify objectives, take care to ensure that evaluation measures reflect the program outcomes desired by those funding the program.

Another way to discover program objectives is to obtain input from others. This method also is helpful even if you identify program objectives through a review of existing documentation. Input from the following three groups often provides the necessary information to develop program objectives:

■ *Decision Makers*
While decision makers may not directly fund the program, they often have a keen interest in program results. Through one-on-one discussions or other communication processes, they make their expectations about the investment of company resources known. Paying attention to what decisions makers communicate—even if they do not communicate expectations directly—can contribute to understanding program objectives.

■ *Program Sponsors*
Program sponsors are the training function's key clients. They fund the program and expect particular outcomes from sending employees to the program. Their input is critical to developing evaluation measures.

■ *Training Suppliers*
Program designers and developers and training facilitators are good sources of information for identifying program objectives. Designers and developers understand the concepts and theory behind the program as well as its intent. Facilitators make up another group that understands the program content due to work with the program prior to implementation and feedback gained throughout the implementation process.

Step 5: Plan Data Collection

Planning the data collection process is critical because the chosen level of evaluation for the program affects data collection methods. To develop a data collection plan, carry out the following six tasks:

1. Connect program objectives with each level of evaluation planned. If you are planning the evaluation before completion of the program design, you need identify only broad objectives at first and update with detailed objectives later.

2. Describe the measures or data descriptors for each objective to define how to determine whether or not an objective has been met.

3. Specify the data collection method for each level of evaluation. Planning data collection methods up front is critical because additional planning will go into their implementation. For Levels 1 and 2, data collection methods include end-of-course questionnaires; written tests and exercises; performance demonstrations under supervisor, facilitator, subject matter expert, and coach observation; peer assessments; self-assessments; and skill-building exercises such as simulation practices. Use surveys and questionnaires, which are relatively easy to administer, to collect Levels 3 and 4 data. The sidebar *Questionnaire Implementation Plan* at right provides a checklist to help you administer the survey and questionnaire process. Other data collection methods include observations on the job, follow-up interviews, follow-up focus groups, assignments related to the program, action plans, performance contracting, follow-up sessions, and performance monitoring.

4. Select sources of data. Deciding on the source of data prevents frustration when the evaluation begins. For the most part, participants are a key source of data especially at Levels 1 and 2. Follow-up data for Levels 3 and 4 comes not only from participants, but also from participant supervisors; peer groups; company records and databases; and, in some cases, external experts and research reports. The key is to know which sources of data are the most reliable and readily available.

Questionnaire Implementation Plan

Gathering data using a questionnaire requires planning not only in the design process, but also in the distribution and collection processes. The goal is to gather the best data from the greatest number of participants possible.

Have you...	Yes	No
1. Pilot-tested the survey with a sample of practitioners?		
2. Gained (and showed) manager support?		
3. Made the questionnaire easy to complete?		
4. Made it easy to respond (for example, by providing self-addressed, stamped envelopes)?		
5. Gained (and showed) executive support?		
6. Prepared follow-up reminders in two different media?		
7. Made the questionnaire anonymous?		
8. Explained how long it will take to complete the survey?		
9. Sent advance communication?		
10. Used third-party data collection?		
11. Personalized the questionnaire as much as possible?		
12. Provided incentives?		
13. Used multiple colors?		
14. Explained "why" (reason for survey)?		
15. Explained "when" (timing)?		
16. Ensured that the printed survey has a professional appearance?		
17. Updated responses?		
18. Provided participants with a copy of the study?		
19. Distributed it to participants and managers?		

5. Determine timing of data collection. Level 1 data is normally collected at the end of the program. Level 2 data also is collected at the end of the program; however, it can be collected prior to the program for a before-and-after-program comparison. Timing becomes most critical when collecting Levels 3 and 4 data. The general rule of thumb is that data is collected when the application of new skills and knowledge becomes a routine part of the participant's performance on the job. The time lag until follow-up data collection takes place depends on the specific skills and knowledge the program is intended to influence, but often takes place about three months after the program's completion.

6. Designate responsibilities. Define and delegate these at the outset to ensure that all parties understand their roles and can take appropriate action at the right time.

Step 6: Plan Data Analysis

Planning the process of analysis is also important, especially in the case of Levels 4 and 5 evaluations.

Measures and Methods to Isolate Effects

Start analysis planning by listing Level 4 measures or data items, which are the business measures that the program is intended to affect. Examples of business measures include turnover rates, absenteeism, unit and operating costs, numbers of defective products, and frequency of safety violations. The next critical step in the data analysis is isolating the effect of the program. Without this step, nothing indicates that changes in the business measure are a result of the program. Consider each data item separately to determine which of the following evaluation methods will be most feasible and appropriate to isolate program effects:

- control groups

- trend line analysis

- forecasting methods

- participant, supervisor, and management estimates

- use of experts and previous studies

- estimates of the effect of other factors

- customer input.

The choice of method is based on time factors, cost, source availability, and need for statistical accuracy. While control groups are generally considered the most scientific, they are not always practical. And while customer input may be the least credible source of data, it also may be the only source of data. So the selection of method must balance a number of issues. However, the primary concerns are to choose the methodology at the outset and to ensure that key stakeholders in the process support the preferred method.

Data Conversion Methods

The purpose of converting Level 4 data items to monetary value in an ROI analysis is to enable a direct comparison of costs and benefits. Use methods such as expert opinions; external studies; links among Level 4 measures and other measures that register monetary value; and participant, supervisor, manager, and training staff estimates to estimate the monetary value of the program's effects. Examples of monetary value measures include profit and savings from output, cost of quality, employee time as compensation, and historical costs and savings. Select your method in advance and gain support from key stakeholders to ensure smooth implementation.

Cost Categories

Capture all cost items when comparing monetary benefits with program costs. Omitting costs negatively affects the credibility of the calculation and the entire evaluation process. Ensure that you are consistent when making cost calculations. An evaluation of one program should not omit costs considered in the evaluation of another program. The sidebar *Tabulating Program Costs* at right lists some common cost items.

Intangible Benefits

Intangible benefits are Level 4 data items that are not converted to monetary value. Intangible benefits are important to the organization, but the process of converting them into monetary value is often too complicated or subjective. Projected intangible benefits are listed in the ROI analysis plan; however, data collection may uncover additional intangible benefits of the program.

Other Influences and Issues

The final step in the analysis plan is projecting issues that may influence the evaluation. For instance, several programs could take place at once that also may influence measures of the program being evaluated. Another influence might be the introduction of a new pay plan, which would shape the mood and attitude of program participants. To address such issues appropriately in the final analysis, try to identify them and anticipate their effects in advance.

Step 7: Plan Communication

The most neglected step in evaluation planning is the development of a communication plan. Develop a communication plan to ensure that you present evaluation results in the appropriate formats to the right stakeholders in a timely manner.

General Communication Policy Issues

To develop the communication policy for training, consider these seven questions:

1. What will actually be communicated?

2. When will the data be communicated?

3. How will the information be communicated?

4. Where will the communication take place?

5. Who will communicate the information?

6. What information should be disseminated to what audience?

Tabulating Program Costs

Tabulating the cost of the program involves monitoring or developing all related costs. The following lists cost categories to include in your analysis.

■ *Design and Development*
This cost category covers all aspects of designing and developing the program, including:

- needs analysis and evaluation
- design and creation of blueprint
- writing, validating, and revising
- typesetting
- illustrating
- reproducing.

■ *Program Materials*
This category covers the cost of program materials per participant, which includes notebooks, handouts, tests, and so forth, and per instructor, which includes videotape, film, software, and overheads. This category also may include equipment costs for projectors, VHS, computers, flipcharts, and other training aids.

■ *Facilities*
Facilities costs include rentals or "fair share" use of classrooms.

■ *Travel*
If applicable, include travel costs as part of the overall calculation. These include airfare, hotel accommodations, meals, shipping of materials, rental of equipment, and so forth.

■ *Salaries*
Salaries costs include:

- participant salaries and employee benefits
- instructor, administrator, and program manager salaries
- consultant or outside instructor fees
- support staff salaries.

■ *Other*
Include any other costs incurred from training, such as administrative and overhead costs or material losses.

Adapted from Jack J. Phillips's In Action: Measuring Return on Investment, *Vol. 1 and Donald L. Kirkpatrick's* Another Look at Evaluating Training Programs.

Sample Communication Plan

The following is an example of a communication plan for a specific program that details the types of communication document, the target audience, and the method of distribution. The specifics for these will vary depending on the program.

Communication Document	Target Audience	Distribution Method
Complete report (100 pages)	• Client team • Training staff	Special meeting
Executive summary (eight pages)	• Senior management	Routine meeting
General interest overview	• Participants	Mail with cover letter
General interest article (one page)	• All employees	Company publication
Brochure highlighting program, objectives, and results	• Team leaders • Potential program sponsors	Marketing materials

7. What specific actions are required?

8. Why is the information being communicated?

Develop the communication plan after the program is approved. It should specify how to develop detailed information, how to communicate the results, and when to communicate them. In addition, the plan should provide details about various audiences and their communication requirements. The program sponsor and training department should agree on the plan's details.

Impact Study Communications

Presentation of the results of an ROI impact study raises additional communication issues and takes place after the overall, detailed results from a major program are known. A couple of major issues are who should receive the results and what form results presentation should take. This is more specific than the general communication plan because it involves the final study from the program.

The sidebar *Sample Communication Plan* at left presents a simple plan. In this example, the evaluation team developed five communication pieces for various target audiences. By planning communication up front, you can ensure that the results are communicated to the right people, at the right time, and in an acceptable format.

Step 8: Develop Project Plan

The final step in evaluation planning is the development of a project plan. Project management is a matter of keeping the scope, schedule, and resources of a given project in balance and on track. In the case of evaluations, it includes planning, organizing, and tracking the various steps in the process. Because evaluation is by itself a cost consideration, it pays, especially with Levels 4 and 5 evaluations, to pay attention to the use of resources and the timeline.

Do most of the work of developing an evaluation project plan in the early planning stages. To develop the project plan, pull together tasks, timeline, resources, and assigned responsibilities. The sidebar *Sample Evaluation Project Plan* at right provides an example of a simple project plan for a comprehensive ROI evaluation.

Sample Evaluation Project Plan

This table shows the data collection components of a simple evaluation project plan. The remaining tasks to include in the plan would be data analysis, report development and presentation, and their subcomponents.

Week Ending:	09/15	09/22	09/29	10/06	10/13	10/20	10/27	11/03	Responsibility
Prepare Data Collection									
Design and test questionnaires.		■							CG/BU
Develop focus group questions, format, and plan.		■							ET
Prepare data integration plan (Levels 1, 2, 3, 4).			■	■					CG/ET
Finalize questionnaires.				■					CG
Implement Data Collection									
Distribute questionnaires.				■					BU
Conduct focus groups.				■					BU
Collect observation data.						■	■		BU
Collect questionnaire data.					■				CG
Summarize reaction and learning data.			■		■				BU/CG
Tabulate questionnaire data (Levels 1, 2, 3, 4).						■	■		CG
Collect business performance data (Level 4).						■			CG
Summarize data for analysis.						■	■		CG
Secure values used in data conversion.		■							ET
Collect program costs.		■							BU

Evaluation Implementation

Until this point, this *Infoline* has focused on developing a comprehensive plan for a program evaluation. The next stage in the process is to specify the actions that will lead to actual implementation of the plan.

Identify and Develop a Leader

Identify a person within the training and development function who will lead the evaluation process. A measurement and evaluation leader usually recognizes the vast potential of the evaluation process.

Next, ensure that the measurement and evaluation leader fully understands the evaluation process, from the specifics of data collection methods and statistical procedures to the broad concept of the process and how the process can be and has been integrated into organizations.

The leader may serve a number of roles, including:

- analyst
- cheerleader
- communicator
- consultant
- coordinator
- designer
- developer
- interpreter
- instructor
- project manager
- technical expert.

These roles require a variety of skills and can be daunting. However, consider developmental opportunities to help measurement and evaluation leaders acquire the necessary skills and serve as an integral part of the training and evaluation process.

Assign Responsibilities

Assign specific responsibilities to avoid the confusion that arises when individuals don't clearly understand their specific assignments in the evaluation process. Clarify responsibilities for two groups: training and development staff and technical support staff.

It is important that training and development staff take an active role in the measurement and evaluation process. Their responsibilities to design, develop, and deliver the programs are an important part of collecting and analyzing data and reporting results. Responsibilities for this group may include:

- ensuring the needs assessment includes specific business impact measures

- developing application objectives

- focusing program content on various objectives

- keeping participants focused on application

- communicating the purposes of the evaluation

- assisting in the follow-up process

- providing technical assistance

- designing data collection instruments and guidelines

- presenting evaluation results.

Depending on the size of the training function, establishing a technical support function may be helpful. This group assists training staff in the evaluation process. The responsibilities of this group may include:

- designing data collection instruments

- providing assistance for developing an evaluation strategy

- analyzing data, including specialized statistical analyses

- interpreting results and making specific recommendations

- developing the evaluation report

- providing technical support in any phase of the measurement and evaluation process.

- designing and developing knowledge, skill, and behavioral assessment instruments to be used before, during, and after training.

Set Targets

Establish evaluation targets to enable staff to focus on improvements needed at specific evaluation levels. This process determines the percentage of course evaluations at each level.

Develop an Implementation Plan

An implementation project plan becomes the master plan for completion of different elements of implementation. In practical terms, the project plan shows the steps in the transition from the present situation within the training process to the desired future situation, which includes the measurement and evaluation process. The more detailed the document, the more useful it is. Items on a project plan may include:

- building staff skills
- developing policy
- setting targets
- teaching managers the evaluation process
- developing support tools
- developing evaluation guidelines
- developing specific evaluation projects.

A key element of planning is developing (or revising) the organization's policy statement on measurement and evaluation. The policy statement addresses critical issues that will influence the effectiveness of the process and describes how to use tools and techniques, guide the design process, provide consistency in evaluation, ensure that appropriate methods are used, and place the proper emphasis on each part of the evaluation.

The final step in planning measurement and evaluation implementation is to assess the organizational climate. Conduct this assessment in cooperation with training staff and the management groups through one-on-one interviews or the use of questionnaires or focus groups. The primary goal is to pinpoint particular issues that the measurement and evaluation process can enhance.

The evaluation process can be time consuming, costly, and sometimes an administrative nightmare. However, careful and thorough planning will reduce time and cost and improve the quality of the evaluation process. Making the effort up front can reduce problems in the end.

References & Resources

Articles

Alampay, R.H., and F.T. Morgan. "Evaluating External Executive Education at Dow Chemical." *Human Resource Development International,* 50, 2000, pp. 489-498.

Alliger, G., S. Tannenbaum, W. Bennett, H. Trave, and A. Shotland. "A Meta-Analysis of the Relations Among Training Criteria." *Personnel Psychology,* Summer 1997, pp. 341-358.

Michalski, G.V., and J.B. Cousins. "Multiple Perspectives on Training Evaluation: Probing Stakeholder Perceptions in a Global Telecommunications Network." *American Journal of Evaluation,* Winter 2001, pp. 37-48.

Warr, P. B., and D. Bunce. "Trainee Characteristics and the Outcomes of Open Learning." *Personnel Psychology,* 48, 1995, pp. 347-375.

Warr, P., C. Allan, and K. Birdi. "Predicting Three Levels of Training Outcome." *Journal of Occupational and Organizational Psychology,* September 1999, pp. 351-375.

Books

Bae, E.K., and R.L. Jacobs. "Three Perspectives of Training Evaluation Based on Organizational Needs." In *Academy of Human Resource Development Conference,* edited by O.A. Aliaga. Tulsa, OK: Academy of Human Resource Development, 2001.

Barksdale, S., and T. Lund. *Rapid Evaluation.* Alexandria, VA: ASTD, 2001.

Basarab, S., J. David, and D.K. Root. *The Training Evaluation Process.* Boston: Kluwer Academic Publishers, 1992.

Bober, C.F. "Utilization of Corporate University Training Program Evaluation." In *Academy of Human Resource Development,* edited by O.A. Aliaga. Tulsa, OK: Academy of Human Resource Development, 2001.

Kirkpatrick, D.L., ed. *Another Look at Evaluating Training Programs.* Alexandria, VA: ASTD, 1998.

Phillips, J.J. *In Action: Measuring Return on Investment.* Volume 1. Alexandria, VA: ASTD, 1994.

———. *In Action: Measuring Return on Investment.* Volume 2. Alexandria, VA: ASTD, 1997.

———. *Handbook of Training Evaluation and Measurement Methods.* Boston: Butterworth-Heinemann, 1997.

———. *Return on Investment in Training and Performance Improvement Programs.* Boston: Butterworth-Heinemann, 1997.

———. *The Consultant's Scorecard.* New York: McGraw-Hill, 2000.

Phillips, P.P. *The Bottomline on ROI.* Atlanta, GA: Center for Effective Performance, 2002.

Reeves, M. *Evaluation of Training.* London: The Industrial Society, 1993.

Rossi, P.H., H.E. Freeman, and M.W. Lipsey. *Evaluation: A Systematic Approach.* 6th edition. Thousand Oaks, CA: Sage Publications, 1999.

Wall, S., and E. White. "Building Saturn's Organization-Wide Transfer Support Model." In *In Action: Transferring Learning to the Workplace,* edited by M.L. Broad. Alexandria, VA: ASTD, 1997.

Infolines

Burkett, H., and P.P. Phillips. "Managing Evaluation Shortcuts." No. 250111.

Long, L. "Surveys from Start to Finish." No. 258612 (revised 1998).

Phillips, J.J. "Level 1 Evaluation: Reaction and Planned Action." No. 259813.

———. "Level 2 Evaluation: Learning." No. 259814.

Phillips, J.J., and R.D. Stone. "Level 4 Evaluation: Business Results." No. 259816.

Phillips, J.J., W. Jones, and C. Schmidt. "Level 3 Evaluation: Application." No. 259815.

Phillips, J.J., P.F. Pulliam, and W. Wurtz. "Level 5 Evaluation: Mastering ROI." No. 259805.

Communication Planning Tools

The following worksheets will help you prepare a communication plan that specifies the what, who, and how of communications. They will also help you to consider content to address in communication documents.

Communication Plan

Developing a communication plan that enables you to specify the form of communication, to identify the audience, and to determine the distribution method will help you to address stakeholder needs.

Communication Document	Target Audience	Distribution Method

Communication Plan Worksheet

Use the following worksheet (adapted from Susan Barksdale and Teri Lund's book, *Rapid Evaluation*) to work through issues to consider in the content of your communication.

Content Considerations	Notes Specific to the Organization
Mission and purpose • What is the purpose of the evaluation? • What is important to the organization about the evaluation? • What is important to the training and development function about implementing the evaluation? • What is the focus of the evaluation? • What is the business linkage of the evaluation? • What are the results or outcomes of the evaluation?	

(continued on next page)

Job Aid

Content Considerations	Notes Specific to the Organization
Measures • What measurement methods will be used? • How will the measurement approach be balanced? • What is important about the approach in terms of individual, business, and financial considerations? • How will the data from the measures help improve training programs?	
Evaluation Structure and Scope Definition • What will be considered part of the evaluation products and processes? • What will be considered not part of the evaluation products and processes?	
Integration With Other Processes • What processes will the evaluation integrate with and how will the evaluation complement other processes?	
Roles and Responsibilities • Who is the owner of the evaluation? • What do those being communicated with expect regarding the evaluation?	
Resource Requirements • What are the resource requirements for the evaluation? • How will these resources be approved? Is approval needed for the resource requirements? What is the approval process?	
Next Steps • Who needs to take action? • What actions need to be taken? • What is the timeframe? • When can results be expected?	

Printed in the United States
121376LV00003B/1-96/A

9 781562 863135